SOCIAL BEHAVIOUR IN ISLAM

SOCIAL BEHAVIOUR IN ISLAM

Muzaffar Husain

ANMOL PUBLICATIONS PVT. LTD.
NEW DELHI - 110 002 (INDIA)

ANMOL PUBLICATIONS PVT. LTD.
4374/4B, Ansari Road, Daryaganj
New Delhi - 110 002
Ph.: 23261597, 23278000
Visit us at: www.anmolpublications.com

Social Behaviour in Islam

First Published, 2004

ISBN 81-261-1892-X

PRINTED IN INDIA

Published by J.L. Kumar for Anmol Publications Pvt. Ltd., New Delhi - 110 002 and Printed at Mehra Offset Press, Delhi.

Contents

Preface

Islam appeared on the world scenario, as a complete faith, with a discipline and a code of conduct. Unlike certain other religions, Islam is not a philosophy or ideology alone. It's not confined to spiritual matters only. On the contrary, it's a perfect system and a way of life. Not only this, Islam has brought with it a complete social organisation. Islamic tenets provide a sort of regulation for all areas in an individual's life and as well as the collective life in a society. It also brings all acts of believers under a law, which controls all actions and operations in the world.

Islam clearly defines all aspects and issues in a social system. It also relates the behaviour of believers in society. The faithfuls have to abide by certain rules, regulations and laws in all matters under the sun. The ideal system leaves no aspect of life, society, polity and even the world hereafter, untouched and no problem unsolved.

The present study deals with social behaviour in Islam and covers all aspects and angles of personal and social life of believers. This small book is meant for guiding, those who follow Islam, in leading a happy, contented prosperous and successful life. Simultaneously, it would educate all those, who may desire to know and understand Islam at the academic level. The approach of the book is objective and empirical, which distinguish it from other works on the subject.

This editor feels honoured in fulfilling a job, which was perhaps most required.

— **Editor**

1

Introduction

To express greatness and pride over mankind is the attribute of their Lord, Who has created them, proportioned them, shaped their destiny, then showed them the path, Whose wrath appears as a terrible punishment and Whose favours and blessing, when manifested, stun human intellect

> Then praise be to Allah, Lord of the heavens and Lord of the earth, Lord and Cherisher of all the worlds! To Him be Glory throughout the heavens and the earth; and He is Exalted in Power, Full of Wisdom.
>
> (*Jathiya : 36-37*)

The bowing of the slaves before their Lord and adopting servility before Him is bowing before Truth and not before Falsehood, because creation, command, Unconcern, and Power are reserved and specific for Him, and the slaves' good or bad fate depends on His will. The slaves are in the best and the most purified condition when their foreheads are lowered in prostration before their Lord, and when they truly pay His dues without committing any excesses or being guilty of any shortcomings.

But the bowing of humans before humans like them is undoubtedly false and wrong and baseless . Here who claims greatness, who is proud and a wrong-doer under a baseless wishful-thinking, and the one who bows does not realise his own value. He has lifted such a heavy burden that he has no strength to carry. That is why Islam, on the one hand, has declared pride as *haram* (forbidden), and on the other hand treated the disgraceful behaviour and undue honouring as equally undesirable, and has enjoined on its followers to be respectable.

Allah's Prophet (S.A.W.) has said:

> "Whoever has pride in his heart equal to a poppy seed, Allah will throw him into the hell face downward."
>
> (*Ahmed*)

In another tradition it is written:

> "In the meanwhile a man was walking in his best clothes. He was very pleased in his heart of hearts. He had combed his hair. There was pride in his gait, and Allah entrenched him in the earth. Now he will go on getting entrenched more and more till the Doomsday.
>
> (*Bukhari*)

The reason for this is that pride and greatness is the attribute of Allah, and it befits Allah only. It is not proper for a man to try to usurp this right of Allah. The foundation of pride is on superficialism and meanness, which include evils like denial of Truth, ignorance of the facts, wicked-living, crossing one's limits and considering others mean.

Islam has declared it haram for a Muslim to consider himself mean, of no significance, weak and disgraceful, and on seeing some rich and powerful person, to feel sorry and inferior.

Anas bin Malik (R.A.A.) has narrated that the Prophet (S.A.W.) has said:

> "A man who has expressed sorrow in connection with the achievement of the material world, he has expressed displeasure against his Lord, and he who creates an uproar and cries loudly on some hardship, he complains against Allah. He who adopts servility seeing somebody rich and powerful, displeases Allah, and he who, after receiving Quran, acts like the people of hell, becomes deprived of Allah's blessings."
>
> (*Tibrani*)

In another *hadith* it is stated:

"Whoever sits in the company of a rich man and adopts an attitude of servility for himself looking to his grandeur and honour in the world, his two-third religion is ruined and he will go to hell.

This *hadith* is a serious warning for those who grumble loudly when they are confronted with hardships, they shout and create big noise when they experience any difficulty and call men for help, and for getting their work done become servile and cringe before the wealthy and rich persons.

To feel pain as a result of lack of facilities is not an inferiority, but the conversion of lack of facilities and riches into disgrace and ignominy is despicable in the eyes of Islam. From the ancient times the sign of manliness is that the wounded bears his pain till he is cured and starts on his journey again, and does not sit accepting defeat and waits for somebody to lift him up from the dust to which he has fallen.

In a *hadith* it is stated: "One who accepts disgrace with willingness and pleasure, is not from among us."

Islam allows a Momin to settle in a place where there is decency and honour, and where full freedom is given to him. It is the duty of every Muslim to act on these righteous ideals, and if it is not possible then he should leave this place of disgrace and dishonour. Allah says :

> When angels take the souls of those who die in sin against their souls, they say: "In what (plight) were you ?" They reply : 'Weak and oppressed were we on the earth.' They say: 'Was not the earth of Allah spacious enough for you to move yourselves away (from evil)?' Such men will find their abode in hell, — What an evil refuge it is ! (*Nina : 97*)

Allah has exempted those helpless persons who were unable to shift and could not find any other way of relief, in these were included women and children

> Except those who are (really) weak and oppressed-men, women and children-who have no means in their power nor (a guide post) to direct their way. For these there is hope that Allah will forgive; for Allah does blot (sins) and forgive again and again.

These verses show how undesirable and reprehensible are tolerance and bearing of disgrace and insults, and these verses create in man, the strength and will to make efforts to seek deliverance from them.

A Muslim's respecting and honouring his self, his religion and his Lord is really a sign of the greatness of his faith. And there is a very big difference between the greatness of the Faith and the greatness of Falsehood. It is really against the selfrespect of a Momin that he should feel inferior before a man in power, or he should be insulted or disgraced at any place, if he should live as a supplement of another person. In it there is an avoidance of transgression and disobedience and also an aversion from disgrace and dishonour. The greater the sense of inferiority before God, the greater is the superiority and elevation before men. This faith is far beyond all the things of the universe, all human beliefs and all false ideas about life. A Momin considers himself a servant for serving the Muslims, for establishing intimate relations with them, and for respecting their rights, he visits their houses and in the true sense of the word nurtures the feelings of greatness and impressiveness

> If any do seek for glory and power,—to Allah belong glory and power. To him mount up (all) words of purity ; it is He who exalts each deed of righteousness. Those that lay plots of evil, for them is a penalty terrible ; and the plotting of such will be void (of result).
>
> (*Fatir : 10*)

The sense of honour, assistance, and self-confidence are those prominent qualities on which Islam has given great emphasis. It has given them a basic place in the formation of the society. For nourishing them and developing them, it has established a never-ending series of instructions. To these qualities had Hazrat Umar Ibn Khattab (R.A.A.) referred when he said: "'That person is extremely dear to me, who, when subjected to digrace and insult, refutes them with all his might."

It is also worth considering why a muazzin repeats the call of greatness of Allah in the beginning and end of his call, five times daily. Why does he repeat these words for the prayers (salat) and why are the movements of qayam (standing) and sujud (Prostration) dependent on these words ?

In order that a Muslim should have an unshakeable faith that every claimant of greatness beside Allah is false, and every proud person beside Allah is mean and disgraceful. In other words this is a spiritual food that is being fed repeatedly to Muslims against problems of the world, attractions of the materialistic gains and the forces of darkness, so that the steps of Muslims may not falter or flounder.

In view of the importance of these attributes and to emphasize that Allah has fixed for Himself the best names, which are called 'Asma-e-Husna' (Beautiful names), so that by repeating them in bowing and prostrating during prayers, the sense of Allah's greatness and uniqueness is fully imbibed into them.

Respect is a man's birth-right, and its achievement is enjoined on every man. It is not proper for a man that he should pay his dues only when they are demanded from him. The better thing is that when a man has been made responsible for a certain job, he should complete that work to the best of his ability, so that nobody should be able to find fault with him, and no one, either a well to1do person or a poor man should criticise him. He should safeguard his honour and respect on that day when from every side there will be showers of curses and reproaches, and his worst enemies will be afraid of him:

> To those who do right is a goodly (reward) yes, more (than in measure)! No darkness nor shame will cover their faces ! They are the people of Paradise ; they will abide therein for ever. But those who (have earned evil will have a reward of like evil; ignominy will cover their (faces); no defender will they have from (the wrath of) Allah ; their faces will be covered, as it were, with pieces from the depth of the darkness of night; they are the people of hell-fire; they will abide therein (for ever) ! (*Yunus : 26-27*)

To disobey Allah and His Messenger is to invite disgrace and dishonour and to throw the individuals and the group into the pit of ruin. In the holy Quran Allah has clearly stated that the defeat in the Battle of Uhad was the result of the disobedience of some individuals.

> Those of you who turned back on the day the two hosts met—it was Satan who caused them to fail, because of some (evil) they had done. But Allah has blotted out (their fault); for Allah is Oft—Forgiving, Most Forbearing.
>
> (*Al-i-Imran : 155*)

When Islam has advised and instructed a Muslim to be respectful and honourable, it has pointed out to him its sources too, and has made the means of achieving it easy. It showed that decency and nobility is on account of Fear of God, superiority and elevation is achieved by worshipping Allah; and honour and power are gained by obeying Allah. A Muslim who finds this recipe, or wants to share its wealth, riches and position, its defence will be considered as a jihad (striving) in the cause of Allah, and it will not be merely a defence of the individual rights, but the defence of the public rights and of the higher values.

That is why in the hadith it is written that the person who is killed in defending his rights should be considered a martyr. A man went to the Prophet and said: "O Messenger of Allah! If someone comes to usurp my wealth, what should be my attitude?" The Prophet (S.A.W.) said :

> "Do not give him your wealth." He asked "If he is prepared to fight with me?" He replied "Then you fight with him." He asked: "If he kills me?" He replied: "You will be a martyr." He asked: "If I kill him, what would be his fate ?" The Prophet replied: "He will go to hell." (*Muslim*)

Yes, it is the demand of the honour and respect of a Muslim that he should not become an easy prey to an oppressor and a usurper. He should not become the target for a greedy and ambitious man, but that he should die fighting in the defence of his life, property and honour. There is nothing wrong if blood is shed in this connection, for it has no value where the defence of higher values are concerned.

Islam has allowed taking of revenge so that the oppressed may be comforted and honoured, and the oppressor may be disgraced and put to shame. Islam has made the rights of Muslims dear and likeable for them and has induced them that they should strive to achieve them, and should not be ready to accept anything less than their rights, except that the oppressor may request for pardon and they themselves, giving a proof of their high moral values and excellent character, forgive him. It will add to their honour.

First the Muslims were taught faith and good moral conduct, and then Allah acquainted them with the high ranks of elevation and kindness, and said:

> And that which is with Allah is better and more lasting; (it is) for those who believe and put their trust in their Lord: those who avoid the greater crimes and shameful deeds, and; when they are angry even then forgive; those who hearken to their Lord, and establish regular prayer ; who (conduct) their affairs by mutual consultation ; who spend out of what We bestow on them for sustenance. (*Shura: 36-38*)

These teachings indicate the honour and greatness of Muslims. Immediately after this, it is said:

> And those who, when an oppressive wrong is inflicted on them, (are not cowed, but) help and defend themselves. The recompense for an injury is an injury equal thereto (in degree); but if a person forgives and makes reconciliation, his reward is due from Allah; for (Allah) loves not those who do wrong.
>
> (*Shura : 39-40*)

The character of a Muslim be such that if he is angry with his inferior, he should forgive him ; and whoever dares to harm him in any way and he is a powerful person, then the demand of good character is that such a person should be taught manners and should be punished, until he is subdued and the balloon of his greatness is pricked. In such a condition it is a Muslim's responsibility that he should display his strength so that the criminal and guilty should be frightened. If a Muslim who is powerful and adopts the policy of forgiveness, it is much better for him, and if he adopts such a policy even if when he is neither weak nor feeble then this is another form of punishing the criminals and the decency of the faithful.

The conduct that has been described in the former verses is different from the one described in the latter verses. In the former verses forgiving the crimes of the criminals has been termed as good conduct, and in the latter verses the criminal has been placed before justice so that he may be punished and the sword of Qasas (revenge) should have sway over him, so that his power is broken and his undue pride is put down, and thereafter the mention of kindness, obligation and forgiveness has been made. It will ensure the due punishment of the criminals and increase the honour and greatness of the Muslims.

Since the elements of weakness and frailty are found in the nature of man, many times he adopts a policy of servility before the concerned persons in order to get his work done and his purpose served. In this way his selfconfidence and honour is adversely affected. Therefore, Allah's Messenger has taught us that in such matters we should not be weak, but should display the character of steel, should have our chins up, and should continue to strive to achieve our objective. He has said : "Try to get your needs fulfilled with self-respect, because these matters are governed by destiny."

And he explained that if all the people of a man's family may try to snatch away from him a thing with which Allah has blessed him, it would not be possible to do so. Similarly it is also not possible to return him a thing which Allah has taken away from him, even if all the people of his family may try to do so. Therefore, it is the duty of a Muslim that he should leave the reins of his affairs in the hands of Allah and have full confidence in Him.

He should understand the importance and greatness of his religion. He should not consider it inferior. He should value himself and should not give an opportunity to an idiot to prove himself superior to him, because whatever happens in the world it is with the will and decision of Allah alone.

> "What Allah out of His mercy does bestow on mankind there is none who can withhold; what He does withhold, there is none who can grant apart from Him; and He is the Exalted in Power, Full of Wisdom". (*Fatir:* 2)

Many times we feel that in our affairs we have been defeated, but this feeling is not correct, for such a feeling negates the existence of the Almighty and All-Powerful Lord of the Universe, Whom nothing can make helpless:

> "And Allah has full power and control over His affairs; but most among mankind know it not". (*Yusuf : 21*)

Nearer to truth, more profitable and helpful in solving the problems is this attitude that a Muslim should maintain his self-respect, should always be mindful of the values, standard and balance, should not bow for getting his needs fulfilled, nor should he surrender in any adversity. He should only pray to the Real Master, should have relationship with Him alone, should display his inferiorty in His presence only, and should not cry before any other creature.

> And if Allah touches you with hurt, there is none who can remove it but He ; and if He designs some benefit for you, there is none who can keep back His favour; He causes it to reach whomsoever of His slaves He pleases. And He is the Oft forgiving, Most Merciful.
>
> (*Yunus: 1-7*)

In the foregoing chapters you have seen how the Prophet (S.A.W.) has been teaching his dear companions to adopt the attitude of disregard for material wealth, unconcern for the riches, and the habit of economy, and how he had been teaching them to avoid asking for even ordinary things from others, so much so that "they were taking so much precaution that if the hunter fell from their hands they did not ask others to pick it up but themselves dismounted and picked it up."

Common men ruin this world and the next and make themselves disrespectable, owing to two causes, or at least one of these two causes : either they are afraid of their poor economic condition or their life is very dear to them. The minds are occupied by earning wealth and property, although Allah has not kept either of these two things in the control of men. In fact the desire to live and the fear of losing the means of livelihood are two such diseases that the superstition arising from them makes a man disgraceful, and when the fear of being disgraced rules the mind then man really is disgraced. Similarly the fear of starvation makes a man lose everything, though Islam has taught men to revert to Allah in happiness as well as in sorrow, and it has built up the edifice of the Unity of Allah on the basis of keeping relationship with Him. What is the use of attaching any desires, aspirations and expectations to humans who, compared to Allah, are not masters of anything, and have no control over any loss or profit:

> Nay, who is there that can help you, (even as) an army, besides (Allah) Most Merciful ? In nothing but delusion are the unbelievers. Or who is there that can provide you with sustenance if He were to withhold His provision? Nay, they obstinately persist in insolent impiety and flight (from truth).
>
> (*Al-Mulk : 20-21*)

Allama Ibn Qayyim (R.A.A.) in his poem pleads to Allah in this way:

"O God, in all my aspirations I think of You alone, And from the things which I fear, I seek Your refuge. All the men of the world cannot join the bone that You have broken, Nor can they break the bone which you have kept joined."

This is perfect belief in the unity of Allah. It is the cure for all those weak and helpless people, who in their tattered and old clothes wander from door to door with begging bowls in their hands, without caring for the reproaches and the curses of the world.

Islam desires to throw away from the hearts the factors of pain and restlessness and to shift them from the environment of narrowness and suffering to a pleasant atmosphere. Allah's Prophet (S.A.W.) says:

> "Livelihood itself searches the man, as death searches man." (*Tibrani*)

The Prophet (S.A.W.) does not mean that the people should be negligent about earning their livelihood. This is the thinking of the ignorants. He has given this assurance so that people should form the habit of getting their desires in a desirable way and should avoid crying before men and placating and being cringy before others. The meaning of this swearing of Allah is the same

> And in heaven is your sustenance, as (also) that which you are promised. Then, by the Lord of heaven and earth, this is the very Truth, as much as the fact that you can speak intelligently to each other.
>
> (*Zariyat* : 22-23)

Abdullah bin Masood (R.A.A.) narrates that the Prophet of Allah has said: "There is nothing that would take you nearer to Paradise but the commands which I have given ; and there is no act that will take you nearer to hell but the forbidden things which I have asked you to avoid. None of you should show any laxity in earning your livelihood, because Jibril(A.S.) has put this thing in my heart that none of you will leave this world unless he takes his full share of the livelihood destined for him. Therefore, O People! fear Allah and earn in a desirable way. If any of you lags behind in the matter of earning his livelihood, he should not try to get it by disobeying Allah, because He does not send down His kindness in exchange for sin."

By these advices Islam has raised the honour of a Muslim, and has urged him to live in this world as 'the leader of the caravan'. He should be like the sky in the depths of this world, and lead his life like a decent gentleman. Then it has also taught that the people whom we approach for fulfilling our needs are merely means of the grace and favours of Allah.

Abdullah bin Masood (R.A.A.) narrates that the Prophet (S.A.W.) has said:

> "Do not please anybody by displeasing Allah. Do not praise anybody for the favour granted by Allah, and for the thing which Allah has deprived you, do not reproach anybody, because Allah's provision cannot reach you by anybody's greed, nor can anybody's dislike stop it from reaching you, and Allah, in His

> justice and fair way, has kept happiness and satisfaction, in belief and seeking His pleasure, and has kept sadness and sorrow in displeasure."
>
> (*Tibrani*)

But it does not mean that man should not thank a person who obliges him, and should reject every offer of obligation from others, when the hadith says:

> "One who does not thank the people cannot be a thankful slave of God." (*Tirmizi*)

The purport of the above quoted hadith is that man should not become a slave of a person who obliges him or shows favour to him, and that his self-respect and decency is trampled, because the first obligation is to Allah. It is also not permissible for the giver to buy men's hearts through his gifts and obligation and use them anywhere he likes. It destroys his obligation and reward. This is the attitude of those whose ideal is not seeking nearness to Allah, therefore, decent and pious people do not accept the gifts of such men.

But those who give for Allah, and pay the dues of the slaves of Allah for seeking His pleasure only, about them Allah's Prophet (S.A.W.) has said:

> "One who has been given a gift should give something in its return, if he has the means, otherwise he should praise it. He who has praised it, has thanked for it . he who concealed it; he was unthankful." (*Abu Daud*)

As regards man's fear of death, and his accepting disgrace for a desire to live, this is foolish, because by cunning away, the life-span cannot be increased and by making efforts it cannot be reduced. How is it possible, when-

> To every people is a term appointed; when their term is reached, not an hour can they cause delay.
>
> (*A'raf : 34*)

2

Purity of Life

Allah the God, Almighty, likes those persons who are very particular about cleanliness. A verse in the Holy Quran says:

> "Allah befriends those persons who are very neat and clean." (9:108)

The Holy Prophet (S.A.W.) has said:

> "Cleanliness is half the creed."
>
> That is to say, half faith comprises personal and environmental cleanliness and the other half pertains to the purity of the soul. The purity of the soul or one's inner self is that one should avoid unbelief or skepticism; should not associate any body with Allah and keep himself free from sinfulness and meanness. As regards personal hygiene and that of the surroundings, one should see that one's person, clothes, articles of use and the environs are clean, tidy and free from all visible filth. One should also learn and adopt good manners.

Neatness and Purity

Clean Hands in Clean Water : Immediately after rising in the morning one should not put one's hand into a pot containing water without first washing his hands.

How to Urinate : One should not urinate on the floor of the bath-room, particularly when the floor, is made of mud or is unplastered. However, if a urinal is not available, soft ground should be used for urination, to be saved from the drops of urine which may rebound. One should, as far as possible, urinate in a sitting posture. In case, the ground may not be fit for sitting or there may be some obstacle or physical disability, one may urinate in a standing position.

How to Defecate : While easing one should not face or have his back towards Holy K'aba. After easing one should clean the affected parts with a piece of hardened but porous piece of clay or tissue paper and water or only water. One should not use a piece of coal, cow dung, bone, etc., for this purpose. Thereafter, one should wash one's hands thoroughly with soap or clay.

Entering the Bathroom : While going to latrine, one should have one's shoes on and head covered with a cap, etc., and before entering the bathroom one should recite the following supplication:

1. "Allah! I seek Thy protection against devils of both the sexes." *(Bukhari, Muslim)*

And after coming out of the bathroom this prayer may be read:

2. "Thanks to Allah Who relieved me from the suffering and granted me relief." *(Nasai, Ibn-Maja)*

Ease First : If one is feeling an urge for easing, he should defecate first, and then sit for eating. An urge for answering call of nature should be fulfilled at once. Delay in this connection adversely affects the stomach and brain.

Use of Right and Left Hands : As far as possible, right hand should be used for eating and ablution and left hand should be used for cleaning; private parts and blowing the nose.

Where to Urinate or Ease : One should not sit by the side of a river or canal, public thoroughfares or shady places frequented by general public for urination or defecation. This not only causes annoyance to the people, it is against good behaviour.

Spitting and Blowing of Nose : (a)In order to clear nose or to eject saliva, proper use of spittoon should be made or one should satisfy his urge in such a way that other persons do not see him doing this.

(b) Avoid inserting finger into the nose to take out the nasal fluid. If cleaning/clearing of nose or blowing the fluid out be necessary, then it should he done out of sight of the people.

Collecting Nasal Discharge, etc.: If one feels the urge for casting off nasal discharge, sputum or phlegm, it should not be done in a handkerchief. It is a very repulsive practice, except in emergencies.

How to Sneeze : While sneezing, put handkerchief on the mouth to avoid the drops of nasal discharge from hitting somebody. After sneezing one should say *Alhamd-o-Lillah*—Thanks to Allah." The other person who hears this, should reply by stating "*Yarhamokal-lah*—May Allah be merciful on you." In reply to this the first person should remark "*Yahdeekal-lah*—May Allah grant you guidance."

Care for Hair, Eyes, Nails, etc : The hair should be regularly combed and oiled. Irregular hair of the beard should be trimmed (so as to make the beard tidy end shapely). Antimony should be applied to the eyes and nails cut and kept clean. Arrange for your garnishment with simplicity and moderation.

Use of Perfumes : Perfumes i.e. itr, the base of which is not alcohol should be liberally used. The Holy Prophet (S.A.W.) was very fond of perfumes. He invariably applied this after finishing his washing, etc., on getting up.

How to Perform Ablution : Ablution (wuzu) is a compulsory pre-prayer function. It is better if one is always in ablution; if it may not be possible to do so, then one should try to be in ablution for as long as possible. The ablution should be performed methodically and like clock-work. If no water be available, then *Tayammum* be done. Ablution should be commenced with the recitation of *Bismillah* i.e.,

3. *Bismillah-hir-Rahman-nir-Rahim*

   (In the name of Allah, the Most Merciful, the Most Beneficent).

And in the course of ablution this prayer be recited:

4. "I hereby testify that there is no god except Allah. He is one and has no associates. and I (further) testify that Muhammad (S.A.W.) is His slave ('Abd) and His Messenger. O Allah! make me among those persons who repent most and are the most clean and tidy."

After finishing ablution the following supplication should be read:

5. "Allah! Thou art immaculate (perfectly clean) and art the Supreme Being. Along with Thine praise and adoration, I testify that there is nobody worthy of worship except Thee. I seek from Thee forgiveness and my redemption and I return to Thee."

The Holy Prophet (S.A.W.) has said:

"On the Day of Judgement my followers will be recognised by their shining foreheads and limbs having been washed by ablution. Therefore anybody who wants the light of his person to be enhanced, may get it enhanced (by means of ablution)." *(Bukhari, Muslim).*

Importance of Bathing : The Holy Prophet (S.A.W.) has once said that cleanliness particularly bathing is a key to paradise. He has called upon his followers to frequently have a wash, and they should invariably have a bath before going to attend the Friday congregational prayers in neat and clean clothes.

Hazarat Abu Huraira states that the Holy Prophet (S.A.W.) has said, "It is the right of Allah on every Muslim that he should wash his body and head and have bath (at least) once a week." According to this saying of the Holy Prophet (S.A.W.) , Allah is much pleased with a person when he has washed and is neat and clean.

Being Fit

Appreciating Health : A good health is a great gift from Allah as well as a trust. It should, therefore, be cherished and should not be neglected. Health, when once goes down, is difficult to regain. Just like the ordinary whiteant which swallows a big library, the slightest neglect in matters of health leads to serious consequences. Carelessness in this regard, amounts to both negligence of one's physical requirements as well as ungratefulness to Allah.

Healthy Persons Constitute a Powerful Nation : The performance of the great task as a Muslim and the discharge of the mission as vicegerent of Allah, require a sound mind in a healthy body with noble ambition and strong will. Only healthy persons with a living heart help constitute a vigorous nation, and only such nations can offer supreme sacrifices and achieve a glorious place in the community of nations. Be always happy, full of vigour and energy and active make your life attractive and full of zest for living, garnished with the help of good manners, cordial smiles and joviality. Keep away from sorrow, anger, concern, envy, ill-will short-sightedness, peevishness and mental confusion. These oral ailments and mental morbidity affect the digestion adversely and cause stomach disorders. They are the worst enemies of health. The Prophet (S.A.W.) has enjoined.

> "Lead a simple life, adopt moderation and be happy." *(Mishkat)*
>
> Hazrat Abdullah Ibn Haris says "I have not seen a person more jovial than the Holy Prophet (S.A.W.) ." *(Tirmizi)*

Healthy Gait : Hazrat Umar once saw a man walking as if he was sick. He asked him if he was unwell. He replied in the negative. Hazrat Umar ordered him to walk well with force.

The Holy Prophet (S.A.W.) used to walk with firm steps as if he was descending from a height.

Not to Overtax the Body : Do not strain your physical system. Since bodily energy has a limit, it cannot stand excessive pressure. It has to be preserved, maintained and used moderately. Hazrat Ayesha quotes a tradition of the holy Prophet (S.A.W.)

> "Work according to your capacity or power. Allah does not want you to be exhausted. It is you who (work so hard) that you get tired."

Hazrat Abu Qais says that once he went to pay his respects to the Holy Prophet (S.A.W.) when he was delivering a sermon. Therefore, the former had to wait for sometime under the sun. The Holy Prophet (S.A.W.) asked him to move towards the shade. He accordingly moved a little towards the shade. (Al Adab Al Mufrad). The Holy Prophet (S.A.W.) has also directed that one should not stay partially in the sun and partially under cover.

Excessive Asceticism : Hazrat Mujiba of the tribe of Bahila, states that once her father had gone to the Holy Prophet (S.A.W.) to seek religious knowledge. After a year he had another audienc with the Holy Prophet (S.A.W.) . The Holy Prophet (S.A.W.) could not recognire him this time. Her father introduced himself to the Holy Prophet (S.A.W.) who therefore said: "What has happened to you? When you visited me last time your appearance and general health were very good." He explained that since his last visit to the Holy Prophet (S.A.W.) he was consecutively fasting and was having only one meal at night. The Holy Prophet (S.A.W.) told him that he had unnecessarily subjected himself to such an ordeal and shattered his health. He further directed him to fast during the whole month of Ramazan and may fast once in each month (during the remaining period of the year). Hazrat Mujiba's father, however, solicited permission for extra fasting days; the Holy Prophet (S.A.W.) said, "You may fast twice in a month." When requested to increase further the number of fasting days, the Holy Prophet (S. A. W.) graciously increased the number of fasting days to three days in a month. Again Hazrat Mujiba's father solicited permission for more fasting days, thereupon the Holy Prophet (S.A.W.) replied, "Very well, you may fast during the sacred months and leave the other months, and do this each year." So saying he made a sign with his three fingers by joining and then separating them. He meant by this that he should keep fast during the months of *Rajab, Shawwal Ziqad* and *Zilhijj*. He further emphasised that he should miss them off and on.

A tradition of the Holy Prophet (S.A.W.) says,

> "It is not proper for a Muslim to belittle himself." When his companions sought elucidation on this point, he

> explained that a Muslim does so by undergoing unbearable hardships."

Habit for Hard Work : Always lead a hard-working life with chivalrous behaviour. Be prepared to face difficult situations in life. Avoid temptation for comfort and ease and love for worldly attractions. The Holy Prophet (S.A.W.) while appointing Hazrat Muaz Ibn-e-Jabal as Governor of Yemen advised him. "Muaz, keep yourself away from living an easy life, because servants of Allah do not run after easy living." *(Mishkat)*

Hazrat Abu Umamah states that the Holy Prophet (S.A.W.) has declared, "Leading a simple life is an article of faith."

Physical Exercise : The Holy Prophet (S.A.W.) always led a simple life like a Mujahid, and he always tried to conserve and increase his energy and capability for' sacrifice and struggle for a just cause.

He was interested in swimming too, because it is an excellent exercise for the whole body. He used to encourage swimming competitions in which he himself participated along with his companions.

Horse-Riding : The Holy Prophet (S.A.W.) liked horse-riding very much. He used to serve his charger himself. While dressing the animal's mane he would say, "His forehead will reflect excellence till the eternity."

> ***Archery*** : Hazrat Aqabah says that the Holy Prophet (S.A.W.) had laid great emphasis on archery and horsemanship. He further declared that he liked the archers more than the horsemen and one who had given up archery, had not done justice to the gift from Allah. *(Abu Dauood)*
>
> Hazrat Abdullah bin Umar quotes a tradition from the Holy Prophet (S.A.W.) "One who guarded the Mujahidin (Muslim warriors fighting in the cause of Allah) during the night for him this night is better than the night of Glory (Lailat-ul-Qadar)." *(Hakim)*

Woman's Life

The Muslim women should also lead an active and hard working life, doing their household chores themselves. They should cultivate a tendency to face difficulties and ordeals, and shun easy life and inactivity. They should teach their children to develop similar habits. Even if there may be servants in the house, the children should be asked to do their work by themselves as far as possible. Muslim women during the days of the Holy Prophet (S.A.W.) used to do their domestic work without any help; they used to look after the kitchen, grind the flour, fetch water, wash clothes, and mend dress. They led a very hard-working life and in emergencies they would undertake the jobs of attending upon the wounded, nursing them and supplying drinking water to the soldiers in the battlefields. This practice enabled them to maintain a very good health. Moreover, it set an excellent example for the younger generation.

Early to Bed, Early to Rise : Develop the habit of early to bed and early to rise in the morning. Bo moderate in sleeping; it should be neither less which may not refresh your body nor excessive which may cause torpidity and sluggishness.

The Holy Prophet (S.A.W.) had prohibited from keeping awake or talking after the night prayers (Isha). He said only those persons can remain awake who have to discuss some religious matters and have to talk over some important topics with his family members.

Exercise and Walking : Offer your morning prayers and then go out for a walk in the open field or a garden. The fresh morning air is good for health. Depending upon your physical capability have some light exercise. The Holy Prophet (S.A.W.) liked walking in a garden.

Control Over Desires : It is necessary to have control over your desires—desire, to your feelings, thoughts, likings, and lusts. Do not dour heart to waver, your ideas to wander and your gination to deviate from the right path. Waywardness of desires and a temptation to throw glances deprive you of your peace of mind.

And the faces of such persons lose the lustre of youth and manly attractions. Such persons prove a failure in all fields of life and they become cowards and timid.

The Holy Prophet (S.A.W.) has said:

> "To look covetously or with an evil desire, is adultery of eyes, and to talk bawdy or indecent language is fornication by the tongue. The psyche coaxes somebody to do something (indecent), his sexual organ either obeys the command or turns it down."

A Wise man has said:

> "O Muslims, do not commit adultery (or fornication). It has got six evils in it. Three of these are evident in this world and three in the hereafter. The evils of this world are: (i) The adulterer loses lustre and charms of his face. (ii) He falls victim to poverty and deprivation. (iii) The span of his life is shortened."

Avoid Intoxicants : Alcoholic drinks in any form, like wine, beer, whisky, etc., are strictly prohibited. All other articles which may cause intoxication should be avoided. These adversely affect brain and digestive system.

Moderation in Life : Moderation and simplicity should govern all aspects of our life, in physical labour, mental exercise, connubial relations, eating and drinking, sleeping and leisure, expressing concern and worries, happiness, and enjoyment, prayers and meditation and in walking and talking one should follow the golden mean.

The Holy Prophet (S.A.W.) has said:

> "How fine is a golden mean in prosperity; in poverty a middle course is a good thing; and in prayers Moderation is preferable."

Care of the Eyes : Take good care of your eyes. Don't expose your eyes to glaring light. Also refrain from looking towards the sun with a set gaze. Always read in a clear and moderate light; avoid glaring or dim light. Do not keep awake till late hours.

Protect your eyes from dust, dirt and smoke. Make the habit of applying collyrium to your eyes and always keep them clean. Enjoy the sights of green fields, gardens and other green pastures. This is good for eyesight. Do not cast evil or covetous eye on anything; this will deprive your eyes of their glow and aparkle and impair your health. The Holy Prophet (S.A.W.) has said "Your eyes too have their rights on you." That is, they need care and protection from impairment.

A Muslim should, therefore, appreciate the value of this gift from Allah, and should use the same in accordance with His Will. That is, he should take care to protect his eyes against hazards by regularly keeping them clean. He should adopt measures which may benefit his eyes and avoid those things which may harm them. In the same way one should take care to protect the other organs of one's body and their vitality.

> The Holy Prophet (S.A.W.) has called upon his followers, "O people, always apply antimony to your eyes. This helps in clearing dirt from the eyes and helps in the growth of hair." *(Tirmizi)*

Care of the Teeth : Be particular about the cleanliness and preservation of your teeth; clean teeth are a source of pleasure and freshness, and a help for digestion and strengthening the roots of the teeth. Cultivate a habit for brushing your teeth with a miswak, and also use some good dental powder. Excessive use of betel leaf and tobacco harms the teeth. Brush and clean your teeth after eating anything.

Dirty teeth are the cause of a number of diseases. The Holy Prophet (S.A.W.) used to brush his teeth and clean his mouth with a miswak after getting up from his sleep.

(Reported by all the traditionists).

Hazrat Ayesha (R.A.A.) says, "We always kept water ready for ablution and miswak for the use of the Holy Prophet (S.A.W.) When with the Will of Allah he used to get up from his sleep, he would perform ablution and clean his teeth and mouth and offer prayers." *(Muslim)*

Hazrat Anas relates that Holy Prophet (S.A.W.) had said:

> "I have already emphasised upon you for brushing your teeth with a miswak so many times." *(Bukhari)*
>
> According to yet another tradition from Hazrat Ayesha (R.A.A.) , the Holy Prophet (S.A.W.) has declared, "*Miswak* is an article to cleanse the mouth and which (i.e., brushing with miswak) pleases Allah." *(Nasai)*

Cleanliness and Tidiness : In view of the importance of cleanliness and tidiness, the Holy Prophet (S.A.W.) has issued detailed and clear instructions on this subject.

Keep all eatables covered. Protect them from getting polluted or rendered unwholesome. Guard them against flies and other insects. Keep the utensils clean; also keep your clothes and bedding-pieces, habitation and environment neat and tidy.

For your personal hygiene, you should regularly take bath and perform ablutions. Cleanliness of your person, clothes and articles of use generates pleasantness to your soul and freshness to the body. As a whole, it has a salutary effect on the health.

Hazrat Adi Ibn Hatim says "Ever since I embraced Islam, I am with ablution for each prayer."

Once the Holy Prophet (S.A.W.) asked Hazrat Bilal, "How you happened to enter the paradise before me yesterday?" He replied: "O Prophet of Allah (S.A.W) whenever I call the Muslims for the prayers (call Azan), I invariably offer two Rakats (sittings) of (optional) prayers, and whenever I am not in the state of ablution, I at once perform fresh ablution and always try to remain in this state."

Preparing for Prayer

It is incumbent on every Muslim to try to advance towards perfection at every hour of his life, and he should continue marching for progress in the material and spiritual worlds, because with Allah his future will be decided according to the stage of progress which he has reached. If he has scaled the peak, and then died, he will be counted among the residents of the Paradise.

And if he died before reaching his destination and if his crimes are pardonable, then he would achieve salvation. But if he has breathed his last in such a condition that instead of advancing forward he has retreated backward and has gone astray, then the angels of severe punishment will snatch him away, and if he had been indifferent to the guidance of Allah in this world, he will be made to rise blind on the Doomsday. And he, who was fully absorbed in evil and wicked acts, will be presented on the Day of Judgment in the same condition.

Allah's Messenger has explained: "The person who would be keen and desirous in this world of keeping his body clean, his parts and person neat and his face shining, when such a man will be made to rise on the Doomsday then his face will be shining, beams of light will be emanating from his forehead, and his body and parts of the body will be clean."

> Abu Huraira (R.A.A.) narrates that when the Prophet (S.A.W.) visited the graveyard, he said: "O faithful people of the household! Peace of Allah be upon you. If Allah wishes we all of us will soon meet you. It is my wish that I may see my brothers." His companious asked : "Are we not your brothers, O Messenger of Allah (S.A.W.) !" He said: "You are my companions. My brothers are those who have not come as yet." The companions asked : "O Messenger of Allah (S.A.W.) ! How will you recognise those people of your Ummah who have not come as yet ?" He said : "If a man has horses that have white marks on their foreheads and legs, and if they are mixed with black horses, then what do you think he will not be able to recognise them?" The people replied: "Why not, O Messenger of Allah (S.A.W.) ! He will certainly recognise them." He said : "So these people will also, when they were made to rise on the Doomsday, will have their all parts of body shining with wuzu (ablutions)."
>
> (*Muslim*)

Health of the body, its beauty and its cleanliness are things to which Islam has given the desired attention, and has included in it the duties of the prophethood. Only that man meets the requirements of Islam who takes care of keeping his body clean and neat, and who avoids dirtiness, filth and hateful things in his food, drink, and in his everyday dealings. The health of the body and its cleanliness is not useful only from the medical point of view but it has also deep effects on man's responsibilities in the battle-field of life and in purification of self. To fulfil the responsibilities of life what can be more important than a strong body and firm and steadfast physique?

Islam has paid due respects to the body, and its complete cleanliness for every prayer has been declared as essential and basic. The prayers have been made compulsory for five times a day, and it has been made incumbent on every Muslim that he should wash his whole body sometimes, and it has been termed full cleanliness, and in ordinary conditions only parts of the body have been asked to be washed so that dust and dirt may be removed, and the body may feel alert and agile:

> "O you who believe ! When you rise up for prayers, wash your faces and your hands up to the elbows, and lightly rub your heads and (wash) your feet upto the ankles. And if you are unclean, purify yourselves." (*Maida: 6*)

The method that Islam has adopted to keep the body clean and tidy all the time is in accordance with man's material temperament and nature. If man were merely a bundle of spirit or soul, there would have been no necessity of bathing, washing and cleaning the body, but since he lives in the material cover made of dust, breathes on this earth, makes use of its vegetables and minerals, and leaves the excreta of his stomach on it ; considering his material existence and temperament, Islam has made wuzu (ablutions) and ghusl (bathing) compulsory for man, so that he may be kept clean of all these dirty and filthy things.

There cannot be a better way of keeping a man clean and neat than the way prescribed by Islam, for the Shariah makes a man habituated to take bath and to wash his parts, even though he may be clean. This does not allow dust and dirt to remain on the body of the Muslim Ummah.

Although Islam has not confined the importance of bathing when it is compulsorily needed, there are some people who do not take bath unless it becomes absolutely necessary. For this purpose at least one day has been fixed in a week for taking bath.

> Allah's Messenger (S.A.W.) has said: "It is incumbent on every adult to take bath on every Friday, and miswak (veg. tooth brush) and fragrance too."
>
> (*Muslim*)

In another hadith it is mentioned:

> "It is the day of the festival which Allah has provided for Muslims. He who comes for the prayers of Friday, he should take a bath." (*Ibn Majah*)

Cleanliness in Eating: Islam has declared it incumbent on Muslims to take care of cleanliness in the matter of eating. It has commanded to wash hands before eating and to remove the remnants of food from the hand after eating. And this is the only way of cleanliness and purity.

> Allah's Prophet (S.A.W.) has said: "The auspiciousness of eating is in washing hands before and after eating." (*Muslim*)

Wherever or in whatever part of the body the remnants of the food after eating may be found, they should be removed. If the food particles are found in the teeth, the teeth should be picked. The Prophet (S.A.W.) has said:

> "Pick your teeth, for it is a means of cleanliness, and cleanliness invites faith. And the heart in which faith resides will go to Paradise." (*Tibrani*)

In the directions given by the Prophet (S.A.W.) this command is for cleanliness of wuzu and in eating.

> Hazrat Abu Ayub has narrates that the Prophet (S.A.W.) came among us and said : "The people of my Ummah who pick their teeth deserve congratulations." They asked : "And who are they, O Prophet of Allah (S.A.W.) " He said : "Those who pick (clean) their teeth in the wuzu and those who do it after eating. Tooth-picking

> after the wuzu is rinsing the mouth, to wash inside of the nose and to pass water through the fingers, and toothpicking after eating is their cleaning. There is nothing more burdensome for the two angels sitting on man's two arms than to see him in the state of prayers while food particles are sticking in his teeth." (*Ahmed*)

The extreme care that the religion has taken for the cleanliness of the mouth and teeth of its followers does nor find a parallel in the history of the old and new medicine and public health.

> The Prophet (S.A.W.) has exhorted: "Brush your teeth with miswak, for it is the means of cleaning the mouth and the method of achieving Allah's pleasure. Whenever Jibril came to me he urged upon me for cleaning of teeth by miswak, so much so that I was afraid that cleaning by miswak might be made compulsory *(farz)* for me and my ummah."
>
> (*Ibn Majah*)

In another tradition it is mentioned : "I was commanded to clean the teeth by miswak, so much so that I surmised that there will come a command in the Quran or a revelation to me."

The diseases that are caused by not cleaning the teeth and the saliva are known to knowledgeable men and they can understand why Islam has stressed so much on their cleanliness, and why it has insisted on the teeth being rubbed and cleaned regularly.

> Allah's Messenger (S.A.W.) has said : "I have been commanded to clean my teeth by miswak in such a way that I was afraid my teeth might fall by rubbing them so much." (*Bazzar*)

Extreme care should be taken to remove the effects of the foods that cause bad breath, etc., like mutton, fish, etc. by cleaning the teeth properly, because it is very important from the point of view of hygiene, personal cleanliness and health.

> The Prophet (S.A.W.) has said: "He who spends the night in such a way that (particles of) flesh, bad smell,

> animal fat remained stuck to his hand, and if he sustains some loss, then he should curse himself."
>
> (*Bazzar*)

There are sayings which indicate that the germs attack the hand and the bad-smelling mouth, because they get their best food from these spots only. These traditions warn us against this kind of losses and damages.

Islam has forbidden, in deference to the welfare of the individuals and the society, men who eat garlic and onions to attend meetings or gatherings, because the bad smell that results from eating them creates aversion and repulsion in the hearts of the addressees, and for this reason Islam has exhorted or induced its followers to dislike the use of these things.

Those who have eaten these things, Islam has suspended the operation of the sunnah of joining the congregational prayers as it has suspended the operation of the sunnah of joining the congregational prayers by the sick, because the bad smell from their bodies and mouths pan create aversion. Such a precaution is really praiseworthy as it is in the interest of both the sick and the healthy.

Islam insists that man should try to be dignified, beautiful and attractive. It has included these things in the requirements of the prayers.

> "O Children of Adam ! Look to your adornment at every place of worship."
>
> (*Al-A'araf* : 31)

The Prophet used to teach every Muslim that he should take care of all these things and he wanted all Muslims to be attentive to these matters in their individual and social affairs, so that Muslims should become popular and beautiful in their external and internal matters, in their clothes and living and in their shape and appearance.

> Allah's Messenger (S.A.W.) has said: "One who has hair must necessarily adorn them" (*Abu Daud*)
>
> Abu Qatada narrates : "I asked: 'O Messenger of Allah (S.A.W.) ! I have long hair, may I comb them?' The

Prophet (S.A.W.) said: 'Yes, adorn them.' Accordingly, Abu Qatada according to this saying of the Prophet sometimes used to apply oil to his hair twice in a day." (*Nisei*)

To comb the hair and to apply fragrance (scent) is the best *sunnah*.

Ata bin Yasar (R.A.A.) has narrated: "A man went to the Prophet in a condition that his hair and beard were dishevelled. The Prophet (S.A.W.) made signs as if saying that he should properly cut his hair. He went, got his hair properly cut and came back. Then the Prophet (S.A.W.) said: 'Is this not a better condition than that some one of you should come in a wretched condition as if he is a Satan' ?" (*Malik*)

Jabir bin Abdulah (R.A.A.) narrates that the Prophet (S.A.W.) found a man with dishevelled hair. He stopped him and said : "Does he not find anything by which he may arrange his hair ?" (*Abu Daud*)

He saw a man in dirty clothes and asked : "Does he not have money that he may wash his clothes ?"

If adornment is done without wasteful spending, if embellishment is arranged without any grandiose formalities and imitation, and if attempts are made to beautify the appearance after reforming the internal life, then this is the teaching of Islam which provides nobility and beauty to its followers.

Allah's Messenger (S.A.W.) has said : "He who has the slightest pride in his heart, cannot enter the Paradise." A man asked : "And if a man likes that his clothes should be good and there should be beauty in his shoes, will this be counted in pride ?" He replied: "Allah is beautiful and He loves beauty."(*Abu Daud*)

In another tradition it is mentioned that a beautiful man came in the presence of the Prophet (S.A.W.) and asked "I like beauty, and I have been blessed by this thing as you are seeing, so much so that I do not like that the lace of any other man's shoe should be better than the lace of my shoe. Then will this thing be counted in pride, O Messenger of Allah (S.A.W.) ?" He replied: "No, pride and conceit is denial of Truth and to think others are inferior."

Allah's Prophet (S.A.W.) used to study people very minutely and carefully. If he saw any Muslim being lax in adornment, embellishment and in cleanliness, he used to point it out and command him to improve matters.

> Jabir bin Abdullah narrates that the Prophet (S.A.W.) saw one of our men who was looking after the animals, and who had two torn sheets on his body. He asked whether there was no other clothes with him?, Jabir replied: "Why not? He has two clothes in the box, which I had given him." The Prophet (S.A.W.) said : "Ask him to wear them." Accordingly he wore them and when he came back, the Prophet (S.A.W.) said : "May Allah behead him (i.e. May he suffer) Is this appearance not better for him?" The man heard the Prophet and said: "Then I am going in the way of Allah, O Messenger of Allah!" The Prophet said : "He is really going in the way of Allah." The narrator says that that man was martyred in the way of Allah.
>
> (*Malik*)

This man understood the humorous advice of the Prophet (S.A.W.) and changed his clothes. It seems that this man was from amongst those whose involvement in their work does not give them time to took after their private life. However heavy burden of responsibilities there may be on a man and whatever may be his involvement in his work, it is not proper for him that he should ignore and overlook the necessity of making himself presentable and clean.

Some professional religious men think that to wear old and torn clothes and to wallow in dirt is a kind of worship. By putting on clothes having patches in them and donning rags and looking wretched they have tried to impress the people that they have no interest in the world and they are totally concerned and involved in working for the Hereafter. Such kinds of hoax are the result of total ignorance of religion and a sort of false accusation of the religion.

> Hazrat Ibn Abbas (R.A.A.) has reported that when the Khawarij rose, he went in the presence of Hazrat Ali (R.A.A.) who said: "Go to them." He put on the best sheet from Yemen and went to meet them. They said : "Welcome O Ibn Abbas! but what chadar have you put on?" He replied :"You are objecting to my wearing this chador, but I have seen the Prophet of Allah wearing the best sheet on his body." (*Abu Daud*)

> Hazrat Bara (R.A.A.) says : "The Prophet was suffering from fever. I saw him clothed in a red *chador*, a better chador than that I had not seen." (*Muslim*)

This campaign of cleanliness and good taste reached homes and roads from the individuals. Islam commanded that the houses should be kept clean from dirt and filth, so that germs and insects may not breed, and diseases may not spread. The Jews were extremely lax in this matter, therefore the Muslims were warned not to copy them.

The Prophet (S.A.W.) has said: "Allah is pure (clean), and likes purity (cleanliness). He is clean and neat. Cleanliness is desired by Him. He is generous and generosity is His desired attribute. He is kind, He likes kindness. Therefore keep your homes and maidans clean and neat, and do not copy the likeness of the Jews."

To remove harmful things from the roads is an aspect of faith. This ordinary but important act has been considered as equivalent to charity.

In the *hadith* it is written:

> "To carry the burden of the weak is equivalent to salat (prayers) and to remove harmful things from the road has the reward of a prayer (Salat)."
>
> (*Ibn Khuzaima*)

> In another hadith it is mentioned:
>
> "Every step that is raised for going to prayers (salat) is equivalent to a charity, and if harmful thing is removed from the road, then it is also a charity."
>
> (*Bukhari*)

That is, if on the road there are stones, or thorns or filth that may be obstructing the coming and going of the people, to remove such an obstruction earns rewards (sawab).

Arrangement for Medical Treatment : The emphasis that Islam has made on man's cleanliness and health is in reality a part of the programme to boost the material and moral power of the Muslims. It requires such bodies in whose veins, instead of blood, currents of power and strength may be circulating, a limitless ocean of alertness and agility may be restless in them. Weak bodies cannot lift any burden, and shaking hands cannot perform any worthwhile act.

Healthy body does not only help in correct thinking and right behaviour, but also plays an important role in providing better men and societies. The Message of Islam cannot spread in the world through the weak hands and helpless steps, in view of its aims and multiplicity of fronts.

This is the reason why Islam has enmity with diseases. It has placed obstructions in the way of all the germs so that they may not spread and with their help the infectious diseases of weakness, helplessness may not gain ground and make headway.

As a measure of safety from diseases, Islam has formulated rules for cleanliness, hygiene and permanent neatness. Thereafter it decided on a well-organized and regulated life for its followers. Every Muslim has to follow these rules and regulations. All Muslims should wake up before the dawn, and therefore, should avoid unnecessary night-watching. They have to remain safe from the waywardness of the carnal desires and have to be balanced and moderate in the matter of their food and drink. In their living, in their character they have to be mindful of economy and moderation, and they have to seek freshness, and agility from the five times daily prayers and the annual onemonth fasting.

It should be remembered that avoiding sin in itself is, to a great extent, a means of being safe from the venereal diseases. If a Muslim becomes a victim of any disease then it is his duty to get medical treatment to remove that disease. Islam invites the attention of its followers to medical treatment in order to get themselves free from all diseases.

> Allah's Messenger (S.A.W.) has said : "Allah has sent down the cure for all diseases." (*Bukhari*)
>
> "Allah has created both medicine and disease, and has provided cure for every disease. Therefore, seek cure for your diseases but do not use in them haram (forbidden) things." (*Abu Daud*)
>
> "For every disease there is a medicine. If a medicine is used in a disease, cure is obtained by the grace of God." (*Muslim*)
>
> Islam has strictly forbidden the use of wrong, absurd and superstitious methods in treating the sick. It is true that there are experts for every branch of learning, and it is necessary to follow their instructions, but dealers in deception and con men try to interfere in every profession. To turn to such persons and to give credence to what they say is not proper for a Muslim.
>
> U'qba bin A'mir (R.A.A.) says that Allah's Messenger (S.A.W.) has said: "He who has hung a talisman, Allah will not fulfil his desire, and he who ties a shell (kaudi) round his neck, may Allah not keep him safe." (*Hakim*)

Inspite of such a severe warning, the use of gandas, talisman and magic has become very common among the Muslims, although Islam has considered it as a kind of polytheism, because all these things are the memento of the non-Islamic days when such superstitions and absurdities were ruling the roost.

> U'qba (R.A.A.) has also narrated that a delegation of ten riders came to embrace Islam to the Prophet (S.A.W.) . Allah's Messenger took the pledge from nine of them and stopped at the tenth one. The people asked what was the matter. The Prophet (S.A.W.) replied "On his arm there is a ganda (talisman)." That man broke and threw away the talisman. Then Allah's Prophet (S.A.W.) took the pledge from him. He said "He who hung these things, he committed polytheism against Allah." (*Ahmed*)

Islam has also fixed a way of preventing diseases by commanding that defecation be done at far off places so that the excreta may be drowned away in a deep pit and the water to be used may not be affected by it, and there should be no filth in the roads and sitting places.

If the Muslims had paid attention to all these things, they would have been safe from all the diseases which have broken their strength, which have ravaged their colonies, and which have made them extremely weak.

> Hazrat Jabir (R.A.A.) has narrated : "The Prophet (S.A.W.) has forbidden from urinating in the stagnant water." (*Muslim*)
>
> He has also narrated that the Prophet (S.A.W.) has forbidden from urinating in the flowing water.
>
> (*Abu Daud*)
>
> Ma'az (R.A.A.) has narratred : "Allah's Messenger (S.A.W.) has said : "Keep away from three reproachable acts: Do not urinate on the river-banks, on the higher portion of the road, and under a shadowy place."
>
> (*Abu Daud*)

That is, the person who is guilty of these acts will be liable to be reproached. The man who defecates in the public, he is bereft of modesty and decency. He has acted in a way which will increase repulsion and anger.

> Allah's Prophet (S.A.W.) has said: "Whoever harmed Muslims in their way, on him the curses and the reproaches of all the Muslims have become incumbent." (*Tibrani*)

In another tradition, it is mentioned:

> "Whoever has washed his excreta in any passage (way) of the Muslims, on him are the curses of Allah, the angels and all humans." (*Baihaqi*)

This restriction has been placed on all these things among Muslims with a view to preventing the spread of diseases, for when the people would start committing this nuisance, then nobody would be safe from trouble.

Islam has drawn a line of the healthy principles. If in any city an epidemic of some disease spreads, it builds up a wall of security around it, till the time the disease is controlled and its area of operation is much narrowed.

> Allah's Messenger (S.A.W.) has said : "If you hear the news of the spread of plague in any town, do not go there at all, and if at any place this disease spreads and you are present there, then do not come out from there." (*Bukhari*)

Islam has advised the residents of the city to remain there and has declared this act as desirable, because the love for security and safety would make a very large portion of the population to leave the city and thus endanger the whole country.

Accordingly, the Prophet (S.A.W.) has said:

> "If a man stays in a plague-afflicted city, he makes patience and Allah's pleasure his policy, and does not run away from there, he believes in the fact that he can receive only that harm which Allah has faced for him, then such a man gets the reward of a martyr." (*Bukhari*)

Some extremists try to travel towards the diseaseafficted city and they argue that the fear of loss is the weakness of faith and belief or it is the name of running away from destiny. But this is a severe mistake, because when in Syria plague was raging, Hazrat Umar (R.A.A.) refused to go there. When he was told that he was running away from the destiny fused by Allah, he said : "We are running away from the destiny of Allah towards His desire."

Provision of means and resources is right and this thing, according to Hazrat Umar (R.A.A.) is within the destiny, and Islam has exhorted to keep away from the infectious diseases.

> The Prophet (S.A.W.) has said : "A sick person should not go to a healthy person." (*Bukhari*)

In another hadith it is mentioned:

"Run away from a leper as you run away from a tiger." (*Bukhari*)

But we must also know that every disease is not an infectious disease. It so happens that a man has germs of a disease in his body but they do not harm him, because the defensive mechanism of his body is strong enough to fight the disease. He is relieved of the disease and he transfers it to others.

If every disease were infectious or communicable, then all the humans on the face of the earth would have died in one day. According to physicians, here there are conditions which nullify the effects of infectious diseases. Probably that is the meaning of the saying of the Prophet (S.A.W.) that "every infectious disease is not fatal." Here the denial is not of its being infectious or

3

Respectable Life

Offer devotions to Allah

Appoint no one His Partner

Be Good to :

Your Mother and Father, Your Kith and Kin, The Orphans, The Needy, The Neighbour—who is a relative, and The Neighbour —who is not a relative, The Companion—in whose fellowship you spend some time, however brief it may be, and Be kind to the traveller, The captives (slaves) who are under your charge. *(4:36)*

Respect for Parents

1. Behave well towards your father and mother and consider this good conduct as a propitious act which will earn Allah's grace in this world as well as in the next. Next to Allah, man owes the greatest obligation to his parents. The greatness and value of this obligation towards one's parents may be realised from the fact that the Holy Quran at several points mentions the rights of parents and the rights of Allah simultaneously at one place. Furthermore, the Holy Qur'an has ordained the duty of offering thanks to the parents along with thanksgiving to Allah.

   "Thy Lord hath decreed that ye worship none save Him and (that ye show) kindness to parents."*(17: 23)*

   Hazrat 'Abdullah ibn Mas'ud [R.A.A.] relates: "I submitted to the Holy Prophet [S.A.W.] which deed will win the highest favour of Allah?" The Holy Prophet [S.A.W.] answered: "The prayer which is offered at the appointed hour." I submitted again: "Next to this which other deed will win the greatest favour of Allah?" The Holy Prophet [S.A.W.] affirmed: "Good conduct towards father and mother." I again submitted: "And next to this?" The Prophet of Allah [S.A.W.] observed: "Jihad (Fighting) in the way of Allah." *(Bukhari, Muslim)*

Hazrat 'Abdullah [R.A.A.] reports: "One day a person went to the Holy Prophet [S.A.W.] and submitted: "I give my hand into your hand and swear allegiance for performing Hijrat and Jihad and I beseech a reward from Allah in return for this." The Holy Prophet [S.A.W.] enquired: "Is one of your parents alive?" He submitted: "Yes, praise be to Allah, both my father and mother are alive." Thereupon the Prophet of Allah [S.A.W.] observed: "Well then do you really want to receive a reward from Allah for performing Hijrat and Jihad'?" The man replied: "Yes, indeed, I beseech reward from Allah in return for these acts." The Holy Prophet [S.A.W.] observed: "Go then. Attend to your parents and serve them well." *(Muslim)*

Hazrat Abu Umama [R.A.A.] relates: "A man enquired from the Holy Prophet [S.A.W.]: "O Prophet of Allah [S.A.W.]! What are the rights of parents over their offspring?" The Holy Prophet [S.A.W.] affirmed: "Your entry into Paradise or Hell depends on your good or bad conduct towards your parents."

(Ibn Majah)

In other words, if you treat them well, you will be sent to Paradise and if you violate the rights that your parents have over you, you will be consigned to serve as fuel for Hell-Fire.

2. Be grateful to your parents. Thanksgiving and an acknowledgement of debt and gratitude are the first duties which a beneficiary owes to the Benefactor. It is a fact that the parents are the palpable cause for our existence. Again, it is under their protection and upbringing that we grow up to an age of maturity. The extraordinary self-sacrifice, unparalleled devotion and deep affection with which they patronise us demand that our hearts should be filled with sentiments of

reverence, indebtedness, love and an acknowledgement of their magnanimity and every fibre of our heart should pulsate with feelings of gratitude to them. It is for this reason that Allah has ordained offering of gratitude to parents along with thanksgiving to Him.

> "(We willed) that you should offer thanks to Me and remain grateful to your father and mother."

3. Always try to make your parents happy. Do not say anything in opposition to their will or temperament which may displease them, especially when they are advanced in age they acquire a peevish and irritable temperament. In old age the parents start making unexpected demands and begin proffering impossible claims. In this case also tolerate their behaviour in good cheer and do not say anything in anger in response to their demands which may cause them pain and may injure their feelings.

> "If one or both of thy parents reach an advanced age with thee, say not 'fie' unto them nor repulse them."

As a matter of fact, the strength to tolerate unpleasant things is sapped during old age and weakness increases the sense of selfimportance in old people. Hence they react sensitively to even the minor offensive matters. Keeping in view their delicate and sensitive nature, do not let your parents feel angry by any of your words or deeds.

Hazrat 'Abdullah b. Amr [R.A.A.] relates that the Holy Prophet [S.A.W.] affirmed: "The pleasure of Allah is contained in the pleasure of the father even as His displeasure is contained in the displeasure of the father."

(*Tirmidhi, Ibn Hibban, Hakim*)

In other words, any one who wants to please Allah should seek the pleasure of his father, for if the father is angry, the favour of Allah cannot be earned. The one who makes his father angry provokes the wrath of Allah."

Another statement of Hazrat 'Abdullah [R.A.A.] runs as follows: "A man left his parents weeping and came to the presence of the Holy Prophet [S.A.W.] for the purpose of offering allegiance to the Prophet [S.A.W.] for Hijrah. The Holy Prophet [S.A.W.] observed to him: "Go back to your parents and return after making them happy as you came after leaving them crying." *(Abu Dawud)*

4. Do service to your parents with heart and soul. If Allah has afforded you the opportunity to serve your parents, it is in fact a favourable opportunity for you to earn entitlement to Paradise and to win the Pleasure of Allah. Good service to parents secures blessings and grace in both worlds and man obtains salvation from the calamities of this world and the next. Hazrat Anas [R.A.A.] relates:

   "Any man who desires that his life should be prolonged and his subsistence may be increased ought to do good service to his parents and show kindness to them." *(Al-Targhib-o-Tarhib)*

   The Holy Prophet [S.A.W.] has observed:

   "Let that man be disgraced, and disgraced again and let him be disgraced even more." The people enquired: "O Prophet of Allah [S.A.W.]! who is that man?" The Prophet of Allah [S.A.W.] affirmed: "I refer to the man who finds his parents old in age both of them or one of them - and yet did not earn entitlement to Paradise by rendering good service to them." *(Muslim)*

   On one occasion, the Holy Prophet [S.A.W.] gave precedence to the obligation of looking after one's parents over one of the supreme forms of worship like Jihad. The Holy Prophet [S.A.W.] forbade a companion [R.A.A.] to proceed on Jihad and urged him to look after his parents.

   Hazrat 'Abdullah ibn 'Amr [R.A.A.] relates that a person came to the presence of the Holy Prophet [S.A.W.] with the intention of participating in the Jihad. The Holy Prophet [S.A.W.] enquired from him: "Are your father and mother alive?" He submitted: "Yes, they are alive." The Holy Prophet [S.A.W.] thereupon observed: "Go and render good service to them. This is the Jihad." *(Bukhari, Muslim)*

5. Respect and adore your parents and do not show disrespect to them by a single word or action. The Holy Qur'an affirms:

   "But speak to them a gracious word." *(17: 23)*

   On one occasion Hazrat 'Abdullah b. 'Umar [R.A.A.] enquired from Hazrat Ibn 'Abbas [R.A.A.]: "Do you wish to ward off Hell and gain entry into Paradise?" Ibn 'Abbas [R.A.A.] answered: "Yes, why not, I swear in the name of Allah I cherish this desire." Hazrat Ibn 'Umar then asked: "Are your parents alive?" Ibn 'Abbas [R.A.A.] replied: "Yes, my mother is alive." Ibn 'Umar [R.A.A.] remarked: "If you talk to them in a polite manner and look after their needs and feed them well, you will certainly be admitted to Paradise provided you abstain from capital evils." *(Al-Adab-ul Mufrad)*

   Hazrat Abu Huraira [R.A.A.] once saw two men. He asked one of them: "What is your relationship with the other man?" The person replied: "He is my father." Hazrat Abu Huraira [R.A.A.] thereupon advised him, "Look, never call him by his proper name, walk ahead of him nor sit before he takes his seat." *(Al-Adab-ul Mufrad)*

6. Be faithful and humble towards your parents.

   "And lower unto them the wing of submission through mercy." *(17: 23)*

   To offer humble obedience to parents implies to pay constant regard to their dignity. Do not assume a haughty attitude towards them, nor treat them with insolence.

7. Love your parents and consider this act as a privilege and a source of reward in the eternal world. Hazrat Ibn 'Abbas [R.A.A.] relates that the Holy Prophet [S.A.W.] observed:

   "The pious offspring who casts a single look of affection at his parents receives a reward from Allah equal to the reward of an accepted Hajj." The people submitted: "O Prophet of Allah [S.A.W.]: If someone casts a hundred such glances of love and affection at his parents, what then?" The Holy Prophet [S.A.W.] observed: "Yes, indeed, even if one does so a hundred time a day, he will get a hundred-fold reward. Allah is far greater than you imagine and is completely free from petty narrow mindedness. *(Muslim)*

8. Obey your parents with full devotion. Even if they show some intransigence, obey their will cheerfully. Keeping in view the great favours which they have done to you, try to fulfil all their demands willingly which may be offensive to your own taste or temperament, provided, of course, they are not derogatory to the tenets of religion.

   Hazrat Abu Said Khudri [R.A.A.] narrates that a person came to the presence of the Holy Prophet [S.A.W.] from Yemen. The Prophet of Allah [S.A.W.] enquired from him: "Do you have any relations in Yemen?" He submitted: "Yes, my father and mother are there." The Holy Prophet [S.A.W.] then asked: "Did they give you permission to leave?" He submitted: "No, I did not take their permission." The Prophet of Allah [S.A.W.] thereupon observed: "Go back then and ask the permission of your father and mother. If they agree, come back and join the Jihad, otherwise, attend on them and render good service to them." *(Abu Dawud)*

   Realise the value of rendering obedience to parents from the facts that a man came from miles intending to join the Holy Prophet [S.A.W.] in Holy war for the glory of religion, yet the Holy Prophet [S.A.W.] turned him back saying: "You can join the Holy War only if both your father and mother allow you to do so."

   Hazrat Ibn 'Abbas [R.A.A.] reports that the Holy Prophet [S.A.W.] observed: "The man who wakes up in the morning having previously discharged all the duties and obligations laid upon him by Allah concerning his parents, he will find the two gates of Paradise open for him on waking up in the morning; and in case there is only one parent, the person will find one door of Paradise open for him. And in contrast if a man wakes up in the morning having previously disregarded any obligations or duties laid upon him by Allah concerning his parents, then he will find two gates of Hell open for him on waking up in the morning; and in case one of the parents is alive, then the man will find one gate of Hell open for him." The man submitted: "O Prophet of Allah [S.A.W.], if the parents are treating him wrongly, what then?" The Holy Prophet [S.A.W.] affirmed: "Yes, even if they are treating him wrongly; yes, indeed even if they are treating him wrongly."

(Mishkat)

Consider your own goods as the property of your parents and spend your capital on them with an open hand. The Holy Qur'an affirms:

> "They ask thee, what they shall spend. Say what ye spend for good must go to parents."

On one occasion a man came to the presence of the Holy Prophet [S.A.W.] and complained that his father took whatever goods he wanted from him. The Holy Prophet [S.A.W.] sent for that man's father. An old, infirm man came walking with the help of a stick. When the Holy Prophet [S.A.W.] interrogated him on the point, the old man submitted: "O Prophet of Allah [S.A.W.]! There was a time when I was strong and he was weak and helpless. I had money and he was empty-handed. I never forbade him then to lay his hands on anything that I possessed. Today, he is strong and healthy and I am old and infirm. He has money and I am empty-handed. He now denies me access to his goods." Upon hearing this tale of the old man, the Benefactor of the humanity [S.A.W.] burst into tears and addressing the son of the old man observed: "You and your goods are the property of your father."

10. Even if your father and mother are non-Muslims, treat them well. Continue to pay them respect and devotion and serve them faithfully. However, in case they command you to become a polytheist or indulge in a sinful act, refuse to obey them and sternly repulse their demand.

> "And if your (parents) pressurise you to associate some one with Me of which you have no knowledge, obey them not, yet continue to treat them well in the world."

Hazrat Asma' [R.A.A.] states: "In the sacred lifetime of the Holy Prophet [S.A.W.], my mother visited me on one occasion. She was a polytheist at that time. I submitted to the Holy Prophet [S.A.W.]: "My mother has come to pay me a visit and she is an unbeliever in Islam. How should I treat her?" The Holy Prophet [S.A.W.] observed: "Yes, you should continue to show kindness to your mother." *(Bukhari)*

11. Offer prayers begging grace for your parents. Bring to mind their fervent appeals to the Allah and beg His mercy for them with a zealous and sincere heart. Allah ordains:

    "And say: My Allah! Have mercy on them both as they did care for me when I was little."

    In other words, say: "O Creator, with mercy, devotion, affection and love my Allah they reared me in childhood and sacrificed their own pleasure and ease for my sake but, they, in their infirmity and helplessness of old age, are more deserving of kindness and love than I ever was. Allah! I can pay them no recompense. Do patronise them and show them mercy in their miserable state."

12. Observe special care in looking after your mother. By nature, the mother is weak and more sensitive and needs your better treatment and devotion. Moreover, her favours and sacrifices are comparatively far greater than the father. Hence religion has conceded preferential rights to the mother and has enjoined upon the believers to treat their mothers with special consideration. The Holy Qur'an affirms:

    "And We have commanded unto man kindness towards parents. His mother beareth him with suffering, bringeth him forth with suffering, bearing of him and weaning of him is thirty months."*(46: 15)*

    While enjoining upon the believers to show good behaviour towards both father and mother, the Holy Qur'an has drawn a poignant picture of constant suffering of pain and hardships by the mother and has excellently pointed out in a psychological manner the fact that the devoted mother deserves comparatively more of your service and kind behaviour than your father. The same fact has been elucidated in greater detail by the Prophet of Allah [S.A.W.].

Hazrat Abu Huraira [R.A.A.] reports: "A man came to the presence of the Holy Prophet [S.A.W.] and submitted: "O Prophet of Allah [S.A.W.]! Who deserves the noblest treatment from me?" The Holy Prophet [S.A.W.] observed: "Your mother." He again submitted: "And next?" The Holy Prophet [S.A.W.] observed: "Your mother." When the man submitted for the fourth time: "And who next?" The Holy Prophet [S.A.W.] observed: "Your father." *(AL-Adabul Mufrad)*

Hazrat Jahma [R.A.A.] paid a call on the Holy Prophet [S.A.W.] and submitted: "O Prophet of Allah [S.A.W.]! I wish to join you in the Jihad and have come to solicit your guidance in this matter. I seek your command." The Holy Prophet [S.A.W.] enquired from him: "Is your mother alive?" Jahma [R.A.A.] submitted: "Yes, she is alive." Thereupon the Holy Prophet [S.A.W.], said "Return to her then and devote yourself to her service, for Paradise lies under her feet." *(Ibn Majah, Nasa'i)*

Hazrat Awais [R.T.A.] was a contemporary of the Holy Prophet [S.A.W.], but he could never attain the privilege of calling on the Holy Prophet [S.A.W.]. He had an old mother to whose service he devoted himself day and night. He cherished a great desire to see the Holy Prophet [S.A.W.] and it was but natural for every Muslim to have a burning desire to catch a glimpse of the Prophet of Allah [S.A.W.]. Hazrat Awais [R.T.A.] indeed wanted to pay a call, yet the Holy Prophet [S.A.W.] forbade him to come. Similarly, Hazrat Awais [R.T.A.] cherished an ambition to discharge the obligation of Hajj, yet as long as his mother remained alive, Hazrat Awais [R.T.A.] never set out for the Hajj alone. He fulfilled the desire to perform Hajj after his mother's demise.

13. Treat your foster mother well. Do service to her and show her respect and adoration. Hazrat Abu Tufail [R.A.A.] states: "I once witnessed the Holy Prophet [S.A.W.] distributing meat at a place called 'Ja'rana'. Presently, a lady arrived and approached near the Holy Prophet [S.A.W.]. The Holy Prophet of Allah [S.A.W.] spread out his sheet for her and the lady sat

on it. I enquired from the people, "Who is this lady?" The people told me: "This lady is the foster mother of the Holy Prophet [S.A.W.]. *(Abu Dawud)*

14. Remember your parents after they have passed away. Observe the following etiquettes to render good service to your deceased parents:

    (i) Offer prayers continuously invoking mercy of Allah upon your dead father and mother.

    The Holy Qur'an enjoins upon the pious to say this prayer:

    > "O our Allah! Grant forgiveness to me and my parents and pardon all the faithful on the day of Reckoning."

    Hazrat Abu Huraira [R.A.A.] states: "When the deceased is elevated to high degrees of favour, he enquires in astonishment: "How so?" He is informed by Allah, "Your offsprings have been offering prayers, begging mercy for you (and Allah has accepted those petitions of mercy)."

    Hazrat Abu Huraira [R.A.A.] also states:

    > "The Holy Prophet [S.A.W.] observed: The opportunity to do something ends with one's death yet there are three things which continue to afford benefit to him after death-a recurring charitable act; knowledge which he has imparted to others from which people derive benefit and thirdly, pious offsprings who continue to offer prayers invoking mercy of Allah upon him."

    (ii) Fulfil all the contracts and promises made by your parents and carry out their will. Your parents must have made many agreements with some people, they might have made a covenant with Allah; they might have taken a vow; they might have promised to deliver goods to someone; they might have owed a debt to somebody but were unable to discharge it before death overtook them; they might have made a will at the time of their death. Fulfil all these obligations to the extent of your means.

Hazrat 'Abdullah b. 'Abbas [R.A.A.] narrates: "Hazrat Sa'd b. Ubaba [R.A.A.] submitted to the Holy Prophet [S.A.W.], "O Prophet of Allah [S.A.W.]! My mother had taken a vow, but she expired before discharging it. Can I carry out the vow on her behalf?" The Holy Prophet [S.A.W.] affirmed: "Why not! You must carry out the vow taken by her."

(iii) Show good conduct to the friends of your father and the female companions of your mother. Treat them with respect. Seek their advice just as you seek the advice of your elders and pay due regard to their opinions and advice. On one occasion, the Holy Prophet [S.A.W.] observed: There is no superior deed of piety than that man should do good service to the companions and friends of his father."

Once Hazrat Abu Darda [R.A.A.] fell ill and his condition continued to aggravate till they lost all hopes of his life. Hazrat Yusuf b. 'Abdullah [R.A.A.] made a long journey and came to enquire after his health. On seeing him, Hazrat Abu Darda asked in astonishment: "How are you here?" Yusuf b. 'Abdullah [R.A.A.] replied: "I have come here only to enquire after your health, for you were on terms of deep friendship with my late father."

Hazrat Abu Darda [R.A.A.] relates: "When I arrived in Madinah, 'Abdullah b. 'Umar [R.A.A.] paid me a visit and said: "Abu Darda, do you know why I have come to see you?" I replied: "No. I have no idea why you have come here." Thereupon Hazrat 'Abdullah b. 'Umar [R.A.A.] said: "I have heard the Prophet of Allah [S.A.W.] as affirming: "The man who wishes to render good service to his father, who is in the grave, ought to show good treatment to his father's companions and friends." Having related this saying of the Holy Prophet [S.A.W.] 'Abdullah b. Umar [R.A.A.] remarked: "Brother, my father

'Umar and your father [R.A.A.] were on terms of deep friendship. I wish to commemorate this friendship and fulfil its duties." *(Ibn Hibban)*

(iv) Show constant good treatment to the relations of your parents and entertain full respect and pay due regard to the sanctity of these connexions. An indifferent and irresponsible conduct towards these relations is tantamount to treating your own parents with indifference and negligence. The Holy Prophet [S.A.W.] observed: "Do not observe indifference towards your forefathers. To show carelessness in your conduct towards your parents is to display ingratitude to Allah."

15. If, Allah forbid, you have been guilty of negligence in treating your parents well or discharging your full obligations towards them during their lifetime, do not despair of Allah's mercy. Offer prayers constantly invoking blessings of Allah upon your deceased parents. It is possible Allah may forgive your sin of negligence and admit you among the ranks of the pious people. Hazrat Anas [R.A.A.] relates: The Holy Prophet [S.A.W.] affirmed:

> "If a person does not observe filial devotion to his parents during their lifetime, and both parents or one of them passes away, the person ought to offer prayers for his deceased parents and beg His Mercy and beseech Him to grant salvation to them till Allah in His Mercy ordains their admission to the rolls of the pious people."

Family Life

The sublime culture and civilisation which Islam envisages can only come into existence when we succeed in building up the structure of a righteous society. And a stable and well-organised family system is a prerequisite for the birth of a righteous society. Family life begins with the sacred matrimonial connexion between husband and wife and the development of this connexion into a permanently happy and pleasant matrimonial life chiefly depends on the full awareness of the etiquettes and duties of marital life in both husband and wife and their zeal, sincerity and devotion to observe those etiquettes and discharge obligations of married life. Let us in the first place deal with those etiquettes and obligations which concern the husband and then we shall proceed to discuss the etiquettes and duties to be observed by the wife.

1. Treat your wife well in life. Discharge your obligations towards her with a liberal heart and adopt a favourable and selfsacrificing attitude in every matter concerning your wife. Allah ordains:

   "And live with them in a good manner."

   In a sermon to a mammoth congregation on the eve of Hajjatul-Widah (Last Hajj) of the Prophet [S.A.W.], the Holy Prophet [S.A.W.] enjoined upon the Muslims:

   "O people! Listen! Behave well towards women, for they are like captives with you. You have no right to give them harsh treatment save in the case when they show open disobedience. If they are guilty of disobedience, keep away from them in the bed room. In case you punish them, take care not to cause them severe injury. When they come round and obey your will, do not find pretexts to harass them. Listen carefully! you have some rights over your wives and your wives have some rights over you. They owe an obligation to you not to let your beds be trampled by anyone whom you dislike and not let anyone trespass into your house whose visit you do not like. And listen, you owe a duty to them to feed them well and provide good clothing to them." *(Riyad-us-Salihin)*

   In other words, make such provisions for their feeding and clothing as are befitting to a marital relationship of unique intimacy, union of hearts and a spirit of companionship.

2. Entertain a good opinion about your wife as far as possible and adopt an attitude of politeness, toleration and magnanimity for the sake of amicable living with her. If she lacks beauty of face or person or is deficient in good manners, morality, good sense or skill in household affairs, bear these faults with patience. Look to her virtues and maintain a harmonious relationship by means of generosity, liberality of

mind and self-sacrifice. Allah ordains:

"And amity contains goodness."

And the believers are enjoined upon as follows:

"For if ye hate them it may happen that ye hate a thing wherein Allah hath placed much good." *(4: 19)*

The same subject has been elucidated by the Holy Prophet [S.A.W.] in the following Tradition:

"No believer should hate his pious wife. If he dislikes one habit of his wife, it is possible he may like her for some other aspects of her character."

As a matter of fact, each woman has some weakness of one sort or another and if the husband turns against her on account of her bearing a certain deficiency and conceives a hatred for her, a pleasant home life becomes impossible for the couple. Common-sense dictates that man should adopt a liberal attitude and reposing his trust in Allah should endeavour to live amicably with his wife. It is possible that Allah may vouchsafe to that man merely for the sake of this woman, such bounties which his limited mind cannot comprehend. For instance, this woman may possess excellent virtues of religion, faith, character and morality in reward for which Allah may shower blessings upon her own family or may be a pious soul is born of this woman who may prove beneficial for the whole mankind and may serve as a Sadaqa Jariah (Continuing Charity) in favour of the father till the end of his life, or perhaps the woman may serve as a means of reforming the character of her man and thus may help him to gain proximity to Paradise or it may be that Allah may bless this man with large subsistence and prosperity because such a blessing of prosperity was destined for his wife. At any rate, do not ruin your married life impetuously on the grounds of an apparent defect in the woman. On the other hand, be wise and try to promote gradually an atmosphere of happiness and concord in the home.

3. Adopt an attitude of forgiveness and kindness. Forget all the faults of omission, stupid actions and disobedient attitude of

your wife. The woman is deficient and weak in wisdom and Common-sense and bears an extremely passionate temperament. Hence try to bring her round with patience, calmness, kindness, affection and devotion. Try to get along with her with patience and restraint. Allah ordains:

> "O ye who believe! verily, among your wives and your children, there are enemies for you, therefore beware of them. And if ye efface and overlook and forgive, then Allah is Forgiving, Merciful." *(Attaghabun: 14)*

The Holy Prophet [S.A.W.] affirmed:

> "Be good to women. The woman has been created out of the rib and the uppermost part of the rib ends in a curve; so if you try to straighten out the curve, it will break, yet if you leave it alone, the curve will remain. Hence, be good to women." *(Bukhari, Muslim)*

4. Treat your wife politely and show love and affection to her. The Holy Prophet [S.A.W.] has affirmed:

> "The believers who possess perfect faith are those who display the best manners, and the best among you are those who treat their wives in the best possible manner." *(Tirmidhi)*

Politeness and tenderness of behaviour can best be judged in the home. People are constantly living amidst their family members and the real temper and moral conduct of man is completely revealed in the free and uninhibited atmosphere of the home. It is a fact that only such believers possess perfect faith who display civility, kindness, and affectionate behaviour towards their family members and who support, sympathise, love and adore inmates of their household.

Hazrat 'Aisha [R.A.A.] reports: "I used to play with dolls along with my playmates in the house of the Holy Prophet [S.A.W.]. On the arrival of the Holy Prophet [S.A.W.] all of them used to hide themselves in the nooks and corners of the house. The Prophet [S.A.W.] used to search out each one of them and send them to join me in the play." *(Bukhari, Muslim)*

Once on the occasion of Hajj, the camel of Hazrat Safiyah [R.A.A.] sat down on the ground and she was therefore left behind while the entire caravan passed on. The Holy.Prophet [S.A.W.] came to her and found her weeping without restraint. The Holy Prophet [S.A.W.] stood there wiping off her tears with the edge of a sheet with his own holy hands. While the Prophet of Allah [S.A.W.] wiped off tears from her eyes, she [R.A.A.] continued to weep unrestrainedly for a long time."

5. Make liberal provisions for all the needs of your wife and do not stint in expenses. Feel a sense of pleasure and comfort in spending your lawful earnings on members of your family. You owe an obligation to your wife to provide her with food and clothing and to struggle energetically, in order to earn enough money to discharge this obligation, is the most pleasant duty of a husband. The performance of this duty with an open and cheerful heart earns for the believer the reward of a happy marital life in this world and a favourable recompense and bounty in the world to come. The Holy Prophet [S.A.W.] has affirmed:

   "You spend a dinar in the way of Allah; you spend another dinar to ransom a slave; you give away one dinar as alms to a beggar; and there is one dinar which you spend on your family. Among all these, the dinar that will earn the best reward and blessings of Allah is the one which you have spent on your family."
   (Muslim)

6. Teach your wife the rules and manners enjoined by religion. Let her observe Islamic morality and make her life graceful. Make every possible effort to train and mould her according to the Islamic pattern of life so that she may prove to be a good wife, good mother and a pious devotee of Allah and may discharge her duties as a wife efficiently and faithfully. Allah affirms:

   "O ye who believe! Save yourselves and your family from the Fire of Hell."

   As the Holy Prophet [S.A.W.] devoted himself to preaching and teaching the laws of religion outside the home, likewise he continued to perform the same function inside his home. Making an illusion to this fact, the Holy Qur'an addresses the wives of the Holy Prophet [S.A.W.] in these words:

> "And remember the verses of Allah and the matters of wisdom that are conveyed to you in your house."

The Qur'an has advised the believers through the ministry of the Holy Prophet [S.A.W.]:

> "And urge upon the inmates of your house to observe prayers and fully abide by this obligation yourself too."

The Prophet of Allah [S.A.W.] affirms:

> "When a man wakes up his wife during the night and they offer two Rak'ats of Prayers together, Allah ordains that the man's name should be included in the rolls of the male remembers of Allah and the woman's name in the register of those females who offer praises to Allah and remember Him."
>
> *(Abu Dawud)*

The second Caliph Hazrat 'Umar [R.A.A.] used to stand all night offering devotions to Allah. Near the hour of dawn he used to wake his wife saying: "Rise, get up and say prayers," and later he [R.A.A.] used to recite this verse also:

> "And urge upon the inmates of your house to observe prayers and fully abide by this obligation yourself."

7. If you possess several wives; show equal treatment to all of them. The Holy Prophet [S.A.W.] used to observe great care in dispensing equal treatment to his wives. On the eve of setting out for a journey the Prophet of Allah [S.A.W.] used to draw lots and took with him the wife whose name was decided by the toss. Hazrat Abu Huraira [R.A.A.] states that the Holy Prophet [S.A.W.] observed:

> "If a man has two wives, but does not treat them with equality and even-handed justice, he shall be resurrected on the Day of Judgement in such a condition that half of his body is paralysed."
>
> *(Tirmidhi)*

'Justice' and 'equality' imply to treat them equally in all matters and show the same kind of behaviour to each wife. As regards the fact that a man may be specially attracted towards one wife or may be drawn to her or cherish deeper feelings of love for her, Allah will award no punishment to the man for it.

8. Obey your husband with a willing heart and feel pleasure and satisfaction in being faithful to him. This is what Allah commands a wife to do and the believing woman. Who acts according to the will of Allah wins His Favour. The Holy Qur'an affirms:

   "The pious wives are those who show obedience to their husbands."

   The Holy Prophet [S.A.W.] observed:

   "No woman should keep fast without the permission of her husband." *(Abu Dawud)*

   Stressing the importance of rendering obedience and devotion to her husband, the Holy Prophet [S.A.W.] has warned the woman:

   "There are two types of persons whose prayers do not rise above their heads-the prayer of a slave who deserts his master until he returns to his service and the prayer of a woman who shows disobedience to her husband until she recants from this behaviour."

   (Al-Targhib-o-Al-Tarhib)

9. Protect your honour and chastity. Keep away from all matters of activities which contain a possible threat to violate your honour or chastity. This is what Allah commands and it is also an essential prerequisite for making your marital life happy and pleasant. No amount of devotion and obedience of the wife can win the heart of her husband if the seeds of suspicion about her infidelity are once sown in his mind. Even an ordinary act of carelessness on the wife's part may prompt the devil to fill the heart of her husband with indelible doubts and suspicions. Hence keeping in view this human weakness, exercise utmost vigilance in such matters.

The Prophet of Allah has affirmed:

> "If the woman offers prayers five times a day, protects her honour and chastity, remains faithful to her husband, she may enter Paradise by whichever gate she likes." *(Al-Targhib-o-Al-Tarhib)*

10. Do not go out of the house without leave or permission of your husband. Do not call at homes of which your husband disapproves, nor admit anyone into your house whom your husband dislikes.

Hazrat Mu'adh ibn Jabal [R.A.A.] narrates that the Prophet of Allah [S.A.W.] observed:

> "It is not lawful for a woman who believes in Allah to admit a man into her house whose visit is disapproved of by her husband or that she should go out of the house against her husband's will or she should obey the will of someone else in opposition to her husband's wishes." *(Al-Targhib-o-Al-Tarhib)*

In other words, obey the wishes of your husband, even watch and be mindful of the slightest indications of his approval or disapproval. Do not follow the counsels of others which are in opposition to the will of your husband.

11. It should be your permanent concern to make your husband happy by your words, actions, behaviour and manners. This is not only the real secret of a successful marriage, but a means to win the favour of Allah and admittance into Paradise. The Holy Prophet [S.A.W.] has affirmed:

> "The woman who dies in such a state that her husband was entirely satisfied and in concord with her, will certainly enter Paradise." *(Tirmidhi)*

Furthermore, the Holy Prophet [S.A.W.] observed:

> "When a man calls his wife to fulfil the sexual urge and she declines and for this reason the husband remains angry with her all night, the angels send curses upon such a wife till dawn." *(Bukhari, Muslim)*

12. Love your husband and value his companionship. He is the adornment of your life, your life's support and a great companion and helper in the course of your life. Give thanks to Allah for this great Bounty and value this Bounty too with all your heart and soul. The Holy Prophet [S.A.W.] observed on one occasion:

 "For the two who love one another there is no better thing than the 'Nikah' (matrimonial tie)."

 Hazrat Safiyah [R.A.A.] cherished deep love for the Holy Prophet [S.A.W.]. When illness overcame the Holy Prophet of Allah [S.A.W.], Hazrat Safiyah [R.A.A.] spoke with genuine concern: "Would Allah that I had fallen ill instead of you, O Holy Prophet of Allah [S.A.W.]!" At this expression of deep love by Hazrat Safiyah [R.A.A.], the other wives of the Holy Prophet [S.A.W.] looked towards her in astonishment. Thereupon the Holy Prophet [S.A.W.] observed:

 "She is not merely making show of her affection; she is expressing her genuine love."

13. Acknowledge the debt of gratitude you owe to your husband and remain grateful to him. Your greatest benefactor is your husband who is always concerned with making you happy, providing for your needs and feels satisfied when he has made all provisions for your comfort.

 Hazrat Asma [R.A.A.] narrates the Tradition: I was once with my neighbour friend when the Holy Prophet [S.A.W.] passed near me. He [S.A.W.] said 'Salam' [peace be on you] to us and observed: "Avoid being ungrateful to those whom you owe a debt of gratitude. One of you, for instance, lives with her parents in an unmarried state for a long period. Then Allah confers upon her a husband. Subsequently, Allah grants her offspring. Yet in spite of all these favours when she feels enraged with her husband on some matter, she utters, 'Never have I received anything good from you." *(Al-Adabul Mufrad)*

 The Holy Prophet [S.A.W.] in a warning statement to an ungrateful and unthinking wife observed:

> "On the Day of Judgement, Allah will not even look at a woman who is ungrateful to her husband, despite the fact that a wife can never get along without her husband." *(Nasa'i)*

14. Feel happy in doing service to your husband and afford maximum comfort to him at the expense of your own inconvenience. Devote yourself to his welfare in all matters and by means of this sincere service capture the deep affections of his heart. Hazrat 'Aisha [R.A.A.] used to wash the clothes of the Holy Prophet [S.A.W.] with her own hands, annointed his sacred head with oil, combed his hair, and rubbed perfume on his holy person. The other contemporary pious ladies [R.A.A.] served their husbands in the same manner.

    On one occasion, the Holy Prophet [S.A.W.] observed:

    > "It is unlawful for a human being to prostrate before another human. If it had been permissible, the wife would have been ordained by Allah to offer prostration to her husband. The husband has the supreme right over his wife, and such is the optimum degree of this right that in case a husband's whole body is covered with wounds and the wife licks them all with her tongue, the obligation she owes to her husband is even then not discharged in full measure."*(Musnad Ahmad)*

15. Safeguard the home, property and goods of your husband. After marriage consider the husband's home as your own and spend the wealth of your husband wisely and economically on the adornment of your home, on the enhancement of the prestige of your husband and on securing a better future for your children.

    Consider the advancement and prosperity of your husband as your own personal achievements. Praising the virtues of the women of the tribe of Quraish, the Holy Prophet [S.A.W.] observed:

    > "How excellent are the women of the tribe of Quraish!

> They are most affectionate towards children and most efficient guardians of their husband's homes."
>
> *(Bukhari)*

Describing the virtues of a pious wife, the Holy Prophet [S.A.W.] observed:

> "Next to the fear of Allah the most useful and the bountiful reward for a believer is a pious wife. When he asks her to do something, she does it cheerfully. When he looks at her, she pleases him to the core of his heart. When he swears upon her trust, she fulfils his oath. When he goes away, she protects her honour and chastity in his absence and finally in superintendence of her husband's goods and property she remains truly faithful and devoted to his interest."
>
> *(Ibn Majah)*

16. Observe cleanliness, manage you household affairs wisely and look after the decoration and furnishing of your homes. Keep your house clean. Arrange everything tidily and use things with proper care and skill. A clean and tidy home, neatly furnished rooms, good management of household affairs and home economy and a beautifully dressed and adorned wife wearing a pleasant smile on her lips ....all this charges the home atmosphere with currents of deep love and affection and the marital life is enriched with happiness and blessings. This is the only way for a wife to gain her personal salvation and to win the favour of Allah.

    On one occasion during a meeting Hazrat 'Aisha [R.A.A.] saw that the wife of `Uthman b. 'Maz'un [R.A.A.] was dressed in plain clothes and wore no adornments. Hazrat 'A'isha [R.A.A.] was taken aback and enquired:

    > "My good lady! Has your husband 'Uthman gone out on a journey?"

    You can judge from the exclamation of Hazrat 'Aisha [R.A.A.] what a propitious act it is for a married woman to adorn and beautify herself for her husband.

Once a Muslim lady of Madinah [R.A.A.] presented herself before the Holy Prophet [S.A.W.]. She was at that time wearing gold bangles. The Holy Prophet [S.A.W.] expressed his disapproval of her wearing the gold bangles. The lady submitted:

> "O Prophet of Allah [S.A.W.]! If a woman does not adorn herself and make her person attractive for her husband, she would soon lose her value for him."
>
> *(Nasa'i)*

Looking for Children

1. Consider your children as a bounty of Allah. Celebrate the birth of a child with joy and exchange messages of congratulation on such occasion. Welcome the birth of children with prayers for grace and blessings of Allah. Offer thanks to Allah that He has conferred upon you the favour of rearing one of His creatures and that He has afforded you the opportunity of leaving behind an heir to represent you in spiritual as well as mundane life.
2. If you are childless, pray to Allah for favour of granting you pious offspring in the same manner as the venerable Prophet of Allah Hazrat Zakaria [A.S.] had prayed to Allah for the grant of pious offspring.

   "Allah! Bestow upon me by Thy bounty goodly offspring. Lo! Thou art the Hearer of prayer." *(3: 38)*
3. Do not feel downcast on the birth of a child. Strictly guard against feeling remorse or considering the birth of a child as a burden on account of financial hardship, ill health or for any other reason.
4. Do not procure an abortion. Abortion or killing a child after birth are both acts of heinous barbarity, gruesome cruelty and extreme cowardice and entail ruination in this world and Hereinafter. Allah affirms:

   > "Those who kill their children out of their foolishness are the great losers." *(6: 140)*

In an impressive condemnation of human shortsightedness, Allah has clearly forbidden the genocide of children:

> "Slay not your children fearing poverty. We shall provide for them and for you. Lo! the slaying of them is great sin." *(17: 31)*

On one occasion a companion [R.A.A.] enquired from the Holy Prophet [S.A.W.], "O Prophet of Allah [S.A.W.]! Which is the greatest sin?" The Holy Prophet [S.A.W.] observed: "Polytheism." The companion [R.A.A.] again asked: "And what next" The Holy Prophet [S.A.W.] observed: "Disobedience to parents." The companion [R.A.A.] enquired the third time: "And which sin is the greatest next to it?" In answer to this, the Holy Prophet of Allah [S.A.W.] observed: "To kill you children fearing that they will share your sustenance."

5. At the time of delivery, recite Ayat-ul-Kursi and the following two verses of Surah Al-A'raf near the pregnant woman. Recite also Sürah 'ALFalaq' and Surah 'An-Nas' repeatedly and after each recitation blow your breath over the woman awaiting delivery:

   "Allah! There is no Allah save Him, the Alive, the Eternal. Neither slumber nor sleep overtaketh Him, unto Him belongeth whatsoever is in the heavens and whatsoever is in the earth. Who is that interecedeth with Him save by His leave? He knoweth that which is in front of them and that which is behind them while they encompass nothing of His knowledge save that what He wills. His throne includeth the heavens and the earth and He is never weary of preserving them. He is the Sublime, the Tremendous." *(2:255)*

   The two verses of Surah A'raf are as under:

   > "Lo! your Lord is Allah Who created the heavens and the earth in six days, and then sat upon the throne of His Kingdom. Who makes the night cover the day which is in haste to follow it and has made the sun and the moon and the stars subservient by His Command. His verily is all creation and command-

ment. Blessed be Allah the Lord of the worlds! (O mankind) Call upon your Lord humbly and in secret. Lo! He loveth not aggressors." *(7: 54, 55)*

6. After birth, bathe the infant and say adhan in its right and Iqamat in its left ear. On the birth of Hazrat Husain [R.A.A.], the Holy Prophet [S.A.W.] had said adhan and Iqamat in his ears." *(Tabrani)*

   The Holy Prophet [S.A.W.] is also reported to have affirmed: "Whenever someone begets a child and says Adhan in its right and Iqamai in its left ear, the child is immunised against the affliction of *Umm-ul-Sibiyan*[1] by this act." *(Abu Ya'la)*

   There is great wisdom in conveying the names of Allah and His Messenger [S.A.W.] to the ears of a new-born infant.

   In his work entitled 'Tuhfa-tul-Wadud', 'Allama Ibn Qayyim observes: "The significance of this act is that the proclamation of the Greatness and Glory of Allah should be the first to reach the ears of a human being. And the affirmation of belief which he will render in full consciousness later in order to enter the fold of Islam should be conveyed to him in the very first day of his life as a man is prompted to recite Kalimah Tauhid (Affirmation of belief in One God) at the time of his death. Another advantage of saying the Adan and Iqamat in the ears of the child is that the devil, who lies in ambush planning to entrap the human being in trials, flees on hearing the sound of Adan and before the devil can draw the soul of the child towards himself, the child is called towards Islam and worship of Allah."

7. After the Adan and Iqamat get a date chewed by some pious man or woman and paste its pulp on the palate of the infant and ask that man or woman to offer a prayer invoking grace and blessings of Allah upon the child. Hazrat Asma [R.A.A.] reports: "When 'Abdullah ibn Zubair [R.A.A.] was born I put him in the lap of the Holy Prophet [S.A.W.]. The Holy Prophet [S.A.W.] asked for a date, chewed it and applied his sacred saliva inside the mouth and pasted the chewed pulp of date on the palate of 'Abdullah ibn Zubair. Afterwards, the Holy

Prophet [S.A.W.] offered a prayer invoking grace and blessings of Allah upon the child."

Hazrat 'Aisha [R.A.A.] states: "Infants were brought to the presence of the Holy Prophet [S.A.W.]. The Holy Prophet [S.A.W.] used to *Tehnik*[2] and pray for the favour and blessings of Allah upon him." *(Muslim)*

When Hazrat Imam Ahmad ibn Hambal [R.A.A.] was blessed with a child, he asked for Meccan date which was available in the home and requested a pious lady Umm 'Ali [R.T.A.] to perform the Tehnik.

8. Give your child a fine name, preferably a name resembling that of the Prophets [peace be upon them] or put a prefix 'Abd with some attribute of Allah, just as 'Abd-Allah or 'Abd-Rahman, to make up a name for your child.

   The Holy Prophet [S.A.W.] has affirmed: "On the Day of Judgement, you shall be called by your names. So prescribe fine names for yourselves." *(Abu Dawud)*

   Furthermore, the Holy Prophet [S.A.W.] observed: "Among all your names 'Abdullah and, 'Abdul Rahman are the favourites of Allah." In addition, the Prophet [S.A.W.] affirmed: "Prescribe those names which resemble the names of the Prophets [A.S.]."

   It is recorded in Bukhari that the Holy Prophet [S.A.W.] also observed: "Name your children after my name, but do not give them my 'Kuniyyat'."

9. If you have prescribed a wrong name due to ignorance, change it and prescribe some good name. The Holy Prophet [S.A.W.] used to alter wrong names. The name of one of Hazrat 'Umar's [R.A.A.] daughter was 'Asiya. The Holy Prophet [S.A.W.] changed it and named her Jamila [R.A.A.]. *(Muslim)*

   The original name of Hazrat Zainab [R.A.A.] the daughter of Abu Salama [R.A.A.] was 'Barrah' which means the pious one'. On hearing this name, the Holy Prophet [S.A.W.] observed: "Do you make a self proclamation of piety?" The people submitted, "What other name shall we prescribe then?" The Prophet [S.A.W.] observed: "Name her Zainab." *(Abu Dawud)*

10. Perform the Aquiqa ceremony on the seventh day of the birth of a child. Sacrifice two lambs for a boy and one if the baby is a girl. However, it is not obligatory to slaughter two lambs for a boy. You may sacrifice one animal also. Get the hair of the head of the baby shaved off and give away in charity gold or silver equal in weight to these hair. The Holy Prophet [S.A.W.] has observed:

    "Prescribe a name for the child on the seventh day after birth and perform 'Aquiqa[3] ceremony after getting the baby's head shaved off." *(Tirmidi)*

11. Get the male child circumcised on the seventh day after birth. However, if for some reason the operation is put off, it is obligatory to get the circumcision performed before the male child reaches the age of seven. Circumcision is part of Islamic faith.

12. When the child learns to speak, teach him first of all to recite: La Ilaha Illallahu. (There is no god but Allah.) The Holy Prophet [S.A.W.] has observed:

    When your offspring starts speaking, teach him to recite: La Ilaha Illallahu. (There is no god but Allah) and never fear about his end. When the milk teeth are uprooted, order your child to observe prayers.

    The Tradition also records that whenever a child in the household of the Holy Prophet [S.A.W.] began to speak, the Prophet [S.A.W.] used to teach him the second verse of Surah al-Furqan in which the concept of the belief in One God has been beautifully expressed in a concise form.

    "He unto Whom belongeth the sovereignty of the heavens and the earth, He hath chosen no son nor hath He any partner in the sovereignty. He hath created everything and hath meted out for it a role."

13. Feed the child on your breast-milk. The mother owes this obligation to the child. The Holy Qur'an has made repeated references to this favour of the mother to her child and has enjoined the pious to treat their mothers with extraordinary devotion in return for their favour. It is the duty of the mother

to inculcate in the soul of the child belief in One God, devotion to the Prophet [S.A.W.] and love of religion along with the drops of her milk which she feeds to the child. She should make sure that the heart and soul of her child completely assimilates the spirit of religion. Do not ease your burden by transferring the duty of rearing the child to a nurse. Perform this pleasant obligation of religion yourself and enjoy spiritual satisfaction and ecstasy.

14. Avoid frightening the children. The fright instilled in the mind of the child in the early years overshadows his mind and intellect for the remainder of his life and these children usually prove incapable of achieving extraordinary success in life.

15. Make it a point not to shout at, reproach or rebuke children on every trifling matter. Make an affectionate endeavour to train the children to form good habits with devotion and good sense instead of expressing annoyance or contempt on the faults of children. However, act in such a way that children must remain in fear that you will not tolerate any of their actions which do not conform to the dictates of religion.

16. Always treat your children with affection, love and tenderness. Keep them happy by providing for their needs and requirements according to you means. Promote sentiments of loyalty and devotion in your children.

    Once Hazrat Mu'awiya [R.A.A.] asked Ahnaf ibn Qais [R.A.A.], "Say, in what manner the offspring should be treated?"

    Ahnaf ibn Qais [R.A.A.] answered: *'Amir-ul-Mo'minin,* the offspring are the fruit of our hearts, a support for our backs; we are like the sky providing a protective shade over them; we are like a soft and harmless ground on which they recline. It is they who give us the incentive to perform great deeds. Hence if they demand anything from you, fulfil their demand with a generous heart. If they are stricken with sorrow, alleviate their grief. Consequently they will love you and appreciate your paternal concern. Do not be an intolerable burden on them to the extent that they should in annoyance wish that you were better dead than alive and hate to come near you."

Hazrat Mu'awiya [R.A.A.] was deeply moved on hearing this wise speech of Ahnaf ibn Qais [R.A.A.] and remarked: "Ahnaf, [R.A.A.] I swear in the name of Allah that when you came and sat beside me I was burning with rage against Yazid."

Later, when Hazrat Ahnaf [R.A.A.] departed Hazrat Mu'awiya's [R.A.A.] anger had cooled down and he felt reconciled to Yazid. He at once sent two hundred dirhams and two hundred dresses as a token of love to Yazid. On receiving these presents, Yazid divided them into two equal portions and despatched one hundred dirhams and a hundred dresses as a gift to Hazrat Ahnaf ibn Qais [R.A.A.].

17. Pat the heads of children with affection; take them up and seat them in your laps, fondle them and treat them in good humour. Do not rule over them as an irate tyrant. Such an attitude stunts the growth of affectionate sentiments towards parents in the hearts of children, destroys their self-confidence and adversely affects the development of their inborn faculties.

On one occasion Aqra' ibn Habis [R.A.A.] came to the presence of the Holy Prophet [S.A.W.]. The Holy Prophet [S.A.W.] was at that time engaged in fondling Hazrat Hassan [R.A.A.]. Aqra' [R.A.A.] felt rather surprised and submitted, "O Holy Prophet [S.A.W.] do you also fondle children. I have ten children and have never shown fondness to even one of them"—The Holy Prophet [S.A.W.] raised his eyes and taking a look at Aqra' observed: "If Allah has deprived your heart of kindness and affection, what can I do!"

Hazrat 'Amir [R.A.A.] held a high post in the government during the reign of Hazrat Umar [R.A.A.]. He once paid a call at the house of Hazrat 'Umar [R.A.A.] and was astounded to see that a few children had mounted the chest of the Caliph and were engaged in play. The Caliph realised the feelings of annoyance writ large on the face of 'Amir [R.A.A.] and enquired, "What manner of treatment do you show to your children?" 'Amir [R.A.A.] now got the opportunity to express his viewpoint on the matter. He said: 'Amir-ul-Mo'minin, as soon as I enter my house the people of my household are struck with terror and stand dumb with fear." On hearing this, Hazrat 'Umar [R.A.A.] said in a deep tone of sorrow:

> "Amir [R.A.A.], you are a follower of the Holy Prophet [S.A.W.] and yet are ignorant of the important injunction that a Muslim should behave towards his family members with extreme love and deep tenderness."

18. Concentrate all your efforts to train and educate your children in piety and honesty and consider the greatest sacrifice too little to achieve this purpose. This is an obligation laid upon you by religion; it is a favour you owe to your children; and it is the greatest good that you can do to yourself. The Holy Qur'an affirms:

> "O Believers, protect yourself and the people of your household from the ire of Hell."

The only means of obtaining salvation from Hell-Fire is that man should be aware of all the requisite knowledge about religion and his life should pass in loyalty and devotion to the commands of Allah and His Messenger [S.A.W.].

The Holy Prophet [S.A.W.] has observed: "The best gift that a father can bestow upon his son is to arrange good education and training for him." *(Mishkat)*

> In addition to this, the Apostle of Allah [S.A.W.] affirmed: "The actions of man cease with his death. But there are three deeds whose reward and blessing continue to reach him even after death: One that he should make a Sadaqa Jariah (Recurring Charity). Secondly, he should leave behind a legacy of knowledge from which people may continue to derive benefit; thirdly, pious offspring who continuously invoke mercy of Allah upon him." *(Muslim)*

In fact the pious offspring are the only means of keeping alive your cultural traditions, religious doctrines and the concept of faith in One God, after you have expired. The believer prays for pious offspring so that the younger generation may keep the message of the old generation ever green and alive.

19. When the children attain the age of seven years, teach the 'Namaz' and urge them to observe prayers. Take them to the mosque with you to arouse their interest. If the children neglect to observe prayers when they have attained the age of ten, administer suitable punishment to them. By word and action make it absolutely clear to them that you will not tolerate their evasion of saying prayers.

20. When the children attain the age of 10 years, give them separate beds to sleep in. The Holy Prophet [S.A.W.] has observed:

    "When your children are seven years old, urge them to observe prayers. When they attain the age of ten and neglect saying prayers, punish them, and after this age provide separate bedding to them."

21. Always keep your children neat and clean. Take care that they are clean, neat and bathed. Keep them dress pure and clean. However, avoid excessive adornment or ostentation in dressing up children. Keep the dress of a female child simple and clean. Do not spoil the nature of your children by dressing them up in gaudy and flamboyant clothes.

22. Do not point out the faults of your children in the presence of others and strictly abstain from degrading or hurting the selfrespect of your children.

23. Do not express your dismay at reforming your children in their presence. Instead praise them generously even for their ordinary virtues in order to boost up their morale. Make constant endeavours to encourage them, and to foster self-confidence and boldness in them so that they may strive for the highest goals in the field of life.

24. Keep telling the children the stories of the Prophets [A.S.], tales of the pious people [R.A.A.] and episodes of the courageous feats of the illustrious companions of the Holy Prophet [S.A.W.]. This must be considered an essential means of training, civilising, character-building and arousing love for religion among the young and despite countless other pre-

occupations you must find some time to talk on these subjects with your children. Recite to them the Holy Qur'an in a sweet rhythmical voice frequently and on occasions relate to them the stirring stories and traditions of the life and work of the Holy Prophet [S.A.W.]. In this manner, you should try to inculcate in the hearts of the young warm sentiments of true love and devotion to the Holy Prophet [S.A.W.].

25. Let the children distribute food or money to the poor with their own hands sometimes so that the virtues of liberality, generosity and charity to the poor may develop in their hearts. On occasions, let brothers and sisters distribute shares of food or other eatables among themselves without your aid. This will create in them an awareness of the rights of others and accustom them to fair-dealing.

26. Do not comply with each legitimate or non-genuine desire of the children. By means of patience and common-sense teach them to give up this habit. Be strict with them at times and do not turn them into obstinate and self-willed youngsters by showering excessive love upon them.

27. Avoid thundering and shouting at the highest pitch of your voice and urge the children to speak softly in a moderate tone and abstain from shouting or railing at each other.

28. Inculcate the habit of self-help in children. They should not look to the servants to do every little job for them. This habit makes the children lazy and crippled in some ways. Foster the habits of sturdiness, hard work and strenuous application among the children.

29. In the event of an altercation taking place among children, do not lend undue support to your own child. You must realise that the sentiments which you cherish in your heart for your child are exactly the same which other people have for their children. Keep in view the faults of your own child and in all untoward circumstances try to pinpoint the error and fault of your own child and then make an earnest endeavour to eliminate these childish shortcomings in a wise manner by exercising constant vigilance.

30. Show equal treatment to all your children and avoid going to extremes in the matter of behaving towards children. If you are naturally drawn towards a particular child then, of course, it can't be helped. Yet in behaviour and dispensation of requirements you must show equal treatment and evenhanded justice. Do not show distinctive favour to a child to the dismay of other children. This will foster inferiority complex, hatred and frustration and all this will finally erupt into rebellious conduct. These evil sentiments greatly retard the development of natural faculties of a child and leave an adverse effect on the moral and spiritual growth of child's personality.

    On one occasion Hazrat Bashir [R.A.A.] took his son Hazrat Noaman [R.A.A.] to the presence of the Holy Prophet [S.A.W.] and submitted: "O Prophet of Allah [S.A.W.]! I possessed one slave and I have transferred that slave to the ownership of this son of mine." The Holy Prophet [S.A.W.] enquired: "Have you given a slave to each of your sons?" Hazrat Bashir [R.A.A.] submitted: "No." Thereupon the Holy Prophet [S.A.W.] commanded him: "Take the slave back from him. Fear Allah and show equal treatment to all of your children." Hazrat Bashir [R.A.A.] returned home and revoked the transfer of ownership of the slave to Noaman. According to another tradition, the Holy Prophet [S.A.W.] had observed on that occasion: "Do not make me a witness of sin. I shall not be a witness to injustice." In yet another tradition it is reported that the Holy Prophet [S.A.W.] observed to Hazrat Bashir [R.A.A.]: "Do you wish that all your sons should behave equally well towards you?" Hazrat Bashir [R.A.A.] submitted: "O Prophet of Allah (S.A.W.]: Yes, why not!" The Holy Prophet [S.A.W.] observed: "Do not act in this manner then."

    (Bukhari, Muslim)

31. Always present a good practical model before the children. Your own life style serves as a mute and permanent precept for your children. Children constantly lean and adopt lessons from your own conduct in life. Do not tell a lie even as a matter of fun before the children.

Hazrat 'Abdullah b. 'Amir [R.A.A.] relates an episode from his own life as follows: "One day when the Holy Prophet [S.A.W.] was present in our house, my mother called for me and said: "Come here, I have something for you." The Holy Prophet [S.A.W.] was watching. He [S.A.W.] observed to my mother, "What is it that you want to give to the child?" My mother submitted: "I wish to give him a date." The Holy Prophet [S.A.W.] observed: "If you had called the boy on the pretext of giving him something and in fact did not give him anything on his arrival, surely this sin of falsehood would have been added to the scroll of your deeds." *(Abu Dawud)*

32. Celebrate the birth of a female child with as much rejoicing as you observe on the birth of a male child. Boy or girl, both are a gift from Allah and only He knows better whether a boy or a girl is propitious for you. It does not behove a faithful of Allah to demure or feel crest-fallen on the birth of a girl. Such behaviour is the height of ingratitude and an insolence towards the Omniscient and Merciful Allah.

    The Tradition records: "When a girl is born to someone Allah sends angels to his home who pronounce: "O inmates of this house! peace be on you." The angels take the baby girl under their wings and passing their hands on her head in a gesture of affection observe: "This is a weak creature born out of a weak creature. Whosoever protects and rears this infant girl, Allah shall sustain him till doomsday." *(Tabrani)*

33. Train and bring up your girls with a sense of great pleasure, spiritual satisfaction and in the spirit of religion. In return for this pious service anticipate from Allah that He will admit you to the uppermost level of Paradise. The Holy Prophet [S.A.W.] has affirmed: "The man who patronises three daughters or three sisters, educates them and teaches them good manners and behaves kindly towards them till they become independent of his care by the will of Allah, is entitled by Allah to enter Paradise." Thereupon a person submitted: "If there be only two daughters or two sisters?" The Holy Prophet [S.A.W.] said: "The same reward will be given for similar conduct towards two daughters or two sisters." Hazrat

Ibn 'Abbas [R.A.A.] observes: "Had the people enquired about the reward for rearing one girl in this manner, the Holy Prophet [S.A.W.] would have given the same glad tidings." *(Mishkat)*

Hazrat 'A'isha [R.A.A.] narrates, "One day a woman accompanied by two small girls came to visit me and begged me to give her something. I had only one date which I handed over to her. The woman divided the date into two halves and gave one half to each girl, leaving nothing to eat for herself. Afterwards she stood up and went out. The same moment the Holy Prophet [S.A.W.] entered the house. I related the whole matter to him [S.A.W.]. On hearing the case, the Holy Prophet [S.A.W.] observed: "Any man who is put to trial on account of daughters being born to him and he comes out of the trial successful by virtue of showing good treatment to his daughters, these girls will serve him as a shield against the fire of Hell on the Day of Judgement." *(Mishkat)*

34. Do not look down upon the female child, nor show preference to the boy over the girl in any matter. Treat both with equal love and behave towards both in an equal manner. The Holy Prophet [S.A.W.] has affirmed: "Anyone who is blessed with the birth of a girl and does not bury her alive in the manner of the pagan days and does not look down upon her; neither shows preference to the boy over the girl nor considers the boy in any way superior to the girl, such a man will surely be admitted into Paradise by Allah." *(Abu Dawud)*

35. Give the prescribed share to the girl out of your property will and with careful attention. This share is ordained by Allah and no one has the authority to increase or decreases the amount of this share. It does not behove a pious believer to make excuses in the matter of paying the share of the girl or to feel content by giving away some fraction of it according to his own personal views. Such an action is a breach of covenant with Allah as well as tantamount to offering an insult to the religion. *(Allah forbid!)*

36. Along with these practical measures, say prayers from the depths of your soul and with sincere devotion of heart for

your offspring. We may trust the Munificent and Kind Allah that He will not let earnest prayers offered by the parents out of the depth of their soul go unanswered.

Interaction with Friends

1. Love your friends and become the object of love of your friends. The man who is held in deep affection by his friends and who cherishes feelings of love for his friends is the most fortunate person. The person who avoids the company of other people and whom the people regard with feelings of disgust is the most deprived man. The man who has no wealth is not poor. In point of fact great poverty consists in being friendless. A friend makes life beautiful, acts as a supporter in the journey of life and is a gift of Allah. Make friends and become friends of others. The Holy Prophet [S.A.W.] has affirmed:

   "The believer is an embodiment of love and affection. And the man who neither loves other nor is loved by others has no good or virtue in him."

   (Mishkat, Bab-al-Shafqat)

   The Holy Qur'an has affirmed:

   "The believing men and believing women are protecting friends of one another." *(9: 71)*

   The Holy Prophet [S.A.W.] used to cherish deep feelings of affection for all his illustrious companions [R.A.A.] so each one of them entertained the happy thought that the Holy Prophet [S.A.W.] loved him more than any one else.

   Hazrat 'Amr b. al-'As [R.A.A.] reports: "The Holy Prophet [S.A.W.] used to converse with me with such deep attention and sincerity and lavished such great care on me that I came to believe myself to be the best person among my people. And one day I submitted to the Holy Prophet [S.A.W.]: "O Prophet of Allah [S.A.W.]: Who is better - Me or Abu Bakr?" The Holy Prophet [S.A.W.] observed: "Abu Bakr is the better one." I submitted again: "Who is better-Me or 'Umar [R.A.A.]?" The Holy Prophet [S.A.W.] affirmed: "Umar is better." I submitted once more: "O Prophet of Allah [S.A.W.]: Who is better - Me or

'Uthman [R.A.A.]?" The Prophet of Allah [S.A.W.] observed: "Uthman is better than you." I then requested the Holy Prophet [S.A.W.] to explain the real matter in detail whereupon the Holy Prophet [S.A.W.] told me the plain truth. I felt greatly ashamed of myself and wondered what impelled me to ask such questions!

2. Maintain amicable social relations with your friends and try to develop sincere links and continue to cement friendships. Avoid adopting an attitude of annoyance with your friends or keeping aloof from them. When a man lives in the society of other men and has to participate in social matters, it is inevitable that he should suffer different kinds of shocks. Sometimes his sentiments are hurt; at other times his reputation is tarnished; one times his peace is disturbed, other times his usual activities are interfered with. Sometimes things are done against his temper and desires; at other times his patience and endurance are severely tried and at times he has to suffer great financial loss. In other words, he has to face all kinds of trials and tribulations. But when a man suffers these hardships, his heart is strengthened and he gains in wisdom and experience. Good morals develop in his personality and passing through a natural process of training and purification he makes rapid spiritual and moral progress. He thus acquires the sublime virtues of patience, forbearance, selflessness, affection, sympathy, humanity, respect, loyalty, devotion and co-operation, sincerity and love, generosity and gallantry, kindness and favour to the highest degree and he becomes an instrument of goodness and blessing for the human society. Every man holds him in esteem and values his friendship; each man considers him a source of blessing in his favour. The Holy Prophet [S.A.W.] has observed:

> "The Muslim who participates in social matters with other men and shows forbearance if he suffers any pain from them is a far better person than the one who isolates himself from the people and is dismayed at the hardships caused by others." *(Tirmidhi)*

3. Form friendships with the pure and righteous people. In the choice of friends do keep in mind the thought as to how far the people with whom you are forging bonds of amity and friendship can prove useful to you from the viewpoint of religion and morality. There is a famous maxim which says: If you wish to ascertain the moral state of a man, look at the moral condition of his friends." And the Holy Prophet [S.A.W.] has observed: "A man follows the beliefs of his friend. Hence each man should deeply consider the question as to what kind of a man is the person with whom he is striking a friendship." *(Musnad Ahmad, Mishkat)*

   The observation that a man will follow the beliefs of his friend implies that when a man keeps the company of his friend he will be affected by the sentiments, thoughts, taste and the mental outlook of his friend. He will inevitably begin to judge things to the standard of likes and dislikes adopted by his friend. Hence a man should exercise utmost care in choosing a friend and should establish bonds of affection and friendship with a person whose taste, temperament,and activities conform to the tenets of faith and religion. The Holy Prophet [S.A.W.] has enjoined: "Develop a relationship of love and friendship with a believer only and eat and drink in his company only." Furthermore the Holy Prophet [S.A.W.] affirmed:

   > "Keep company with the believer and only the righteous should eat from the Dastar Khwan[4] of a believer."

   Eating together naturally stimulates sentiments of warm affection and love between friends and these links should only be developed with the believers who are Allah-fearing and righteous people always keep away from those who have forgotten Allah and are irresponsible and indifferent in carrying out the commands of religion and are immersed in immorality. The Holy Prophet [S.A.W.] has described the nature of relationship with a good and bad friend in a sublime allegory:

"The example of a good or a bad friend is like that of a dealer of musk-perfume and an ironsmith who stokes the furnace. In the company of the perfumer you will certainly derive some benefit i.e. you will buy musk perfume or at least its sweet odour will afford pleasure to you. On the other hand, the furnace of the ironsmith will burn your house or set your clothes ablaze or the foul fumes emitted by the furnace will give you a headache." *(Bukhari, Muslim)*

The Tradition is recorded by Abu Dawud in the following words:

"The example of a pious friend is like that of a muskperfumery shop-keeper. If nothing, at least the benefit of sweet smell can be derived from this friend. The example of an evil friend is like that of a furnace. Even if your clothes are not set ablaze, your dress will certainly be blackened by the fumes of the furnace."

4. Love your friends for the sake of Allah. The favourites of Allah are those who join together on the basis of Allah's religion and struggle shoulder to shoulder with perfect unity of mind and soul to discharge their obligation of establishing the religion of Allah and stand like a solid wall in defence of their creed.

The Holy Qur'an affirms:

"Lo! Allah loveth those who battle for His cause in ranks as if they were a solid structure." *(61: 4)*

And the Holy Prophet [S.A.W.] has affirmed:

Allah will ordain on the Day of Judgement: Where are those people who used to love their fellows for my sake only. I shall place them under My own shadow." *(Muslim)*

The enviable state of dignity in which these people will find themselves on the Day of Judgement has been described by the Holy Prophet [S.A.W.] in these words:

"There are some loyal servants of Allah who, though they are not Prophets or martyrs, yet they shall be elevated to such high status by Allah on the Day of Judgement that the Prophets and martyrs will envy their good fortune." The illustrious companions [R.A.A.] submitted: "O Prophet of Allah [S.A.W.]! Who will be these fortunate persons?". The Holy Prophet [S.A.W.] affirmed: "These will be the people who loved each other on the basis of the religion of Allah - they were not related to one another by blood, nor had any commercial connection with each other. I swear by Allah, the faces of these people will be glowing with radiance nay they will be the emblems of pure light. When all the people shall be trembling with fear, they shall be free from fear. When all the people will be grief-stricken, they shall know no sorrow."

Afterwards the Holy Prophet [S.A.W.] recited this verse of the Holy Qur'an:

> "Lo! verily the friends of Allah are (those on whom fear (cometh) not, nor do they grieve." *(10: 62)*

Hazrat Abu-Darda [R.A.A.] states that the Holy Prophet [S.A.W.] observed: "Some people shall be raised from their graves on the Day of Judgement in a state that their faces will be glowing with radiant light. They shall be seated on pulpits made of pearls. Other people shall envy their elevated state. These dignified people, however, will neither include Prophets nor martyrs." The companions submitted: "O Prophet of Allah [S.A.W.]! Who are these people? Tell us their distinguishing qualities." The Holy Prophet [S.A.W.] observed: "These are the people who love each other for the sake of Allah only." *(Tabrani)*

5. Consider the love of pious people as a source of salvation in the eternal life and a means of winning the favour of Allah. Pray to Allah to bless you with the love of righteous people and beseech His favour to admit you to the ranks of the pious. Hazrat 'Abdullah ibn Mas'ud [R.A.A.] narrates: "A person came to the presence of the Holy Prophet [S.A.W.] and submitted: "O Prophet of Allah [S.A.W.], a person loves a pious

man for his piety, yet himself does not emulate the good deeds of this pious man, how shall he be treated in the next world?" The Prophet of Allah [S.A.W.] affirmed: "It does not matter at all. Man shall find himself in the company of that person whom he loves." *(Bukhari)*

One night the Holy Prophet [S.A.W.] was blessed with the vision of Allah. Allah said to the Holy Prophet [S.A.W.]: "Ask what thou wilt?" Thereupon the Holy Prophet [S.A.W.] said this prayer:

"Allah! I beseech Thy favour to perform good deeds and avoid evil deeds and I seek the love of the poor and implore Thee to grant me forgiveness and show me Thy Mercy. When you wish to send a calamity over a people, lift me in a state in which I may enjoy Your protection from the calamity. I implore Thy love and I beseech Thee to grant me love of that person who loves Thee and grant me the favour to perform deeds which may serve as means of obtaining nearness to You."

Hazrat Mu'adh ibn Jabal [R.A.A.] states that the Holy Prophet [S.A.W.] affirmed: "Allah ordains that I owe love to those people who develop links of love and friendship among themselves for My sake and assemble at one place to recite My name and meet each other for the love of Me and show good treatment to each other in order to win My favour." *(Ahmad, Tirmidhi)*

The Holy Prophet [S.A.W.] giving an inspiring description of the meeting of two friends, observed:

> "A man set out to call on his friend who lived in another habitation. Allah appointed an angel to await him on the way. The angel enquired of him: "Where are you going?" The man made the answer: "I am proceeding to that village to see my brother." The angel further enquired: "Does he owe you a debt of favour which you are now going to receive from him?" The man replied: "No, I am going to meet him only because I love him for the sake of Allah." The angel thereupon told him: "Listen then! God has sent me to convey to

you the glad tiding that Allah loves you as much as you love your friend for Allah's sake." *(Muslim)*

6. Make friendship with those who deserve to be your friends from the viewpoint of Islam and then by your utmost to maintain a loyal and devoted friendly relationship throughout your life. As the choice of pious people as friends is a matter of utmost importance, so equally is the continuous endeavour to maintain and strengthen these bonds of friendship.

   The Holy Prophet [S.A.W.] has affirmed: "On the Day of Judgement when there will be no shade anywhere except under the heaven of Allah, only seven types of people will find place under the shade of Allah's heaven. Of the first type will be two persons who were friends of each other for no other purpose except for the sake of Allah. The love of Allah would have forged a common link of friendship between them and they would separate from each other in the same condition. In other words, their friendship would be based on their common love of Allah and they would endeavour to maintain and cement this bond of friendship throughout their lives. And when one of them would be near the end of his life, their friendship would be intact at that time and they would part in this world as friends.

   Trust your friends. Behave cheerfully while you are in their company. Avoid being gloomy and making your friends gloomy. Be informal, frank and good natured amidst friends. Do not frown; nor stand on formality. Try to act as an informal companion, a good-natured mate and a cheerful comrade among your friends. Your friends should not feel bored with your presence; rather they should feel happy and alive in your company and should feel drawn towards you.

   Hazrat 'Abdullah ibn Harith [R.A.A.] relates: "I have never seen a person who smiled more often than the Holy Prophet of Allah [S.A.W.]." *(Tirmidhi)*

   Hazrat Jabir b. Samrah [R.A.A.] narrates: "I was present in over hundred sittings with the Holy Prophet [S.A.W.]. In these sittings the illustrious companions [R.A.A.] used to recite verses and related stories and anecdotes dating back to pagan times. The Holy Prophet [S.A.W.] used to hear all this in silence and even joined in laughter himself at times." *(Tirmidhi)*

Hazrat Shuraid [R.A.A.] reports that "on one occasion I was sitting behind the Holy Prophet [S.A.W.] on the back of an animal. During the journey I recited a hundred verses of Umaiya ibn as-Salt to the Holy Prophet [S.A.W.]. After each verse the Holy Prophet [S.A.W.] asked me to recite some more verses and I complied." *(Tirmidhi)*

Similarly, the Holy Prophet [S.A.W.] sometimes himself used to relate stories in his company. Hazrat 'A'isha [R.A.A.] reports: "Once the Holy Prophet [S.A.W.] related a story to the members of his household. A lady submitted: "This strange tale resembles the stories of Khurafa." The Holy Prophet [S.A.W.] asked her: "Do you know the real story of Khurafa?" and then himself narrated the true story of Khurafa in great detail. Similarly, the Holy Prophet [S.A.W.] once related a very interesting story of eleven women to Hazrat 'A'isha [R.A.A.].

Describing the informal conduct and cheerful temper of the illustrious companions [R.A.A.] Hazrat Bakr ibn 'Abdullah [R.A.A.] relates:

> "The illustrious companions [R.A.A.] used to throw the peelings of melon at each other in playful fun, yet when the time came for attack or defence the valour of the companions [R.A.A.] outweighed others in this field also." *(Al-Adab-ul-Mu frad)*

Hazrat Muhammad b. Ziyad [R.A.A.] reports: "I have seen the times of the righteous forebears. Several families of them lived in a single mansion. On many occasions it so happened that a family received a visit from a guest. At that moment food would be cooking in a pot in the quarter of another family. So, the host who had received a guest would go to the quarter of his neighbour and bring over the food without informing the family. The owners of the pot would then go about searching for their pot of food and would ask the people: "Who has taken away my pot?" The host who had taken the pot would then confess to him. "Brother, I had received a visit from a guest so I took away your pot of food." The owner of the pot of food would thereupon say, "May Allah bless you by increasing the quantity of this food." Muhammad ibn Ziyad [R.A.A.] also states that when these people baked bread, the same thing happened. *(Al-Adab-ul-Mufrad)*

A saying of Hazrat 'Ali [R.A.A.] is as follows:

> "Let your heart be free at time. Let your mind conceive pleasant notions, for mind also gets weary even as the body is fatigued."

8. Do not be dull and spiritless. Be of good cheer and keep your spirits high. Beware, however, that your cheerful temper and humour does not exceed proper limits. Along with a cheerful temper, fun and recreation, you should never forget to observe sanctity of religion, prestige and self respect, balance and moderation in your activities.

   The illustrious companion of the Holy Prophet [S.A.W.], Hazrat Abdul Rahman [R.A.A.] reports that the illustrious companions of the Holy Prophet [S.A.W.] neither were devoid of humour nor talked about in a lifeless manner. They used to recite verses and narrate tales and legends of pagan times in their sittings. But when in any matter something was demanded of them which did not conform to justice and truth, the pupils of their eyes were inflamed with such intense anger as if they were seized with a fit of madness."

   (Al-Adab-ul-Mufrad)

   Somebody remarked to the renowned traditionist Hazrat Sufyan b. Uyaina [R.A.A.] that humour is a nuisance. He answered: "No, humour is a Sunnah, but only for the man who knows the suitable occasion on which to practise it and has the ability to indulge in good jokes." (Sharh Shama'il Tirmidhi)

9. If you love someone, you must express your love to that person. Its psychological effect on that person will be that he will develop a sense of nearness to you. The exchange of feelings and passions on both sides will augment love and sincerity

to an extraordinary extent. Love then will no longer be merely a feeling confined within the heart but will begin to play a potent role in practical life. Thus people will have an opportunity of taking deep interest in the individual lives of each other and coming nearer to each other.

The Holy Prophet [S.A.W.] has affirmed: "Any person who cherishes in his heart sentiments of love and sincerity for his brother, he should express these sentiments to his brother and tell him clearly that he holds him in love and affection."

(Abu Dawud)

On one occasion a man passed in front of the Holy Prophet [S.A.W.]. Some people were at that time in attendance on the Prophet [S.A.W.]. One of them submitted; "O Prophet of Allah [S.A.W.]! I love this man for the sake of Allah alone." On hearing this the Holy Prophet [S.A.W.] enquired from him: "Have you told this to the man?" The man submitted: "No, I have not." Thereupon the Holy Prophet [S.A.W.] urged the man: "Go and tell the man that you love him for the sake of Allah." The man stood up at once and approaching the passer-by expressed to him his sentiments. The passer-by made the answer: "May Allah love thee for whose sake you entertain feelings of love for me." *(Tirmidhi, Abu Dawud)*

In order to cement the bonds of friendship and to bring friends closer to each other for their mutual benefit, it is essential that you should take proper interest in the individual and private matters of your friends and express to them your special feelings of devotion and concern.

The Holy Prophet [S.A.W.] has observed:

> "When a man establishes ties of friendship and fraternity with another person he should ascertain from him his name, father's name and particulars about his family as this strengthens the roots of mutual friendship." *(Tirmidhi)*

10. Adopt a moderate course in expressing your love and in the conduct of mutual relationship. Do not display such unconcern that your love and connexion may appear doubtful, nor

permit yourself to go to such extremes of passion that your love and friendship may assume the form of craziness and perchance you may suffer a shock at times (Allah forbid!) Always observe moderation and keep your feelings at balance. Adopt a moderate attitude which may be enduring and long-lasting. Hazrat Aslam [R.A.A.] states that Hazrat 'Umar [R.A.A.] observed: "Your love should not assume the form of madness, nor should enemity excite you to perpetrate torture on other." I submitted: Sir, how should we de so?" Hazrat 'Umar [R.A.A.] observed: "In this manner that if you love someone you start hugging him in a childlike fashion and display other forms of childish behaviour. And if you feel angry with someone, you resolve upon the destruction of his life and property and utter ruination." *(Al-Adab-ul-Mufrad)*

Hazrat 'Ubaid Kindi [R.A.A.] reports: I heard Hazrat 'Ali [R.A.A.] observing: "Adopt a tender and moderate attitude towards your friend; he might turn your enemy tomorrow. Likewise, follow a tender and moderate course in your conduct towards the enemy; he might become your friend sometime later." *(Al-Adab-ul-Mufrad)*

11. Be loyal and devoted to your friends. The best form of devotion to your friend is that you should increasingly try to elevate his morals. You should be more concerned with his salvation in the eternal world than his advancement in the material world. The Holy Prophet [S.A.W.] observed: "Religion wholly consists in seeking the welfare of others." The real test of a well-wisher is that one should wish for his friend the same thing that one wishes for his own self, for a man can never be his own illwisher.

The Holy Prophet [S.A.W.] has affirmed:

"I swear by Him Who hath power over my life, no man can be truly pious unless he wishes for his brother the same thing that he wishes for himself."

Laying down six obligations which each Muslim owes to the other, the Holy Prophet [S.A.W.] observed: "And the believer should act as a well-wisher of his brother both in his presence and absence." Furthermore, the Holy Prophet [S.A.W.] affirmed:

> "Without doubt Allah has ordained the ordeal of fire for that man and He has forbidden his entry into Paradise who forfeits the right of a brother Muslim after having sworn to fulfil his obligation." Someone from among the illustrious companions [R.A.A.] submitted: "What if that obligation relates to a very minor thing?" The Holy Prophet [S.A.W.] affirmed: "Yes, even if he owes an ordinary branch of the 'Pelu' tree to another Muslim."

12. Share the grief and sorrow of your friends. Likewise, participate actively in their joyous occasions. The purpose of your sharing their grief should be to alleviate their suffering and the aim of your participation in their festivities ought to be to enhance their joy. Every friend rightly expects from his sincere associates that they will stand by him in times of trial and will never desert him in the hour of need. Similarly, he anticipates that his friends will add to his felicity by increasing the grace of his festive parties with their presence and active participation.

    The Holy Prophet [S.A.W.] has observed:

    > "The Muslim fraternity is like a mansion. Even as each brick supports and cements the other brick, so does a Muslim act as a supporter and a source of strength for the other Muslim." So saying the Holy Prophet [S.A.W.] interlocked the fingers of his both hands and thus explained the mutual link and close connexion that ought to subsist among the Muslim community.
    >
    > *(Bukhari, Muslim)*

    The Holy Prophet [S.A.W.] enjoined:

    > "In their sense of mutual love and affection and perception of common distress, you will find Muslims as one body; if one organ of this body is afflicted, the whole body is affected by fever and sleeplessness."
    >
    > *(Bukhari, Muslim)*

13. Meet your friends in a cheerful, amicable, joyous and sincere manner. Greet them warmly and observe proper etiquettes in receiving them. Avoid showing an indifferent, cold and unconcerned behaviour. These evils create a rift in the hearts. Say words of praise and thanks and joy and satisfaction during meetings with your friends. Abstain from talk which reveals sorrow, grief and low spirits. Behave in such a manner during meetings with your friends that they should be thrilled with feelings of joy and liveliness. Do not greet them with such a gloomy face that they may feel crestfallen and may come to regard your fellowship as intolerable nuisance.

    The Holy Prophet. [S.A.W.] has affirmed:

    > "Do not look upon any pious deed as insignificant, may it be greeting your brother with a cheerful heart." *(Muslim)*

    > On another occasion, the Holy Prophet [S.A.W.] observed: "Your smile on seeing a brother is also an act of sacrifice on your part." *(Tirmidhi)*

    Tenderness, politeness and civility generate feelings of affection and love in the heart and it is on the basis of these virtues that a good society can be formed.

    The Holy Prophet [S.A.W.] observes:

    > "I tell you the distinguishing marks of a person for whom the fire of Hell has been made unlawful and who is a forbidden person for the Hell Fire to consume: He is a man who bears a sweet temper, tender heart and is soft-spoken." *(Tirmidhi)*

    The illustrious companions [R.A.A.] relate that the Holy Prophet [S.A.W.] used to be attentive with his whole posture towards the person with whom he was talking and listened to the talk in rapt attention. Once the Holy Prophet [S.A.W.] was sitting in the mosque. A man paid a call and the Holy Prophet [S.A.W.] shifted his posture and shrank a little. The man submitted: "O Prophet of Allah [S.A.W.]! there is ample room here." The Holy Prophet [S.A.W.] observed:

> "A Muslim owes it to his brother that on seeing him, he should move for him a little." *(Baihaqi)*

Describing the virtues of the believers, the Holy Qur'an affirms:

> "They are always very gentle to the believers."

The Holy Prophet [S.A.W.] has elucidated the same fact in the following words:

> "The believers are forbearing and soft-hearted like a camel who is tied with a nose band; the camel is drawn to whichever direction his nose-band is tugged and if he is made to sit on a stone, he complies." *(Tirmidhi)*

14. Whenever you differ among yourselves on any matter resolve it at once. Always take the initiative to seek forgiveness and to admit your fault.

    Hazrat Abu Darda [R.A.A.] reports: "Once there was an exchange of hot words between Hazrat Abu Bakr and Hazrat 'Umar [R.A.A.]. Hazrat Abu Bakr [R.A.A.] felt it hard and went to the Holy Prophet [S.A.W.] in a very sad and sorry mood and submitted: "O Prophet of Allah [S.A.W.]! A difference arose between 'Umar and myself whereupon I flew into rage and we exchanged some bitter words. Later, I felt greatly ashamed of myself and solicited 'Umar [R.A.A.] to forgive me. But, O Prophet of Allah [S.A.W.]! 'Umar was not reconciled and declined to forgive me. I am feeling very much upset and uneasy so have I come to you. The Holy Prophet [S.A.W.] observed: "Allah will grant you forgiveness and salvation". Meanwhile Hazrat 'Umar [R.A.A.] also realised his fault and rushed to Hazrat Abu Bakr's [R.A.A.] house. He was informed that Abu Bakr [R.A.A.] has gone to the presence of the Holy Prophet [S.A.W.]. Whereupon 'Umar [R.A.A.] also hurried to the presence of the Holy Prophet [S.A.W.]. Signs of anger and displeasure appeared on the countenance of the Holy Prophet [S.A.W.] on seeing Hazrat Umar. Noting the displeasure against Hazrat 'Umar, Hazrat Abu Bakr [R.A.A.] felt deeply perturbed. He fell on his knees and submitted to the Holy Prophet [S.A.W.] in great humility "O Prophet of Allah [S.A.W.]! 'Umar is not at fault. All blame rests on me. I committed the fault. It was I 'who spoke harshly to him." Thereupon the Holy Prophet [S.A.W.] observed: "Allah sent me as His Prophet among you and when in the early days you refuted me, it was Abu Bakr who affirmed his faith in me and stood by me at the cost of his life and property. Would you now aggrieve my companion?"

Do not lose time in making peace. The longer the delay in resolving quarrels, the deeper grow the roots of contention, and the wider grows the gulf of separation between the hearts. The following precept of Hazrat 'Isa [A.S.] contained in the Bible is intensely heart-warming:

> "So if you are engaged in offering sacrifice at the altar and you suddenly recall to mind that your brother has some complaint against you, leave your offering at the altar and return at once to your brother to make peace with him. Then go back to the altar and make your offering."

The Holy Prophet [S.A.W.] has observed:

> "The deeds of the people are presented to Allah on every Monday and Thursday and every believer is granted pardon except the one who nurses a grudge against any of his believing brothers. Allah ordains: "Leave them so that they may resolve their quarrel."

Who knows whether the next moment will bring death or life! Who knows whether he will witness the next Monday or Thursday! Why and on what hope do you delay in purifying your heart and settling the complaints of your friends? Is any sensible person who believes in the Day of Judgement ready to present himself with an impure, dark and gruesome heart before the Almighty Allah?

Beware also that if your friend admits his fault and requests pardon, you should accept his excuse and forgive him from the core of your heart.

The Holy Prophet [S.A.W.] has affirmed:

> "The Muslim who declines to accept the confession of his fault and a request for forgiveness from his brother

Muslim is held guilty of a sin as grave as the sin of cruelty and oppression committed by an Octroi man who extorts an illegal cess."

15. Restrain your tongue even if friends talk or behave in a manner which is offensive to your temper or taste. Do not utter harsh or offensive speech in retaliation. Instead let the matter pass with tact and gentle conduct.

    The Holy Prophet [S.A.W.] observed:

    > "Hazrat Moosa [A.S.] submitted to Allah: My Allah: 'Which one is the dearest to you among your creatures?' Allah affirmed: 'That one who hath the power to take revenge' yet forgives." *(Mishkat)*

    In addition to this, the Holy Prophet [S.A.W.] observed:

    > "The heaviest thing put in the balance of a believer on the Day of Judgement will be his politeness. Allah looks upon that person with intense wrath who utters indecent and foul speech."

    Hazrat 'Abdullah ibn Mubarak [R.A.A.] had defined the virtue of politeness in three ways:

    (i) A person should meet others with a bright, smiling face.

    (ii) A man should spend his wealth on the destitute and needy persons.

    (iii) A person should not cause harm to any one.

    Hazrat 'A'isha [R.A.A.] reports: "The Holy Prophet [S.A.W.] observed: "The worst man in the eyes of Allah on the Day of Judgement will be the one whom the people avoid on account of his indecent and foul speech." *(Bukhari, Muslim)*

16. Do not shirk your duty to reform your friends and train them in righteousness. Do not let vanity and pride take root in the character of your friends which is the greatest hurdle in their reformation and moral uplift. Always try to persuade your friends to realise their omissions and errors and develop moral courage to confess their faults. They should always be mindful of the fact that failure to realise one's shortcomings and

insistence upon one's faultlessness mars one's spiritual development.

As a matter of fact it is very easy to show off false humility, to call oneself as insignificant and to display submissiveness in style and manners, but it is extremely difficult to sustain an injury to your feelings, to listen to and admit your shortcomings with a cool mind and to tolerate the criticism directed by your friends against your personal faults. Yet true friends are those who keep an enlightened eye on the conduct of their friends and are always alert and alive to the task of protecting each other from the evils of vanity and pride by sincere counsel and practical example.

The Holy Prophet [S.A.W.] affirms:

(i) The passion which is allowed to prevail upon one's good sense.

(ii) The greed and lust which is allowed to become the guiding principle of one's life.

(iii) And vanity-the most dangerous of the three ills."

(Baihaqi, Muslim)

Criticism and accountability are lancets which purge the moral existence of man from all undesirable elements. They augment moral strength and infuse new life into the individual and the society. To take offense, to get irritated and to consider oneself as above the criticism and accountability of friends is detrimental to one's moral being as well as to evade healthy and constructive criticism of one's friends to check and protect them from moral degradation. Do feel uneasy if you find hideous faults and shortcomings in your friends and take wise measures to eliminate those blemishes on the characters of your friends. Similarly, give a chance with genuine humility and urge to your friends that they should expose to you your own foibles and faults. When your friends discharge this unpleasant duty towards you, do not be vainglorious, but welcome their criticism with large heartedness, cheerfully and with a grateful heart. Express your gratitude to them for their sincerity and kindness. The Holy

Prophet [S.A.W.] has described this exemplary friendship in a most eloquent allegory.

> "Each one of you serves as a mirror to his brother. Hence if your see any fault in your brother, eliminate it." *(Tirmidhi)*

There are five illuminating points in this allegory which can make your friendship exemplary in genuine terms:

(i) The mirror reflects the spots and stains on your person when you stand before it with the intention of locating these spots and stains. When you stand aside, the mirror ceases to reflect these blemishes. Similarly, you should expose the foibles of your friend only if he willingly presents himself before you for criticism and chastisement with an open mind. At the same time, make it sure that his mind is receptive to your criticism and that his heart is eager to accept suggestions for the correction of his faults. In the absence of these conditions, you should keep silent and put off the matter wisely for a later occasion. In the absence of your friend especially you should exercise the utmost care not to utter a single word pointing to any shortcoming of your friend, for this would be counted as back-biting and backbiting divides the hearts rather than uniting them.

(ii) The mirror reflects very honestly all such spots or stains which are really present on the face; it neither hides their number nor makes an addition to them. Furthermore, the mirror reflects only those deformities which are outwards and apparent; it does not expose the hidden blemishes, neither probes inward, nor presents an illusory picture of your demerits. Likewise, you should also present a genuine and true picture of the inadequacies and faults of your friends. Moved by sentiments of undue politeness and flattery you should neither suppress the exposure of a few foibles of your friends nor exaggerate their dimensions or add to their number in the heat of your passionate oratory and declamation. Moreover, point out only those faults of your friends which are exposed in the normal conduct of life. Do not display curiosity or an eagerness to spy into the secrets of others. To expose the secret faults of your friends is no moral service, in fact it is a perilous and immoral act on your part.

The Holy Prophet [S.A.W.] once ascended the pulpit and warned the congregation in a very high tone of his holy voice:

> "Do not pry into the vices of Muslims. Allah exposes the hidden vices of a person who seeks to expose the faults of his brother Muslims; and when Allah decides to expose the faults of someone, He inevitably reduces the man to disgrace, even if such a man hides himself in the inner recesses of his home." *(Tirmidhi)*

(iii) The mirror discharges its duty unaffected by any sort of motives. Any one who faces the mirror, the mirror shows him his true image without any reservations. The mirror nurses no grudge or vendetta against anyone, nor wreaks vengeance on anybody. You should also chastise your friends unaffected by personal motives, feelings of vendetta grudge, pique, or dishonesty. Your only motive in criticising your friends should be to enable him to reform himself, as a man adorns himself by eliminating spots and stains from his person by locating them through their reflection in the mirror.

(iv) No one feels annoyed at seeing his true image in the mirror, nor commits the blunder of breaking up the mirror in a fit of rage. Instead most people on looking into the mirror begin to adorn themselves by removing the apparent defects on their persons and in fact realising the valuable services of the mirror in this regard are thankful to it in their hearts. They are fully conscious of the fact that the mirror has proved extremely helpful to them in the task of embellishing their persons. They believe that the mirror has done its natural duty remarkably and they put it away carefully for use at another time. Similarly when someone presents your true picture before you in his own words, do not retaliate in annoyance. Instead express your gratitude to him for his sincere performance of the obligation of friendship. Feel grateful to him in your heart also, apart from offering him thanks in words and set about reforming yourself at once. Realising the value and greatness of your friends with an open mind and with a sense of extreme gratitude, request your friend to continue to show you the favour of his valuable suggestions.

(v) The final point is that "every Muslim selves as a mirror unto his brother Muslim." A brother is an emblem of sincerity and love for his brother. A brother is loyal, devoted, sympathetic a well-wisher and a helper in grief to his brother. He feels restless on seeing his brother in trouble and is overjoyed at his happiness. Hence the criticism of a brother and a friend if motivated by feelings of extreme sincerity, devotion, sympathy and love. It will be characterised by a desire for the welfare and extreme concern for the best interests of his friend. Every word of this friendly criticism will reflect the spirit of reformation. Such a form of criticism may be rightly expected to unite the hearts and correct the wrongs.

17. Exchange gifts in order to express your feelings of sincerity and love for your friends and to deepen the relationship of love and affection. Mutual exchange of gifts unites the hearts and cements the bonds of love. The Holy Prophet [S.A.W.] has observed:

> "Exchange gifts with each other. This will generate mutual feelings of love and eliminate feelings of animosity and estrangement from your hearts."
>
> *(Mishkat)*

The Holy Prophet [S.A.W.] himself often used to send gifts to his illustrious Companions [R.A.A.]. The Prophet's Companions [R.A.A.] also frequently exchange presents and gifts among themselves. In the matter of exchanging gifts always keep within your means. Whatever the status of the receiver, do not think that your gift should necessarily be a costly one. Give according to your means and whatever is easily available. The real worth of your gift depends on your sincerity and the nature and depth of feelings with which you have presented the gift. It is the feelings of sincerity and deep passions of love and devotion which unite the hearts and the cost or value of the gift is insignificant in this regard. Do not regard the gift of your friend as insignificant, however cheap in cost it may be. Instead put a high value on the feelings of love and sincerity reflected by the gift of your friend.

The Holy Prophet [S.A.W.] observed:

> "Even if someone offers me the leg of a goat as a gift, I shall accept it and if someone invites me to a dinner consisting of a cooked leg of goat, I shall certainly join the feast." *(Tirmidhi)*

You must answer a gift with a gift. The Holy Prophet [S.A.W.] used to observe this rule strictly. The Holy Prophet's [S.A.W.] favourite gift was perfume. You should also consider the present of a perfume as a propitious gift. In the present-day circumstances, the presentation of a book can also be regarded as a propitious gift. In this connection, you should hold common feasts at times. Invite your friends to dinner at home. When friends invite you to functions at their homes, make it a point to join their parties. Mutual entertainment promotes feelings of love and affection, and bonds of fraternity are further cemented. However, on these occasions instead of observing excessive formalities and laying out lavish quantities of food and drink, you should put more emphasis on displaying and augmenting the feelings of love and sincerity.

18. Look after your friends. Stand by them in their hour of need, even at the cost of your own life and property. Asbahani relates in a tradition: "A person came to Hazrat 'Abdullah b. 'Umar [R.A.A.] and asked: Which one is the most favourite of Allah among the people?" Hazrat 'Abdullah b. 'Umar [R.A.A.] answered: "The most favourite person of Allah among the people is he who affords the greatest benefit to his fellow men. The deed which wins the greatest favour of Allah is that you should make a Muslim happy in such manner that you should alleviate his suffering or hardship or make a provision

of food to satisfy his hunger. I would go out with a brother Muslim in order to help him in his need rather than sit in the mosque of the Holy Prophet [S.A.W.] and perform I'tikaf. Allah shall fill the heart of that man with His favour on Doomsday who controlled his rage at a time when he could give vent to his fury, if he so wished. And the person who accompanied his brother in order to help satisfy his need and actually provided for his need shall be rewarded with the favour of Allah on Doomsday when the other people will be staggering, this person will walk with a firm gait."

The Holy Prophet [S.A.W.] has affirmed:

> "Any man who provides for the need of his brother, Allah shall always keep fulfilling the need of that man. And any person who alleviates some hardship of a Muslim, Allah on Doomsday shall remove one of his hardships out of the many hardships of that day."
> *(Bukhari, Muslim)*

The Holy Prophet [S.A.W.] also affirmed:

> "Allah continues to help a man as long as he continues to help his brother." *(Tirmidhi)*

Hazrat 'Abdullah b. 'Abbas [R.A.A.] has reported that the Holy Prophet [S.A.W.] observed:

> "The reward and blessing for the act of providing for the need of a brother Muslim exceeds the reward and blessing for performing an I'tikaf for a period of ten years." *(Tabrani)*

Hazrat Anas [R.A.A.] states that the Holy Prophet of Allah [S.A.W.] observed:

> "A Muslim who conveys a message of felicity and happiness to a brother Muslim and thus affords him happiness, Allah shall, on Doomsday, make this messenger happy." *(Tabrani)*

19. Be a trustworthy confident. If a friend, relying on your good faith, confides his secret to you, you should safeguard his secret. Do not betray the confidence of your friend. Make your

heart an iron vault for the safe keeping of secrets, so that friends may take counsel with you without hesitation and also in order that you may proffer good advice to your friends and extend your full cooperation to them.

Hazrat 'Umar [R.A.A.] narrates:

> "When Hafsa [R.A.A.] was widowed, I called on 'Uthman [R.A.A.] and said to him: "If you are agreeable I should give Hafsa in marriage to your." 'Uthman [R.A.A.] answered: "I shall think over the matter." I waited for his message for many nights. Later 'Uthman [R.A.A.] met me and said: "I have no intention of marrying at the moment." I then went to see Abu Bakr [R.A.A.] and proposed: "If you wish you may take Hafsa [R.A.A.] as your wife." Abu Bakr [R.A.A.] kept silent and make no answer. I was offended at the silence of Abu Bakr. I was more deeply offended with him than even at the response of 'Uthman [R.A.A.]. Many days passed and one day the Holy Prophet [S.A.W.] sent me a proposal to marry Hafsa [R.A.A.]. I accepted the proposal and gave Hafsa [R.A.A.] in marriage to the Holy Prophet [S.A.W.]. Later one day Abu Bakr [R.A.A.] met me and said: "You talked to me concerning Hafsa [R.A.A.] and I kept silent. My response might have caused you some pain." I replied: "Yes, I did feel sore at your silence." Abu Bakr [R.A.A.] thereupon told me: "I knew that the Holy Prophet [S.A.W.] himself intended to send a proposal for marriage with Hafsa [R.A.A.]. The Holy Prophet [S.A.W.] had confided this secret to me and I did not intend to reveal it. If the Holy Prophet [S.A.W.] had not expressed his intention concerning Hafsa [R.A.A.], I would certainly have accepted your proposal."
>
> *(Bukhari)*

Hazrat Anas [R.A.A.] relates: "One day I was playing with boys of my age when the Holy Prophet [S.A.W.] arrived and blessed us with 'salam' [peace be on you]. The Holy Prophet [S.A.W.] told me his need and sent me on some errand. The errand took rather a long while. When it was over and I reached home late my mother enquired: "Where have you been for so long?" I answered: "The Holy Prophet [S.A.W.] had sent me on an errand." She asked: "What for?" I said: "It is a secret matter." Thereupon my mother advised me: "Look, do not reveal the secret of the Holy Prophet [S.A.W.] to anyone." *(Muslim)*

20. Your moral conduct towards the people should be characterised by a cosmopolitan, vast, comprehensive, and tolerant outlook, so that people of every taste and temper, thought and ideal may feel an uncommon sense of attraction towards you. Keeping in view the particular taste, viewpoint and temperament of every one, behave towards each person so wisely that no one's feelings are hurt. Do not adopt the unwise attitude of measuring everyone according to your own particular standard of propriety, nor make an absurd and unsuccessful attempt to mould every one according to your own taste and temperament. The variety of tastes and temperaments is a beauty of Nature. Do not deform the beauty. Keep your relations according to the nature of acquaintance and the temperament of your friends, give them respect and importance accordingly and keep them attached in bonds of friendship with you by means of your own liberal behaviour and good character.

    An all-round genius as the Holy Prophet [S.A.W.] was, men of all tastes and temperaments found consolation and contentment in his august company. Nobody felt any uneasiness due to the magnanimous toleration and extraordinary charitable nature of the Holy Prophet [S.A.W.]. The august company of the Holy Prophet [S.A.W.] included embodiments of toleration and affection like Abu Bakr [R.A.A.] and men of iron nature and courage like 'Umar Farooq [R.A.A.], pacifists who trembled at the prospect of war like Hassan b. Thabit [R.A.A.] as well as the gallant victor of Khybar Hazrat 'Ali [R.A.A.]. There was Abudhar Ghifari [R.A.A.] a saintly, gloomy figure as well as 'Abdul Rahman b. 'Auf [R.A.A.], sumptuously rich and elegant in person. It was by virtue of the cosmopolitan outlook, excellent conduct, deep love for humanity and the highest degree of statesmanship of the Holy Prophet [S.A.W.] that men of divergent personalities were extremely devoted to the person of the Holy Prophet [S.A.W.] and the Prophet of Allah [S.A.W.] himself treated everyone of them with such deep .consideration that every one thought himself the most favourite friend of the Holy Prophet [S.A.W.]. Again, it was owing to this cosmopolitan moral view-point, statesmanship, wisdom and unique selflessness that the Holy Prophet [S.A.W.] formed that matchless group of illustrious companions [R.A.A.], who despite their variegated natures and temperaments, were welded together in a unique combination characterised by uncommon unity, cooperation and enviably deep mutual love and affection. The mankind as a whole may rightly consider this era as the essence and substance of its long existence so far.

Your friendships, in fact, can only be successful and longlasting when your collective attitudes and behaviour reflect rationality, liberalism, patience and tolerance, forbearance and magnanimity, forgiveness and selflessness, mutual understanding and humility, submissiveness, mutual accommodation of each other's sentiments and due consideration of each other's interests in every day life. You may judge from the following few references from the life of the Holy Prophet [S.A.W.] how considerate, magnanimous, liberal, forbearing and tolerant was the Prophet of Allah [S.A.W.] towards the natural needs, feelings and frailties of human beings:

> "I come to offer prayer and wish to prolong the prayers. But I hear some infant crying on the woman's side and I shorten my prayers, for I cannot afford to put the mother of the child to inconvenience by prolonging the prayers." *(Bukhari)*

Hazrat Malik bin al Huwarith states:

> "Some of us young men of the same age group paid a visit to the Holy Prophet [S.A.W.] in order to learn

religion from him. We stayed with the Holy Prophet [S.A.W.] for twenty days. The Holy Prophet was very kind and tender in his dealings. At the end of our twenty days' stay, the Holy Prophet [S.A.W.] felt that we were anxious to return home. The Prophet of Allah [S.A.W.] enquired from us: "Tell me about the people you have left behind at home." we related to him [S.A.W.] the affairs of our households in detail. Whereupon the Holy Prophet [S.A.W.] commanded us: "Go back to your wives and children. While living among them teach them everything you have learnt here and urge them to observe piety. Tell them the proper timings for offering prayers. When the time for prayer comes, one of you should call the people for prayers by saying Adhan and he who excels in knowledge and good morals among all of you, should act as leader (Imam) in the prayer."

(Bukhari, Muslim)

Hazrat Mu'awiya b. Hakam Sulami [R.A.A.] relates one of his own experiences as follows:

"I was saying prayers behind the Holy Prophet [S.A.W.] when a man sneezed. Forgetting that I was saying my prayers I spontaneously replied *Yarhamakallah* whereupon the people started rebuking me. I said to them: "May Allah protect you, why do you stare at me?" I felt, however, that the people wanted me to observe silence, so I kept mum. When the Holy Prophet [S.A.W.] had finished the prayers-May my father and mother be sacrificed for him, for never had I seen nor saw afterwards anyone who was a better teacher and guide than the Holy Prophet [S.A.W.]-he did not reproach me, neither beat me, nor rebuked me. He [S.A.W.] only observed: "This is worship and it is not proper to talk in the prayer. Prayer is meant to announce the purity of Allah, to acknowledge His Greatness and to recite the Qur'an." *(Muslim)*

21. Be very much particular in prayers. Pray for your friends and request them to remember you in their prayers. Pray for your friends in their presence as well as in their absence. Think of your friends and pray for them by name in their absence. Hazrat 'Umar [R.A.A.] reports: "I requested leave of the Holy Prophet [S.A.W.] to perform 'Umrah. Granting the leave, the Holy Prophet [S.A.W.] observed: "O My brother, do not forget us in your prayers." Hazrat 'Umar [R.A.A.] said: "I felt so happy on hearing this observation of the Holy Prophet [S.A.W.] that I would not have felt happier had I been offered the whole world."

    The Holy Prophet [S.A.W.] has affirmed:

    > "When a Muslim says a prayer for his brother Muslim in absentia, Allah accepts his prayer and appoints one of his angels on the Muslim who is offering the prayer so that when this Muslim prays for his brother Muslim the angel says: "Amen, you shall receive from Allah for yourself too what you are asking for you brother." *(Muslim)*

    Beseech Allah in your sincere prayers: "Allah, clear our hearts of all grudge, vendetta, enemity and misunderstanding and tie us with bonds of sincerity and love. Make our relationships pleasant by means of mutual cooperation and love." Say this prayer of the Holy Qur'an also:

    > "Our Allah! Forgive us and our brethren who were before us in the faith, and place not in our hearts any rancour towards those who believe. Our Allah; Thou art full of pity, Merciful."*(59.' 10)*

Hospitality

1. Express your joy and love on the arrival of a guest. Greet him with a cheerful heart. Welcome him with open arms and show him every mark of respect and honour. Do not display stinginess, indifference, cold attitude or resentment.

    The Holy Prophet [S.A.W.] has observed:

> "The people who believe in Allah and the Day of Judgement should show hospitality to their guests."
> *(Bukhari, Muslim)*

Hospitality includes all those matters which are essential for showing due respect and honour to the guest and to make provisions for his comfort, peace, happiness and fulfilment of his needs. Showing respect to your guest means treating your guest with politeness and in good cheer; to entertain him with pleasant conversation, to make provisions for his rest and relaxation; to introduce him to your other respectable friends; to look after his needs, to arrange provisions of food and drink for him with a liberal and generous mind and to give personal service and attention to all the requirements of your friend.

> "Whenever respectable guests paid a visit to him, the Holy Prophet [S.A.W.] used to attend to their hospitality himself."
>
> "Whenever the Holy Prophet [S.A.W.] served meals to his guest he [S.A.W.] used to prompt the guest repeatedly to partake more of the food. When the guest had taken to his fill and expressed inability to eat more, it was then that the Holy Prophet[S.A.W.] ceased urging him to take more.

2. When a guest arrives, say Salam [peace be on you] to him and pray for him. Then enquire about his health.

   The Holy Qur'an affirms:

   > "Hath the story of Abraham's honoured guests reached thee (O Muhammad) when they came in unto him and said: "Salam" Hazrat Ibrahim answered salam."
   >
   > *(51: 24-25)*

3. Show generous hospitality to your guests and offer them the best that is readily available. On arrival of his guests, Hazrat Ibrahim [A.S.] at once got busy in making arrangements for their dinner. He [A.S.] had a fat calf in his home, which he slaughtered and got it roasted for his guests.

> "Then he went apart unto his house folk and brought a fatted calf roasted for the guests; and presented it before them." *(51: 26, 27)*

Faragha ila ahlihi also bears the meaning that Hazrat Ibrahim [A.S.] went inside his home to make arrangements for the feast without informing any one lest the guests should feel informal or forbid preparation of food for them for fear of causing inconvenience to the host. In that case, it would not be possible for the host to entertain his guests.

Hazrat Abu Sharih, in his report of the manner in which the Holy Prophet [S.A.W.] has urged the Muslims to show hospitality to their guests, states as follows:

> "I saw with my two eyes and heard with mine two ears when the Holy Prophet [S.A.W.] was delivering this counsel: "The people who believe in Allah and Day of Judgement should show hospitality to their guests. The first night and first day of his stay is the prized day and night for you." *(Bukhari, Muslim)*

To attribute 'In'am' (reward) to the first night and first day of the guest's stay implies that as the munificent feels spiritual contentment on giving away (reward) with deep sentiments of joy and love, similar behaviour should be displayed by the host towards the guest on the first night and first day of his stay with him. Likewise as the beneficiary receives the (reward) with joy and happiness deeming it as his rightful due and appreciates the munificence of his benefactor, a similar attitude should be adopted by the guest towards his host during the first night and first day of his stay with him. The guest should not stand on formality and ought to accept the offerings of the host with sentiments of joy and close fellowship considering the host's hospitality towards him as his rightful due.

4. As soon as the guest arrives, think first of his natural human needs. Make discreet enquiries as to whether he wishes to use the toilet or bathroom. Arrange a bath for him, if it is required. Even though it may be a late hour for meals, ask

your guest if he wants to eat or drink in such a discreet manner that he should not decline as a matter of formality. Show your guest his bedroom where he is to stay.

5. Do not pester your guest with your constant company. Similarly do not keep him awake late in the night talking or discussing matters. Allow him sufficient time to rest so that he may not feel inconvenient. When the guests paid a visit to him, Hazrat Ibrahim [A.S.] left them alone for a while and went inside his home to prepare a feast for the guests.

6. Do feel pleasure when the guests are dining with you. Do not show any signs of stinginess, annoyance or weariness. The guest is not a burden, but a source of blessing, grace and Divine favour. Whomsoever Allah sends to you as a guest, He sends provisions for the guest also. The guest eats with you whatever was decreed for him; he does not eat your share of the Divine bounty. The visit of a guest adds to your honour and dignity.

7. Protect the honour and dignity of your guest and consider his honour and dignity as vital as your own. In case any one poses a threat to the honour of your guest, you should consider it a challenge to your own honour and conscience.

   The Holy Qur'an affirms that when the people of the habitation assaulted the guests of Hazrat Lut [A.S.] with evil intentions, Hazrat Lut [A.S.] rose up in their defence and declared: "These people are my guests. Do not disgrace me by treating them offensively. I hold their disgrace as an offence against my own person."

   "He said:

   Lo! they are my guests. Affront me not! And fear Allah and shame me not." *(22: 68-9)*

8. Observe all the etiquettes of hospitality with deep enthusiasm and eagerness for three days. The guest has a right over you to entertain him for three days and a believer should always be extremely generous in discharging their obligations. On the first day the guest should be shown special hospitality. Hence make sumptuous arrangements for the entertainment

of your guest. On the subsequent two days it does not matter if that level of sumptuous entertainment cannot be maintained. The Holy Prophet [S.A.W.] has observed:

> "And hospitality is ordained for three days. Later whatever entertainment the host offers to his guest is a charity on his part." *(Bukhari, Muslim)*

9. Consider rendering service to the guest as your moral duty. Do not consign your guest to the care of your servants and children. Instead devote yourself personally to the service of your guest. The Holy Prophet [S.A.W.] used to look after the entertainment of the guests personally. When Hazrat Imam Shafi [R.T.A.] paid a visit to Imam Malik [R.T.A.] he was received with every mark of honour and respect due to a guest and was lodged in his bedroom to sleep for the night. At dawn Imam Shafi heard a knock on the door and a voice said in affectionate tones: "May Allah show you His Mercy! Arise, the hour of prayer has come." Imam Shafi at once got up and found Imam Malik standing on the door with a vessel full of water in his hand. At this, Imam Shafi [R.T.A.] felt some embarrassment, noticing which Imam Malik [R.T.A.] remarked in deep affection "Never mind, brother, it is my obligation to look after the guests."

10. Having lodged the guest, tell him the location of the toilet; provide him with a vessel of water; point out the direction of the Qiblah, and supply him with a prayer-mat. The servant of Imam Malik [R.T.A.], having lodged Imam Shafi [R.T.A.] in a room submitted to him: "Hazrat! This is the direction of the Qiblah; the vessel of water is placed here and the toilet is located this way."

11. At dinner time wash your hands first and reach the table before your guests wash their hands. When Imam Malik [R.T.A.] observed this etiquette, Imam Shafi [R.T.A.] asked him the significance of this gesture. Thereupon Imam Malik [R.T.A.] observed, "Before starting the meal the host should wash his hands first and reach the dining place before his guests in order to greet them at the meal. At the end of the

meal, however, it is the guests whose hands should be washed first and the host should wash his hands last of all lest some more guests should drop in before the host gets up from the dinning place."

12. The quantity of food and the number of plates should be somewhat in excess of the actual number of guests. It is possible that someone might turn up during the meal. In that case, the host will have to get up and take the extra trouble of making further arrangements. If the provisions and plates are already there the new guest will be saved from embarrassment and will rather feel happy and honoured.

13. Show selflessness and sacrifice in the case of a guest. Provide comfort to him at the cost of your won convenience.

One day a person came to the Holy Prophet [S.A.W.] and submitted: "O Prophet of Allah [S.A.W.]! I am in a terrible agony of hunger." The Holy Prophet [S.A.W.] sent word to one of his holy wives [R.A.A.]: "Send whatever food is available," The answer he [S.A.W.] received was: "In the name of Allah Who has sent you as His Apostle, there is nothing except water available here." The Holy Prophet [S.A.W.] thereupon sent the same message to a second wife and received the same reply. The Holy Prophet [S.A.W.] made enquiries from each of his wives, but answer was invariably the same. The Holy Prophet [S.A.W.] then turned towards his companions [R.A.A.] and observed; "Who among you will accept this man as his guest for tonight?" A companion [R.A.A.] from among the Ansar submitted: "O Prophet of Allah [S.A.W.], I accept this man as my guest."

The Ansari [R.A.A.] thereupon took the guest to his house and told his wife: "I have brought a guest from the Holy Prophet [S.A.W.] with me. Show him some hospitality." The wife answered: "I have just enough food for children and no more." The illustrious companion said: "Put the children to sleep by diverting their attention to some thing else and when you serve the meal before the guest, extinguish the lamp on some pretext and sit down beside the guest so that he may feel we are sharing the meal with him." In this manner, the guest ate to his fill, but the hosts passed the night on an empty stomach. Next morning when this illustrious companion [R.A.A.] reached to the presence of the Holy Prophet [S.A.W.], the Prophet [S.A.W.] on beholding him observed: The goodness both of you displayed towards your guest has won you the immense pleasure of Allah."

(Bukhari, Muslim)

14. Even if your guest has treated you with bad manners and given you a cold shoulder on some occasion in the past, behave towards him with generosity, liberality and magnanimity.

    Hazrat Abul Ahwas Jashmi [R.A.A.] relates about his father that once he submitted to the Holy Prophet [S.A.W.]: "If I come across someone and he does not perform his duty of hospitality and entertainment towards me and later if he happens to meet me, is it obligatory upon me to show him hospitality? Or should I act towards him in the same impolite and indifferent manner? The Prophet [S.A.W.] observed: "No, you should perform your obligation of hospitality towards him in any case." *(Mishkat)*

15. Make a request to your guest to offer a prayer invoking the favour and grace of Allah on you, especially when the guest is a man of piety, a devotee of religion and a person of excellent faith. Hazrat 'Abdullah b. Busr [R.A.A.] reports: "The Holy Prophet [S.A.W.] once stayed as a guest with my father. We presented to him a dish of 'Harisa'. The Holy Prophet [S.A.W.] ate some of it. Afterwards we offered some dates. The Holy Prophet [S.A.W.] ate the dates and taking the kernels between the two forefingers of his hand, cast them away. Finally we presented a drink. He [S.A.W.] took some draughts of it and passed it on to the next person sitting on his right. When the Holy Prophet [S.A.W.] got up to leave, my father took hold of the bridle of his horse and submitted: "O Prophet of Allah [S.A.W.]! Pray for us." Thereupon the Holy Prophet [S.A.W.] prayed for him.

> "O Allah! Bless the provisions you have vouchsafed to them with Thy increased bounty, grant them salvation and show them Thy Mercy." *(Tirmidhi)*

1. When you pay a visit to someone as a guest, do take some gifts for the host or for his children according to your means. Keep in mind the taste and liking of your host while choosing gifts for him. Exchange of presents and gifts augments sentiments of love and promotes intimate relationship. The gift creates a soft corner in the heart of the receiver for the donor.

2. Do not stay for more than three days as a guest with any one, save under special circumstances or when the host insists on your staying with him for a longer period. The Holy Prophet [S.A.W.] affirms:

   > "It is not permissible for a guest to stay so long with the host as to cause him trouble." *(Al-Adab-ul-Mufrad)*

   'Sahih Muslim' reports:

   > "It is not permissible for a Muslim to stay so long with his brother as to make him a sinner." The people submitted: "O Prophet of Allah [S.A.W.]! How will a Muslim make his brother a sinner in this manner?" "By staying so long with his brother that his brother may be exhausted of all means of entertaining him."

3. Do not always be a guest of others. Invite others also to be your guests and entertain them liberally.

4. When you go to stay as a guest with somebody, take necessary baggage and bedding etc. according to the season along with you. In winter, especially, never forget to take the bedding with you, otherwise the host will be put to extreme hardship. It is highly improper that the guest shall in any way become an unbearable burden for the host.

5. Keep in mind the engagements and duties of your host. Take care that your host's occupation, duties and engagements are not in any way disturbed by your presence as a guest with him.

6. Do not make all sorts of demands on your host. Be content with whatever provisions he makes for your comfort and entertainment and thank him for this. Do not put him in any extraordinary trouble.
7. If your host's women are not your close or blood relation, avoid entering into conversation with them without reason. Do not eavesdrop on the mutual conversation of your host's women. Behave yourself in such a manner that your conversation or conduct does not become a nuisance for them. Do not violate the privacy and the limitations of Purdah in any case.
8. If for some reason you do not wish to eat with your host, or you are observing a fast, excuse yourself politely and say a prayer invoking the Grace and Blessings of Allah upon your host.

   When Hazrat Ibrahim [A.S.] presented a sumptuous meal to his venerable guests and the guests would not partake of it, Hazrat Ibrahim [A.S.] said to them: "Gentlemen, why don't you eat?" In a bid to put Hazrat Ibrahim at ease the angels submitted: "Please do not take it ill. As a matter of fact, we cannot eat. We have come only to convey the glad tidings of the birth of a talented son to you."
9. When you attend a feast, say a prayer at the end of the meal invoking Allah to bless the host with extensive means, grace, favour, salvation and His Mercy. Hazrat Abu Athhim b. Tahan [R.A.A.] once invited the Holy Prophet [S.A.W.] and his illustrious companions [R.A.A.] to a feast. When the meal was over, the Holy Prophet [S.A.W.] observed: "Reward your brother." The illustrious companions [R.A.A.] submitted: "How can we reward him, O Prophet of Allah [S.A.W.]?" The Holy Prophet [S.A.W.] observed:

   > "When a man pays a visit to his brother and eats and drinks there, he can reward his brother by praying for Allah's favour and blessings upon his brother:
   >
   > *(Abu Dawud)*

The Holy Prophet [S.A.W.] once visited the house of Hazrat Sa'd b. 'Ubadah [R.A.A.]. Hazrat Sa'd [R.A.A.] presented to the Holy Prophet [S.A.W.] bread and olive oil. The Prophet of Allah [S.A.W.] took the meal and then prayed for him:

> "May the fasting people break their fasts with your provisions! May the pious partake of your meals and may the angels pray for Allah's Mercy and forgiveness for you." *(Abu-Dawud)*

Social Life

1. Try to keep company with persons of good character.
2. Join in the conversation that is going on among those present in the company. To exclude yourself from the conversation and to sit in company with a frowning face betrays a haughty attitude. The Holy Prophet [S.A.W.] used to take an active part in the conversation among his illustrious companions. Do not adopt a gloomy attitude or a posture of depression while sitting in a company. Wear a smile on your face and sit in the company in a fresh and joyous mood.
3. Try that the remembrance of Allah and the life in the Hereafter should form part of discussion in each of your meetings. When you feel that the interest of the participants is lagging in conversation on religious matters, change your topic to worldly issues. Later when a suitable opportunity arises make a discreet effort to bring the talk round to religious topics again.
4. When you go to a meeting take seat wherever you find room. Do not make a bid to move ahead by pushing through or jumping over the heads or shoulders of the people. Such conduct causes inconvenience to those who came early and took their seats first and the man who indulges in such impolite behaviour reflects a sense of self-importance and haughtiness.
5. In a meeting, do not try to dislodge a person from his seat in order to occupy it yourself. This is a very bad habit. Such conduct provokes hatred and ill-will in the hearts of others

and betrays a sense of self-assertion and a haughty attitude towards others.

6. In a meeting where people are sitting around in a circle, do not sit in the centre of the circle. Such a behaviour is not only ridiculous, but extremely improper. The Holy Prophet [S.A.W.] has cursed such defaulters.
7. Do not try to grab the seat of a person who leaves his seat for a while. Keep his seat reserved until he returns. However, if it is known that the person will not return, you are free to take the seat previously occupied by him.
8. Do not separate two persons sitting together in some gathering without seeking their permission. They might be sitting together because of intimacy, love or for some other reason and separation may hurt their feelings.
9. Avoid sitting at a place of distinction in a gathering. If you pay a visit to somebody's house, don't by to take a seat of distinction, save in case the host himself insists on your taking such a seat. Always sit in the meeting in a respectful manner. Do not spread your feet or stretch your legs.
10. Do not make a bid to always sit near the person presiding the meeting. Sit wherever you find room, and leave space for those who arrive after you to find a place to sit conveniently. In case a greater number of people arrive to attend the meeting, you should try to adjust yourself .in a smaller space and generously leave room for the new comers to find a seat.
11. Do not stand before or around someone, even to show respect as it is against Islamic etiquette.
12. No two persons should talk to each other in confidence in a gathering or sitting. This annoys others and creates a feeling that they do not deserve to be taken into confidence. It may also create a misunderstanding among others that the two persons are perhaps engaged in backbiting against others present over there.
13. Seek the permission of the chairman before you say anything in a meeting. While you speak or take part in question and

answers, do not assume such role as if you are presiding over the meeting. It may be taken as an attempt to impose yourself upon others as well as an insult to the chairman of the meeting.

14. Only one man should speak at a time. Each one should be heard with full attention. Eagerness to express himself first in a meeting may create chaos and pandemonium.
15. The matters discussed in confidence in the meeting must not be spread everywhere. The participants are under obligation to guard the secrets of the meeting.
16. Do not broach another issue until the meeting concludes discussion about the matter under consideration. Do not interrupt a speaker in order to start speaking yourself. In case, it is imperative for you to speak up at once, you should do so with the permission of the speaker.
17. In the course of the proceedings, the Chairman of the meeting should pay equal attention to all members. He should address the meeting turning towards right and left so that each side receives the benefit of attention. The Chairman should allow the participants a right to express their views.
18. Say this prayer before dispersing the meeting. The meeting should not end without offering this prayer:

    "Allah, grant us Thy Fear and Mercy which may stand betmean us and disobedience to Thee. Vouchsafe to us that devotion which may entitle us to Thy Paradise. Give us such deep Faith which may render all wordly losses as worthless for us. Allah, grant us the favour of utilising our sense of hearing, sight and physical strength to our advantage and continue this favour even after we are no more. Take our revenge from him who oppresses us. Grant us victory over him who shows enmity towards us. Do not put us to trial concerning religion. Do not make worldly goods the chief objects of our lives. Do not make this world the limit of our knowledge and wisdom, nor entrust us under the charge of a person who shows no mercy to us." *(Tirmidhi)*

1. Say 'Assalamo-'Alaikum on meeting a Muslim brother in order to express your feeling of attachment and felicity.

   The Holy Qur'an affirms:

   > "And when those who believe in our revelations come unto thee say: Peace be unto you." *(6: 45)*

   This verse which is addressed to the Holy Prophet [S.A.W.] indirectly teaches a moral etiquette to the entire Ummah i.e. whenever two Muslims meet each other, they should exchange feelings of love and felicity with each other, and the best means of doing this is that they should pray for the salvation and wellbeing of each other. One should say 'Assalamo-'Alaikum'; the other should respond with 'Wa 'Alaikumus salam'. Offering the salam is a means of maintaining and augmenting love and affection.

   The Holy Prophet [S.A.W.] affirmed:

   > "You cannot enter Paradise until you acquire piety and you cannot attain piety unless you learn to love each other. Let me tell you a novel way. If you practice it, you will learn to love each other. Make the practice of offering salam to each other common among you." *(Mishkat)*

2. Always say 'salam' after the Islamic fashion. In personal conversation or in correspondence, you must use these words of greeting which have been prescribed by the Holy Quran and Sunnah. Do not avoid the usage of this Islamic etiquette of greeting, nor use substitute words or expressions prescribed by modern society. This Islamic mode of greeting is not only very simple, meaningful and impressive but also a comprehensive prayer for salvation and peace. The significance of your offering a salam to your Muslim brother is very vast. 'Assalamo-'Alaikum' implies 'May Allah bless you with all kinds of peace and salvation'; 'May Allah protect your life and property'; 'May Allah protect your hearth and home'; 'May He keep your family and relations in safety'; 'May Allah safeguard your faith and belief ; May you live in peace in this world and in the world Hereafter'; 'May Allah vouchsafe to

your graces of which I know and graces of which I have no knowledge'; I bear deep sentiments, good-will, love and sincerity, safety and peace for you. Hence do not have fear on my account. You will never come to harm from any deed of mine'. By adding 'Alif and 'Lam' to the world *'salam'* and saying *'Assalamo-'Alaikum'* can be used for expressing heartfelt felicity, sincerity, love, goodwill and devotion to the person whom you meet, provided these words are uttered with full awareness of their significance. When you greet your brother with the words 'Assalamo-'Alaikum', you in fact invoke the blessings of Allah to protect your brother; you invoke the blessings of Him Who is the Fountain of all good and Whose Being is synonymous with peace and salvation. 'Assalam' is one of the attributes of Allah and a person can attain peace and salvation only at the goodwill of the Almighty and whomsoever He denies salvation is deprived of it in both worlds.

The Holy Prophet [S.A.W.] has affirmed:

> *'Assalam* is one of the attributes of Allah. It has been sent unto the world for the benefit of the people. Hence make the use of Assalam common among you."
>
> *(Al-Adad-ul-Mufrad)*

Hazrat Abu Huraira [R.A.A.] has reported that the Holy Prophet [S.A.W.] observed: "When Allah created Hazrat Adam [A.S.], He ordained that Adam [A.S.] should approach a group of angels and offer them 'salam'. Allah also counselled Adam [A.S.] to listen carefully the answer given by the angels and to remember it, because the same prayer would be prescribed for Adam [A.S.] and his progeny. Hence Hazrat Adam [A.S.] approached the angles and said: 'Assalamo-'Alaikum'. The angels in reply said: 'Assalamo-'Alaikum Wa Rahmatullah." In other words, the angels in their answer added the words 'Rahmatullah' to *'Assalamo-'Alaikum'*. *(Bukhari, Muslim)*

The Holy Qur'an affirms that when the angels come to extract the souls of the believers they say 'Salamu 'Alaik' on their arrival:

Thus Allah repayeth those who ward off (evil).

> "Those whom the angels cause to die (when they are) good. They say: Peace be unto you! Enter the garden because of what ye used to do." *(16: 31, 32)*

When these God-fearing people will arrive at the gates of Paradise, the sentinels of Paradise will accord them a magnificent welcome with the same words:

> "And those who keep their duty to their Allah are driven unto the gardens in troops till when they reach and the gates thereof are opened and the warders thereof say unto them: Peace be unto you! You are good so enter you (the garden) to dwell therein forever." *(39: 73)*

And when they shall have entered Paradise, the angels will enter from all the Gates of Paradise and say 'Assalamo 'Alaikum' to them.

> "And the angels shall arrive to offer them welcome from each Gate of Paradise and say to them: Salamun-'alaikum. This is the recompense for your patience and steadfast conduct. Hence how excellent is this eternal home."

The people of Paradise will also greet each other with the same words:

> "And therein their tongues shall pronounce. "O Allah! Thou art Pure and Supreme" and they shall pray for each other in these words: "Salam be on you."

Even Allah shall send them greetings of 'Salam' and 'Blessings'.

> "Lo! those who merit paradise this day are happily employed, they and their wives in pleasant shade on thrones reclining! Theirs the fruit and theirs that they ask; the word from a Merciful Lord is peace!" *(36: 55-58)*

In reality, there shall be greetings of 'Salam' for the believers from all sides in Paradise.

> "They shall not hear improper absurdities there, nor (talk) of sin. There shall only be greetings of 'Salam" 'Salam', on all sides."

In view of these clear injunctions and evidence of the Holy Qur'an and Sunnah, it is not lawful for a believer to forsake the manner prescribed by Allah and His Prophet [S.A.W.] under any circumstance and adopt other modes of expressing love and felicity.

3. Say Salam to every Muslim, whether you have a prior acquaintance or connexion with him or not. The condition that he is your Muslim brother suffices for establishing a relationship or making an acquaintance and a Muslim must cherish sentiments of love, sincerity,.goodwill and loyalty for his brother Muslim. A person submitted to the Holy Prophet [S.A.W.]: "What is the most commendable deed in Islam?" The Holy Prophet [S.A.W.] observed: "To feed the poor and to offer Salam to every Muslim, whether you have a prior acquaintance with him or not." *(Bukhari, Muslim)*

4. On entering your house, say 'Salam' to members of your family. The Holy Qur'an affirms:

> "But when ye enter houses salute one another with a greeting from Allah blessed and sweet." *(24: 61)*

Hazrat Anas [R.A.A.] reports that the Holy Prophet [S.A.W.] had advised him: "Dear son! On entering your house, you should first say 'Salam' to members of your family. This is an act of goodness and blessings for you and your family." *(Tirmidhi)*

Similarly, when you call at somebody's house, say 'Salam' before entering the house. Do not go into the house without saying *'Salam'* first.

> "O ye who believe! Enter not houses other than your own without first announcing your presence and invoking peace upon the folk thereof." *(24: 27)*

When the angels called on Hazrat Ibrahim [A.S.] as his venerable guest, they offered 'Salam' and in response Hazrat Ibrahim [A.S.] also said 'Salam' to them.

5. Say 'Salam' to small children also. This is the best means of teaching the children the manner of offering 'Salam' as well as an observance of the Sunnah of the Holy Prophet [S.A.W.]. When Hazrat Anas [R.A.A.] passed near the children, he said '*Salam*' to them and observed that the Holy Prophet [S.A.W.] used to do the same." *(Bukhari, Muslim)*

   Hazrat 'Abdullah b. 'Umar [R.A.A.] used to write *'Salam'* in his letters to children also. *(Al-Adab-ul-Mufrad)*

6. Women can offer 'Salam' to men; likewise men can offer '*Salam*' to women. Hazrat Asma Ansaria [R.A.A.] states: "I was sitting among my lady friends when the Holy Prophet [S.A.W.] passed by us. He [S.A.W.] offered 'Salam' to us.

   (Al-Adab-ul-Mufrad)

   Umm Hani [R.A.A.] states: "I came to the presence of Holy Prophet [S.A.W.]. He [S.A.W.] was taking a bath at that time. When I offered 'Salam' to the Holy Prophet [S.A.W.] he en quired about me. I submitted: Umm Hani. The Holy Prophet [S.A.W.] said: "Most Welcome." *(Al-Adab-ul Mufrad)*

7. Accustom yourself to say 'Salam' as often as possible and never miss the opportunity of saying 'Salam'. Say 'Salam' to each other as often as possible. The act of offering 'Salam' promotes love and in recompense for this act, Allah grants protection from all pain or loss.

   The Holy Prophet [S.A.W.] has affirmed:

   > "Let me tell you a device, which will promote love and friendship among you. Say Salam to each other as often as possible." *(Muslim)*

   In addition, the Holy Prophet [S.A.W.] also observed:

   > "Make the practice of offering 'Salam' common among you. Allah shall grant you salvation in recompense."

   Hazrat Anas [R.A.A.] reports that the illustrious Companions of the Holy Prophet [S.A.W.] used to say 'Salam' to each other very often. So common and widespread was the practice that if at times a Companion went out of sight behind a tree and appeared in view again, he offered 'Salam' again. The Holy Prophet [S.A.W.] has observed:

> "Any person who meets a Muslim brother should say *'Salam'* to him. Later if one of them goes out of sight behind a tree, wall or a stone and reappears, he should offer 'Salam' once again on seeing his brother."
> *(Riyad-us-Salihin)*

Hazrat Tufail [R.A.A.] reports:

> "I used to call on Hazrat 'Abdullah b. 'Umar [R.A.A.] often and also accompanied him on his trips to the bazar. When both of us went to the bazar it was the common practice of Hazrat 'Abdullah ibn 'Umar [R.A.A.] to say 'Salam' to every passer-by, may he be a junk-man, a shopkeeper or a poor or destitute person. In fact he invariably offered 'Salam' to every person whoever he may be."

One day when I called on him, he said:

> "Let us go to the bazar." I submitted: Hazrat what will you do in the bazar? You never stop to make any purchases, neither enquire about any goods; nor strike a bargain; nor attend any company in the bazar. Come, sir, let us sit here and talk." Hazrat Tufail [R.A.A.] observed: "O Abu Batan (fat-bellied)! I go to the bazar merely to offer 'Salam'. Whoever happens to meet me I say *'Salam'* to him." *(Muwatta Imam Malik)*

8. Beware that each Muslim has a right over you to offer him 'Salam'. Discharge this obligation towards a brother Muslim open-heartedly and never miss an opportunity to say 'Salam' to another Muslim.

The Holy Prophet [S.A.W.] has observed:

> "Each Muslim owes an obligation to another Muslim to offer him 'Salam' when ever they happen to meet."
> *(Muslim)*

Hazrat Abu Huraira [R.A.A.] states:

> "The most niggardly person is he who lets go an opportunity to say 'Salam'." *(Al-Adab-ul-Mufrad)*

9. Always be the first to say 'Salam'. If, Allah forbid, you are not on good terms with someone, even then you should take the initiative in offering 'Salam' and making up the quarrel.

   The Holy Prophet [S.A.W.] observed:

   > "He who takes the initiative in offering 'Salam' is the nearest to Allah." *(Abu Dawud)*

   Furthermore, the Holy Prophet [S.A.W.] affirmed:

   > "It is not lawful for any Muslim to severe all connexions with his brother Muslim for a period of more than three days to such extent that if they happen to come across each other, one should turn towards one side and the other should change his course towards the other side. Between these two, he is the superior who is the first to say 'Salam' to the other." *(Al-Adab-ul-Mufrad)*

   Someone submitted to the Holy Prophet [S.A.W.]:

   > "When two persons happen to meet each other, who should say *'Salam'* first?" The Holy Prophet [S.A.W.] observed: "He who is better than the other in the eyes of Allah." *(Tirmidhi)*

   Hazrat 'Abdullah b. 'Umar [R.A.A.] was so much particular in being the first to offer 'Salam' that no one ever succeeded in beating him in this respect.

10. Do offer the 'Salam' by word of mouth and say Assalamo-*'Alaikum* in a distinct voice so that the addressee may hear it clearly. There is nothing wrong with making a sign with your hand or nodding your head if need be along with saying the *'Salam'*. For example if the person to whom you wish to offer *'Salam'* is out of the reach of your voice, or he is unable to hear your because of deafness, you must make a gesture of 'Salam' along with uttering *Assalamo-Alaikum*.

    Hazrat 'Abdullah b. 'Umar [R.A.A.] has observed:

    > "When you offer 'Salam' to someone, make sure that he hears it, for *'Salam'* is the purest and the most blissful prayer vouchsafed by Allah to man."
    >
    > *(Al-Adab-ul-Mufrad)*

Hazrat Asma, daughter of Yazid, [R.A.A.] has reported:

> "One day the Holy Prophet [S.A.W.] passed near the mosque where a group of women were seated. While passing by the Holy Prophet [S.A.W.] offered 'Salam' to the women with a gesture of his holy hand."

It is evident that the Holy Prophet [S.A.W.] made a gesture of the hand along with uttering the words Assalamo-'Alaikum. The Tradition recorded in the Abu Dawud also confirms this point. Hazrat Asma [R.A.A.] states that when the Holy Prophet [S.A.W.] passed by us, he offered us *'Salam'*." It is proper, therefore, to make a gesture of the hand or nod the head if need be, but the words of 'Salam' must be uttered all the same.

11. Be particular in offering *'Salam'* to your elders. If you are walking along and some people are sitting on the way, you should be the first to offer them 'Salam'. When you are part of a small group and your small group comes across a large number of people, the smaller group must take the initiative in saying the 'Salam'. The Holy Prophet [S.A.W.] has affirmed:

"A Muslim has five rights over another Muslim:

(i) To make a response to the 'Salam'.

(ii) To visit him if he is lying ill.

(iii) To join in the funeral procession.

(iv) To accept the invitation.

(v) To respond to a sneeze.

Furthermore the Holy Prophet [S.A.W.] enjoined: "Avoid sitting on the road sides." The people submitted: "O Holy Prophet [S.A.W.]: It is an unavoidable necessity for us to sit on the roadside." The Holy Prophet [S.A.W.] observed: "If it is unavoidable for you to sit on the roadside, then you must discharge certain obligations concerning the roadside." The people submitted: "What are those obligations concerning the roadside? O Prophet of Allah [S.A.W.]?" The Holy Prophet [S.A.W.] observed: "To keep your eyes cast down, not to cause inconvenience, to respond to the 'Salam, to preach piety and to forbid people to indulge in wicked deeds."

18. In response to 'Salam" do not just confine yourself to saying 'Wa Alaikumus salam, but utter the words *Wa rahmamatullahi Wa barakatuhu.*

The Holy Qur'an affirms:

> "And when ye are greeted with a prayer greet ye with a better prayer than it or repeat it." *(4: 86)*

The implication is that you should never miss the opportunity of responding to the 'Salam'. Say a better prayer in response by adding more words to the 'Salam', or at least utter the same words. In any case a response to 'Salam' must be made. Hazrat 'Imran b. Haseen [R.A.A.] relates: "The Holy Prophet [S.A.W.] was seated when a man came and said *Assalamo-'Alaikum*. The Holy Prophet [S.A.W.] responded to the 'Salam' and observed: 'Ten' (in other words the man had earned ten virtues). Than a second man arrived and said, *Assalamo-Alaikum Wa Rahmatullah*. The Holy Prophet [S.A.W.] responded to the *'Salam'* and observed: `Twenty' (in other words the man had earned twenty virtues). Later a third man came to the presence and said: *Assalamo 'Alaikum Wa Rehmatullahi Wa Barakatuhu*. The Holy Prophet [S.A.W.] responded to him and observed 'Thirty' (in other words that man had earned thirty virtues). *(Tirmidhi)*

Hazrat 'Umar [R.A.A.] has reported:

> "Once I was riding behind Abu Bakr [R.A.A.] and Abu Bakr said: *Assalamo 'Alaikum* to every one whom we passed by and every one responded with the words *Wa 'Alaikum Assalam Wa Rehmatullah*. And when Abu Bakr [R.A.A.] said: Assalamo 'Alaikum Wa Rehmatullah, the people responded with the words: *Wa 'Alaikum Assalam Wa Rehmatul lahi Wa Barakatuhu*. Thereupon Abu Bakr [R.A.A.] observed: Today the people have surpassed us in excellence to a great extent. *(Al-Adab-ul-Mufrzd)*

19. On meeting someone say 'Assalamo 'Alaikum' first. Do not start conversation straight-away. Start conversation only after offering the 'Salam'

The Holy Prophet [S.A.W.] has enjoined:

"Do not respond if somebody starts talking before saying the *'Salam'*.

20. Avoid saying 'Salam' under the following conditions:
    (i) When people are engaged in reading, listening to or teaching the Holy Qur'an and Hadith.
    (ii) When some one is either delivering a sermon or is listening to it.
    (iii) When some one is announcing *'Adhan'* or *'Takbir'*.
    (iv) When a religious topic is being discussed in a meeting or some one is telling what Allah has ordained to us.
    (v) When the teacher is engaged in giving a lesson.
    (vi) When somebody is relieving himself of excretions.

    Moreover, under the following conditions, you should not only avoid saying 'Salam' but also express your unconcern and spiritual agony in a discreet manner:
    (i) When somebody is engaged in licentiousness and evil acts or mercy-making such as is forbidden by Shariah and is thus guilty of contempt of religion.
    (ii) When someone is defaming religion by uttering abuses, mean and sameless talk, fabricated lies and nonsense or is indulging in obscene jokes.
    (iii) When someone is propagating views and philosophies which are repugnant to religion and is trying to proselytise people or inciting them to anti religious activities and immoral and unethical manners.
    (iv) When some one is desecrating religious beliefs and manners and is indicating his inner wickedness and hypocrisy by making fun of the principles and injunctions of the Shariah.
21. Do not take the initiative in offering 'Salam' to the Jews or Christians. The Holy Qur'an affirms the fact that the Jews are

the worst nation as regards their disbelief, denial of truth, tyranny and savagery, falsehood and deception. Allah showered countless bounties upon this nation, yet they always displayed ingratitude to Him and persisted in their foul practices. It is the same nation which assassinated the venerable Prophets sent by Allah. Hence the believer should eschew all such conduct which shows even the slightest trace of respect or esteem for the Jews. On the other hand, the believers should adopt such conduct towards the Jews that they should be repeatedly reminded of the fact that recompense for offering the most hideous opposition to Truth is always disgrace and humiliation.

The Holy Prophet [S.A.W.] has observed:

> "Do not take the initiative in saying 'Salam' to the Jews and Christians. When you meet them on the way, force them to move over to the edge of the road."
> *(Al-Adab-ul-Mufrad)*

The implication is that you should walk with such dignity and in a stately manner that the Jews and Christians should move over to the edge leaving the road open for you.

22. However, say 'Salam' on arrival at a mixed meeting of the Muslims and polytheists. The Holy Prophet [S.A.W.] once passed near a meeting in which Muslims and polytheists were all taking part. On that occasion the Holy Prophet [S.A.W.] had said: 'Salam' to the whole meeting."*(Al-Adab-ul-Mu frad)*

23. In case an occasion arises to greet a non-Muslim with some words of respect, do not say Assalamo-'Alaikum. Use words like-'Adab Arz ; 'Taslimat' (respect or honour to you) etc. Do not make a gesture of your hand or nod your head or make any other sign which is repugnant to the tenets and spirit of Islam.

    The letter which the Holy Prophet [S.A.W.] had addressed to Heracles contained the following words of greetings:

    > "Salam be on him who follows Guidance (of the Allah)."

24. Do shake hands after saying the 'Salam' in order to express feelings of love, felicity and reverence. The Holy Prophet [S.A.W.] himself used to shake hands with people and his illustrious companions [R.A.A.] also used to shake hands whenever they met each other. In fact, the Holy Prophet [S.A.W.] had enjoined upon his Companions [R.A.A.] to adopt the custom of shaking hands with each other, and had explained the merits and importance of this etiquette in many different ways.

    Hazrat Qatada [R.A.A.] enquired from Hazrat Anas [R.A.A.]: "Was the custom of shaking hands current among the illustrious companions [R.A.A.]?" Hazrat Anas [R.A.A.] replied: "Yes, it was." *(Bukhari)*

    Hazrat Salama b. Dardan [R.T.A.] states: "I saw that Hazrat Malik b. Anas [R.T.A.] was shaking hands with people. He asked me 'Who are you?' I answered: "I am the slave of Bani Laith." Thereupon he passed his hand three times over my head and observed: "May Allah bless you with goodness and bounty."

    On one occasion when some visitors from Yemen arrived, the Holy Prophet [S.A.W.] observed to his illustrious companions [R.A.A.]: "The people of Yemen have come to you and they deserve handshakes more than other visitors." (Abu Dawud)

    Hazrat, Huzaifa b. Yaman [R.A.A.] reports: "The Holy Prophet [S.A.W.] observed: When two believers meet each other and after exchanging 'Salam' shake hands with each other they are shorn of their sins as dry leaves fall off from the trees." *(Tabrani)*

    Hazrat 'Abdullah b. Mas'ud relates: "The Holy Prophet [S.A.W.] affirmed: "To shake hands is to complete your Salam."

25. When a friend, near relative or elder returns from a journey, embrace him in greeting. On reaching Madinah Hazrat Zaid b. Haritha [R.A.A.] went to the Holy Prophet's [S.A.W.] house and knocked at the door. The Holy Prophet [S.A.W.] dragging

his covering sheet behind him reached the door and embraced him and kissed his forehead." *(Tirmidhi)*

Hazrat Anas [R.A.A.] states:

> "When the illustrious Companions [R.A.A.] happened to meet each other, they shook hands and when any of them returned from the journey he was greeted with an embrace." *(Tabrani)*

Attending the Sick

1. You must enquire after the health of the patients. To visit a patient is not only a social requirement or a means of promoting mutual cooperation and sympathy, but it is also a right of a Muslim over another and an essential pre-requisite to devotion to Allah. He who is devoted to Allah cannot remain unconcerned with the creation of Allah. To evade the obligation of offering sympathy, consolation and assistance to the sick is tantamount to forsaking the remembrance of Allah.

   The Holy Prophet [S.A.W.] has affirmed:

   > "On the Day of Judgement Allah shall ordain: "O son of Adam! You did not visit me when I was ailing?" The man will submit: "O Creator! You are Lord of the whole universe. How could I dare enquire after your welfare!" Allah shall ordain: 'Such and such person from among My creatures fell ill and you did not enquire after his health. If you had gone to enquire after his welfare, you would have found Me there. (In other words you would have earned My Favour and Blessing)." *(Muslim)*

   In addition, the Holy Prophet [S.A.W.] observed:

   > "A Muslim has six rights over another Muslim." The people submitted: "O Holy Prophet [S.A.W.]! What are those rights?" The Holy Prophet [S.A.W.] affirmed:
   >
   > (i) Say 'Salam' to your brother Muslim whenever you meet him.

(ii) Accept the invitation of your brother Muslim whenever he invites you.

(iii) Offer proper advice with all sincerity to your brother Muslim whenever he seeks your good advice.

(iv) When your Muslim brother sneezes and says *'Al-Hamd-o-Lillah'*, respond with saying *'Yar hamo-kallah'*.

(v) Visit your brother Muslim whenever he falls ill and enquire about his health.

(vi) When a Muslim brother dies, join in his funeral procession." *(Muslim)*

Furthermore, the Holy Prophet [S.A.W.] affirmed:

"He who enquires after the health of an ailing Muslim brother will find a dwelling place on the highest level of Paradise." *(Al-Adab-ul-Mufrad)*

Hazrat Abu Huraira [R.A.A.] has reported that the Holy Prophet [S.A.W.] observed:

"When a person goes to enquire after the health of a Muslim brother or just pays a call on him, a caller from the Heaven pronounces, "You have done well; your walking is propitious; you have earned a dwelling place in Paradise." *(Tirmidhi)*

2. Sit towards the head of the patient, pass your hand over his head or body and utter words of sympathy and consolation, so that the patient may start thinking about the reward and recompense awaiting him in the eternal world; and he may abstain from uttering any remarks showing impatience, or feelings of anguish and complaint.

   Hazrat 'A'isha bint Sa'ad [R.A.A.] reports that her father related: "Once while in Mecca I fell gravely ill. The Holy Prophet [S.A.W.] came to enquire after my health. I submitted: "O Holy Prophet [S.A.W.]! I am leaving behind a great deal of wealth and I have only one daughter. Should I will away two-third of my wealth and leave one-third for my daughter?"

The Holy Prophet [S.A.W.] observed: "No." I submitted: "Should I then will away half of my property and leave half portion for my daughter?" The Holy Prophet [S.A.W.] observed: 'No'. Thereupon I submitted: "O Holy Prophet of Allah [S.A.W.]! Should I then will away one third of my wealth?" The Holy Prophet [S.A.W.] observed: "Yes, will away one-third of your wealth and this is enough." Afterwards, the Holy Prophet of Allah [S.A.W.] placed his hand on my forehead and passed it over my face and belly and then said the following prayer:

"O Allah, bless Sa'ad with health and complete his Hijrat." Since then whenever I recall to mind that moment I feel the soothing sensation of the holy hand of the Holy Prophet [S.A.W.] to the depth of my inner-self." *(Al-Adab-ul-Mufrad)*

Hazrat Zaid b. Argam [R.A.A.] relates:

"Once my eyes became sore. The Holy Prophet [S.A.W.] visited me to enquire after my health and said: "Zaid, what do you do when you are suffering from sore eyes." I submitted: "I endure this illness with patience." The Holy Prophet [S.A.W.] observed: If you observe patience and endurance while you are afflicted with sore eyes, Allah shall admit you into Paradise as a reward for this."

Hazrat Ibn 'Abbas [R.A.A.] states: "Whenever the Holy Prophet [S.A.W.] visited a patient to enquire after his health, the Prophet [S.A.W.] used to sit at the head of the ailing person and repeated the following prayer seven times:

"I beseech Allah Almighty Who is the Lord of Exalted Heavens to grant you health!"

The Holy Prophet [S.A.W.] observed:

"The patient will certainly be restored to health if this prayer is offered seven times, except in case the hour of his death has come." *(Mishkat)*

Hazrat Jabir [R.A.A.] reports that the Holy Prophet [S.A.W.] paid a visit to an old lady Umm-as-Saib [R.A.A.] to enquire after her health. Umm-as-Saib [R.A.A.] was shivering with intense fever. The Holy Prophet [S.A.W.] enquired: "How are you feeling?" The lady submitted: "May Allah curse this fever which is oppressing me." On hearing this, the Holy Prophet [S.A.W.] observed: "Don't curse the fever. It purges the pious of sins just as the furnace smelts the iron and purifies it of rust." *(Al-Adab-ul-Mufrad)*

3. When you visit a patient, enquire about his condition and pray for his recovery. Whenever the Holy Prophet [S.A.W.] visited a patient he first enquired about his health and then used to observe: *L ba'sa tuhurun inṣha Allahu.* "There is no need to worry. By the Will of Allah, this illness will disappear and will prove a means of purging you of all sins." Afterwards, the Holy Prophet [S.A.W.] used to pass his right hand over the region of pain and discomfort and say this prayer:

   "Allah! Remove this pain. O Lord of mankind, grant health to this person. You are the Healer. There is none from whom we expect recovery from illness save You alone-Grant such recovery that this disease may be completely uprooted."

4. Do not sit beside the patient for long, nor make noise near him. However, if the sick person is your intimate friend or a near relation and himself insists on your sitting beside him for a longer time, you should comply with his wishes.

   Hazrat 'Abdullah b. 'Abbas [R.A.A.] states:

   "It is part of the Sunnah not to sit for long beside a patient, nor to make noise near him."

5. Do ask the relations of the patient about his condition and express your sympathy. Offer them all possible assistance or cooperation. For example, fetch the doctor, or convey a message about the condition of the patient, or fetch medicines etc. or if required, extend financial help also.

Hazrat Ibrahim b. Abi Habla [R.A.A.] relates: "Once my wife fell ill. In those days I used to pay frequent visits to Hazrat Umm al-Darda [R.A.A.]. Whenever I called on her, she used to enquire: "Say, how is your wife?" I answered: "She is still indisposed." Thereafter, she used to send for food. I sat down and dined at her home and then came back. One day, when I called on her and she enquired about my wife's health, I replied: "By the grace and favour of Allah, she has nearly recovered from her illness. "Hazrat Umm-al-Darda [R.A.A.] thereupon observed: "When you used to say that your wife was unwell I used to arrange a meal for you. Now that she has gained her health, I need not arrange a meal for you."

6. Do visit a non-Muslim patient to enquire after his condition. Whenever you get an opportunity invite his attention towards Islam in a discreet manner as illness makes a man more inclined towards Allah and he gets more receptive to the truth.

   Hazrat Anas [R.A.A.] reports:

   > "A Jewish boy used to attend on the Holy Prophet [S.A.W.]. Once he fell ill. The Holy Prophet [S.A.W.] visited him to enquire after his health. The Holy Prophet [S.A.W.] sat at the head of the boy and conveyed to him the message of Islam. The boy looked to his father, who was standing nearby, as if to seek his opinion. The father said to the boy: "My son, submit to what Abul-Qasim says." So the boy accepted Islam. The Holy Prophet [S.A.W.] came out of his house saying. "Thanks Allah Who saved the boy from Hell-Fire." *(Bukhari)*

7. When you visit the house of a patient to enquire after his health, avoid-looking about in the house. Sit in a manner that the inmates of the house, particularly the women are not within your sight.

   Once Hazrat 'Abdullah bin Mas'ud [R.A.A.] went to the house of an ailing person to enquire after his health. He was accompanied by some others also. One of his companions started gazing a lady of the house. When Hazrat 'Abdullah [R.A.A.] perceived it, he observed to his companion: "It would have been better for you to gouge out your eyes."

8. Do not go to enquire after the health of those who openly indulge in sinful acts and flout the Commands of Allah unashamedly and obstinately.

   Hazrat 'Abdullah b. 'Amr [R.A.A.] observes:

   > "When the drunkards fall ill, do not go to enquire after their health."

9. When you go to enquire after the health of a patient, request him to pray for you also. It is recorded in Ibn Majah: "When you visit a patient to enquire after his health, request him to pray for you. The prayer of a patient is as much effective as the prayer offered by angels." (The implication is that the angels offer prayers only at the Command of Allah and hence their prayers are always granted).

1. Whomsoever you meet, greet him with a smiling face. Express your sentiments of felicity and take initiative in offering Salam. It will invoke great blessings of Allah on you.

2. Use no words of greeting other than those enjoined by the Holy Prophet [S.A.W.] i.e., 'Assalamo-'Alaikum'. Shake hands if possible and enquire after his health as well as the welfare of his family. The greetings 'Assalamo-'Alaikum' taught by the Holy Prophet [S.A.W.] are comprehensive in their connotations and cover all the blessings of this material life as well as our spiritual life and religion. These words signify complete peace and salvation. While shaking hands with somebody, keep it in your mind that the Holy Prophet [S.A.W.] never withdrew his hand first, but waited for the other one to release his hand.

3. Put on a clean dress when you go to call on someone; do not go out in dirty dress nor wear expensive garments while going to visit someone in order to impress him with your costly dress.

4. When you intend to visit someone, make an appointment with him first. Never visit anybody at inconvenient hours. Such a

visit is not only an interference in others' engagements but also degrades you in their eyes.

5. When someone calls on you, greet him with an affectionate smile. Offer him a seat in a respectful manner and entertain him according to the occasion.
6. When you call on someone, confine yourself to talking about useful matters. Do not waste time in useless conversation, otherwise the people will dislike and avoid you.
7. When you call on somebody's house, stand outside the gate and ask for permission to enter. When permitted to enter, say *'Assalamo-'Alaikum'* and enter the house. If you get no response after pronouncing *'Assalamo-Alaikum'* three times, don't mind it and return cheerfully.
8. While visiting somebody, do not forget to carry some suitable gifts with you. Exchange of gifts deepens feeling of mutual love and affection.
9. If a needy person calls on you, try to fulfil his need to the extent of your means. If he requests you to recommend his case to someone, do it. However, if you cannot comply with his request, you should decline in a polite manner. Do not keep him in hopeful illusions.
10. If you call on someone to seek his assistance in need, tell him your requirement in a courteous manner. If he fulfils your need, thank him. But if he declines, never mind, say *'Salam'* to him and return cheerfully.
11. Do not always expect others to call on you. You should also pay visits to others off and on. It is the most pleasant thing to develop social relations and to serve others in need. Keep in your mind that brothers in faith always develop relations for good ends.
12. If you notice a little straw or any other thing clinging to the face, beard or clothes of the person whom you happen to meet, remove it with your own hands. If the other persons does the same for you, thank him and pray for him:

    "May Allah remove all such things from you as are displeasing to you."

13. When you visit someone at night, be mindful of his comfort. Do not sit with him for long. If you come to know that he has gone to bed return cheerfully without feeling resentment.
14. When a group of people call on someone, the man who is talking should represent all his companions. Never try to press your importance or give prominence to your own self ignoring the presence of your other companions.

Discussion

1. Always speak the truth. Never hesitate speaking the truth even at the greatest risk.
2. Speak only when you must, and always talk with a purpose. Too much talk and useless conversation betrays lack of seriousness. You are accountable before Allah for every word you utter. The angel of Allah records.

   "A supervisor remains vigilant to preserve on record every speech that is uttered by his tongue."
3. Always speak politely. Wear a smile on you face and a sweet tone in your speech. Always speak in a moderate voice. Do not keep your voice so low as to be inaudible to the addressee, nor raise it so loud that the addressee might be over-awed by your voice. The Holy Qur'an affirms:

   Lo! the harshest of all the voices is the voice of the ass." *(31: 19)*
4. Do not spoil your tongue with dirty talk. Do not speak ill of others. Never indulge in backbiting. Do not complain against others. Never indulge in mimicking others to ridicule them. Do not make false premises. Never laugh at others, nor boast of your own superiority or indulge in self-praise. Never get unreasonable and rash in conversation. Do not pass remarks on others or satirize them. Do not call someone by a disgraceful name. Avoid swearing frequently.
5. Always say what is just and fair regardless of any loss to your self, your friend or relative.

   "And when you say something, speak what is just even if you are talking about your relative."

6. Be soft-spoken, reasonable and sympathetic in your conversation. Do not utter sharp, harsh and teasing remarks.
7. When women happen to talk with men, they should speak in a clear, straight and rough manner. They ought not speak in delicate, sweet tone lest the listener should entertain any foul expectation.
8. If the impudent wish to entangle you in dialogue or altercation offer them 'Salam' politely and leave them. Those who indulge in loose talk and absurd conversation are the worst lot of the Ummah.
9. Keep in view the mental level and outlook of the man you are talking to so as to make him understand. If the addressee cannot hear or is unable to catch your meaning, repeat what you have said before without any resentment.
10. Always be brief and to the point in your talk. It is unfair to prolong discussion without rhyme or reason.
11. When you wish to explain the tenets of Islam; want to speak on the teachings of Islam be simple and clear and speak in a passionate and heart-warming style. To seek reputation through oratory, to try to impress people with flowery language, to seek popularity among people, to adopt a proud and haughty mien, or to deliver speeches only for the sake of fun or recreation all these are the worst habits that corrupt the man to the core of his heart.
12. Never indulge in flattery, nor ingratiate with anybody. Always mind your honour and respect and avoid any thing below your dignity.
13. Do not interrupt and interfere in others' conversation without their permission, nor intercept others' conversation in order to say something yourself. If, however, you must speak, do so with the permission of other.
14. Speak slowly in a proper and dignified manner. Do not speak in a hurried manner nor indulge in fun and jokes all the time as it degrades you in the eyes of others.

15. If somebody puts a question to you, listen carefully to him and make an answer after careful thought. It is simply foolish to answer the questions without due consideration. If the questions are being put to somebody else, do not be so officious as to give answers yourself.
16. When someone is narrating something, do not say 'we know already'. May be he reveals something new and impresses you by his sincerity and piety.
17. When you talk to someone, give due regard to his age, status and his relationship to you. Do not talk with your parents, teachers and elders in a manner in which you would talk to your friends. Likewise, when you are talking to youngster, speak with affection and elderly dignity.
18. While engaged in conversation, do not point out towards any one lest he should conceive any misunderstanding or suspicion. Abstain from eavesdropping on others.
19. Listen more and talk less. Do not reveal your secrets to others. Once you disclose a secret to someone, never expect it to remain a secret any more.

Letter Writing

1. Always begin your letter with the words.

   In the name of Allah the most Beneficent, the most Merciful

   If you wish to use an abbreviation, you may write.

   In the name of Allah, the Exalted

   The Holy Prophet [S.A.W.] has affirmed: "Any undertaking, which does not commence with utterance of the attribute of Allah 'Bismillah' remains incomplete and unblessed." Some people write the numerals 786 in place of the words. This practice should however be avoided, because it is the words that carry blessings not the number.
2. Do write your own address in each letter. Never omit your address under the impression that the addressee already knows your address. Your address may not be necessarily

preserved by the addressee nor can you be sure that the addressee remembers your address.

3. Write your address on the right hand side leaving a little space in between the margin and the lines of the address. Write your address clearly and take care that it is correct and the spellings of each word are also correct.
4. You must indicate the date below your address.
5. After indicating the date, write a brief 'salutation' to the addressee. Keep your 'salutation' brief and simple, such as may communicate feelings of sincerity and close relationship. Avoid words of salutation, which smack of artificiality and convey a formal sense. Along with the salutation or on the next line after it write *'Salam Masnoon'* or *'Assalamo- 'Alaikum'*. Do not write words like *'Adab'* or *'Taslimat'*.
6. If you are sending a letter to a non-Muslim, write words like 'Adab' or `Taslimat' instead of 'Assalamo-'Alaikum' or *'Salam Masnoon'*.
7. After the salutation, write down your message or purpose which you wish to convey to the addressee. Close your letter with a suitable compliment which indicates your relationship to the addressee such as yours obediently, yours sincerely, yours truly etc.
8. Your letter must be legible, clear and simple, so that it may be easily read and understood, and may impress the addressee.
9. Use fluent and polite language in your letter.
10. Be brief, but never miss necessary details to make your point clear.
11. Throughout the letter, from the salutation to the complimentary close, pay due regard to the status of the addressee.
12. Start with a new paragraph for every new point.
13. Adopt a serious style in correspondence and avoid frivolity.
14. Avoid writing letter in hot temper. Never write anything offensive. Always adopt a courteous style in letters.
15. Do not discuss secret matters in general correspondence.

16. Put a dot at the end of each sentence.
17. Do not read a letter addressed to someone else without his permission. This is a grave violation of trust. However, the elders and guardians should, as a matter of duty, go through the letters written or received by their children so that they may correct and guide them. Islam does not give free licence to the teenagers to indulge in activities that do not conform with the norms and ethics of Islamic society. Before marriage, boys and girls, having no blood relations, are not allowed to mix freely or to write private letters to each other. Hence it is the responsibility of the parents to keep an eye on the letters written to or by their children till they are married.
18. Keep up a regular correspondence with your relatives and friends conveying to them your welfare.
19. When someone falls ill, or, Allah forbid, is injured as a result of an accident or some other calamity, do send a letter of concern and sympathy to him.
20. On occasions of ceremony, festivity or any happy development, do send letters of congratulation and joy.
21. Always use blue or black ink for the purpose of writing letters. Do not use a pencil or red ink for correspondence.
22. When some one gives you a letter for the purpose of posting it, never forget to post it without delay. Negligence and delay in such matters speaks of irresponsibility.
23. Send a return card or stamp to those with whom you are not familiar.
24. If you wish to cancel a portion of what you have written already, just cut it with a faint line.
25. While writing a letter, keep in view the interest of the addressee as well, and do not concentrate on the matters of your own choice and interest. You should not only communicate news of the peace and welfare of your own family but enquire about the peace and welfare of the family of the addressee and do not make too many demands even in letters. A man who makes too many demands degrades himself.

1. Conduct your business diligently and with interest. Earn your living by the sweat of your own brow and do not live as a parasite on others. On one occasion, a man from the tribe of Ansar came to the Holy Prophet [S.A.W.] and begged for assistance. The Holy Prophet [S.A.W.] enquired: "Do you have anything at home?" The companion [R.A.A.] submitted: "O Holy Prophet of Allah [S.A.W.]! We have two things only —a canvas which we use as bedding as well as a covering sheet and a bowl for drinking water." The Holy Prophet [S.A.W.] commanded: "Bring those two things to me."

   The companion [R.A.A.] at once brought both the things to him. The Holy Prophet [S.A.W.] auctioned them for two dirhams and handing over the money to the companion, observed: "Go, buy some food for one dirham and leave it with your family, and buy an axe for the other dirham."

   The Holy Prophet [S.A.W.] fused a handle to the axe with his own auspicious hands and observed to the companion: "Go to the jungle daily, cut some wood and sell it in the bazar. Come back after fifteen days and report your condition to me." At the end of a fortnight when the companion [R.A.A.] returned, he had accumulated a sum of ten dirhams. The Holy Prophet [S.A.W.] was overjoyed and observed: "This hard earned income is better for thee than begging from others which might leave a stigma of begging on thy face on the day of Judgement."

2. Carry on your business in right earnest and earn as much as you can so that you may be free from dependence on others. Once the people submitted to the Holy Prophet [S.A.W.]: "O Holy Prophet of Allah [S.A.W.]! Which is the best form of earning?" The Holy Prophet [S.A.W.] observed: "Earning with your own hands and income from the business which is free from dishonesty and fraud." Hazrat Abu Qalaba [R.T.A.] observed: "Conduct your business in right earnest in the bazar. This is the way to remain attached to religion and free from all dependence upon others."

3. Promote your business by truthful means. Strictly avoid swearing falsely in the name of Allah. The Holy Prophet

[S.A.W.] affirmed: "On the Day of Judgement Allah shall neither address, nor look at, nor admit that man to Paradise after purging him of sins who endeavours to expand his business by swearing falsely in the name of Allah." (Muslim). Moreover, the Holy Prophet [S.A.W.] observed: "Avoid swearing falsely in order to sell your goods. Apparently it looks like promoting your business but in fact it lets your business down and damages the goodwill of your business."

(Muslim)

4. Be honest and truthworthy in business dealings. Do not turn your lawful earnings into unlawful income by supplying defective goods or by indulging in profiteering. The Prophet of Allah [S.A.W.] has affirmed: "A truthful and honest trader will be a companion of the Prophets, the righteous and the martyrs on the Day of Judgement." *(Tirmidhi)*
5. Try to supply the best quality of goods to the customers. If a customer seeks your counsel, give him the best possible advice.
6. Take your customers into confidence so that they may trust you as their well-wisher who will never deceive them. The Holy Prophet [S.A.W.] has observed: "He who lived on lawful earnings, observed my Sunnah and did not cause mischief to the people will be admitted to Paradise." The people submitted: "O Holy Prophet [S.A.W.]! There is a great number of such people at the present time." The Holy Prophet [S.A.W.] observed: Such people will exist even after me." *(Tirmidhi)*
7. Be punctual. Arrive at your place of business in time and remain there steady. The Holy Prophet of Allah [S.A.W.] has observed: "Set out in search of livelihood and lawful earnings early in the morning, for work in the morning is auspicious and brings prosperity,"
8. Work hard and demand hard and sincere work from your employees. Discharge your obligations towards your employees with selflessness and generosity and in a liberal and polite manner. Avoid scowling at them frequently or adopting an attitude of suspicion towards them in every matter. The Holy Prophet [S.A.W.] observed: "Allah never

blesses a nation with piety where the weak do not get their right."

9. Be polite and liberal to your customers. Never be harsh to those who ask for loan from you neither disappoint them, nor press them unduly hard for return of your loan. The Holy Prophet [S.A.W.] has affirmed:

   "May Allah bless the person who observes politeness and courtesy in business dealings and in demanding his money back." *(Bukhari)*

   Moreover, the Holy Prophet [S.A.W.] observed:

   "Any person who craves for the protection of Allah against the affliction and oppression of the Day of Judgement should allow enough time to the hard-pressed debtor or relieve him of the burden of debt altogether." *(Muslim)*

10. Avoid concealing the defect of the goods and making false representations to the customer. You should openly declare the defects or inferior quality of your goods to the customer. Once the Holy Prophet [S.A.W.] passed by a heap of grain. The Holy Prophet [S.A.W.] put his hand into the heap and felt that his fingers had caught some dampness. The Prophet of Allah [S.A.W.] enquired from the grain dealer, "What is this?" The dealer submitted: "O Holy Prophet of Allah! Some rain poured over this heap." Thereupon the Holy Prophet [S.A.W.] observed: "Why did you not put the wet grain on top of the heap so that people may readily notice it. The man who deceives people has nothing to do with me."

11. Do not hoard foodstuffs anticipating a rise in prices. Strictly avoid causing distress to the people by such a vicious act. The Prophet [S.A.W.] observed: "The hoarder is a sinner." On another occasion, the Holy Prophet [S.A.W.] observed: "How wicked is the hoarder! When Allah makes goods cheap, the hoarder is afflicted with sorrow, and when the prices go up, he rejoices." *(Mishkat)*

12. Give the customer full value of his money. Be honest in weights and measures. Stick to one standard of give and take.

Addressing the dealers on weights and measures, the Holy Prophet [S.A.W.] warned:

> "You have been charged with two duties while the people before you have perished only because they failed to fulfil these duties:

The Holy Qur'an affirms:

> "Woe unto the defrauders; those when they take the measure from others they demand it full, but if they measure unto them or weigh for them they give less. Do such (men) not consider that they will be raised again unto an awful Day, the day when (all) mankind stand before the Lord of the Worlds?" *(83: 1-6)*

13. Do compensate for lapses of business ethics and give away in cash and kind as much as you can in the name of Allah without fail. The Holy Prophet [S.A.W.] enjoined upon the traders:

    > "O traders and businessmen! There is every chance of exaggeration and lie in selling your commodities. Hence compensate (your faults) by spending as much as you can (to help the poor and needy).*(Abu Dawud)*

14. And never lose sight of that business which will secure you from the fearful tortures in the life Hereafter and pay you in terms of eternal prosperity, peace and pleasure. The Holy Qur'an affirms:

    > "O ye who believe! shall I show you a Commerce that will save you from a painful doom; ye should believe in Allah and His Messenger and should strive for the cause of Allah with your wealth and your lives. That is better for you, if ye did but know." *(61: 10, 11)*

4

Everyday Manners

Islam, etiquettes cover all the following :

• Purity and Neatness • Maintenance of Health • Dress • Eating and Drinking • Going to Bed and Getting up • Walking • Travelling • Mourning and Grief • Fear and Panic • Rejoicing

> Hazrat Jabir [R.A.A.] stated: "One day the Holy Prophet [S.A.W.] visited our home to see us. He [S.A.W.] beheld a man who had dishevelled his hair and was covered all over with dust. The Holy Prophet [S.A.W.] observed: "Has this fellow no comb with which to set his hair." And the Holy Prophet's [S.A. W] gaze fell on another man who was wearing very soiled garments. The Holy Prophet [S.A.W.] observed: "Can't this man procure even that thing with which to wash his clothes clean." *(Mishkat al-Masabih)*

Cleanliness

Allah's favourites are those who make constant efforts to be neat and clean. The Holy Prophet [S.A.W.] has observed: "Purity and neatness are half of faith." In other words, Faith partly consists in cleans ing one's soul and partly in keeping physically clean and pure. The purity and neatness of soul implies cleansing the soul of all impurities such as infidelity, polytheism, sin and vice, and embellishing it with righteous beliefs and pure morals. The purity and neatness of the body denotes keeping it clear of all external filth and adorning it with neatness and good manners.

1. On waking up, clean your hand before putting it in a pot of water. You can never tell where your hands lay during sleep.
2. Do not discharge urine on the floor of bathroom/toilet.
3. When passing stool or urine, do not sit facing the direction of Qiblah, nor with your back to Qiblah. Having relieved yourself, use a clod or water to clean the private parts or purify yourself with water only. Do not use the dung, bone or charcoal for cleaning purpose. When the private parts have been cleaned, scrub your hands with soap or earth and wash them.
4. Do not sit down to eat when your bowels are under pressure. Relieve yourself of urine or stool before eating.
5. Use your right hand for eating and drinking. For cleaning the private parts of the body or for cleaning the nose, use your left hand only.
6. Discharge urine on soft ground, so that its drops do not splash around. Always pass the urine in a sitting posture. However, if the condition of the ground or some real hardship prevents from sitting down, you may urinate in a standing posture. Otherwise, in normal circumstances, it is a very dirty habit and should be strictly avoided.
7. Do not sit down to answer the call of nature on the riverside, the quay, on the thoroughfares or in shaded places. Such a practice causes inconvenience to others and is derogatory to rules of propriety and good manners.
8. Put on shoes and cover your head with a cap etc. before going to the lavatory and read the following prayer on your way:

   "Allah! I seek Thy protection against the devils of the masculine as well as the feminine species."

   (Bukhari, Muslim)

   On emerging from the lavatory, read this prayer:

   "I thank Allah who relieved me of the burden and granted me ease." *(Nasai, Ibn-e-Majah)*
9. Discharge your nose or phlegm with care in a spittoon, or do so in a place out of the sight of people.

10. Avoid putting your finger in the nostrils and clearing the wax of your nose too often. Clear the nose and clean it well out of the sight of people, whenever the need arises.
11. Strictly avoid the practice of spitting phlegm into the folds of a handkerchief and rubbing them together. This is a despicable habit and must be avoided except when it cannot be helped.
12. While chewing betel leaf, do not talk in such a manner as to splash saliva on the person you are talking to, thus causing discomfort to him. If you chew tobacco or betel leaf frequently, you should take great care in observing the rules of oral hygiene. Beware also, lest you should talk with your mouth too close to the person addressed.
13. Perform ablution with great care and try to keep in a state of ablution most of the time, if not at all hours. Where water is not available, you may perform Tayammum. Recite:

    'In the name of Allah, the Most Beneficent, the Most Merciful' at the commencement of ablution and say the following prayer in the course of its performance:

    "I bear witness that there is no god save Allah and He has no partner. And I testify that Muhammad is the servant of Allah and His Messenger. Allah! Join me with those people who repent most and take great care in keeping themselves pure and clean." *(Tirmidhi)*

    When the ablution is over, say the following prayer:

    "Allah! Thou art Pure and Supreme in Thy Praiseworthiness. I testify that there is no deity beside Thee. I seek Thy for giveness and I appeal to Thee." *(Nasai)*

    The Holy Prophet [S.A.W.] observed:

    The hallmark of my Ummah on the Day of Judgment will be that their foreheads and other parts of the body on which ablution is performed will be radiant with light. Hence whosoever wishes to enhance his light is free to do so." *(Bukhari, Muslim)*

14. Brush your teeth with miswak (twig) regularly. The Holy Prophet [S.A.W.] has affirmed:

    "I would have decreed the brushing of teeth with a miswak (twig) during all ablutions but for the inconvenience it would have caused to the Ummah."

    On one occasion, some people arrived to see the Holy Prophet [S.A.W.]. Their teeth were stained with yellow grease. On observing their teeth the Holy Prophet [S.A.W.] urged them to form the habit of using miswak.

15. You must bathe at least once a week. Make it a point to bathe on Friday and join the Friday congregation in clean and neat dress. The Holy Prophet [S.A.W.] said:

    "Discharging of trust leads to Paradise." The Companions [R.A.A.] submitted: O Apostle of Allah! What is meant by Trust?"

    The Apostle of Allah observed:

    "Allah has appointed no greater trust than cleansing oneself of impurity by taking bath." Hence a person must take bath when he needs one.

16. Do not go into or pass through the mosque in a state of impurity. If no alternative is available, perform the Tayammum before entering the mosque or passing through it.

17. Dress your hair with oil and comb. Trim the overgrown. hair of your beard with scissors; apply collyrium to your eyes; clip your nails and keep fingernails clean. Adorn yourself with propriety, simplicity and moderation.

18. Cover your face with a handkerchief on sneezing, so that the excretion is not splashed on anyone else. After sneezing say:

    "Praise be to Allah"!

    The listener should say:

    "May Allah show you Mercy"!

    In response to this, you should recite:

    "May Allah guide you."

19. The Holy Prophet [S.A.W.] was very fond of perfume. After finishing the toilet on arising from sleep, the Holy Prophet [S.A.W.] invariably used perfume.

Hygiene

1. Health is not only a great blessing of Allah but also a valuable trust from the Almighty. Regard your health as of great value and take every care to safeguard it. Health once lost is hard to recover. As the whiteant eats into the books and destroys great libraries, similarly a little negligence or an ordinary sickness ruins the life. To neglect the rules of hygiene and to be indifferent towards proper maintenance of health is callous, even it is an act of ingratitude to the Almighty. The essence of human life is reason, morality, faith and knowledge. It is only the physical health which ensures the proper functioning of human faculties of reason, morality, faith and knowledge. In fact, physical health is the basic factor in the development of mind and the growth of reason. It is also a pre-requisite for the performance of sublime acts of morality and the discharge of religious obligations. A weak and sick body has a feeble mind whose faculty of reason cannot but be unsound. When life is devoid of longing and ardour; when there is no courage and the will is weak; when the urges are exhausted - such spiritless existence is a drag on the infirm body. The true believers have to perform lofty deeds in life and discharge heavy responsibilities of state. It is imperative, therefore, that they should have robust physique, sturdy intellect and sound mind, firm will, high morale and a life full of spirit, enthusiasm and sublime passions. Healthy and spirited individuals make dynamic nations and such nations by offering supreme sacrifices in the struggle for existence achieve preeminent position and are a living symbol of the value and dignity of life.

2. You should always be cheerful, glad, alert and active. Made your life well-ordered, elegant, and healthy by means of good living, cheerful manners, joyful smiles and lively disposition. Avoid sorrow, anger, grudge or anxiety, envy, jealousy, slander,

narrowmindedness; don't lose your spirits and keep your mind clear of all complexities. These moral ills have an adverse effect on the digestive system and a defective digestive system is the major cause of poor health. Allah's Apostle observed:

> "Lead a simple life, adopt moderate habits and keep yourself cheerful." *(Mishkat)*

The Holy Prophet [S.A.W.] once saw an old man who was dragging on support on either side by two of his sons. The Holy Prophet [S.A.W.] inquired: "What has happened to this old man." The people told him: "This man had vowed to travel to the House of Allah on foot." The Holy Prophet [S.A.W.] observed: "It is not the will of Allah that this old man should torment himself " and then urged the old man to ride towards his destination.

Hazrat 'Umar [R.A.A.] once saw a youth walking along slowly like a sick man. 'Umar stopped the youth and inquired: "What sickness afflicts you?" He replied: "I am not ailing." Thereupon 'Umar took hold of a whip and threatening him with it said to the young fellow: "Walk on the way energetically with firm foot."

The Holy Prophet [S.A.W.] used to walk with a firm foot and stepped on the ground as if he were descending a slope.

Hazrat 'Abdullah bin Harith reports: "I never met a man who smiled more often than the Prophet of Allah [S.A.W.]."

The Holy Prophet [S.A.W.] taught the following prayer to his people and you should say this prayer more often:

> "O Allah! I seek refuge in Thee from the anxiety and grief, from inability and sloth, from the burden of indebtedness and the domination of men."
>
> *(Bukhari, Muslim)*

3. Do not lift more burden than your strength can bear. Do not waste your physical energy. It is obligatory that you should save and protect your physical strength and use it with moderation according to your capability.

Hazrat 'A'isha [R.A.A.] reports that the Holy Prophet [S.A.W.] observed:

> "Act as much as is within your strength, for the Lord will not feel wearied but you will get weary."
>
> *(Bukhari)*

> Hazrat Abu Qais [R.A.A.] reports that he went to see the Holy Prophet [S.A.W.] when the Prophet [S.A.W.] was delivering a sermon. Hazrat Abu Qais [R.A.A.] stood waiting in the sun. At the bidding of the Holy Prophet [S.A.W.] he stepped into the shade.
>
> *(Al-Adab Al-Mufrad)*

The Holy Prophet [S.A.W.] forbade that a person should stand in a position where a part of his body is under the shade and the other part in the sun.

A lady of the Bahla tribe, Hazrat Mujiba [R.A.A.] relates:

> "Once my father called on the Holy Prophet [S.A.W.] to seek religious knowledge. Having learnt some important matters about religion, my father returned home. A year later, he again went to see the Holy Prophet [S.A.W.]. The Holy Prophet did not recognise his visitor. Upon this, my father submitted: "O Prophet of Allah! Don't you remember me." The Holy Prophet [S.A.W.] said: No, I do not recognise you. Introduce yourself." My father submitted: "I belong to the tribe of Bahla. I came to see you last year also." The Holy Prophet [S.A.W.] observed: "Why are you in such a bad shape. When you came here last year you were in a much better state and looked fine." My father replied: "Since our last meeting, I have been continuously observing fasts. I eat only at night." The Holy Prophet [S.A.W.] observed: "It was utterly needless for you to torment yourself and ruin your health." Then the Prophet [S.A.W.] urged my father, "You should keep fasts during the whole of the month of Ramadan and in addition observe fast for one day during each

> month." My father submitted: "O Prophet of Allah! Permit me to keep more fasts." The Holy Prophet [S.A.W.] enjoined: "You should observe two fasts during each month." My father asked permission for more. The Holy Prophet [S.A.W.] said: "You can keep three fasts during each month." My father entreated for a further addition in the number of fasts. The Holy Prophet [S.A.W.] replied: "Well then, you may observe fasts during sacred months each year and then leave a gap. You may follow this course every year." While observing this, the Holy Prophet [S.A.W.] made a sign with three fingers, joined them and moved them apart.

The point that the Holy Prophet [S.A.W.) wanted to bring home to his visitor was that he should observe fasts during the months of Rajab, Dhiqa'dah and Dhulhijah and leave a gap in fasting during the intervening years. The Prophet [S.A.W.] has affirmed:

> "It does not behove a believer to degrade himself." The people inquired: "In what manner does a believer degrade himself." The Holy Prophet [S.A.W.] observed: "He subjects himself to intolerable sufferings and thus degrades himself." *(Tirmidhi)*

4. You should always be industrious, energetic, hard-working, painstaking and bold in your daily life. You should form the habit of facing all forms of hardship and tackling with the most difficult situations. Prepare yourself to lead the hard and simple life of a Mujahid (a fighter in the service of True Faith). Don't be ease-loving, careless, indolent, voluptuous, timid and a materialist. While dispatching Hazrat Mu'adh bin Jabal [R.A.A.] as Governor of Yemen, the Holy Prophet [S.A.W.] gave him the following instruction:

> "Mu'adh Deny yourself the love of pleasure for the servants of Allah are not pleasure-seekers." *(Mishkat)*

> Hazrat Abu Umama [R.A.A.] reports the Holy Prophet [S.A.W.] as having said: "Simple living symbolises true Faith." *(Abu Dawud)*

The life of the Holy Prophet [S.A.W.] was ever a simple and hard one, like a Mujahid. The Holy Prophet [S.A.W.] took care to preserve his physical energy and strive to enhance it. The Prophet [S.A.W.] also liked to swim, for this sport provides the best physical exercise. Once the Holy Prophet [S.A.W.] and some Companions [R.A.A.] were swimming in a pool. The Holy Prophet [S.A.W.] arranged the Companions in pairs of two and desired that each man should swim towards his partner. Hazrat Abu Bakr [R.A.A.] was paired with the Prophet, [S.A.W.]. The Holy Prophet [S.A.W.] swam towards Abu Bakr [R.A.A.] caught him and held him by the neck.

Horse was the Prophet's favourite riding animal. The Holy Prophet [S.A.W.] himself tended his horse. He used to rub and clean the mouth of his horse with his own sleeve. He would tie the hair of its mane into knots and used to say:

> "Goodness remains attached to its forehead till Doomsday."

Hazrat 'Uqba [R.A.A.] reports that the Prophet of Allah observed:

> "Learn archery and horse-riding. I like the archers more than the horse-riders. He who learns the art of shooting arrows and then gives it up has paid scant regard to a Divine blessing." *(Abu Dawud)*

Hazrat 'Abdullah bin 'Umar [R.A.A.] reports that the Holy Prophet [S.A.W.] stated:

> "He who guards the soldiers of Islam against danger in the night passes a night better than Shab-e-Qardr."

In an address to his Companions, the Holy Prophet [S.A.W.] observed: "A time will come when the other nations will fall upon my followers as diners scramble over food."

Someone inquired: "O Prophet of Allah [S.A.W.]! Will our numbers so dwindle that other people will join forces in order to annihilate us?"

The Holy Prophet [S.A.W.] answered: "Not that your numbers will be small. In fact you will be much larger in number, but then your number will carry no weight, just as so many straws floating in flood-tide are weightless. Your enemies will no longer fear you, cowardice will creep into your hearts."

At this point a man enquired: "O Prophet of Allah [S.A.W.]! what will be the cause of this cowardice?"

The Holy Prophet (S.A.W.] observed: "The cause will be that you will grow to love the worldly life and hate death."

Hazrat Abu Huraira [R.A.A.] reports that the Holy Prophet [S.A.W.] observed:

> "He who holds the reins of his horse firmly and rides to serve the cause of Islam, lives the best life. From whichever spot the news of threat to the cause of Islam reaches him, he mounts his horse and rushes thither. He is so fearless of death as if he is after it." *(Muslim)*

5. Women should also lead hard and strenuous life. They should perform all household chores with their own hands. They should form the habit of being active and train themselves to bear hardships. They should abstain from being work-shy, indolent or voluptuous. They should raise their children so that they learn to be sturdy, energetic and tough from the very beginning of their lives. Even when there are servants in home, do not encourage your children to depend on them for odd jobs. Teach children to cultivate the habit of self-help. The ladies of the Companions of the Holy Prophet used to perform house-hold tasks with their own hands. They would work in the kitchen; they would grind at the millstone; they fetched water for use in the home, washed clothes, sewed and led a strenuous life. In the hour of need, they took the responsibility of rendering medical aid to the wounded in the battle-field and supplied water to the fighting forces. Hard work keeps women fit; it ensures the purity of their morals and the good example of the mothers being as a model for character building of their children. From the Islamic point of view, a good wife is the one who keeps herself busy in housekeeping tasks. She should be so engrossed in household activities that signs of exhaustion due to hard work, the blackness of the kitchen

and the soot of fire-smoke should be evident from her face. The Holy Prophet [S.A.W.] has stated:

> "I and the woman whose cheeks are besmeared with kitchen smoke will be close together on the Day of Resurrection." (While saying this, the Prophet made a sign by joining his index finger with the middle finger).

6. Be an early riser. Keep your sleeping hours within limits of propriety. Don't sleep little, for in that case your body will not get proper rest and your limbs will feel exhausted and weary. On the other hand, do not sleep for long hours, for in that case you will become lazy and inactive. Follow the maxim: "Early to bed and early to rise, is the way to be healthy, wealthy and wise."

   Get up early in the morning and offer prayers. Go for a stroll into the field or garden and relax there. The fresh air of the morning has a salutary effect on health. Make it a point to do some light exercise daily according to your physical strength and endurance. The Holy Prophet [S.A.W.] liked to divert himself by visits to the gardens. He used to go for a stroll in the garden once in a while. The Prophet [S.A.W.] forbade to remain awake and engage in conversation after 'Isha' (night prayer) and observed:

   > "Only that person is permitted to remain awake after 'Isha' who is either engaged in talk concerning religion or has to discuss some important matter with the members of his household."

7. Learn self-control. Keep your passions, fancies, desires and lusts under control. Guard against your ideas getting distracted or your eyes going astray. Peace of mind and contentment of the heart evaporate when the passions are given free rein and eyes begin to wander astray and the faces of such people lose all the beauty, grace and attractiveness. Having lost these attributes, these persons prove to be timid, weak-minded and cowards in every sphere of life.

   The Holy Prophet [S.A.W.] has stated:

> "To cast a lascivious eye is the adultery of eyes and shameless talk is the adultery of tongue. Your lust presses a demand on you and your genitals either affirm or contradict this demand."

A sage observes:

> "O Muslims! Keep away from sin. Sin entails six evils: three evils relate to this world and the other three are concerned with the eternal world. Those evils that relate to this world are:

* Beauty and grace vanish from the face of man.
* The man is seized by the torment of poverty and destitution.
* It shortens the life of man.

8. Save yourself from intoxicants. They affect the brain as well as the stomach. Liquor, of course, is forbidden, but you should refrain from using all other things having an intoxicating effect.

9. Observe the rules of simplicity and moderation in all your activities. In physical labour, mental exertion, marital relations, eating, drinking, sleep and rest, anxiety, merriment, recreation, worship, walking and conversation - in short, in all your activities always follow a middle course, and regard it as the main source of virtue and well-being.

   The Holy Prophet [S.A.W.] has said:

   > "How wonderful it is to be moderate in the midst of plenty! And what a fine thing it is to follow a middle course in deprivation, and what a better course it is to be moderate in offering prayers."
   >
   > *(Musnad Bazaz/Kanz al'Amal)*

10. Eat at the proper time. Abstain from over-eating. Don't munch all the time. Take food only when you feel the appetite and stop eating before your stomach is filled, so that you should still feel slightly hungry when the meal is over. You must never indulge in over-eating. The Holy Prophet [S.A.W.] observed:

> "The believer fills only one intestine while the non-believer eats to fill seven intestines." *(Tirmidhi)*

Good health depends on proper functioning of the stomach. Overeating makes the stomach sick. The Holy Prophet [S.A.W.] has explained this point in an allegory as follows:

> "The stomach serves as a cistern. The veins receive their life-blood from this reservoir. Hence if the stomach is healthy, the veins will be irrigated with the juices of health, and in case the stomach is ill, the veins will only suck the juice of sickness." *(Baihaqi)*

Persuading the people to be abstemious in taking food the Prophet [S.A.W.] observed:

> "One man's dinner is sufficient for two."

11. Always eat simple food. Eat whole wheat bread. Do not eat while the food is piping hot. Avoid spiced and pungent foods and have no unnecessary craving for tasty delicacies.

Make it a point to eat simple, easily digestible, nourishing and healthful diet. Do not crave for delicious foods or foods that leave a pungent taste on the tongue.

The Holy Prophet [S.A.W.] preferred whole-wheat bread. He did not like bread made of soft flour or thin. He never ate while the food was piping hot, but waited till it cooled. Referring to the eating of food while it is piping hot, the Prophet [S.A.W.] some times observed: 'Allah has not ordained us to eat fire'; and some other time he would say: "There is no virtue in eating piping hot food."

Meat (especially joints of leg, pieces of neck and flesh of the backside) was the Prophet's [S.A.W.] favourite food. In point of fact, meat is an important and essential food for the nourishment of body and for forging a bold attitude of mind; and the believers should always be bold and sturdy.

The Holy Prophet [S.A.W.] has affirmed:

> "One who died without fighting in the cause of Allah and had no desire for such a fight has in a way died in the state of hypocrisy." *(Muslim)*

12. Eat with perfect peace of mind and in a relaxed mood and chew the food well. Avoid eating in a mood of sorrow, anger, anxiety or perplexity. The food that is eaten in a cheerful and peaceful state of mind nourishes the body, whereas food that is gulped down in a state of anxiety or grief has an adverse effect on the stomach and affords no strength to the body. Don't be silent, sad or woe-begone while taking meals nor show undue mirth by raising loud guffaws. Laughter during meals proves fatal sometimes.

    Talk and laugh with moderation while taking meals. Eat in a pleasant and cheerful mood and offer thanks to the Almighty and when ill, take every precaution with regard to your meals.

    Umme Mundhir [R.A.A.] relates:

    > "The Holy Prophet [S.A.W.] once visited me. Bunches of date-fruit were hanging in the home. The Holy Prophet [S.A.W.) plucked the fruit and started eating it. Hazrat 'Ali [R.A.A.] did the same. The Holy Prophet [S.A.W.] however, forbade 'Ali [R.A.A.] and said: "You have just recovered from illness; you should not eat this fruit." So 'Ali [R.A.A.] stopped. Meanwhile, the Prophet [S.A.W.] continued to eat the fruit." Umme Mundhir [R.A.A.] further relates: "Later, I cooked some barley and beet-root. The Holy Prophet [S.A.W.] said to 'Ali [R.A.A.] "'Ali, take this. This food will do you good." *(Shama'il Tirmidhi)*

    "When he [S.A.W.] had a guest at meals, he used to prompt the guest repeatedly to eat more and until he had eaten to his fill and insisted on taking more, the Holy Prophet [S.A.W.] then stopped to prompt him."

    During meals, the Holy Prophet [S.A.W.] used to be engaged in amiable talk and maintained an atmosphere of joy and cordiality.

13. Take a nap after the mid-day meal and go for a stroll after dinner. Avoid strenuous physical and mental exertion immediately after the meals. There is a well-known maxim in Arabic which runs thus:

"Stretch out after the midday meal and take a stroll after taking dinner."

14. Take good care of your eyes. Don't expose your eyes to glaring light. Don't set your gage upon the sun. Don't read in either faint or intense light. Always study under a clear and soothing light. Avoid keeping yourself awake for too long. Protect your eyes from filth and dust. Apply collyrium to your eyes and always try to keep your eyes clean. Go for a walk in the fields, gardens and green pastures and amuse yourself. The sight of greenery has a pleasant effect on eyes. Guard against casting evil glances, for this practice will dim the sparkle of your eyes and your general health will decline. The Holy Prophet [S.A.W.] has said:

    "Your eyes have a right on you."

    It is, therefore, incumbent upon a believer to value this Divine blessing. He should use this blessing according to the will of the Almighty. He should be particular about the protection of his eyes and keeping them clean. He should use all means which may be of benefit to his eyes and avoid everything that may cause injury to them. Similarly, a true believer should take care to preserve the strength of other limbs and organs of his body. The Holy Prophet [S.A.W.] observed:

    "O people! You should apply collyrium to your eyes. It clears away all wax from your eyes and helps in the growth of hair." *(Tirmidhi)*

15. Be careful about dental hygiene and protect your teeth. Clean teeth keep you fresh, produce a good effect on digestion and cleanliness makes the teeth firm too. Form the habit of cleaning your teeth with a miswak (twig); use dental powder also. Don't spoil your teeth by too frequent chewing of betel leaf or using tobacco. Clean your teeth well after every meal.

    Unclean teeth cause various diseases. It was customary with the Holy Prophet (S.A.W.] that on getting up from sleep, he used to clean his teeth with a miswak (twig). *(Agreed upon)*

Hazrat 'A'isha [R.A.A.] states:

> "We used to keep the water for ablution and the miswak (twig) ready for the use of the Holy Prophet [S.A.W.]. By the will of Allah when the Prophet [S.A.W.] got up from sleep he used to clean his teeth with the miswak (twig). Later, he performed ablution and then offered prayers." *(Muslim)*

Hazrat Anas [R.A.A.] has reported that the Holy Prophet [S.A.W.] observed:

> "I have already laid much stress upon the need to clean your teeth with miswak (twig)." *(Bukhari)*

Hazrat 'A'isha [R.A.A.] relates that the Holy Prophet [S.A.W.] stated:

> "The miswak (twig) cleans the mouth and the Lord is pleased by this act of cleanliness."

The Prophet [S.A.W.] is. reported to have said:

> "Had I not considered it a great inconvenience for my Ummah, I would have enjoined upon people to brush their teeth with a miswak (twig) before each prayer." *(Abu Dawud)*

> Some Muslims once came to see the Holy Prophet [S.A.W.]. Their teeth were unclean and were encrusted with yellow grease. Noticing this, the Holy Prophet [S.A.W.] said to them: "Your teeth look so yellow! You should clean them with a miswak." *(Musnad Ahmad)*

16. When the need arises to answer the call of nature fulfil it promptly. Delay in answering the call of nature affects the brain and the stomach badly.

17. Pay full attention to keeping yourself pure, clean and tidy. The Holy Qur'an says:

> "Allah's favourites are those who take great care in keeping themselves pure and clean." *(At-Tauba)*

The Holy Prophet [S.A.W.] has said:

> "Cleanliness and purity are the half of Iman (Faith)."

In view of the great importance of cleanliness and purity, the Holy Prophet [S.A.W.] has given detailed injunctions about neatness and has stressed the need for observing purity and cleanliness in every matter. Keep all articles of food under cover. Protect them from being soiled and keep the flies away. You should have clean utensils. Keep your dress and bed-covers tidy and spotlessly clean. Keep your body clean by performing ablution and taking a bath. Cleanliness of body, neatness of dress and tidiness of all articles of use is refreshing and pleasant for the soul. The body also feels delightfully fresh. On the whole, purity and neatness have a salutary effect on human health.

Hazrat 'Adi bin Hatim [R.A.A.] stated: "I always remain in a state of ablution for each salat (prayer) since I embraced Islam."

The Holy Prophet [S.A.W.] once asked Hazrat Bilal [R.A.A.]: "How did you manage to reach Paradise before me yesterday?" Hazrat Bilal [R.A.A.] submitted: "Whenever I proclaim the call for prayer, I invariably offer two Rak'ats of Salat (prayer) and as soon as I am out of the state of ablution, I perform ablution afresh and try to remain in this state always."

Hazrat Abu Huraira [R.A.A.] reports the Prophet [S.A.W.] as having said:

> "It is Allah's right upon every Muslim that he should take bath once a week and wash his head and body."
> *(Bukhari)*

Dress Code

1. You should wear a dress which covers and protects your body and meets the requirements of modesty, honour and virtue. Your dress should also be an expression of culture, elegance and beauty. In respect of this blessing, Allah says in the Holy Qur'an:

> "O children of Adam! We have sent unto you raiments to conceal your shame and to serve as protection and adornment." (7: 26)

As a matter of fact, the word 'Rish' in the verse, literally means the wings of the bird. The wings of a bird lend beauty and grace to it and also seen as a means of protection for its body. The word, however, is commonly used when referring to beauty, elegance and fine dress. Of course the purpose of dress is to lend beauty and grace and to serve as protection against climatic effects. But the foremost use of dress is to cover private parts of the body. Allah has inculcated modesty and diffidence in the nature of man. It was for this reason that when Hazrat Adam and Hazrat Hawwa (Eve) [A.S.] were deprived of the elegant robes of Paradise, they began to use leaves of trees to cover their bodies. Hence consider this as the principal use of dress and choose a dress which conforms to the requirements of modesty. You should also make sure that your dress, besides affording adequate protection against climatic conditions, should also be such that it should lend an aura of grace, elegance and culture to your personality. Do not wear such dress which should make you an object of ridicule or provoke satirical comments from the people.

2. You should keep in mind while putting on clothes that dress is a blessing which Allah has conferred on man only. It has been denied to all other living creatures. Offer thanks to Allah for this special favour and blessing. Endowed as you are with this distinctive bounty, you should never act contrary to the decrees of Allah or show ingratitude. Dress is a remarkable favour from the Lord. While putting on dress, re-kindle this feeling in your heart and express your sense of gratitude in the words which the Holy Prophet [S.A.W.] had taught to the believers.

3. Piety is the best apparel. Piety signifies purity of soul as well as righteous physical appearance. In other words you should wear dress of the kind which the Shari'ah has prescribed for the believers, which does not display arrogance or pride, which does not lend a feminine air to men nor a masculine appearance to women. The dress should be an emblem of your righteousness and devotion to Allah. The women should strictly conform to the rules set by Shari'ah in respect of

female dress and men must observe the laws of Shari'ah with regard to their dress.

4. Put on a new dress with feelings of joy. Give some name to it when you don a new apparel and acknowledge the munificence and blessing of Allah. Inspired by a sense of gratitude to the Lord, recite the prayer which the Holy Prophet [S.A.W.] used to offer while putting on a new dress.

   Hazrat Abu Said Khudri [R.A.A.] reports: "Whenever the Holy Prophet [S.A.W.] put on a new dress, head dress, shirt or a sheet covering, he used to recite the following prayer and insert the name of the garment in the recitation:

   > Allah! Unto Thee belongeth all praise. Even as Thou hast clothed me in this (garment), I ask of Thee the good thereof and I seek refuge in Thee from the evil thereof, and the evil of that wherefor it hath been made." *(Abu Dawud)*

   The prayer bears the following meaning: Allah! Make me use this dress which You have bestowed on me for the purposes which You deem righteous. Enable me to cover my modesty with this dress and to protect my soul and body against immodesty and shamelessness; to make it a means of adornment and grace for my body; to eschew displaying ostentation, pride or arrogance and let me not transgress the bounds set by you for men and women in the use of dress.

   Hazrat 'Umar [R.A.A.] stated: "The Holy Prophet [S.A.W.] observed: "Whosoever puts on a new dress and has means, should give away his old dress to the poor. On wearing a new dress, a person should recite the following prayer:

   "Praise be to Allah Who clad me with that wherewith I cover my shame, and where with I adorn myself in my life."

   > Whosoever reads the above prayer at the time of putting on a new dress, Allah will keep him under His care and protection in this life and in the life Hereinafter." *(Tirmidhi)*

5. Take care to put on the dress with the right side first. While putting on the shirt, Kurta, shervani or coat, wear the right

sleeve first. Similarly while putting on a pyjama enter the right foot first. The Holy Prophet [S.A.W.] while putting on the shirt used to wear the right sleeve first and then put the left arm into the left sleeve. Similarly, the Holy Prophet [S.A.W.] used to put the shoe on his right foot first and then wore the left shoe. On taking off his shoes, the Holy Prophet [S.A.W.] first took off from his left foot and then from the right one.

6. You must shake the garments before putting them on, lest there be deadly insect hidden in them which might cause you harm. The Holy Prophet [S.A.W.] was once wearing socks in a jungle. He put on a sock and was intending to put on the second one when a crow dived and carried off the sock. The crow soared to a great height and dropped the sock on the ground. The shock of landing threw out of the sock a snake which fell at some distance. On seeing this, the Holy Prophet [S.A.W.] offered thanks to Allah and observed: "It is the duty of every Muslim that on intending to wear socks, he should shake them first." *(Tabarani)*

7. Wear white dress. White dress is ideal for men, especially. The Holy Prophet [S.A.W.] observed: "Wear white dress. It is the best. You ought to wear white clothes in life and bury your dead in a shroud made of white cloth." *(Tirmidhi)*

   On another occasion, the Holy Prophet [S.A.W.] observed: "You should wear white clothes, for the white clothes stays cleaner and put your dead in white coffins."

   The phrase 'white-cloth stays cleaner' implies that white cloth shows off the slightest stain instantly, which a person may clean immediately. If the cloth is dyed, the stains will not be seen instantly. Hence a person will not pay immediate attention to wash a dyed garment.

   It is recorded in Sahih Bukhari that the Holy Prophet [S.A.W.] used to wear white clothes. In other words he [S.A.W.] not only liked to put on white dress himself, but also enjoined upon the male members of his Ummah to wear white clothes.

8. The length of your pyjama, or lungi should fall above the ankles. The Holy Prophet [S.A.W.] holds such people as the doomed ones and deserving of severe torment who out of pride and haughtiness let their pyjamas or lungis fall below their ankles. The Holy Prophet [S.A.W.] has affirmed: "There are three types of people with whom Allah shall not speak on the Doomsday, nor look at them, nor will He admit them to Paradise after purifying them; rather He shall ordain a painful torment for them." Hazrat Abudhar Ghifari [R.A.A.] submitted: "O Apostle of Allah who are these unfortunate people?" The Holy Prophet [S.A.W.] observed:

   "Firstly, he who out of pride and haughtiness lets his lower garments fall below his ankles.

   Secondly, the man who reminds others of the favours he has done to them.

   And thirdly, the one who wishes to promote his business by misrepresentation on oath." *(Muslim)*

   Relating a personal anecdote, Hazrat 'Ubaid ibn Khalid [R.A.A.] says: "I was once walking in the holy city of Madinah when a voice said from behind: Lift up your lower garment - by so doing a man not only guards himself from physical filth but also from the impurity of soul." Looking over my shoulder, I saw the Allah's Apostle [S.A.W.]. I submitted: "O Apostle of Allah [S.A.W.]! It is a simple sheet of cloth that I am wearing. How can it show haughtiness and pride?" The Holy Prophet [S.A.W.] observed: "Is it not obligatory for you to follow my example?" On hearing these words of the Holy Prophet [S.A.W.] my eyes at once fell towards his lower garment and I saw that it came to the middle of his calf."

   The Holy Prophet's [S.A.W.] observation that by keeping the length of his pyjama or lower garment above the ankles the man is guarded against not only physical dirt but also impurity of soul, is highly significant. It implies that when the length of a garment falls below the ankles, it gathers filth from the ground and becomes dirty. Soiled clothes are always offensive to a person of neat and clean taste. Moreover, the habit of wearing garments whose length falls below the ankles betrays arrogance and pride and these two evils are symptoms of the impurity of soul. These considerations apart, the Qur'anic injunction 'The life of the Prophet is the best model for you to follow' should suffice for a pious believer.

According to a Tradition reported by Abu Dawud, the Holy Prophet [S.A.W.] has given warning of terrible punishment for this offence. The Holy Prophet [S.A.W.] observed: "The pious believer should wear the length of his 'lower garment' up to the middle of his calf; there is no harm if the length falls to the ankles; but any part of the length which falls below the ankles shall burn in the fire. And on the Doomsday, Allah shall not even look at the man who out of pride and arrogance wears an apparel whose length falls below his ankles."

9. Do not wear silk. Garments of silk are befitting for females only. The Holy Prophet [S.A.W.] has strictly forbidden men to wear female dress or to put on effeminate airs.

   Hazrat 'Umar [R.A.A.] reports that the Holy Prophet [S.A.W.] observed: "Do not wear silk garments, for he who wears them in this world shall not wear them in the next." (Bukhari, Muslim) The Holy Prophet [S.A.W.] once observed to Hazrat 'Ali [R.A.A.]:

   > "Cut this silk cloth into scarves and distribute them among the Fatimahs." *(Muslim)*

   This also shows that silk dress is desirable for women. It was for this reason that the Holy Prophet [S.A.W.] urged Hazrat 'Ali [R.A.A.] to cut the silk cloth into scarves for the ladies, otherwise the cloth could have been used for some other purpose.

10. Women should not wear thin dress which should make their forms visible, nor should they put on a tightly fitting dress which might make their figures prominent and alluring. In this way, they would be exposing their bodies, despite having worn garments. The Holy Prophet [S.A.W.] has warned such immodest women of dire punishment.

> "Woman who are nude in spite of having garments on them, who allure others and are allured by others shall be consigned to Hell. Their heads are coquettishly inclined on one side like the humps of the Bakht camels. These women shall not enter Paradise, nor shall enjoy the sweet odour of Paradise, although the sweet odour of Paradise can be savoured from a long distance off." *(Riyad-us-Salihin)*

On one occasion Hazrat Asma [R.A.A.] came to the Holy Prophet [S.A.W.] wearing thin clothes. On seeing her, the Holy Prophet [S.A.W.] turned his face at once and observed:

> "Asma, when a woman comes of age it is not lawful for her to expose any part of her body except face and hands."

11. When wearing a Tehbund or pyjama do not lie down or sit in such a posture as to make prominent or lay bare any part of your body. The Holy Prophet [S.A.W.] has observed: "Do not walk with one shoe on. Do not squat with one knee raised while you are wearing a Tehbund. Do not eat with your left hand. Do not wrap up your whole body in a sheet in such a manner as to make it impossible for you to move your hands freely for performing your work or for offering prayers. Do not lie flat and put one leg over the other lest it should uncover your body.

12. Men and women should not adopt the same fashions in dress. The Holy Prophet [S.A.W.] affirmed: "Allah sends curses on those men who adopt feminine fashions and on such women who adopt a masculine style." *(Bukhari)*

> Hazrat Abu Huraira [R.A.A.] states: "The Holy Prophet [S.A.W.] pronounced a curse upon a male who puts on female dress and has cursed a female who dresses herself in masculine fashion." *(Abu Dawud)*

Someone once mentioned to Hazrat 'Aisha that there was a certain woman who wore masculine shoes, whereupon Hazrat 'A'isha observed: "The Holy Prophet [S.A.W.] has pronounced a curse upon such women who adopt masculine habits."

13. The women must cover themselves with a scarf and keep their head and bosom veiled. They should not wear scarf of such transparent stuff as to reveal their hair. The scarf is meant to veil the beauty of the person. Allah ordains in the Holy Qur'an:

    "And draw their veils over their bosoms." (24: 31)

    The Holy Prophet [S.A.W.] once received fine Egyptian veil. He cut out a piece and handing it to Hazrat Yahya Kalbi [R.A.A.] observed: "Cut a piece and make a shirt for yourself and give the other piece to your wife to use as a scarf, but tell her to stitch another layer of cloth under it so that her form may not be exposed to view." *(Abu Dawud)*

    Bearing this clear injunction of the Holy Book and Sunnah in mind, you should scrupulously follow the purport of Divine Command. Do not make a mockery of the Ordinance of Allah and His Messenger by wearing only a small strip of cloth around your neck.

    Hazrat 'Aisha [R.A.A.] states: "When this injunction was revealed, the women discarded thin garments. They started making their scarves out of coarse cloth." *(Abu Dawud)*

14. Dress yourself in keeping with your means and status. Do not dress up to show off vanity and to display an attitude of haughtiness towards others or to make an indecent show of your affluence. On the other hand, your dress should not cost more than your means permit, for thus you will be guilty of the sin of extravagance. Do not look shabby and crest-fallen so as to make an impression of penury and helplessness upon others. Do not make a show of destitution, despite having everything. Put on proper, suitable and neat garments in keeping with your means and position. Some people appear destitute by wearing rags or patched garments and consider it an act of piety or virtue. Moreover, they view those who put on clean and neat dress as worldly-minded and irreligious.

This conception of religion is wholly fallacious. Hazrat Abu Hasan 'Ali Shazli [R.A.A.] was once clad in very fine clothes. A destitute Sufi took exception to this and remarked: "What need have the servants of Allah to put on such elegant dress?" Hazrat Shazli [R.A.A.] answered: "Brother, I have put on this elegant dress to express my gratitude and homage to the Grand and Magnificent Allah. Your shabby appearance is a show of misery. You appear as if you were begging alms from the people." In reality, virtue does not consist in wearing rags, patched garments or clothes of inferior quality, nor does it require wearing luxurious apparel. The ingredients of virtue are the pious intentions and right thinking of the man. The truth is that every man should adopt a moderate and balanced attitude in all matters in consonance with his means and position. He should not let his soul grow dull by putting on destitute airs, nor should he display vanity and pride by wearing resplendent garments.

Hazrat Abul Ahwas [R.A.A.] reports a Tradition from his father, "Once I went to the Holy Prophet [S.A.W.]. I was then clad in very poor and mean dress. The Holy Prophet [S.A.W.] asked me: "Do you possess wealth and means?" I submitted: "Yes, I do." The Holy Prophet [S.A.W.] then enquired: "What kind of goods do you possess." I submitted: "Allah has blessed me with all kinds of goods - camels, cows, goats, horses besides slaves." The Holy Prophet [S.A.W.] observed: "When Allah has blessed you with wealth and means, your person should manifest His Bounty and Favour." *(Mishkat)*

The implication, is that when Allah has conferred ample means to you, why do you put on the garb of a beggar and destitute person? This is an act of ingratitude to Him.

Hazrat Jabir [R.A.A.] reports: "Once the Holy Prophet [S.A.W.] visited our house to see us. He chanced to see a man who was covered all over with dust and his hair was dishevelled. The Holy Prophet [S.A.W.] observed: "Does this man possess no comb with which to set his hair." The Holy Prophet [S.A.W.] then happened to see a man who was clad in a dirty dress. whereupon the Holy Prophet [S.A.W.) observed: "Does this man not possess even that (soap etc.) with which to wash his clothes clean." *(Mishkat)*

A man submitted to the Holy Prophet [S.A.W.] "O Messenger of Allah! I like to have fine clothes and I like to dress my hair with oil, and wear nice shoes. In this manner, he named several niceties he was fond of and even mentioned that he wished that his lash should also be of the best quality. The Holy Prophet [S.A.W.] listened to him and then observed: "All these things are desirable and Allah views this fine taste with favour." *(Mustadrak Hakim)*

Hazrat 'Abdullah bin 'Umar [R.A.A.] states: "I submitted to the Holy Apostle of Allah: "O Apostle of Allah! Would I be guilty of vanity and haughtiness if I wore fine and nice clothes." The Holy Prophet [S.A.W.] observed: "No, it is elegant to wear nice dress and elegance of dress pleases Allah."

(Ibn Majah)

The following Tradition has also been reported by Hazrat 'Abdullah bin 'Umar [R.A.A.] "The Holy Prophet [S.A.W.] observed: Put on both garments when saying prayers (in other words, dress yourself in full suit). Man owes it to Allah more than to any one else that he should go into His presence in his best apparel and in the neatest state." *(Mishkat)*

Hazrat 'Abdullah bin Mas'ud [R.A.A.] states: "The Holy Prophet [S.A.W.], observed: "He who has even a little bit of pride in his heart shall not enter Paradise." A man submitted: "Every man wishes that he should put on fine clothes and wear nice shoes." The Holy Prophet [S.A.W.] observed: "Allah Himself is Graceful and elegance pleases Him. In other words, elegant dress does not connote haughtiness. Haughtiness consists in ignoring the rights of others and looking down upon others as mean and base." *(Muslim)*

15. Observe good taste and propriety in dress and make-up. It is improper and offensive to good taste to go about with shirt unbuttoned at the chest, to wear buttons without proper arrangement, to roll up one leg of the trousers and keep the

other down, to walk with one shoe on or to keep the hair dishevelled.

One day, the Holy Prophet [S.A.W.] was seated in the mosque when a man with dishevelled hair, and unkempt beard came into his presence. The Holy Prophet [S.A.W.] made a gesture with his hand towards the man signifying that he should go and set the hair of his head and beard. The man went away and returned having put his hair in better shape. Whereupon the Holy Prophet [S.A.W.] remarked: 'Isn't it better to look elegant and fine than to wear unkempt hair. A man with dishevelled hair wears the look of the devil." *(Mishkat)*

Hazrat Abu Huraira [R.A.A.] states: "The Holy Prophet [S.A.W.] observed: No one should walk with one shoe on; either wear both shoes or take off both." *(Tirmidhi)*

It is in the light of this Tradition that the Ulama have forbidden the wearing of only one sleeve and only one sock.

16. Avoid wearing red, gaudy or resplendent dress or showy black or yellow apparel. Red, gaudy and resplendent dress is suited only to women and even women should observe proper rules about wearing such dress. As regards assuming superior airs by donning flowing robes and yellow garments, for the sake of displaying one's distinction, it is a sure sign of pride and haughtiness. Similarly, do not put on strange and funny clothes which may lend you an outlandish appearance and you may become an object of public ridicule.

17. Always put on simple, dignified, civilised dress and spend moderately on your clothes. Avoid luxury and extravagant finance in matters of dress. The Holy Prophet [S.A.W.) has observed:

    "Keep away from luxury, for the favourites of Allah are no lovers of ease and luxury." *(Mishkat)*

    The Holy Prophet [S.A.W.] also affirmed: "Allah will adorn that man with the dress of honour and nobility who, in spite of possessing means and power, observes simplicity in dress out of humility and obedience to Allah." *(Abu Dawud)*

The illustrious Companions were one day sitting together discussing worldly matters. The Holy Prophet [S.A.W.] remarked: "Simplicity of dress is one of the signs of Faith." *(Abu Dawud)*

Once the Holy Prophet [S.A.W.] observed: "There are many a servant of Allah in the world whose outward appearance is humble; their hair are dishevelled and dusty and their dress is ordinary and simple, yet in the sight of Allah their stature is very high. Should they take a vow to do something, Allah fulfils their oath. Bra' bin. Malik [R.A.A.] is one among this type of people." *(Tirmidhi)*

18. Give clothes to the destitute by way of expressing thanks to the Lord for having conferred the bounty of dress on you. The Holy Prophet [S.A.W.] has observed: "Whosoever gives clothes to a Muslim to cover his body, Allah shall clothe that man on the Day of Judgement in the green dress of Paradise." *(Abu Dawud)*

    The Holy Prophet [S.A.W.] also affirmed: "A Muslim who gives clothes to another Muslim shall be afforded protection and safety by Allah as long as those clothes serve as a covering for the beneficiary." *(Tirmidhi)*

19. Give fine clothes according to your means to your servants who serve you day and night.

    The Holy Prophet [S.A.W.] observed: "The slaves, male and female, are your brothers and sisters. Allah has given them under your charge. Hence to whomsoever Allah has given power and control over some one, he should give him the same to eat as he eats himself and the same kind of dress to wear as he wears himself and he should not give him work to do which is beyond his capacity, and if the slave be unable to cope with the load of work, the master should share his burden." *(Bukhari, Muslim)*

Eating Habits

1. Wash your hands before taking your meals. It is in keeping with the rules of cleanliness and neatness that your mind

should be satisfied about the cleanliness of your hands before starting the meal.

2. Say, Bismillah hirrahma nirrahim 'In the Name of Allah, the Most Beneficent, the Most Merciful', while starting the meal. If you forget this, then say as soon as you realise the oversight during the meal. Remember, the meal which is not consecrated by the Name of Allah is made lawful by the devil for himself.
3. Do not lean against anything when sitting down for a meal. Sit in a humble position with your knees raised or joint on the floor or with one knee prostrate and the other one raised. The Holy Prophet [S.A.W.] used to sit for meals in this posture.
4. Always eat with your right hand. However, the left hand may be used simultaneously with the right hand, if needed.
5. Use three fingers while eating. If required, use four fingers except the little finger. Do not put your fingers in the food up to their roots.
6. Do not take a big morsel, nor a small one. Put the second morsel into your mouth only after swallowing the first one.
7. Do not wipe your fingers with bread. This is a filthy habit.
8. Avoid brushing off the loaves and refrain from knocking them about also.
9. Eat out of the plate from the side nearest to you. Do not put your hand in the middle of the plate nor extend your hand to eat from that edge of the plate which is nearer to other diners.
10. If the morsel drops from your hands pick it up and eat it after cleaning or washing it.
11. Eat in company. Dining in company promotes cordiality and love and is a source of blessing.
12. Do not find fault with the food. Leave it if you don't like it.
13. Do not eat while the food is piping hot or simmering.
14. Avoid breaking into guffaws or indulging in too much conversation during taking food.
15. Do not sniff the food needlessly, it is a bad habit. Do not often open your mouth so wide during dinner that the other people

may see the food you are munching between your teeth, nor should you pick your teeth repeatedly in the course of eating. The other diners will find this habit disgusting.

16. Sit down to eat and sit down also while taking a drink of water. However, if needed, you may eat fruit or drink water while standing.
17. If some soup is left over in the plate, drink it; otherwise clear the sediments from the plate with a finger and lick the finger.
18. Do not blow on the articles of food. The breath that we exhale is polluted and poisonous.
19. Take three breathing pauses while drinking water. By this method you can drink according to your need and get full satisfaction. Beware, drinking all the water in one breath may be harmful.
20. While eating in company pay due regard to the needs of the slow diners as well as those who eat at a rapid pace and rise only when all others have finished eating.
21. When you have finished eating, lick your fingers and then wash your hands.
22. Do not pick up two pieces or slices at once while eating fruit.
23. Do not drink water from the spout of a water pot or a goblet etc. Drink from such a container that you may clearly see the water that you are pouring into your mouth in order that no filth or harmful substance goes into your stomach.
24. Say this prayer at the end of the meal:

    "Praise be to Allah Who fed us and gave us drink and made us Muslims."

Daily Routine

1. When the dusk falls, call your children inside and do not permit them to play outside the home. It is safe not to let the children go out at night except in the case of an urgent need. The Holy Prophet [S.A.W.] has observed:

"When the night falls make your children stay at home, for at this hour evil spirits stalk the earth. However, after an hour has passed you may permit the children to move out."

2. At the hour of nightfall, say the following prayer. The Holy Apostle [S.A.W.] used to instruct his Companions [R.A.A.] to say the same.

   "O Allah! with Thy help do we enter upon the morning and with Thy help do we enter upon the evening. With Thy help do we live and with Thy help do we die. And unto Thee shall be the Resurrection." *(Tirmidhi)*

   At the hour of the call for Maqhrib (evening) prayer, say this prayer:

   "Allah, this is the hour of the approach of Thy night and the departure of Thy day and this is the time of Thy Mu'addhin's call. Hence grant me salvation." *(Tirmidhi, Abu Dawud)*

3. Do not go to bed before saying 'Isha prayers. Often the 'Isha prayer may be missed if you take a nap before prayer for who knows Allah will return life to man after this sleep (akin to death) or He forfeits his life for ever while he slumbers in deathlike sleep. The Holy Prophet [S.A.W.] did not like to sleep in a house which was not lit up at night.

4. Soon after the fall of night, light up your homes. The Holy Prophet [S.A.W.] abstained from sleeping in a house which was not lit up at night.

5. Do not keep awake till late hours in the night. Adopt the habit of going to bed early at night and rising early at dawn. The Holy Apostle [S.A.W.] observed in this regard: "After the time of 'Isha prayers, you may either keep awake for the purpose of remembering Allah or to talk over necessary matters with the members of household."

6. Abstain from keeping awake at night and making up for sleep during the day. Allah has appointed the night a time for peace and rest. He has made the day a time for keeping awake and a time for labour to earn one's living. Surah al-Furqan affirms:

> "And He it is Who created night a covering for you and sleep for repose and made the day (a time for) waking up."

And Surah-an-Naba affirms:

> "And We made your sleep for repose and We made the night a covering and We appointed the day for livelihood."

And in Surah al-Namal (86) Allah says:

> "Have they not observed how We have made the night that they may rest therein and the day bright (so that they may strive during its course). No doubt, there are signs in it for a people who believe."

The implication of making the night dark so as to serve as a time of peace and rest and making the day bright so that man may labour and strive is that one should keep a strict schedule of sleeping at night and working hard for earning one's livelihood during the day. In the light of day devote yourself energetically to work and make strenuous efforts to earn your living till your faculties and limbs begin to feel tired. Then in the night when an atmosphere of peace and privacy reigns, repose in bed in a calm and comfortable state. As soon as dawn breaks, arise and invoking the blessings of Allah enter into the field of practical endeavour with renewed vigour. People who due to indolence and lethargy drone in day time or keep awake throughout night enjoying sensuous pleasures and making merry are guilty of violating the law of nature. They ruin their health and undermine their lives. Those who sleep long during the hours of the day not only neglect their daily work but also deprive their body and soul of necessary repose and rest; for sleep during the day cannot serve as an alternative for repose at night in providing rest and nourishment. The Apostle of Allah [S.A.W.] even disapproved of the idea that a man should remain awake all night for offering worship to Allah and thus suffer an unbearable hardship.

The Apostle of Allah [S.A.W.] once said to Hazrat 'Abdullah bin 'Umar [R.A.A.]: "Is it true what I have heard that you regularly keep fast during the day and pass all night in offering prayers?" Hazrat 'Abdullah [R.A.A.] submitted: "I confess this to be true." The Holy Prophet [S.A.W.] observed: "No, don't go on like that. Keep fast sometimes and eat and drink at other times. Similarly get some sleep and then rise and say prayers. You owe a duty to your eye." *(Bukhari)*

7. Do not sleep on a very soft bed. The true believers should for bear love of ease, indolence and luxurious living in the world. Life is a Jihad (straggle) for the true believers. The true believers should, therefore, follow an energetic, strenuous and a hard-working pattern of life. Hazrat 'Aisha [R.A.A.] related: The Holy Prophet [S.A.W.] slept on a bed made of a hide-skin filled with the bark of a palm tree." *(Shama'il Tirmidhi)*

Someone asked Hazrat Hafsa [R.A.A.]: "What kind of a bed did you make for the Holy Prophet [S.A.W.] in your house?" She replied: "There was a canvas cloth which we used to fold up and spread under the Holy Prophet [S.A.W.]. One day, I thought that if I folded the cloth into four layers it would make a softer bed. So 1 folded up the canvas into four layers and spread it for the Prophet [S.A.W.] to sleep on. Next morning the Apostle [S.A.W.] enquired: "What was it that you spread beneath me last night?" I submitted: "It was the same canvas cloth. However, I had folded it up into four layers to make a softer bed." The Holy Prophet [S.A.W.] observed: "No, keep it folded in two layers. The softness of the bed proved a hindrance in arising up for midnight prayers last night. *(Shama'il Tirmidhi)*

Hazrat 'Aisha [R.A.A.] reports: "One day a lady from the Ansar visited our house and saw the bed of the Holy Prophet [S.A.W.]. She returned home and prepared a bedding and heavily padded it with wool to make it extra soft. She.sent it as a gift for the Holy Apostle [S.A.W.]. When the Holy Apostle [S.A.W.] returned home, he saw the bedding and enquired: "What is it?" I submitted: "O Prophet so and so lady from the

Ansar came and saw your bed. She went back and has sent this bedding as a gift for you." The Holy Prophet [S.A.W.] said: "No, return it to her." I liked that bedding so much that I did not really want to return but the Holy Prophet [S.A.W.] insisted so hard that I had to return it back to the lady."

(Shama'il Tirmidhi)

The Holy Prophet [S.A.W.] was one day sleeping on a mat. The mat left some marks on his august body. Hazrat 'Abdullah bin. Mas'ud [R.A.A.] relates: "On seeing the marks of mat on his body I broke into tears." The Holy Prophet [S.A.W.] looked at me and enquired: "Why do you weep?" I submitted: "O Prophet of Allah [S.A.W.]! The Emperors of Rome and Persia rest on silk and velvet cushions and you go to sleep on such a rough mat." The Holy Prophet [S.A.W.] observed: "There is no point in weeping for it. They love the world and we crave for the Hereafter."

On one occasion, the Holy Prophet [S.A.W.] observed: "How can I lead a luxurious, easy and carefree life while the angel Israfil with a trumpet to his lips, with ears open, head bowed, stands waiting for the Lord's Command to blow the trumpet to usher in the Day of Doom." *(Tirmidhi)*

The precedent of the Holy Prophet [S.A.W.] requires the true believers to lead a strenuous life in the world and to abstain from luxurious, carefree living.

8. Perform ablution before going to bed and sleep in a clean and pure state. If your hands are greasy wash them well before going to bed. The Holy Prophet [S.A.W.] has said: "The person whose hands are greased and goes to sleep without washing his hands has only himself to blame if he comes to harm (if he is bitten by some insect)."

   The Holy Prophet [S.A.W.] used to perform ablution before going to sleep. On occasions when he wanted to sleep while in a state when a bath is obligatory, then he used to wash the unclean part and go to bed after performing ablution.

9. When going to bed, close the doors of your house, extinguish the wick lamp or lantern, and put out the burning fire. Once

fire broke out in the home of a person in Madinah at night. On that occasion, the Holy Prophet [S.A.W.] enjoined upon the people: "Fire is your enemy. Be careful to put it out before going to bed."

The Apostle of Allah [S.A.W.] further observed: "Do not permit your little children to go out at the hour of evening, for at that hour evil spirits stalk the earth. When an hour or so of the night has passed, let them go out if need be. Close your doors at night reciting (Bismillah) the name of Allah and extinguish the light after reciting (Bismillah) Allah's name, and tie the mouth of the waterskin with the recital of Allah's name and again recite (Bismillah) the name of Allah and cover the vessels in which you eat and dank. If there is no cloth cover available for this purpose, cover the puts and pans with something else.

10. Take care to keep the following things within reach of your bed at the time of going to sleep. Drinking water and a glass, a jug, a stick, a box of matches or torch for lighting purposes, a miswak (twig for cleaning the teeth), a towel etc. If you are staying as a guest in a home, ask the host for directions to toilet rooms etc. You may thus save unnecessary inconvenience if a sudden need arises during the night. Seven things were always kept ready near the bed when the Holy Prophet [S.A.W.] was in repose:

    • A bottle of oil. • A comb. • Collyrium container. • Scissors. • A twig for cleaning the teeth (miswak). • A Mirror. • And a small wooden needle used for scratching the head etc.

11. Keep your shoes and clothes near at hand while going to bed. This will save you from the trouble of looking for them on arising. Do not put on shoes at once after leaving the bed. Similarly, do not put on clothes without shaking them briskly. It is possible that some deadly insect may have crept into your shoes or clothes and, Allah forbid, may cause you harm.

12. Clean and give a brisk shake to your bed covers before lying down for sleep. If you get up from sleep and leave your bed for any reason, then shake the bed covers once again when you return to the bed. The Holy Prophet [S.A.W.] observed:

"When a person leaves the bed at night and returns to it again, he should dust it thrice with the edge of his wrapping cloth, for he does not know what creature may have crept on to the bed in his absence." *(Tirmidhi)*

13. Say the following prayer, when you get into bed. The Prophet's [S.A.W.] close attendant Hazrat Anas [R.A.A.] reports that on going to bed, the Holy Prophet [S.A.W.] used to recite the following prayer:

    "Praise be to Allah Who gave us food and drink, provided us sufficiently, and gave us (a place for) shelter! How many there are who have neither a provider nor shelterer." *(Tirmidhi)*

14. Recite some portion of the Holy Qur'an at the time of going to bed. The Holy Prophet [S.A.W.] invariably used to recite a portion of the Holy Qur'an before going to sleep. He has observed: "Allah sends an angel to a man who recites a portion of the Book of Allah before going to sleep to protect him from all harm till the time of his rising." *(Ahmad)*

    The Holy Prophet [S.A.W.] has further observed: "When a man lies down on the bed, an angel and the devil call on him. The angel says to him: "Close thy deeds of the day with a virtuous act." And the devil says: "Close thy deeds of the day with an evil act." If that man then recites the name of Allah before going to sleep, the angel stands guard over him all night."

    Hazrat 'Aisha [R.A.A.] has reported: "When the holy Prophet [S.A.W.] went to bed, he used to join his arms in the style of prayer and having recited the *Surahs* (last three Surahs of the Qur'an) used to blow upon his hands and then starting from his head, face and the front he passed his hands over his body as far as it could go. The Holy Prophet [S.A.W.] repeated this act three times." *(Tirmidhi)*

15. While going to sleep put your right hand under the right cheek and turn on the right side. Hazrat Bra [R.A.A.] relates: "The Holy Prophet [S.A.W.] used to rest his right hand under his right cheek. While retiring to sleep, the Prophet [S.A.W.] used to say the following prayer:

"O Allah! Save me from Thy doom on the day Thou wilt raise Thy bondmen."

It is recorded in Hisn-e-Hasin that the Holy Prophet [S.A.W.] used to recite this prayer three times.

16. Do not lie down on your belly nor take a turn to the left side of your body when going to sleep. The father of Hazrat Mu'ish Tafkhat-al-Ghifari [R.A.A.], relates: "I was lying on my belly in the mosque. Presently a person startled me with a touch of his foot and observed: "Allah disapproves of this posture." When I looked up I saw he was the Holy Prophet [S.A.W.]. *(Abu Dawud)*

17. Sleep in place where fresh air is accessible. Do not sleep in closed rooms where there is no opening for letting in fresh air.

18. Do not keep your face covered when asleep. This habit is harmful for health. Sleep with your face uncovered so that you may inhale fresh air.

19. Take care not to sleep on roofs which are not surrounded with a ridge of the wall or railing. Put on light before stepping down the stairs as a little oversight often causes grave consequences.

20. Even in the freezing cold, do not keep the stove burning while you are asleep, nor keep the lantern on in a closed room. The gases produced by fire are deeply injurious to health; sometimes they may even prove fatal."

21. Say the following prayer before falling asleep. Hazrat Abu Huraira [R.A.A.] has reported: "The Apostle of Allah [S.A.W.] used to say this prayer before going to sleep.

    "In Thy name, my Lord! I lay my side (on the bed) and in Thy name I raise it. If Thou withhold my soul, then have mercy thereon. If Thou send it back, then guard it even as Thou dost guard Thy righteous bondmen." *(Bukhari, Muslim)*

    In case memory does not retain this prayer, here is a short prayer:

"O Allah! In Thy name do I live and die." (Bukhari, Muslim)

22. Form the habit of waking up in the small hours of the night. It is essential to rise in the last quarter of the night and remember Allah to master your desires and physical demands and to establish communion with Allah. The distinctive trait of the favourites of Allah, as Allah has Himself affirmed, is that they wake up in the night and bow in humility to Him and make prostrations and seek His forgiveness for their sins. It was the practice of the Holy Prophet [S.A.W.] that he reposed in the early part of the night and got up in the small hours and engaged himself in devotion to Allah.

23. Say this prayer on arising from sleep:

    "Praise be to Allah Who restored us unto life, having caused us to die and unto Him shall be the Resurrection." *(Bukhari, Muslim)*

24. Offer thanks to the Lord on seeing a happy dream and take it as a good omen. The Holy Prophet [S.A.W.] observed: "Prophethood now bears glad tidings and nothing besides." The people enquired: "What do the glad tidings signify?" The Apostle of Allah observed: "A happy dream" (Bukhari). The Holy Prophet. [S.A.W.] further remarked: "Whoever is more truthful among ye will see a more truthful dream." The Prophet [S.A.W.] instructed the people, "Offer thanks to the Lord and praise Him whenever you see a happy dream. And relate your happy dreams and relate them to your friends only." Whenever the Holy Prophet [S.A.W.] saw a happy dream, he related it to his Companions and he used to say to his friends. "Recount your dreams to me and I shall tell you their interpretation." *(Bukhari)*

25. Invoke blessings frequently upon the Holy Prophet [S.A.W.]. Perchance Allah may bless you with a visit n of His Apostle [S.A.W.].

    Hazrat Maulana Muhammad 'Alt Mongiri once asked Hazrat Fazal Rahman Ganj Muradabadi, "Teach me some special Darud (prayer of Benediction) by which I may be blessed with the vision of the Holy Prophet [S.A.W.]." Hazrat Fazal replied: "There is no special prayer of Benediction. You need to cultivate deep devotion only." Later, after some deliberation he observed: "However, with the following Benediction Hazrat Syed Hassan [R.A.A.] had the vision of the Prophet:

> "Allah! shower Thy Grace upon Muhammad and his family to the ultimate extent of numbers which are in Thy Knowledge."

The Holy Prophet [S.A.W.] observed:

> "He who sees me in dream does actually sees me, for the devil cannot appear in my form."
>
> *(Shama'il Tirmidhi)*

Hazrat Yazid Farsi [R.T.A.] used to calligraph the Holy Qur'an. Once he was blessed with the vision of the Holy Prophet [S.A.W.] in a dream. Hazrat Ibn 'Abbas [R.A.A.] was alive at that time. Hazrat Yazid mentioned his dream to him. Thereupon Hazrat Ibn 'Abbas related this Tradition to him, "Whoever sees my vision in a dream actually sees me, for the devil can never appear in my form." Then 'Abbas asked Yazid: "Can you describe the person you saw in your dream?" Hazrat Yazid recounted: "His frame and height were of fine proportions. He had a brown complexion inclined towards fairness. He had dark eyes and a smiling, handsome, round face. He had a thick beard covering his whole visage and flowing down to and spreading over his bosom." Hazrat Ibn 'Abbas affirmed: "Yes, if you had seen the Holy Prophet [S.A.W.] in his life you could not have given a better description of him" (i.e., the description given by you fits the actual appearance of the Apostle) [S.A.W.] *(Shama'il Tirmidhi)*

26. When, Allah forbid, you see an unhappy or terrifying dream, never relate it to any one. Beseech Allah to protect you from the menace of the dream. If it pleases Him, you will be safe from any evil. Hazrat Abu Salama relates: "I often used to fall ill on seeing unhappy dreams. One day, I told of it to Hazrat Abu Qatada [R.A.A.] who related to me the following Tradition

of the Holy Prophet [S.A.W.] "A happy dream is a blessing from Allah. If any of you sees a happy dream, he should not relate it to any one other than his sincere friend. If any of you sees a bad dream, he should not mention it to any one. On the other hand, as soon as he wakes from sleep he should recite." (A'audhu blillahi minashshaita nirrajim three times and breathe a 'tut-tut' towards his left side and then take a turn over to the other side. In this manner, he will remain safe from the evil effects of the dream" *(Riyad-us-Salehin, Muslim)*

27. Do not relate false dreams conceived by your own imagination. Hazrat 'Abdullah bin 'Abbas [R.A.A.] states that the Holy Prophet [S.A.W.] observed: "The person who relates concocted dreams shall be awarded a punishment to bind two grains of bar ley in a knot and he will never be able to do it."*(Muslim)*

    And the Holy Prophet [S.A.W.] observed: "It is a great calumny that a man should relate what he has not seen with his own eyes." *(Bukhari)*

28. When a friend relates his dream to you, give him a favourable interpretation and say a prayer to invoke the blessing of Allah upon him. A man once related his dream to the Holy Prophet [S.A.W.]. He observed: "You have seen a good dream and it shall have a happy outcome."

    After the dawn prayers the Holy Prophet [S.A.W.] used to sit cross-legged and asked the people to relate to him if anyone had seen a dream and before listening to anyone's dream, the Holy Prophet [S.A.W.] used to say:

    "May the goodness of this dream be bestowed on you and may you be protected from its evil effects. May this dream prove favourable to us and may it bring curse upon our enemies. Praise and thanksgiving is due to Allah alone Who is the Lord of all worlds."

29. If a dream strikes feelings of terror into you or an awkward dream perplexes you, you should recite the following prayer to get rid of fear or perplexity and ask your grown-up children also to learn it by heart.

Hazrat 'Abdullah bin 'As [R.A.A.] related that whenever a person saw a terrible or awkward dream, the Holy Prophet [S.A.W.] used to instruct him to say the following prayer:

> "I seek the protection of the perfect words of Allah against His wrath and anger and punishment; against the evil-doings of His creatures; against the fears of evil spirits and against the possibility that these evil spirits or their fears should assail me."
>
> *(Abu Dawud, Tirmidhi)*

Morning Walk

1. Walk with a medium pace. Do not rush to become an object of ridicule for the onlookers, nor drag your feet so wearily that people might think you are ill and start making anxious enquiries after your health. The Holy Prophet [S.A.W.] used to take long steps when walking and placed his feet firmly on the ground; he never dragged his feet while walking.
2. Walk with poise and dignity with eyes cast down. Do not continue to look sideways at everything along the path. It is childish and improper. The Holy Prophet [S.A.W.] used to walk with his holy self inclined forward as if he were descending a slope. He [S.A.W.] used to move with dignity at a rather quick pace and kept an alert but self-possessed posture of body. He [S.A.W.] seldom looked sideways, right or left, on the road.
3. Walk humbly with even steps. Do not walk arrogantly and proudly. You can't split the earth with a kick nor are you going to scale the heights of mountains. What is the sense then, for striking arrogant and haughty postures in walking?
4. Walk with shoes on. Do not walk bare foot. Shoes protect the feet from injury by thorns, pebbles or other harmful bits and pieces lying on the way, as well as from the bites of deadly insects. The Holy Prophet [S.A.W.] observed: "Keep your shoes on most of the time. A person who keeps his shoes on is a kind of rider."

5. Be mindful of good taste, propriety and dignity when walking along the road. Walk with both shoes on, or with both feet bare. It is ridiculous to walk with a shoe on one foot and the other foot bare. Observe utmost care not to display such bad' taste or improper behaviour unless it is inevitable. The Holy Prophet [S.A.W.] observed: "No one should walk with one shoe on. Walk with both shoes on or with both feet bare."

   (Shama'il Tirmidhi)

6. Keep the ends of your dress folded in the course of walking to avoid the danger of entanglements. The Holy Prophet [S.A.W.] used to roll up his attire a bit while walking.

7. Walk shoulder to shoulder with your companions. Do not walk ahead of your companions to show off your higher rank. Sometimes walk hand in hand with your fellows in a spirit of close friendship. The Holy Prophet [S.A.W.] never displayed his distinguished rank while walking with his Companions [R.A.A.]. Often the Prophet [S.A.W.] would walk behind his Companions [R.A.A.] and sometimes took the hand of a Companion into his own sacred hand as a mark of intimate companionship.

8. Observe the following etiquettes strictly while walking along the road. Do not stop or sit on the way with the object of staring at the passers-by. If on occasions you must stop or sit on the way, you should follow the following six rules:

   (i) Keep your eyes downcast. (ii) Remove harmful bits and pieces out of the way. (iii) Respond to the salutation of others. (iv) Persuade the people to do good and prevent them from doing evil. (v) Show the way to travellers who have lost direction. (vi) Help those who are in trouble or are facing hardship.

9. In the course of a journey, seek the companionship of the good and avoid travelling with the wicked.

10. Men and women should not walk in a mixed company on the road. The women should avoid the middle path and walk along the edge of the road. The men should walk apart from the women. The Holy Prophet [S.A.W.] affirmed: "Collision

with a mud-stained swine drenched in stinking slush is tolerable, but it is undesirable that a stranger should rub shoulders with a female."

11. Whenever righteous women have to pass along the road they should cover their bodies, garments and all pieces of adornment carefully with a 'burqa' or a sheet and cover their faces with a veil.

12. Do not wear a piece of ornament which gives out a tinkling sound while you walk, or otherwise, walk with sod steps so that the tinkle of your ornaments may not invite the attention of those unrelated to you.

13. Women should not use strong perfumes if they intend to go out on the road. The Holy Prophet [S.A.W.] has disapproved of such women in strong terms.

14. When you emerge from your home, look up to the sky and say the following prayers:

    "In the name of Allah, I rely upon Allah. O Allah! We seek refuge in Thee lest we slip, or go astray or wrong or be wronged, or act foolishly or any one should act foolishly with us." *(Musnad Ahmad)*

15. On going to the bazar, say this prayer :

    > "In the name of Allah. O Allah! I ask of Thee good of this market and the good of that which is therein and I seek refuge in Thee from the evil thereof and the evil of that which is therein. O Allah! Behold I seek refuge in Thee lest I take a false oath or strike a bargain incurring loss."

    Hazrat 'Umar bin Khattab [R.A.A.] stated that the Holy Prophet [S.A.W.] had observed: "The man who says this prayer on entering the bazar, Allah adds ten lakh virtues to his account and forgives his ten lakh sins and raises his merits by ten lakh degrees"

    > "There is no deity save Allah. He is One. No partner hath He. His is the Sovereignty and His is the praise. He giveth life and He giveth death. He is the Ever

Living that never dieth. In His hand is all the good and He hath power to do all things." *(Tirmidhi)*

Journey

1. You should set out on a journey at a suitable hour so that the journey may be completed in the shortest possible time and prayer times may also be properly observed. The Holy Prophet [S.A.W.] generally held Thursday to be a propitious day to start on a journey himself or for sending someone else on a journey.
2. Do not go on a journey alone. If possible, travel in the company of three persons. This ensures proper care of baggage and needs are easily met by mutual cooperation. Companionship during a journey also ensures safety from several dangers and mishaps. The Holy Prophet [S.A.W.] once observed: "If the disadvantages of travelling alone that I am aware of are made known to the people, no rider would go on a journey alone during the night." (Bukhari). On one occasion, a man having made a long journey came to the Holy Prophet [S.A.W.]. The Prophet [S.A.W.] en quired from the traveller, "Who is thy companion?" The traveller submitted: " O Prophet of Allah [S.A.W.] I have no companion. I have come alone." Thereupon the Holy Prophet [S.A.W.] ob served: "A lone rider is a devil; two riders are devils, too; but three riders are riders all right." *(Tirmidhi)*
3. A woman must go on a journey in the company of her spouse or lawful kith and kin. In the case of ordinary travelling for a day or half, she may go alone, but it is always discreet for a woman not to move out alone. The Holy Prophet [S.A.W.] has observed: "It is not permissible for a woman who believes in Allah and the Day of Judgement to go on a journey lasting for three or more days alone. She may, however, undertake such a long journey if she is accompanied by her father, brother, husband, her own son or any other lawful kith or kin." (Bukhari). The Holy Prophet [S.A.W.] is reported to have remarked on one occasion: "A woman should not go alone even on a journey of one day and one night." *(Bukhari, Muslim)*

4. Setting out on a journey when you get on to the vehicle of transport and it begins to move, say this prayer:

   "Glory be unto Allah Who hath subjugated this (beast) unto us, though we were unable to subdue it. Behold we are assuredly to return unto our Lord. O Allah! Behold, we beg of Thee in this journey of ours righteousness and piety and a conduct wherewith Thou wilt be well pleased. O Allah! Make this journey of ours easy for us, and roll up for us the distance thereof. O Allah! Thou art (our) companion in this journey, and representative in (our) household. O Allah! Behold, I seek refuge in Thee from the toil of this journey, from holding a sad sight and a bad reverse in my wealth and household and from deficiency after plenty, and from the curse of the oppressed.

   (Muslim, Abu-Dawud, Tirmidhi)

5. Pay due regard to the comfort and convenience of others on the way. Your fellow-travellers have a right on you. The Holy Qur'an affirms: *Was-sahibi bil-jahanbi.* ("Be nice to the companion beside you"). The term `companion beside you' includes all such persons who happen to be your fellowtravellers any time, anywhere. The brief fellowship in the course of a journey imposes a duty on you to show the best conduct towards your fellow-traveller and take the utmost care not to cause him any physical or mental distress by word or deed. The Holy Prophet [S.A.W.] affirmed: "The chief of the nation is the servant of the people. The person who excels others in rendering good service to his fellow men can be surpassed in piety by no one, save those who attain martyrdom in the way of Allah." *(Mishkat)*

6. Say two Raka'ats of Thanksgiving on leaving for a journey and on returning from it. Such was the practice of the Holy Prophet

7. When your train or bus ascends a slope or your aeroplane takes off and is air-borne, say this prayer:

"O Allah, Thou art supreme over all heights and elevations. Praise and Thanks giving under all circumstances is due to Thee alone."

8. If you have to halt in your journey at night, stay at a safe place where your life and goods are sufficiently safeguarded against thieves and brigands as well as from the menace of deadly animals or insects.
9. Having achieved the purpose of your journey, make haste to return home. Do not linger about aimlessly.
10. On return from a journey, do not enter your house suddenly without sending in advance information of your arrival. Offer two Raka'ats of prayers in the mosque, thus affording time to the members of your household during which they may make preparations to accord you a befitting welcome.
11. Take care of the comfort of the animals accompanying you during the journey and look after the needs and protections of the rider who accompanies you.
12. In the cold weather, carry your bedding with you. Do not cause unnecessary trouble to your host.
13. Carry a tumbler and a prayer mat during the journey to avoid inconveniences at times of need like purification, ablution, prayer and taking a drink of water.
14. When some persons are travelling together they should appoint one person from among themselves to act as their "Ameer" (leader). But each one should keep his ticket, money for necessary expenses and other baggage in his own custody.
15. When night falls in the course of a journey, you should say this prayer:

   "O earth! My Lord and Thy Lord is Allah. I seek refuge in Allah from three evil, and evil of that which is in thee, from the evil of that which bath been created in thee, and from the evil of that which moveth over thee. I also seek refuge in Allah from the lion and the Aswad, from the serpent and the scorpion, from the evil of the dweller in the land, from the begetter, and that which (the begetter) begetteth." *(Abu Dawud)*

16. At the time of returning home from a journey, say this prayer:

    "We are returnees, penitents before our Lord, penitence that may not let any effect of our misdeeds remain on us." *(Hisn Hasien)*

17. On sending off someone on a journey, accompany him for some distance. On taking leave, ask him to say a prayer and say this prayer for him when the traveller departs:

    "Unto Allah' I commend your faith, your trust, and the corgi elusion of your deeds." *(Hisn Hasien)*

18. Extend a warm welcome to the traveller when he returns from the journey. Make affectionate remarks and shake hands with him or embrace him as need be or as the occasion demands.

Behaviour in Sorrow

1. Endure calamities with fortitude and calmness. Do not lose heart and never let your grief and sorrow exceed moderate proportions. No person in the world can remain safe and unaffected by sorrow, grief, calamity, hardship, affliction, failure or loss. The response of the believers and unbelievers is, however, different in this respect. The non-believer loses his sense under the burden of pains and sorrows and is completely immobilised by feelings of hopelessness and dismay. Sometimes he succumbs to grief and commits suicide. In contrast, the believer remains undaunted in the face of the greatest calamity and never loses his patience. At such times he becomes a symbol of patience and fortitude and remains firm like a rock. He takes the view that whatever has occurred was decreed by Allah and no command of Allah is without wisdom or purpose. Hence whatever Allah commands is for the ultimate good of man and surely there is always an aspect of mercy in all the dealings of Allah with man. This reasoning produces a state of spiritual calm and the bitter taste of sorrow turns into sweetness. This faith in the predetermined destiny makes the burden of hardship light and calamity becomes easy to bear. Allah has affirmed:

> "Naught of disaster befalleth in the earth or in yourselves but it is in a Book before We bring it into being. Lo! that is easy for Allah that ye grieve not for the sake of that which hath escaped you."
>
> *(Al Hadeed 22, 23)*

In other words one of the merits of putting faith in a divinely-appointed destiny is that the believer finds solace even amidst the greatest suffering deeming it to be the decree of the Providence. He remains unshaken and in all matters looks towards the Merciful Allah and thinks only of His Grace and endeavours to seek good out of every evil by employing the virtues of patience and contentment under all circumstances. The Holy Prophet [S.A.W.] has observed:

> "How excellent is the state of the true believers! He wins Grace under all conditions. If he is afflicted with grief, sickness or poverty, he bears them with fortitude and such trials bring good to him, If he is rewarded with happiness and prosperity it becomes the cause of goodness for him." *(Muslim)*

2. On hearing a tragic or painful news or if you suffer loss or sustain grief or injury or are beset with a sudden misfortune, recite at once:

> "Lo! We are Allah's and Lo! unto Him are we to return." *(al-Baqarah)*

The implication is that all our possessions belong to Allah; Allah has given us everything and He is the One Who will take away everything. We are his creatures and we must return to Him. We submit to the Will of God in all matters and are content with His Dispensation. All acts of Allah contain certain purpose, wisdom and justice. He acts with greater good in view. It is the duty of His faithful servant never to resent the actions of the Lord. Allah has said:

> "And surely We shall by you with something of fear and hunger and loss of wealth and lives and crops; but give glad tidings to the steadfast who say, when a misfortune striketh them: Lo! we are Allah's and lo!

> unto Him we are to return. Such are they on whom are blessings from their Lord and Mercy. Such are the rightly-guided." *(al-Baqarah: 155-157)*
>
> The Holy Prophet [S.A.W.] has affirmed: "When a man is afflicted with hardship and says this Allah removes his affliction and blesses him with a happy outcome and bestows on him what his heart desires in reward for it."

On one occasion when his lamp went off, the Holy Prophet [S.A.W.] said. *inna lillahi wa inna ilaihai raji'un* someone enquired: "O Holy Prophet [S.A.W.] Is it a calamity if the lamp goes off?" The Holy Prophet [S.A., W.] observed: "Yes, everything that causes hardship to a believer is a calamity." And the Holy Prophet [S.A.W.] has observed:

> "Allah forgives all the sins of those Muslims who suffer a torment of the soul or physical pain, illness, sorrow, grief or afflic tion, even the injury on account of the piercing of a thorn (and bear all these trials with patience)." *(Bukhari, Muslim)*

Hazrat Anas [R.A.A.] reports:

> The Holy Prophet [S.A.W.] observed: "The more severe the trial and hardship, the greater its reward. When Allah cherishes love for a group of people, He puts them to trial to cleanse them more and to make them pure. Hence those who submit to the Will of Allah win His pleasure. And those who harbour resent ment against Allah in the hour of trial, Allah also is displeased with them." *(Tirmidhi)*

Hazrat Abu Musa Ash'ari [R.A.A.] relates that the Holy Prophet [S.A.W.] observed: "When the child of a person dies, Allah enquires from His angels: "Did you extract the soul of the child of one of my Creatures?" They submit: "Yes." Allah again asks them: "Did you extract the soul of the most beloved of my creature?" They submit: "Yes." Allah then enquires from them: "What did my creature say?" They submit: "In his hour of affliction, he praised Thee. Allah commands the angels: 'Build a dwelling for this creature of Mine in the Paradise and call it 'Bait ul-Hamd' (The House of Thanksgiving)." *(Tirmidhi)*

3. It is natural to show grief on suffering from pain or meeting an accident. However, care should be taken that even under the stress of extreme pain and grief the tongue should not utter an unbecoming remark, nor the virtues of patience and contentment be forsaken.

   The Holy Prophet [S.A.W.] had his son Hazrat Ibraheem [R.A.A.] in his lap when the child was about to depart from this earthly life. On seeing this piteous sight tears started trickling down the eyes of the Holy Prophet [S.A.W.] and the Prophet observed: "O Ibraheem! we grieve over thy separation, but our tongue shall utter only that which conforms to the Will of Allah." *(Muslim)*

4. Even in the throes of grief, do not commit an act which may smack of ingratitude or complaint or which transgresses the limits of Shari'ah. It is unlawful for a believer to give vent to loud weeping, tearing off clothes, slapping cheeks, crying and shouting or beating of head or the chest in mourning. The Holy Prophet [S.A.W.] has said: "The man who tears off his clothes, slaps his cheeks and raves and shouts like pagans and wails is not a member of my ummah." *(Tirmidhi)*

   When Hazrat Ja'far Tayyar [R.A.A.], the cousin brother of the Holy Prophet [S.A.W.] attained martyrdom and the news reached his home, the women of his household began to shout and cry and started wailing loudly. The Holy Prophet [S.A.W.] sent word, "Stop wailing." But the women continued their lamen tations. The Holy Prophet [S.A.W.] forbade them a second time, but the women would not comply. Thereupon the Holy Prophet [S.A.W.] observed: "Fill their mouths with dust." *(Bukhari)*

   On one occasion, the Holy Prophet [S.A.W.] was accompanying a funeral procession. A woman came carrying a stove. The Holy Prophet [S.A.W.] reprimanded her so severely that she ran away at one. *(Shat-un-Nabi Vol. VI)*

The Holy Prophet [S.A.W.] observed:

> "No one should carry fire or funeral music behind a bier."

There was a custom in Arabia that people who walked behind a bier used to cast away their cloaks as a mark of grief and kept only their shirts on. On seeing people in this state once the Holy Prophet [S.A.W.] observed: Are you observing a pagan custom! I was thinking of invoking such a curse upon you that your appearances might be deformed." The people at once put on their cloaks and never acted in that fashion again. *(Ibn Majah)*

5. Do not curse your illness, nor utter any word of complaint. Exercise utmost restraint and self-control and pray for the reward in the Hereafter.

The sins, of the believers are washed away by suffering illness or enduring tortures. The soul of the believer is purged and he attains capital reward in the Eternal world. The Holy Prophet [S.A.W.] has affirmed:

> "All pain that the believer endures on account of physical torture, illness or some other cause is rewarded by Allah in such fashion that Allah purges the believer of all his sins even as a tree sheds its leaves." *(Bukhari, Muslim)*

Once on seeing a lady shivering, the Holy Prophet [S.A.W.] enquired from her, "O Umm Sa'ib (or Musayyib)! Why are you shivering so?" She replied: "I am seized with fever. May Allah curse it!" The Holy Prophet [S.A.W.] advised her, "No, don't curse the fever. Fever purges the progeny of Adam of sins even as fire melts the ore to extract pure iron." *(Muslim)*

Hazrat 'Ata bin Rabah [R.A.A.] describes a first-hand account as follows: "On one occasion when we were near the Ka'ba,. Hazrat 'Abbas said to me, "Would you like to see a woman who will go to Paradise?" "Yes, certainly." Hazrat 'Abbas [R.A.A.] said: "Look at that black woman. She once went to the Holy Prophet [S.A.W.] and submitted, "O Prophet of Allah [S.A.W.] I am seized with such deep fits of epilepsy that I lose all consciousness and in that state I become completely naked: O Prophet of Allah! Pray to Allah in my behalf." The Holy Prophet [S.A.W.] observed: "If you continue to endure this affliction with patience, Allah will send thee to Paradise or if you wish I shall pray to Allah to cure thee." On hearing this, the lady submitted; "O Prophet of Allah [S.A.W.]! I am willing to endure this affliction. However, please pray to Allah to save me from the humiliation of becoming naked when gripped with fits." The Holy Prophet [S.A.W.] thereupon prayed to Allah on behalf of this lady. Hazrat 'Ata [R.A.A.] reports that he saw this tall lady, Umm Rafz, on the steps of the Ka'ba."

6. Do not observe mourning for more than three days on the death of any one. It is natural to be stricken with grief and to weep on the death of relations, yet the period of mourning should not exceed three days. The Holy Prophet [S.A.W.] observed: "It is not lawful for a believer to mourn the death of someone for a period of more than three days. However, the lawful mourning period for a widow is four months and ten days: During this period, she should not put on a colourful dress, nor use any perfume nor should bedeck herself."

   (Tirmidhi)

   On the fourth day after the death of the brother of Hazrat Zainab bint Jahsh [R.A.A.], some ladies visited her to offer condolences. Hazrat Zainab [R.A.A.] applied perfume to her person in the presence of everyone and remarked: "I did not need to use perfume at this time. However, I have done so now because I have heard the Holy Prophet [S.A.W.] to say, "It is not lawful for a Muslim lady to observe mourning for more than three days for any relation except her husband."

7. Advise each other to bear sorrow, grief or calamity calmly and patiently. When the Holy Prophet [S.A.W.] returned from the battle of Uhud, the ladies came to his holy presence to enquire after their relations and kin. When Hazrat Hamna bint Jahsh [R.A.A.] appeared, the Holy Prophet [S.A.W.] instructed her to bear her grief calmly, and said: "Be patient over the martyrdom of your brother 'Abdullah, [R.A.A.] and

she recited: (It is from Allah and we have to return to Allah) and prayed for the salvation of her brother." Then the Holy Prophet [S.A.W.] instructed her, "Be patient over the martyrdom of your maternal uncle Hamza [R.A.A.]." Hazrat Hamna [R.A.A.] again recited and prayed for the salvation of her uncle.

The son of Hazrat Abu Talha [R.A.A.] was gravely ill. Leaving his son in this precarious state, Hazrat Talha [R.A.A.] had to go out to work. The child died in his absence. Abu Talha's wife [R.A.A.] instructed the people not to report the news to Abu Talha [R.A.A.]. When he returned home in the evening after work, he enquired from the wife: "How is the child?" She replied: "He is in a more restful state." Then she brought dinner for Abu Talha [R.A.A.]. He ate it in peace and went to bed. Next morning the pious wife conveyed the sad news to her husband in a very wise manner. She asked him: "If someone lends something to somebody and then demands it back, what right has the possessor to withhold the thing from the real owner?" Abu Talha [R.A.A.] replied: "It is improper for the borrower to claim such a right." Thereupon the patient wife observed: "Be patient over the loss of your son then."

(Muslim)

8. Welcome all hardships in the way of righteousness in good cheer and feel joy rather than sorrow at whatever distress befalls you in this way. Offer thanks to the Lord that He thus accepted your sacrifice in His way. Hazrat Asma' [R.A.A.] the illustrious mother of Hazrat 'Abḍullah-bin-Zubair [R.A.A.] once fell gravely ill. Hazrat 'Abdullah [R.A.A.] came to enquire after her health. The mother said to him "Son! in the first place, I wish that Allah should keep me alive until I witness one of the two things that either you should attain martyrdom on the field of battle and I should obtain the Grace of being patient on hearing the report of your martyrdom or you should gain victory and seeing you a victor I should be happy. As Allah willed it so Hazrat 'Abdullah-bin-Zubair [R.A.A.] attained martyrdom in the lifetime of his mother. Hajjaj ordered

to keep his dead body hanging on the stake. Hazrat Asma' [R.A.A.] was at that time too old and weak yet in spite of her old age and weakness she arrived to look at this piteous sight. Instead of crying and wailing on seeing the dead body of her dear son, she addressed Hajjaj and said to him: "Has not the time yet come for this rider to dismount the horse"?

9. Support one another in grief and pain. Share the sorrows and afflictions of your friends and lend all help you can to alleviate their suffering. The Holy Prophet [S.A.W.] observed: "All Muslims are like one human body. If the eye becomes sore, the entire body feels distress. If there is pain in the head, all organs of the body suffer the agony." *(Muslim)*

   At the time when Hazrat Ja'far Tayyar [R.A.A.] attained martyrdom, the Holy Prophet [S.A.W.] observed:

   > "Let food be sent to Ja'far's house, for the inmates of his house, in the abundance of their grief will not be able to cook food". *(Abu Dawud)*

   Hazrat Abu Huraira [R.A.A.] reports that the Holy Prophet [S.A.W.] observed:

   > "A man who offers condolences to a woman whose child is dead shall be admitted in Paradise and he shall be wrapped in the sheet of Paradise". *(Tirmidhi)*

   And the Holy Prophet [S.A.W.] also observed:

   > "The man who solaces an afflicted person shall be rewarded in the same degree as the afflicted one". *(Tirmidhi)*

   In the same connection the Holy Prophet [S.A.W.] enjoined upon the people to join the funerals. Hazrat Abu Huraira (R.A.A.] has reported: "The Holy Prophet [S.A.W.] observed:

   > "The person who joins the funeral and says the funeral prayer will get a reward equal to one Qirat (Carat) and the person who after the funeral prayers attends the burial also will get reward equal to two Qirats (Carats)." Someone asked: "What will be the mass of

these two Qirats?" The Holy Prophet [S.A.W.] observed: "The mass of these two Qirats will be equal to two mountains". *(Bukhari, Muslim)*

10. When you are pressed under the burden of calamities and afflicted with sorrows, turn to Allah; offer worship and bow in humility to Him and say prayers to Him. The Holy Qur'an affirms:

    "O ye who believe! Seek help through perseverance and prayer." *(al-Baqarah)*

    It is natural to be sorrowful and shed tears in a griefstricken state. However, avoid weeping loudly. The Holy Prophet [S.A.W.] used to weep in a muffled voice. He [S.A.W.] used to heave a cold sigh; tears would stream down the eyes and the voice which came out of his holy bosom used to be similar to the sound of a bubbling kettle or the turning of a grinding wheel. The Holy Prophet [S.A.W.] has himself described the state of his grief and weeping:

    "The eye sheds tears; the heart is filled with sorrow; yet our tongue utters only those words which are pleasing to our Lord."

    Hazrat Abu Huraira [R.A.A.] reports that whenever the Holy Prophet [S.A.W.] felt worried, he used to look up to the heavens. and said repeatedly (Gloried by the Lord the Magnificent) and when the sorrow deepened the Holy Prophet [S.A.W.] devoted himself to prayer with greater fervour, and used to say: (The Alive, The Eternal) *(Tirmidhi)*

11. Say these prayers in the moments of intense grief and sorrow, when calamities befall and you are under heavy stress of grief and unrest. Hazrat Sa'd-bin-Waqqas [R.A.A.] reports that the Holy Prophet [S.A.W.] affirmed: "The prayer which Dhun-nun[3] offered to Allah from the belly of the fish was as follows:

    "There is no deity except Thee. Be Thou glorified! Lo I have been a wrong doer." (21: 87)

    Hence any Muslim who says this prayer to Allah in times of distress or hardship, Allah surely accepts his prayer. It is reported by Hazrat Ibn'Abbas [R.A.A.] that in moments of sorrow or grief, the Holy Prophet [S.A.W.] used to say this prayer:

> "There is no deity except Allah. He is the Master of Great Heaven. There is no deity except Allah. He is the Master of Heaven and Earth and the Master of High Heaven." *(Bukhari, Muslim)*

Hazrat Abu Musa [R.A.A.] states that the Prophet [S.A.W.] observed:

> "This prayer is a panacea for ninety-nine ills. The least benefit to be derived from saying this prayer is that he who says this prayer remains safe from grief and sorrow."

Hazrat 'Abdullah b. Mas'ud [R.A.A.] reported that the Holy Prophet [S.A.W.] affirmed: "Any one who is afflicted with pain or distress and says this prayer, Allah will surely turn his sorrow and grief into happiness and felicity:

"Allah! I am Thy servant. My father is Thy servant and so is my brother. Thou hast power over my whole being. It is Thy Law which rules my life. All Thy Commands in my case are most just. I beseech Thee in the name of all Attributes which thou have mentioned. Thy own or those which Thou revealed inThy Book or revealed to some among Thy creatures or kept them hidden in Thy veiled Treasures, to make the Great Book, the Qur'an, the pleasure of my heart, the light of my eyes, the balm for my affliction and a cure for my anxiety."

(Ahmad, Ibn Habban Hisn Hasien)

12. If, Allah forbid, matters come to such a pass that the calamities and hardships oppress you so hard that life becomes unbearable and distress assume such fearful proportions that the burden of life hangs heavy on you, even under such circumstances do never call for death nor should you ever think of the disgraceful act of taking your own life. The act of suicide is a symptom of cowardice; it is the worst form of breach of trust and the most heinous sin. Under such conditions of perplexity and unrest, pray constantly to Allah in these words:

> "Allah! Keep me alive as long as it is better for me to live and if there be goodness for me in death, send me death." *(Bukhari, Muslim)*

13. Say this prayer when you find any one afflicted with hardship. Hazrat Abu Huraira [R.A.A.] related: The Holy Prophet [S.A.W.] observed:

> "He who says the following prayer on seeing the other afflicted with trouble will, Allah willing, himself remain safe from this trouble:
>
> "Praise be to Allah Who saved me from that where with He hath afflicted thee and made me to excel with a marked excel lence most of those whom he created." *(Tirmidhi)*

Happy and Fearless Life

1. Assailed by the threat of slaughter, devastation, tyranny, barbarity, mischief and strife unleashed by the enemies of faith or panic-stricken by the catastrophic effects of natural calamities under all circumstances use the insight of a true believer and probe into the real causes of these visitations. Instead of wasting time on superficial remedies, focus all your energies on putting into effect the injunctions contained in the Book of Allah and the Sunnah. The Holy Qur'an affirms:

> "Whatever of misfortune striketh you it is what you have earned by your own deeds. And He forgiveth much." *(Ash-Shura: 30)*

And the Holy Qur'an itself reveals the remedy:

> "And all of you together should turn to Allah in repentance, O Believers, so that you may get salvation."

'Tauba' (Repentance) denotes: 'To return', 'To have recourse to'. Immersed in the fearful cesspool of sins and vices, when the Ummah (Muslim Nation) feels a sense of shame and turns to Allah in a spirit of devotion and having washed the stains of her vices by tears of repentance, renews her pledge of allegiance to Allah - this state is described in the Holy Qur'an

by the term 'Tauba'. This 'repentance' and 'petition for mercy' is the most efficacious and genuine remedy against the fear and dread of all forms of evil and strife.

2. Do not degrade the honour of your national life by adopting a cringing attitude before the tyranny, oppression and mischiefs of the enemies of faith; do not reduce yourself under their awe to the indignity of begging the cruel enemy for mercy. Gird up your loins; strengthen your faith and remove weakness which produces cowardice in you and encourages the enemies of faith to oppress and extinguish you. The Holy Prophet [S.A.W.] has identified two causes for this weakness: *Attachment to the world; *Fear of Death.

   Make a resolve that you will not rest in peace until you have eliminated these two weaknesses from your own self as well as from the general body of the Muslims. The Holy Prophet [S.A.W.] observed:

   "My Ummah will pass through a time when other nations, considering you an easy prey, will fall upon you just as the hungry rush towards food. Someone asked: "O Prophet [S.A.W.]: Will our number diminish encouraging other nations to make an assault to devour us?" The Holy Prophet [S.A.W.] observed: "No, you will not then be less in number but will render yourself weightless like straws that float helplessly in the flood water. Your enemies will no longer fear you and your hearts will be stricken with cowardice." At this stage, a man enquired: "O Prophet [S.A.W.]! What will be the cause of such cowardice?" The Holy Prophet [S.A.W.] observed: "There will be two causes: (a) You will start loving the world and; (b)You will feel allergic to death and hate the very idea of it."
   (Abu Dawud)

3. Purge your society of sensuality, frivolity, rule of women, and wickedness. Make your collective strength impregnable and use it to eradicate evil and mischief. Make a determined effort to inculcate and promote bravery, zest and courage in each and every individual of your fraternity. The Holy Prophet [S.A.W.] has affirmed:

> "When your rulers are righteous, and the rich among you are generous and large-hearted and when your collective affairs are decided by mutual consultation, then the surface of the earth is better for you than its belly (life is worth living). But when your rulers are persons of wicked character and the rich in your society are lovers of wealth (miserly), and when your affairs are determined by your women, then the belly of the earth is better for you than its surface.
>
> *(Tirmidhi)*

4. Never fail to support the right even under the most adverse circumstances. To give away one's life in support of right is far better than to lead a godless and ignominious existence. Do not shrink from upholding the truth in the severest of trials and in the face of the greatest threat. Respond to the threat of death with a smile and welcome the chance of attaining martyrdom with zest and eagerness. The Holy Prophet [S.A.W.] has said:

   > "The wheel of Islam is on the move, beware you must turn towards the direction given by the Holy Qur'an. Be vigilant! The Qur'an and the political power will shortly part company. Beware lest you should forsake the Qur'an. In the times to come there will be rulers who will impose their will on you. If you obey them, they will lead you astray from the path of righteousness. And if you rebel against them, they will put you to death." A Companion [R.A.A.] submitted: "What should we do then, O Prophet [S.A.W.]!" The Holy Prophet [S.A.W.] replied: "Do what the companions of Jesus [A.S.] did. They were cut through with saws and hanged on the cross. It is far better to give one's life obeying the commandments of Allah than to live a life of disobedience to the Almighty."

5. Strive constantly against those evils of the society which produce an atmosphere of fear and panic in the people and lead to poverty, famine and violence reducing the whole

nation to a miserable and helpless lot suffering the oppressions and tyranny of their enemies.

Hazrat 'Abdullah b. 'Abbas [R.A.A.] remarks: "Wherever dishonesty becomes the order of the day, the people lose heart and courage and are afraid of their enemies, and wherever adultery becomes common, the people are destined to perish. Whenever people start cheating in weights and measures, they certainly face famine and starvation and where justice is denied blood is inevitably to be shed there. And nation which commits breach of promise is doomed to become the slave of its enemy." *(Mishkat)*

6. When you are assailed by the dread of the foes, say this prayer:

   "O Allah! Behold, we place Thee in front of them and seek refuge in Thee from their mischiefs."

   (Abu-Dawud, Nasai, Hisn Hasien)

7. When you are surrounded by the enemy, say this prayer: "Allah! Do safeguard our honour and respect, and bless us with peace in this state of fear and harassment."

   (Ahmad, Hisn Hasien)

8. On seeing the windstorm rising or a cloud overcasting the sky, you should feel apprehension and fear. Hazrat 'Aisha' [R.A.A.] reports that "I never beheld the Holy Prophet [S.A.W.] breaking into laughter in such a manner as to make his sacred mouth wide open. In moments of joy, a thin smile used to play on his august face. When a windstorm arose or a cloud darkened the sky, he [S.A.W.] used to feel apprehension, he alternately stood up or sat down and this mood lasted until the clouds had burst into rain. I submitted: "O Prophet [S.A.W.]! I see that other people rejoice when they see a cloud and look forward to raining with joyous hope, yet I see that your holy face shows feelings of heaviness and anxiety on watching a cloud." Thereupon the Holy Prophet [S.A.W.] observed: "Aisha, how can I avoid the apprehension that this cloud will not bring down a calamity, when I have the precedent before me that the nation of 'Ad were visited with a

calamitous windstorm. On beholding this cloud, the people of 'Ad had said: This cloud will pour rain over us." (Bukhari, Muslim). Say this prayer when you see a cloud or a windstorm rising.

If the windstorm fills the horizon with deep darkness say:

I seek refuge with the Lord of the Dawn and I seek refuge with the Lord of Men (Surah 113: 114)

Hazrat 'Aisha [R.A.A.] relates:

> "Whenever the Holy Prophet [S.A.W.] beheld the windstorm rising, he used to say the following prayer:
>
> "O Allah! Behold, I beg of Thee the good of this (wind) and the good of that which is therein, and the good of that which hath been sent therewith. And I seek refuge in Thee from the evil thereof and the evil of that which is therein and the evil of that which hath been sent therewith." *(Muslim, Tirmidhi)*

9. When excessive rain threatens loss and destruction, say this prayer: "O Allah! let there be downpour in our suburb; but not on us. Let the rain fall on hillocks, in the thickets on the mountains, rivers, and on the hot beds of plantations." *(Bukhari, Muslim)*

10. On hearing the roar of clouds and the thunderbolt, stop conversation and begin reciting the following verse of the Holy Qur'an:

> "And the thunder (of the clouds) hymneth His praise and (so do) the Angels for awe of Him." *(Al-Ra'd: 13)*

Hazrat 'Abdullah ibn Zubair [R.A.A.] on hearing the thunderbolt used to stop talking and recited the same verse. *(Al-Adab al-Mufrad)*

Hazrat Kab [R.A.A.] states that any one who recites this verse three times on hearing the thunderbolt will remain safe from its danger. *(Tirmidhi)*

The Holy Prophet [S.A.W.] on hearing the roar of the clouds and the thunderbolt used to say this prayer:

"O Allah! Slay us not with Thy wrath and destroy us not with Thy punishment but take us unto Thy protection."

(Al-Adab-al-Mufrad)

11. When fire breaks out, make energetic efforts to extinguish it and continue to say:

    (Allah is Great, Allah is Great). The Holy Prophet has observed: "When you see a fire blazing out say: "Allah-u-Akbar" (Allah is Great). 'Takbir' Glorification of Allah extinguisfies the fire."

12. When you are seized with fear and panic, say this prayer. Godwilling fear will vanish and you will attain peace of mind. Hazrat Bra' b.'Azib reports: "A person once complained to the Holy Prophet [S.A.W.] "I suffer from panic all the time." The Holy Prophet [S.A.W.] enjoined upon him to say the following prayer. He recited this prayer frequently and Allah freed his heart from panic.

    "Pure and Supreme is the Lord, the Real Sovereign, Faultless. Oh Creator of Angels and Jibrail! Your Power and Awe reigns over the Heavens and Earth."

1. You must celebrate occasions of joy in a befitting manner. Rejoicing is a demand of human instincts and a natural urge. Religion gives due importance to the satisfaction of natural instincts and permits their fulfilment subject to some useful restraints and conditions. Religion disapproves of marring the attractiveness of your personality by assuming artificial postures of dignity, unnecessary sombreness, and constant moroseness. Religion allows you to be joyous on all lawful such occasions and enjoins upon you to keep your spirits high and live with zest. It is misunderstanding the religion if it is thought that giving expression to joy and to rejoice on lawful occasions does not conform with the dignity of religion.

   If Allah grants you the favour of performing some religious duty; you or one of your relations attains high honour in learning and excellence; Allah blesses you with prosperity, wealth or some other bounty; you return safe from a long journey or any of your relations comes back from his travels to distant parts; you receive a visit from an honourable guest; a marriage comes off or the birth of a child takes place in your home; you receive report of the health and well-being of a near relative or the happy news of the victory or glorious achievement of the people of Islam; or on festivals - it is your natural right to celebrate these occasions with rejoicing. Islam not only allows the holding of festivities, but regards this act as in perfect harmony with the spirit of religion.

Hazrat Ka'b ibn Malik [R.A.A.] relates: "When Allah had accepted my prayer for forgiveness and I received the glad tidings of it, I at once went to the Holy Prophet [S.A.W.] offered my salam. At that moment, the holy face of the Prophet [S.A.W.] was radiant with joy. Whenever the Holy Prophet [S.A.W.] attained some happiness, his face would glow like the radiance of moon and we used to take the brightness and radiance of his face as index of exceedingly joyous feelings in him, [S.A.W.]. *(Riyad-us Salihin)*

2. Feel free to do arrangements to celebrate a festival and join the festivities without inhibitions. On arrival at Madinah, the Holy Prophet [S.A.W.] observed:

 "You used to celebrate festivities on two days during a year. Allah has now blessed you with two better days, i.e., *'Id-al-Fitr* and *'Id-al-Adha."* Therefore you should celebrate these two festivals of the year with great happiness and rejoicing and arrange reunions and indulge in recreation in joyous mood and give vent to your feelings of happiness in a natural manner. It is because of this injunction of the Holy Prophet [S.A.W.] that fasting is forbidden on the occasions of these two festivals.

 The Holy Prophet [S.A.W.] observed:

 "These two days are meant for feasting, celebration of joy in union with other people and to remember Allah." *(Sharah M'aani-ul-Athar)*

 On the day of 'Id, be neat and clean and take a bath, put on the best dress according to your means, use perfume, eat good food and let the children enjoy themselves with proper means of recreation and games and permit to observe fun freely and without any hindrance.

Hazrat 'Aisha [R.A.A.] relates:

> "It was the 'Id day and some slave girls were singing the verses which the Ansar had composed about the battle of Bu'ath.[6] While the girls were thus engaged in singing, Hazrat Abu Bakr [R.A.A.] came and exclaimed in astonishment: "How strange! Singing in the household of the Prophet [S.A.W.]!" The Holy Prophet [S.A.W.] answered: "Abu Bakr, never mind. Each nation has a festival day and today we celebrate our 'Id."

Once on 'Id day some negro acrobats were giving a demonstration of their skill. The Holy Prophet [S.A.W.] himself watched these exercises and let 'Aisha [R.A.A.] also see them from behind his back. The Holy Prophet [S.A.W.] cheered also. When 'Aisha [R.A.A.] grew weary, the Holy Prophet [S.A.W.] permitted her to depart. *(Bukhari)*

3. Observe the injunctions and mores of Islam in your rejoicings. Offer thanks to your Benefactor and prostrate before Him in gratitude. In the excitement of your joy, do not perform any act nor adopt any attitude which does not conform to the spirit of Islam or is contrary to Islamic manners and injunctions. You must express your joyous sentiments, but observe the rule of moderation and do not let your expression of happiness take the better of the duty of obedience, devotion and humility and turn into a display of haughtiness and pride. The Holy Qur'an directs:

> "And exult not because of that which hath been given. Allah loveth not all prideful boasters." *(57: 23)*

Do not be so intoxicated by happiness as to forget Allah. The supreme happiness of the pious is to remember the Best of happiness all the more and offer prostration before Him in gratitude and acknowledge by action and speech the Benefactions, Greatness and the Glory of Allah.

After observing fasts during the month of Ramadan and securing the blessings of reciting the Holy Qur'an and saying 'Taravih' prayers during the month, when you sight the 'Id-moon, your happiness knows no bounds. On realising that you have been successful in carrying out the injunctions of Allah by His Grace, you at once give away the share of your poor and needy brethren out of your wealth so as to make amends for any negligence in worship or error in discharging the duty of Devotion to Allah and also to enable the poor people to participate with others in the joys of the 'Id. In acknowledgement of this favour of Allah, you express your befitting sentiments of joy by offering two prayers of thanksgiving to Allah and on the day of *'Id-al-Adha,* you commemorate the great and unique sacrifice of Hazrat Ibraheem and Hazrat Isma'il [A.S.] and thus finding your own heart filled with the eagerness to make sacrifice when need arises you offer prostration to Allah in gratitude. And then the hymns of 'Praise be to Allah', *'Takbir* and 'Thanksgiving' resound through every community and are heard in all streets, lanes and roads. And when on 'Id days you eat well and put on your best clothes and celebrate in lawful fashion according to the injunctions of the *Shari'ah* all these activities of yours are recorded as submission to and acknowledgement of the authority of Allah.

4. Invite others to join your celebrations and share your joy and similarly participate in the rejoicing of others to enhance their feelings of happiness. Exchange messages of felicitation on occasions of joy.

When the repentance of Hazrat Ka'b-b-Malik [R.A.A.] was accepted by Allah and the Muslims got news of it they came in crowds to offer congratulations to Hazrat Ka'b [R.A.A.]. They expressed their unbounded joy. Hazrat Ka'b was so deeply moved by the felicitation and expressions of rejoicing displayed by Hazrat Talha [R.A.A.] that it remained fresh in his memory all through the rest of his life. In his old age Hazrat Ka'b [R.A.A.] related the case of his trial and repentance to his son 'Abdullah and especially mentioned about Hazrat Talha's [R.A.A.] expressions of joy. He remarked: "I can never forget Talha's manner of congratulating me and his feelings of joy."

The Holy Prophet [S.A.W.] on conveying to Ka'b [R.A.A.] the glad tidings of the acceptance of his repentance expressed his personal feelings of great happiness and observed: "Ka'b, this is the happiest day of the life!" *(Riyad-us-Salihin)*

On occasions of marriage or birth of a child or on similar events of joy in the homes of other people, join in their celebrations and felicitate them on the happy occasion.

Hazrat Abu Huraira [R.A.A.] reports that the Holy Prophet [S.A.W.] used to congratulate the newly-wedded in these words:

> "May Allah keep you in prosperity and confer His blessings upon both of you and may He grant you the favour of living together in perfect harmony."
>
> *(Tirmidhi)*

On one occasion Hazrat Husain [R.A.A.] instructed someone to felicitate others on the birth of a child in the following manner:

> "May Allah grant you grace in this gift. May Allah grant you the favour of offering gratitude to Him. May Allah develop this child into a full-blended youth and raise him submissive to you."

5. When a near relative or an acquaintance return from a long journey, go and welcome him and express your feelings of joy on his safe return and successful conclusion of his mission. If he holds a function to celebrate the happy occasion of his safe return from the journey, go and join the party. On the other hand, when you return home safe from your travels and arrange a function to celebrate the occasion, invite your near relatives to the party. However, you must avoid unnecessary expense or ostentatious and lavish display. Do not incur expenditure which is beyond your means. When

the Holy Prophet [S.A.W.] returned from the battle of Tabuk, the Muslim men and children had gone up to Thaniyyatul-Wada ' to receive him [S.A.W.]. *(Abu Dawud)*

When the Holy Prophet [S.A.W.] migrated from Makkah and reached Madinah and prepared to enter the city from the southern side, the Muslim men, women, boys and girls came out of their homes to greet him [S.A.W.]. The small girls of the Ansar were singing this happy song:

> "Today, the moon arose upon us from the southern hill, Thaniyyatul Wada'.[7] It is our duty to offer thanks for the call and teaching of the Apostle who guided us towards Allah. O Prophet! You have been sent among us, you have brought a religion that we will bear allegiance to it."

Once on his return to Madinah from a journey, the Holy Prophet [S.A.W.] slaughtered a camel and a cow and arranged a feast for the people. *(Abu Dawud)*

6. Celebrate the occasions of marriage with joy and happiness and invite your relatives and friends to participate in the celebration of the happy event. The Holy Prophet [S.A.W.] permitted singing and playing of music on weddings. This injunction is meant to serve a two-fold purpose: the expression of the feelings of joy and the public announcement of the news of wedding.

   Hazrat 'Aisha [R.A.A.] married one of her female relations to a man from the Ansar. At the time of the departure of the bride, the Holy Prophet [S.A.W.] observed: "Why didn't these people send a slave-girl with her to play duff and sing some songs on the way." *(Bukhari)*

   On the occasion of the wedding of Hazrat Rabi' bint Mu'awwadh [R.A.A.] some girls were sitting with her and playing on duff. They were singing some verses in praise of their fathers who had attained martyrdom in the battle of Badr. One of the girls recited this line: "And there is a prophet in our midst who knows what is to happen tomorrow." On hearing this, the Holy Prophet [S.A.W.] observed: "Leave this bit out and sing those verses which you were singing earlier." *(Bukhari)*

7. On the happy occasions of wedding, arrange a feast for your relatives and friends according to your position and means. The Holy Prophet [S.A.W.] established the precedent of arranging 'Walima' feasts on his own marriages and enjoined upon others to follow the same practice. The Holy Prophet [S.A.W.] observed: "If nothing else, slaughter a goat and serve its meat to guests." *(Bukhari)*

   If for some reason you cannot attend a wedding party, do send a message of congratulations. The practice of exchanging gifts on nuptials, weddings and on similar occasions of joy, renews and deepens the relationship and augments love and lends warmth to it. Nonetheless be careful to send gifts of the value which your means can afford and avoid ostentatious display.

5

Routine of Life

How to Dress

Appropriate Dress : The dress you put on should meet the requirements of modesty, self-respect and moderation. It should protect your body and cover concealable parts adequately, and may reflect your culture, elegance and beauty. This has been enjoined in the Holy Quran in these words:

> "O the offsprings of Adam, We have bestowed upon you garments to cover such parts of your body which need covering, and also to protect them (from vagaries of the seasons) and which may also serve as a piece of decoration." (7 : 26)

Purpose of Clothing : The purpose of clothes is, no doubt, the garnishment and gracefulness of one's person and to protect him from the effects of the seasons. But the foremost use of the clothes is to provide covering for those parts of human body which have to be covered. The tendency to be modest and not to exhibit one's private parts is inherent in human nature. When Adam and Eve were stripped off their heavenly dress, they at once covered their bodies with the leaves of the tree of the paradise. Therefore while, choosing a dress one should keep these requirements in mind. Also one should not use an apparel which may make a fool of him.

Clothes a gift from Allah : While putting on your dress you must bear in mind that clothings are a gift from Allah, which have been bestowed upon humans only and no other creatures. Therefore, you must express your gratitude to Allah for this favour.

Clean and Pious Dress : **The best dress is to be pious.** The dress of piety also means inner cleanliness or sanctity of soul and apparent saintliness. This means that one should wear such clothes which may conform to the principles laid down by the Sharia, and which may not reflect ostentation and false pride. The dress should present the person as devout and God-fearing person.

Thank Allah for New Dress : When you put on a new dress express your pleasure and gratitude to Allah for this favour. Imbued with thankfulness recite the following prayer which the Holy Prophet (S.A.W.) used to recite while putting on a new apparel:

> "Allah! All praise belongs to Thee, Thou hast given me this dress. I pray for the goodness of this dress and the goodness for which it has been made. I seek Thy refuge against all evils that may be in this dress and from the evils for which it has been made."

Giving Old Clothes to the Poor: Hazrat Umar (R.A.A.) reports that the holy Prophet (S.A.W.) had said:

> "A person who is putting on a new dress may present his old clothes to a poor person, if he can afford to do so; and he should recite this prayer while putting on a new dress.
>
> "All praise and eulogy is due to Allah, who has bestowed upon me this apparel, without any ability or power on my part." Anybody who recites this prayer while putting on new clothes will remain under the protection of Allah in this world as well as in the next world.

Start from the Right Side : While putting on clothes be careful to start from the right side. That is, if you have to wear a shirt, kurta, sherwani or coat, insert your right hand into the right sleeve first and then the left hand into the left sleeve. In the same way when wearing a pyjama or pant, put your right foot first and the left foot afterwards. The Holy Prophet (S.A.W.) used to wear clothes in this way. While putting on shoes he (S.A.W.) would put his right foot into the right shoe first and then left foot into the left shoe; and while disengaging his feet, he would take away his left foot first and then the right foot from his shoes.

Precaution Against Insect Bites : While putting on your clothes, shoes and socks you must take care to" thoroughly shake them, lest some venomous insect or worm may be hidden in them and may cause you harm.

White Dress : If possible, use white clothes. This colour is good for males. The Holy Prophet (S.A.W.) has said, "Wear white clothes. This is the best. Only white clothes should be worn in lifetime, and in a white shroud one should be buried."

Holy Prophet (S.A.W.) Preferring White Dress: According to Sahih Bukhari, the Holy Prophet (S.A.W.) used to wear clothes of white colour. He (S.A.W.) not only himself used such clothes, he (S.A.W.) exhorted the male members of his ummah to use them.

Avoiding Arrogance through Show of Dress : You should not use pyjamas, trousers, etc., which have long sleeves and touch the ground. The Holy Prophet (S.A.W.) has condemned such persons who, in order to show off their arrogance and haughtiness, deliberately allow their trousers or gramments covering their lower body, to fall below their ankles and touch the ground. He (S.A.W.) has declared them as "unsuccessful and unfortunate and deserving severe punishment," He (S.A.W.) further holds "There are three kinds of persons, with whom Allah will neither talk nor look at them, and also will not purify them and allow them to enter the paradise on the Day of Judgment. They will rather get a severe punishment."

Hazrat Abuzar Ghifari, a companion of the Holy Prophet (S.A.W.) sought a clarification from the Holy Prophet (S.A.W.) on this point, who elucidated by saying:

> "Firstly that person who allows the garment of his lower body to fall and touch the ground as an indication of pride and arrogance; secondly the man

who recounts the favours done by him to somebody; and thirdly the person who tries to develop or flourish his business on falsehood." (*Muslim*)

Arrogant Persons not to Enter Paradise : Abdullah bin Mas'ud quoted the Messenger of Allaḥ (S.A.W.) as having said "Whoever has a grain of vanity, will not enter paradise. A person said that every one desires that he should have good clothes, fine shoes, etc. The Prophet of Allah (S.A.W.) replied, "Allah is beautiful and likes beauty. Putting on fine clothes is not pride. In reality arrognace is disregard of truth and contempt for others."

(*Muslim*)

Following the Holy Prophet in Dress : Hazrat Obed Ibn Khalid recounting an incident says: "Once I was passing through a street in Madina when I heard a voice from my rear, saying "Raise your Tahmad (sheet for the lower part of body) - this helps a man to protect himself from all visible and invisible impurities. I turned back and saw it was the Holy Prophet (S.A.W.). I said "O Messenger of Allah! It is an ordinary piece of cloth which I have put on. How can it reflect arrogance and pride?' The Holy Prophet (S.A.W.) remarked: "Is it not your duty to follow me?" On hearing this I at once glanced on the Tahmad he was wearing then I noticed that his garment did not go beyond half the length of his calf."

Raising the Ends of Trousers : The instruction of the Messenger of Allah (S.A.W.) for raising the pyjama, pant or loin cloth up to your ankle-joints to guard you from all internal and external impurities, is very significant. It means that when the cloth trails on the ground, it will be spoiled by the filth lying on the ground. This is against the etiquette of cleanliness. purity and decency. Moreover, this is an indication of pride and arrogance which is internal impurity. Besides. whatever is commanded by Allah's Messenger (S.A.W.) is to be obeyed because in him we have indeed "the best pattern (of conduct)." (*Al Quran*, 33: 21)

Punishment : On another occasion the Prophet of Allah (S.A.W.) had announced a very horrible punishment for this dereliction. He has said:

"The tahmad (piece of cloth round the waist) of the believer should be up to half of his shin. There is no harm if it is upto his ankle joint. But whatever portion trails below the ankle joint that cloth will burn in the (Hell) Fire. Anybody who keeps his cloth trailing on the ground exhibiting pride and arrogance, Allah will never cast His sight on him on the Day of Resurrection." *(Abu Dawood)*

Prohibition for Silken Cloth : Do not wear silken clothes as these are meant for women. The Messenger of Allah (S.A.W.) has strictly prohibited the use of womanly dress by males and thereby to assume a womanly appearance and vice-versa. Hazrat Umar (R.A.A.) narrated that the Messenger of Allah (S.A.W.) has said: "Do not put on silken dress: one who (man) wears it, will not be able to wear the same in the Hereafter." *(Bukhari and Muslim)*

Proper Use : Once Ukaider, the Ruler of Dommah sent a piece of silken cloth to the Holy Prophet (S.A.W.) as a gift. The Holy Prophet (S.A.W.) asked Hazrat Ali to cut this silk cloth into short pieces and distribute them among the following three ladies who bear the name of Fatimah. *(Muslim)*

1. Fatimah Zahraa, daughter of the Messenger of Allah (S.A.W.) and wife of Hazrat Ali. 2. Fatimah bint-e-Asad severed mother of Hazrat Ali. 3. Fatimah, daughter of Hazrat Hamzah, uncle of the Prophet of Allah (S.A.W.).

It is clear from the above, that the Prophet of Allah (S.A.W.) liked only the women-folk wearing silken clothes. For this reason, the Prophet of Allah (S.A.W.) directed that the shawls should he made of the silken cloth, else that same could have been utilized for other purposes.

Dress for Women : Females should put on neither such fine clothes through which their bodies may be visible, nor their dress be so tight as to make their bodies more attractive and charming and as such they may appear naked even though dressed. The Holy Prophet (S.A.W.) has cautioned women of doubtful character of their dreadful end in these words: "Such coquettes are doomed to hell who look naked even though they appear to be dressed: they entice others, and are enticed by others; their heads are filled with pride and are crooked like the humps of Bukhti camels. These women will not enter paradise nor will have even a smell of the same, although the fragrance of the paradise comes from afar."

(Riaz-us-Sali-heen)

Once Hazrat Asma (R.A.A.) appeared before the Prophet of Allah (S.A.W.) dressed in fine clothes; but he (the Prophet) turned his face from her and said, "O Asma! It is not permissible for a woman, after having attained the age of puberty, that any part of her body except her face and hands could be seen (while she is out among strangers)."

Proper Way : Pyjama, pant or cloth worn round the waist should not be used in a way as to expose some part of the body.

The Prophet of Allah (S.A.W.) has said:

> "Do not walk wearing a shoe in one foot only, while wearing the cloth round the waist, do not sit in a posture that may expose some part of your body; and do not wrap your shawl in a manner that you may not be able to move your hands in prayers or daily work, etc., nor lie down flat on the back, keeping your foot on each other."

Separate Dress for Men and Women : The males and, females should not adopt opposite sex's style in dress or manners. The Prophet of Allah (S.A.W.) has said:

> "Allah has cursed those men who like to adopt womanly ways and also cursed the women who imitate the ways and manners of men." *(Bukhari)*

Once a person reported to Hazrat Ayesha (R.A.A.), "There is a woman who wears the shoes meant for men." She said, "The Prophet of Allah (S.A.W.) has cursed such women, who try to imitate men."

Ladies should be very particular to cover their heads and bosoms with a shawl. It should not be so fine as to allow their hair to be seen. The purpose of shawl is to cover their beauty spots and decorations. In the Holy Quran, Almighty Allah says, "To draw their veils over their bosoms."(24 : 31)

Once a piece of Egyptian soft muslin was presented to the Prophet of Allah (S.A.W.), who gave away some of its portion to Dehya Kalbee (R.A.A.) and said:

> "Out of this make a long shirt for yourself and give the other part to your wife for her shawl, but ask her to have another cloth beneath it so that the form of her body may not be visible." *(Abu Dawood)*

Keep in view the clear directive of the Holy Quran and Sunnah and the purpose of the Divine commandments and do not make a fun of these orders by putting a small piece of cloth round your neck.

Hazrat Ayesha (R.A.A.) is reported to have said:

> "When this commandment was revealed, the women-folk made their shawls (sheets of cloth for coverage of the body) from coarse cloth and abandoned finer varieties." *(Abu Dawood)*

Dress According to Status : Always dress yourself according to your means and status. The dress should be neither ostentatious as if you are running down others by an extravagant show of your wealth nor it should be beyond your means to make you a spendthrift; or put on such dress that may make you appear indigent, needy and poor. Always dress yourself in a proper, clean and neat manner, of course, according to your position and capacity.

Ungratefulness to Allah : According to some, it is a sign of ungratefulness to put on old, tattered and worn-out clothes: over and above this, they consider those persons who use neat, decent and proper clothing as running after the world and ostentatious. This is absolutely an erroneous view of religion and piety.

Father of Abul-Ahwas states that once he presented himself before the Prophet of Allah (S.A.W.) with ordinary clothings. The Holy Prophet (S.A.W.) asked him, "Have you sufficient means?"

He replied, "Yes sir." The Holy Prophet (S.A.W.) enquired, "What type of riches have you?" He replied, "Allah the Exalted has given me all kinds of wealth-camels, cows, goats, horses and slaves." The Prophet of Allah (S.A.W.) said: "Since Allah has graced you by granting you wealth, your physical body should reflect the effects of His bounty and benevolence."

Meaning thereby that when Allah has given His bounties to you, then why you assume the role of the indent and the down-trodden. This is clear ingratitude to Allah, the Almighty.

Allah Likes Fine Taste : Once a person said to the Prophet of Allah (S.A.W.) "O Messenger of Allah, I wish that my dress should be decent, neat and clean; hair of the head properly oiled; my shoes be fine and shining," and in this way he named many other articles. He even desired that his whip might also be extremely nice. The Prophet of Allah (S.A.W.) heard his talk and said: "All these are approved and Allah likes this fine taste."

(Mustadrak Hakim)

Full Dress in the Mosque : According to Hazrat Abdullah bin Umar (R.A.A.), the Messenger of Allah (S.A.W.) has said,

> "Put on both the pieces of clothes during prayers (adorn yourself with full dress while praying) as it is most befitting that His servant should appear before Him well dressed and chic." *(Mishkat)*

Good Taste : Follow the proper etiquette in the use of clothes and decorum in dressing. To go about with open skirt of the shirt, uneven buttons or keep one leg of the trousers up and the other down, wearing shoe in a foot and keeping the other bare, or having dishevelled hair, are all against etiquette, and good taste.

Well-Dressed Hair and Beard : Once the Prophet of Allah (S.A.W.) was sitting in the mosque, when a man with twisted hair and knotted beard came. The Holy Prophet of Allah (S.A.W.) rasied his hand meaning thereby that he should go and get his hair and beard trimmed. The person went away and returned having his hair and beard duly put in order. Thereupon the Prophet of Allah (S.A.W.) said, "Is this adornment and orderliness not better than the disarranged and twisted hair, which gives one the appearance of a devil." *(Mishkat)*

Improper for Men : Red, bright, and dark-coloured and glittering clothes, black or saffron-coloured dress should be shunned by men. 'These are meant for females only, and that too within limits. To wear long, black robes and yellow costumes trailing the ground, is to emphasise one's superiority over others and is a sure sign of arrogance and conceit. So also do not use such unusual clothes which may make you the laughing-stock of the people.

Simple and Appropriate : Always use simple, civilized and dignified dress, and be always moderate in expenses on your garments. Avoid elegance and delicacy in dress. The Messenger of Allah (S.A.W.) has said: "Be away from ease and comfort because the pleasure-loving persons are not the beloved ones of Allah. *(Miskhat)*

Simplicity in spite of Means : The Prophet of Allah (S.A.W.) also said: "Anybody who adopted simplicity in his dress in spite of his means and affluence, only on account of humility and modesty, Allah Almighty will adorn him with the raiment (clothing) of nobility and wisdom." *(Abu Dawood)*

Sign of Faith : One day, when the companions of the Holy Prophet (S.A.W.) were talking about the affairs relating to this world, the Holy Prophet of Allah (S.A.W.) remarked, "Simplicity in dress is one of the signs of faith, (Iman) in Allah." *(Abu Dawood)*

Reward for Providing Clothes : To express thanks to Allah for this bounty of (decent) clothings bestowed upon you, you should also clothe the indigent and needy persons who have nothing to put on. The Messenger of Allah (S.A.W.) said,

> "A Muslim who clothes another Muslim, shall be clothed with a green heavenly dress by Allah on the Day of Judgment." *(Abu Dawood)*

The Holy Prophet (S.A.W.) has also said:

> "So long as the clothes given by a Muslim to his fellow Muslim brother remain on his body, Allah will keep in safety the provider of the same." *(Tirmizi)*

Social Equality : Provide clothing for the servants, serving you day and night, according to your status. The Prophet of Allah (S.A.W.) has said, "Slaves are like your brothers, whom Allah has placed under your control. It is your responsibility to give them the food you eat, the clothes you wear, and make them work according to their capacity. If a slave is not able to do his master's work, the master should give him a helping hand."

(Bukhari and Muslim)

What to Eat ?

Etiquette of Eating and Drinking : Be punctual and regular in taking meals. Avoid gluttony and incessant eating. Eat only when you feel hungry and stop eating when some hunger is still left; and under no circumstances do not resort to overeating. The Holy Prophet (S.A.W.) has said:

> "A believer eats in one intestine and a non-believer, in seven intestines." *(Tirmizi)*

Healthy Stomach : Good health depends upon the health of the stomach. Overeating harms the digestive system. The Holy Prophet (S.A.W.) has elucidated this point as follows:

> "The stomach is like a reservoir for the body. The veins and arteries receive their supply of life—blood from this reservoir. As such, if the stomach is in good health, they will receive healthy material and if the stomach is unhealthy, they will circulate unhealthy material."
>
> *(Behaqui)*

Under-eating Encouraged : Encouraging under-eating the Holy Prophet (S.A.W.) has also said.

"A meal of one person should suffice for two."

Prefer Simple Fare : Always have a simple fare; use bread made from flour containing roughage. Avoid food containing too much spices, and unnecessarily very tasty dishes. The food should be easily digestible which may furnish energy and health to the body. Don't go after very much savoury meals.

Unsieved Flour Preferred : Our Holy Prophet (S.A.W.) preferred bread made of unsieved flour. He did not relish a thin loaf or one prepared from fine flour. Similarly, he did not like very hot and teaming food and waited till it got cool. About hot food, he often said, "Allah has not given us fire to eat," and occasionally he would say:

"There is nothing divine in a hot food."

He was fond of meat specially forelegs, pieces of neck or collar and back. In fact, meat is an essential diet for supplying energy to the body, and developing the spirit of a chivalrous Mujahid. And a Muslim should always keep his heart full of the spirit of a Mujahid.

A meal should be taken in a serene and peaceful mood; each morsel should be thoroughly chewed. Refrain from eating while you are in a state of gloom, anger or agitation. Food eaten in a placid and unperturbed state is wholesome, and that taken under some strain and stress of sorrow, concern and disturbance adversely affects the belly, and does not supply sufficient energy to the body. As such do not sit on the dining table while in a state of gloom or dullness. Exhibition of too much joviality causing loud giggle sometimes proves fatal.

One should enjoy ones meal cheerfully and may cut jokes moderately. Do not forget to thank Allah for gifts and favours bestowed by Him. If and when you feel sick, be very careful about your diet.

Be Careful in Eating While Sick : Hazrat Umm Munzar says that once the Holy Prophet (S.A.W.) visited her house. This was the time when date trees had borne fruits and bunches of dates were hanging from the trees. The Holy Prophet (S.A.W.) plucked some fruits and started eating. Hazrat Ali, who accompanied him, followed suit and also started eating dates. Since he had recently recovered from sickness, the Holy Prophet (S.A.W.) forbade him from eating dates as the same would have harmed him. Hazrat Ali accordingly stopped eating dates. The Holy Prophet (S.A.W.), however, continued eating.

In the meanwhile, the distinguished hostess prepared a fare with barley and beet root for the August visitors. The Holy Prophet (S.A.W.) this time invited Hazrat Ali to partake of this preparation saying, "Ali, take this, it will do you good." (*Shamail Tirmizi*)

Entertaining a Guest : Whenever the Holy Prophet (S.A.W.) had a guest at meals with him, he (S.A.W.)' used to be very solicitous and called upon the guest to eat to his fill, and when the latter had eaten to his satisfaction, the Holy Prophet (S.A.W.) then only would refrain from pressing him to eat. It was the Practice of the Holy Prophet (S.A.W.) that he used to talk with those who joined him (S.A.W.) in eating, in a happy and cordial atmosphere.

Siesta after Mid-day Meal and Stroll after Dinner : After mid-day meal, take a short nap; and after the evening dinner, go for a walk. Do not take up any hard physical or mental work after meals. According to an Arabic Hakim, 'Take rest after mid-day meal and go out for a stroll after evening meal."

Wash your hands before starting to eat. The norms of personal hygiene and cleanliness requires this. It is natural that one should be mentally satisfied about the cleanliness of his hands which are going to touch the food-stuff.

Begin eating with the recitation of

Bis-mil-laa-h ir-rah-maa-nir-ra-ha-heem.

i.e. in the Name of Allah, the Most Compassionate the Most Merciful.

If we forget to recite it, we may recite the following words as soon as we are reminded of it.

Bis-mil-laahe Awwa-lo-hoo wa aa-khiro-hoo,

i.e. in the name of Allah from beginning to end.

Remember that the meals upon which the name of Allah has not been recited, turns into devil's food.

Do not take recourse to a prop while eating; sit in an unassuming style with your knees pointing outwards, or with one foot up and the other down, because the Prophet of Allah (S.A.W.) sat like this while eating. However, if you have to sit on a chair, sit straight without leaning while eating.

Always eat with your right hand, using the left hand only when necessary.

Eat with three fingers only : if necessary, use fourth one, except the small one. Do not soak the fingers to their roots in the soup etc.

Moderate Size Morsels : Do not take too big or too small morsels; take the next morsel, only after swallowing the first one.

Do not wipe your fingers with loaves. This is a very dirty habit.

Eat from the corner of the plate facing you neither eat from the middle of the plate nor from the other side.

Wash the Fallen Morsel : If a morsel falls down, clean it, if necessary by washing, and then eat it.

Eat collectively along with others, as eating in company generates mutual love and affection and mates the meat enough and to spare.

Never find fault with the food; if you do not relish, leave it.

Avoid laughing very loudly and too much talking at meals.

Eat and drink in a sitting posture : Fruits, desserts and drinks can be taken in a standing position, if necessary.

Clean the Plate : Drink off the left-over from the plate, if liquid; and clean the same with a finger, if thick, and lick the finger.

Do not blow your breath on the food as the breath coming out of your mouth is putrifying and poisonous.

Take water in three breaks as it will slake the thirst and is more convenient to the person drinking water; whereas gulping it off in one breath may lead to complications.

Consideration for the Company While Eating : While eating in company, be considerate to both slow eaters and fast eaters. Make allowance for both and leave the dinner-table along with others.

Etiquette While Eating in Company : Do not smell the food unnecessarily. It is a bad habit. Neither open your mouth too often during the course of eating so as to make the chewing matter visible; nor put your finger frequently in your mouth for picking the teeth as it is repulsive to other participants of the meal.

Don't Go Uninvited, but Do Go if Invited : The Holy Prophet (S.A.W.) has said: "Anyone who has been invited but has rejected the invitation has transgressed the commands of Allah and His Prophet. He who has gone to a party uninvited, has in reality entered as a thief and come out like a robber (from there)."

Take one Piece at a Time : While eating fruit, do not pick up two slices together nor pick up two fruit pieces at a time.

Do not drink water directly from the tap or, faucet, waterspout or a long-necked vessel. Take water in a widemouth utensil or tumbler, so that it may be visible and no impurities may slip into the mouth.

Having finished the food, recite the, following prayer:

> "All praise for Allah who has fed us, given us drinks, and has made us Muslims."

Bed Time and Wake-up Time

Children to be Called in Before Nightfall : When the sun is setting, the children should be asked to come in and they may not be allowed to remain outside. However, they may go out, if necessary, only after a part of night has passed away. The Holy Prophet of Allah (S.A.W.) has said:

"Keep the children at home when the evening has fallen, as satanic forces descend (on earth) at this time. But if some night has passed, they might be allowed to go out."

(Sihah-Sitta quoted by Hisn-e-Haseen)

Prophet's Evening Prayers : The Holy Prophet of Allah (S.A.W.) used to recite the following prayer at evening and taught the same to be read out by his followers:

> "O Allah (only) with Thy grace we could pass evening and (only) with Thy help we will pass morning. We are living with Thy favour and will die when Thou so command. And at last long, we shall return to Thee."
>
> *(Tirmizi)*

The following supplication is to he recited at the time of the Azan (the call for prayers) of Maghrib (evening) prayers:

> "O Allah this is the moment of the arrival of Thy night and the departure of Thy day and the time of the Calls of Thy Muazzins (the persons who call the Muslims for prayer) and the presentation of prayers to Thee. So forgive me."

Avoid going to sleep before 'Isha prayers as there is likelihood of the same being missed. The Holy Prophet of Allah (S.A.W.) did not go to bed before 'Isha prayers'.

The house should be lighted up as soon as the night falls. The Holy Prophet of Allah (S.A.W.) avoided sleeping in a house that was not lighted.

Day Sleep No Substitute for Night Sleep : Sleep early in the night and also rise early in the morning. Do not make up the deficiency of late sleeping in the night by sleeping in the day. Allah has created night for rest and peace, and the day is meant for work for the necessities of life.

> ***The Holy Quran says*** : "And it is He (Allah) Who has made the night a covering for you, and deep (a means of) repose and tranquillity and made the day for rising (work)." (25 : 47)

And also at another place, it is said:

> "And We have made sleep (as a means) of rest and peace for you, and have made the night as a cover, and the day for the struggle for the livelihood." (78 : 9 to 11)

Again in Soora 'An-Namal, it is said:

> "Have they not observed that We have made the night dark so that they may rest therein and the day alight and brilliant (so that they may struggle and0 work for their livelihood). Certainly there are indications (in this arrangement) for the believers to ponder." (27 : 86)

The idea behind making the night dark and a time for refit and the day bright for toiling and working is that one should take rest in the night and engage himself in the business of daily life in the light of the day till his body begins to feel tired and he may get peaceful and soothing sleep in the night. At dawn, we should get up duly refreshed and reciting the name of Allah ready for our work. The persons who sleep during the day due to sluggishness or keep awake in the night for enjoyment and pleasure, act contrary to the law of nature, and harm their health and life. Those who sleep during the day, do so at the cost of their daily obligations and deprive their body of natural rest and relaxation, as sleep of the day is no substitute for a night's sleep. The Holy Prophet (S.A.W.) has not even liked that a man should pray the whole night and place himself under undue ordeal.

The Messenger of Allah (S.A.W.) once asked Hazrat Abdullah bin 'Amr :

"I have been told about your fasting during the day and offering optional prayers throughout the night. Is it correct?" Hazrat Abdullah said: "O Prophet of Allah (S.A.W.), it is true." The Holy Prophet (S.A.W.) thereupon said: "Do not act like this. Keep fast occasionally and at times eat and drink. Similarly go to sleep and offer prayers, for your body too has right upon you: the eyes as well have their privilege." *(Bukhari)*

Please do not use too comfortable and cosy bed. The Momin (believer in Allah) should shun worldy comforts, self ease and luxury. For him, the whole life is a Jihad (continuous struggle).

Holy Prophet's (S.A.W.) Bedding : Hazrat Hafsah (R.A.A.) was asked by someone as to the nature of the bedding of the Holy Prophet of Allah (S.A.W.). She replied:

> 'It was made of a coarse jute cloth that we used to fold twice and spread under the Holy Prophet (S.A.W.). One day I thought that it could be a little more comfortable if it were folded four times. So I did the same. Early in the morning the Messenger of Allah (S.A.W.) asked: 'What had you spread under me last night?' I replied, 'The same piece of jute cloth was your bedding but I folded it four times instead of two foldings so that it may become a little cosier.' The

Messenger of Allah (S.A.W.) said: 'No, let it remain twice folded only. The softness of the bedding was a source of hindrance in getting up for the Tahajjud (after mid-night prayer) last night. *(Shamail-e-Tirmizi)*

The Holy Prophet (S.A.W.) disliked a cosy bed : Hazrat Ayesha narrates: "Once an Ansar lady came and saw the bedding of the Holy Prophet (S.A.W.). On reaching home she prepared a very soft bedding for the Holy Prophet (S.A.W.) stuffing it with wool and sent it for his use. When the Holy Prophet (S.A.W.) saw this he enquired, 'What is it?." I said, 'O Messenger of Allah, the Ansari lady who had come 'to see you had noticed your (hard) bedding. She prepared a soft one and has sent it for you." The Holy Porphet (S.A.W.) said: 'No, return it to her." Hazrat Ayesha further stated, "I liked the bedding very much and wanted to retain it, but the same had to be returned due to the insistence of the Holy Prophet (S.A.W.)." *(Shamail-e-Tirmizi)*

Hereafter Preferred to This World : Once the Holy Prophet (S.A.W.) was sleeping on a (bare) mat. This mat had caused some impressions on his body. Hazrat Abdullah Bin Masud says: "On seeing this, I began to weep." The Holy Prophet (S.A.W.) saw me weeping, so he asked, "Why are you weeping?" I submitted, "O Messenger of Allah, Emperors of Rome and Iran sleep in the soft cushioned beds of silk and velvet and the Holy Prophet of Allah (S.A.W.) on a mat (of date-palm leaves)." The Messenger of Allah said, "This is not the point to weep; for them is this world only, and we have the Hereafter."

Any Day May be Doomsday : The Holy Prophet (S.A.W.) once remarked: "How can I pass a life of comfort, ease and leisure when Hazrat Israfeel may blow the trumpet which is ever ready on his lips, and his ears are all attentive to the command of Allah to announce the Doomsday." *(Tirmizi)*

This excellent pattern of conduct of the Holy Prophet (S.A.W.) demands that the Muslims should lead a hard and strenuous life, avoiding pleasure-seeking and luxuriant way.

Before going to bed, perform ablution (wuzu) and go to sleep duly cleansed and purified. Any fat or grease sticking to the hands should be well washed off. 'The Holy Prophet of Allah (S.A.W.) said: "If anyone goes to bed without washing his hands and removing the greasy material from them, and he suffers on this account (bitten by some insect or animal) he should reproach none but himself (why he slept without washing his hands?)" It was the routine of the Holy Prophet of Allah (S.A.W.) that he performed wuzu (ablution) before going to sleep.

When the Holy Prophet (S.A.W.) intended to go to bed while obligatory bath was due, he used to wash away the filth from its place and then went to bed after performing wuzu (ablution).

Close Doors, put out Light and Fire and Cover Pots before Retiring : Before retiring to sleep, shut the doors of your house, cover up the utensils containing eatables; put out the candle or lantern and extinguish the fire burning in the kitchen, etc. Once, a fire broke out in one of the houses in Madina, thereupon the Holy Prophet (S.A.W.) said: "Fire is your enemy, extinguish it when you go to bed." The Holy Prophet (S.A.W.) also said, "While shutting the door, putting out the light, closing the mouth of the water-bag (or pot), covering the kitchen utensils containing foodstuffs, recite Bismillah (in the name of Allah). If there is no cloth to cover the utensils they should be covered with something else."

Requisites for the Bed and Bedside : The follwing articles should be kept ready at hand near bedside: water for drinking, a jug and a tumbler, a stick, a match-box or a torch for light, and a towel. If one is putting up as a guest, he should ask about the location of the toilet so that he may be saved from the inconvenience of not knowing the same at night, if necessary.

Holy Prophet's (S.A.W.) Routine : The Holy Prophet (S.A.W.) kept the following articles by his bedside: (a) a bottle of hair oil, (b) a comb, (c) a collyrium container and stick, (d) a pair of scissors, (e) one miswak, (f) a mirror, and (g) a small stick such as one used for scratching the head, etc.

Clothes and shoes should be kept nearer to your bed, so that on waking up, you may not have to look for them. The shoes should not be put on immediately on getting up from the bed. Shake up the shoes and clothes before using them.

The bed should he shaken up before going to sleep and also whenever one leaves it momentarily for some work, he should shake it up again. The Messenger of Allah (S.A.W.) said "If anyone gets up from the bed and goes to it again, he should sweep it with a piece of cloth, as he is not aware as to what may have crept into the bed in his absence."

Bedtime Prayers : When going to bed, the following prayer should be recited. It has been reported by Hazrat Anas, the chief attendant companion of the Holy Prophet (S..A.W.) that while going to sleep he (S.A.W.) used to say:

> "All praise is for Allah, who gave us food and water, helped us fully in our chores and labours, gave us shelter for living. There are numerous others, who have nobody to help them or to accommodate them."
>
> *(Shamail-e-Tirmizi)*

According to Hazrat Abu Hurairah(R.A.A.), the Messenger of Allah (S.A.W.) used to recite the following prayer before going to bed:

> "Allah with Your name, O my Lord, I have put my side on the bed and with Your help shall raise it from the bed. Have mercy on me if You will to take away my life at night and if You grant further reprieve it be under Your protection as You guard Your pious servants." *(Bukhari and Muslim)*

The following short prayer can also be recited in place of the above:

> "O Allah, with Your name, I go into the fold of death, and in Your name shall I rise alive."
>
> *(Bukhari and Muslim)*

Bedtime Recitation from the Holy Quran : While going to sleep recite a passage from the Holy Quran. The Messenger of Allah (S.A.W.) invariably recited a portion of the Holy Quran before going to bed. The Holy Prophet (S.A.W.) has said, "When a person in bed recites a surah (chapter) from the Holy Quran, Allah sends an angel who guards him against all evils till he gets up."

Further, the Messenger of Allah (S.A.W.) said: "When a person goes to his bed, an angel and a Satan come up to him. The angel says, 'Let your actions come to an end with virtuous deeds'. Satan says, 'Be through your deeds with something bad.' If the person goes to sleep remembering Allah, the angel guards him the whole night."

> Hazrat Ayesha narrates: "When the Prophet of Allah (S.A.W.) went to bed, he used to combine and stretch his hands as in prayers and used to recite the three surahs of the Holy Quran i.e., Al-Ikhlas (112) Al-Falaq (113) and An-Naas (114). Having recite d these, blew his breath upon both hands beginning from head, face and front portion of the body. He repeated this routine thrice." *(Shamail-e-Tirmizi)*

Mode of Sleeping : When you intend to sleep, lie on the right side and put the right hand below your right cheek. Hazrat Baraa' narrates:

"When the Prophet of Allah (S.A.W.) used to repose, he would put his right hand below his right cheek and recite the following supplication:

> "O Allah: save me from: Thy punishment on the Day when Thou will resurrect Thy servants before Thee (for reckoning)."

It is reported in Hisn-e-Hasin that the Holy Prophet (S.A.W.) recited the above words three times.

Avoid sleeping flat and lying on the left side. Father of Hazrat Ma'eesh, Taf-khatul-Ghifaree narrates:

> "I was lying in the mosque with my belly touching the ground, when somebody shook me by the foot and said:
>
> "Allah does not like this mode of sleeping." When I looked up, it was none but the Holy Prophet ofAllah (S.A.W.) himself." *(Abu Dawood)*

The sleeping room should be airy; place for sleeping not accessible to fresh air should be avoided.

While sleeping do not cover the face. It adversely affects the health. Always sleep with uncovered face so that you may get fresh air.

Sleeping on an open roof without railing or protective wall should be avoided. While coming down the stairs, arrange for light. Sometimes a minor slip results in considerable suffering.

Burning Coal or Lantern in the Sleeping Room : In spite of intense cold one should not sleep in a closed f room with the coal burning in a grate, or a lantern on, as the gas thus released, is harmful to health and might result in death.

Cultivate the Habit of Tahajjud (Late Night Optional) Prayer: It is highly commendable to get up towards the end of the night, for Tahajjud (Optional) prayers. In order to discipline yourself and to develop concord with Allah, it is essential to wake up towards the close of the night and offer prayers. Allah has spoken of this distinctive quality of his beloved servants, that they rise up in the night, pray and prostrate to Him and beg forgiveness of their sins. It was usual with the Holy Prophet (S.A.W.) that he went to sleep early and prayed towards the close of the night.

On waking up, the Holy Prophet (S.A.W.) used to recite the following prayer:

> "All praise and thanks are for Allah who gave us life after death (sleep) and surely we are to be resurrected before Him (on the Day of Judgment)."

Praise Allah and consider it as good tidings for the future. The Prophet of Allah (S.A.W.) has said, "Out of Prophethood, nothing has remained now except good tidings." The companions of the Prophet of Allah (S.A.W.) enquired, "What is meant by good tidings?" The Messenger of Allah (S.A.W.) replied, "A good dream" *(Bukhari)*

> And the Messenger of Allah (S.A.W.) also said, "One Who is more truthful among you, will see truer dreams." And the Messenger of Allah (S.A.W.) furthermore advised his followers, "Whenever you see a good dream, glorify your Lord (Allah) and describe it to your friend only.' Whenever the Prophet of Allah

(S.A.W.) saw a dream, he used to mention it to his companions and also advised his companions to mention dreams to him so that he would interpret the same. *(Bukhari)*

Vision of the Holy Prophet (S.A.W.) : Recite Darud or Salat (invoking bessings of Allah and offering salutations) to the Holy Prophet (S.A.W.) as much as possible. It is quite likely that Allah Almighty may graciously enable you to see the vision of the Holy Propht (S.A.W.) in dream. The Prophet of Allah (S.A.W.) is reported to have said "Whosoever saw me in the dream, he did actually see me in the vision, as the Satan cannot impersonate me in dream."

God forbid, if you see an unpleasant dream, do not mention it to anybody. Seek the protection of Allah from its evil effects: God Willing, you will remain immune from its adverse effects. Hazrat Abu Salam said that he often remained sick due to harmful effects of dreams. One day he complained about it to Hazrat Abu Qatadah who narrated the following Hadis of the Holy Prophet (S.A.W.)

"A good dream is divine (from Allah) : if anyone of you sees such a vision, he should mention the same to none except to a sincere friend; but perchance one sees a disquiet dream, it should never be told to anyone, but on the other hand immediately after awakening, he should recite thrice:

A'oo-zubillaa-hi minash-shai-taa-nir-rajeem.

"I seek refuge with Allah from (the mischief) of the Satan, the cursed" and should spit three times on the left side and also change his side on the bed; and thus he shall be safe from the-evil effects of the dream. *(Riaz-us-sali-heen, Muslim)*

Do not concoct imaginary dreams : Hazrat Abdullah Ibn Abbas .narrates the Messenger of Allah.(S.A.W.) as having said, "Whosoever narrates false dreams, will be asked by way of punishment to knot together two pieces of barley grains which he will never be able to do." And the Holy Prophet (S.A.W.) also said: "It is a big calamity to describe a scene which one has not witnessed."

Interpretation of Dreams : When a friend narrates his dream, that should be interpreted favourably and blessings of Allah be invoked for him. Once a person narrated his vision to the Prophet of Allah (S.A.W.) who said: "You have seen a good dream and it will augur well." The Prophet of Allah (S.A.W.) used to sit with folded feet (cross-legged) on the floor of the mosque after the morning prayers and would ask his companions to narrate their dreams if any and recite the following prayer before hearing them:

> "May you be blessed with the good of this dream and be immune from its evil. It may be a blessing for us and a curse for the enemy. All praise is for Allah, the Creator and Sustainer of the worlds."

Pray on Seeing a Nightmare : If one had an evil and horrifying dream, the following prayer should be recited. Grown-up children in the family be asked to memorise it. Hazrat Abdullah Ibn-i-Amr bin-Al 'Aas narrated that the Holy Prophet Muhammad (S.A.W.) recommended this prayer to him to be recited whenever he had a nightmare:

> "I seek shelter in the perfect words of Allah; from His wrath, from His punishment, from the evil of His creatures, from the instigations of the Satans and from their advance towards me."

Using the Road

One should walk with a moderate speed neither so swiftly that he should become a spectacle for the passers-by nor as slowly as if crawling and may look like a sick person, and the people may stop and enquire after his health. The Holy Prophet (S.A.W,) always walked steadily with long steps and never dragged his foot.

One should walk with decorum keeping his eyes downwards, and not glancing here and there unnecessarily. Casting eyes at random is against good manners. The Holy Prophet (S.A.W.) walked carrying his weight forward as if descending from an elevation. He walked gracefully with a slightly swift step with the body kept compact and collected, never looking sideways.

Walk modestly without making any noise or ostentation. One should never strut. It is impossible for anybody to rend the ground he walks upon, nor scale the mountain peak. Then why to swagger and show off?

Avoid walking barefooted. Shoes offer protection against gravel, thorns and other dangerous things, insects and crawling creatures.

The Holy Prophet (S.A.W.) said: "Put on footwears as far as possible. One who uses footwear is a sort of rider."

Walking with one shoe is a ridiculous practice, unless some special circumstance has made it unavoidable. Have due regard for good manners and decorum.

The Holy Prophet (S.A.W.) has said "Never walk with one shoe on. Walk either with bare feet or with both shoes on.

(Shimail-e-Tirmizi)

The garments should be gathered and collected while walking. The Holy Prophet (S.A.W.) walked with his shirt slightly raised.

One should always walk with the spirit of companionship and informality with his friends, and not try to be ahead of them, as if to have himself singled out as superior to others. It is better to be fraternal and walk hand-in-hand with friends. The Holy Prophet (S.A.W.) walked thus and never tried to make his presence felt. He often walked behind the companions, and occasionally clasped their hands.

It is not proper to stand or sit on the road and stare at the passers-by. If one by necessity has to stall himself on the roadside or sit thereon, one should have the following rules in mind.

(i) To keep the eyes down.

(ii) To remove impediments that might prove troublesome to others, from the roadside.

(iii) To offer greetings.

(iv) To preach good and to check from doing evil things.

(v) To guide those who have gone astray from the proper road.

(vi) To help one who needs one's help.

Good company on the Road : It is advisable to have the company of good people on the roadside and to shun the undesirables.

Men and women should not walk together : Women should walk on one side of the road and men should keep themselves at some distance from them.

The Holy Prophet (S.A.W.) said: "It might be tolerable for one to collide with a filthy pig smeared with mud, but not that the shoulders of a man should brush against a stranger woman."

Noble ladies while walking on the road, should cover their dress and all articles of decoration and put veils over their faces.

Ladies should not walk with such ornaments on their bodies which may give out jingling sound. They should rather walk softly so that their walking may not. attract the attention of strangers.

Ladies should avoid the use of strong and enchanting perfumes before going out in the street. The Holy Prophet (S.A.W.) has condemned this practice vehemently.

Recite the following prayer when leaving home:

> "In the Name of Allah (I have stepped out) and Him alone 1 trust. There is no power nor strength except in Allah."

While Going to the Market recite the following prayer:

> "In the name of Allah (I enter the market place), I beg for the good of this market and the good of all that is in it and seek Thy shelter from the evil of this market and from the evil of all that is in it, and seek Thy protection from taking a false oath here, or from entering into a bargain that may result in a loss."

Another Prayer : According to Hazrat Umar Ibn Al Khattab (R.A.A.), the Holy Prophet (S.A.W.) said that anyone who recites the following prayer while stepping into the market, shall have a million blessings credited, and a million sins debited in his account, and further he will be elevated by a million grades.

> "There is no God except Allah, His is One: He has no partner and His alone is the sovereignty. He alone is

> deserving of all thanks and praises. He is Who gives and takes life. He is Everlasting. He will never die. All that is good is in His possession and He has authority over everything."

Code for Travelling

One should start on a journey at such a time that he may have to spend the least period in travelling and may be able to offer his prayers in time. The Holy Prophet (S.A.W.) whenever undertook a journey or sent someone on it, regarded Thursday as the most appropriate day for the same.

Travel in company as far as possible. One should arrange for a company of at least three persons. Such a company will provide means of looking after the luggage, ensure mutual cooperation and safety from dangers. The Holy Prophet (S.A.W.) has said: "If people know the dangers inherent in travelling alone that I know, then even a rider would not negotiate a journey at night."

> If a group of persons is travelling, then they should appoint one of them as their leader. Nevertheless, each member of the party must retain his travelling documents, ticket, etc., some cash and other essential articles with him. Once a traveller who was proceeding on a journey to a distant place came to the Holy Prophet (S.A.W.). When asked as to who was accompanying him, he said, "None". Thereupon the Holy Prophet (S.A.W.) said: "A single rider is a Satan, two riders are also satans, but three riders are riders."
>
> *(Tirmizi)*

A woman should always travel with someone (i.e. *Mahram*) whose company is pemitted by the Shariah. She can, however, travel alone if the journey is of half a day's or one day's duration. But discretion requires that she should not travel unaccompanied.

> The Holy Prophet's (S.A.W.) Tradition is: "A woman who believes in Allah and in the Day of Judgment is not permitted to travel alone for a period of three days or more. She can undertake such a long journey only

> if she is accompanied by her father, brother, spouse, son, or someone who is *Mahram*." *(Bukhari)*

> On one occasion he even said: "A woman should not go alone on a journey extending over one day and one night." *(Bukhari, Muslim)*

Prayers on Starting on a Journey: The following prayer should be recited on boarding a vehicle or mounting an animal and when it starts moving.

> "Glorified be Allah who enabled us to keep in control this (animal or vehicle) although we were not in a position to control it. Verily, we are to return to our Lord."

Consideration for Fellow-travellers : It is necessary to care for the convenience of fellow travellers during journey. A companion during the journey has a right upon the fellow-travellers. The Quran says: "Treat your companion in the flank well." A companion in the flank means a person who becomes one's companion during the course of a journey anywhere, any time. Such a companion deserves all courtesies and help, and every effort should be made not to cause him any mental or physical harm.

The Holy Prophet (S.A.W.) has said:

> "The leader of the people is their servant. The person who tries to serve others the best, is only second to a martyr." *(Mishkat)*

Prayers at the Beginning and End of a Journey : On starting for or on returning from a journey two rak *'ats* of prayers in thanksgving to Allah should be offered. This was the practice of the Holy Prophet (S.A.W.).

One should stay at night at a place which is safe from thieves, robbers and harmful animals.

Quick Return from Journey : As far as possible, you should return home after having completed your business. Do not unnecessarily prolong your sojourn.

Convenience for Animals Accompanying the Traveller : If animals or cattle accompany a traveller or a rider is keeping company, every convenience and protection should be provided to them.

While travelling during cold weather take necessary bedding and clothes with you so that the host is not unnecessarily inconvenienced.

Carry a pot for water and a prayer carpet with you, so that you may not be inconvenienced when necessity for toilet, ablutions, prayers and drinking may arise.

Prayer to be Recited if Night Falls En Route : The following prayer is to be recited if night falls during the journey:

> "O earth, thy Sustainer and mine is Allah. I seek the protection of Allah from three evils and that which is in thee, and from the evils of creatures which Allah has created in thee, and from the evils of the creatures that crawl and walk on thee. And I'seek the protection of Allah from the lion, the black python, serpent, the scorpion, the inhabitants of this land, and the evils of every begetter and which is begotten in this land."

On returing home from journey recite the following prayers:

> "We return to Allah penitents, worshippers and adorers of our Lord."

When seeing off someone, you should accompany him up to a reasonable distance. At the time of departure he may be requested to offer the following prayer and you should also recite this:

> "I commit to Allah's care your faith, your trusts and the consequences of your actions."

A peson returning from a journey should be welcomed with words appropriate to the occasion. He should be greeted with a handshake, or, if the occasion so dictates, an embrace as well.

6

Domestic Life

"Worship Allah and be obedient to Him: and do not associate any partner with Him. And be benevolent to:

Your parents, near kindred,

and the orphans, and needy persons,

the neighbour who is related to you,

and the neighbour who may not be related to you,

and the companion of the journey, and the traveller,

and slaves your right-hand possess." (4 : 36)

Serving the Parents

Parents are to be treated well, and Allah's blessings in having enabled you to do this virtuous act, be considered as a great asset in this world as well as in the Hereafter. After Allah and the Holy Prophet (S.A.W.) you have the greatest duty towards your parents. The respect we ought to pay to our parents has been time and again emphasised in the Qur'an wherein duties towards parents have been enumerated alongwith the duties towards Allah, and the Muslims have been commanded to render thanks to Allah and also to their parents. Allah has decreed:

"Your Allah has decreed that you worship none save Allah, and (that you should) be kind to your parents." (17 : 2 3)

> Hazrat Abdullah Ibn Masud (R.A.A.) narrates: "I asked the Prophet of Allah (S.A.W.) as to which act Allah likes best. The Holy Prophet (S.A.W.) said: "the prayer offered in time." I asked "What, is it that Allah likes next best. "The Holy Prophet (S.A.W.) said, "Good treatment of your mother and father." When I asked him about the third most excellent act, he (S.A.W.) said, "Fighting in the way of Allah."
>
> *(Bukhari - Muslim)*

Hazrat Abdullah Ibn Masud (R.A.A.) futher says: "A man once presented himself before the Holy Prophet (S.A.W.) and said, "I affirm solemnly before you for Hijrat and Jihad and wish for recompense from Allah." The Holy Prophet (S.A.W.) thereupon enquired: "Is anyone of your parents alive?" He said: `Yes, O Prophet of Allah, and by the grace of Allah both are living." The Holy Prophet (S.A.W.) then asked "Do you really wish for recompense from Allah for your Hijrat and Jihad?" When he said he did want it, the Holy Prophet (S.A.W.) commanded: "Go and stay with your parents and serve them well." *(Muslim)*

> Hazrat Abu Umamah says that once a person asked the Holy Prophet (S.A.W.) about the rights of the Parents upon their children. The Holy Prophet (S.A.W.) said, "Your parents are your Paradise and they are your Hell," *(Ibn Majah)*

That is by doing good to them you will earn Paradise and if you ignore their rights you will go to Hell.

Be grateful to your parents : It is among the cardinal principles of good manners and acknowledgement of debt that one should be grateful for all the acts of kindness one has received. It is a fact that the main reason for our physical existence are our parents. We grow up under their tender care and reach adulthood. They suffer great hardships and show extraordinary love and suffer unparalleled sacrifices in bringing us up and it is, therefore, befitting that we should be grateful to them from the core of our hearts. This is why Allah has decreed that when we render thanks to Him, we should express gratitude to our parents as well.

> "(We have decreed) that you should render thanks unto Me and unto your parents." (31 : 14)

You should always try to please your parents and not do anything that may hurt their feelings, particularly when they get old, and become somewhat peevish and short tempered. In old age, parents very often make such claim., and demand which may seem to be unusual. This be tolerated cheerfully, and do not retort in anger which may cause annoyance to them. Allah has specifically commanded:

> "If one or both of them (your parents) attain old age with thee, say not "Fie" unto them nor repulse them." (17 : 23)

In fact, in old age a person becomes weak in nerves, and consequently touchy and somewhat irascible; and on slightest excuse start feeling as if they are being ignored. As such, they should not be given any chance for being annoyed.

According to Hazrat Abdullah bin Umar (R.A.A.), the Holy Prophet (S.A.W.) has said:

> "The pleasure of Allah is in the pleasure of the father and His displeasure in father's displeasure."
> *(Tirmizi, Ibn Habban, Mustadrak Hakim)*

> Hazrat Abdullah bin Umar (R.A.A.) also narrates an incident in which a man left his parents crying, and presented himself before the Holy Prophet (S.A.W.) seeking permission for Hijrat (migration). The Holy Prophet (S.A.W.) thereupon commanded him to go back to his parents and to return after making them happy as he had made them sad earlier.*(Abu Dawood)*

Parents should be served earnestly and with sincerity : Even if they appear to be a bit hard and inflexible, you should be kind to them. Keeping in view the unparalleled kindness and affection shown by them, you should fulfil even such demands which may be contrary to your taste and liking, but not against religion. It is our service to the parents that would lead to our redemption and earn for us Allah's blessings making us immune from calamities in both the worlds.

> According to Hazrat Anas (R.A.A.), the Holy Prophet (S.A.W.) has said that he, who wishes for long life and greater prosperity, should be good to his parents and be)fine towards his kith and kin.
>
> *(Al-Targhib wat Tarhib)*

The Holy Prophet (S.A.W.) has also said that:

> "That man may be disgraced; again disgraced and again disgraced.," The companions asked: "O Prophet of Allah (S.A.W.), who is that man?" The Holy Prophet (S.A.W.) said: "He who found his parents in old age, both or one, but could not enter the Paradise due to his failure to serve them." *(Muslim)*

Entry into Paradise : Fully respect your parents, and do not say a word or commit an act which may be derogatory to them. Be humble and modest before them. The Holy Qur'an says:

> "Speak to them (parents) with grace and respect."
>
> (17 : 23)

And again the Holy Qur'an enjoins:

> "And lower unto them the wing of submission through mercy!" (7 . 24)

This means that you should always be mindful of your parent's position and dignity, and never talk boastfully in presence nor in any way belittle them.

> Once Hazrat Abdullah Ibn Umar (R.A.A.) asked Hazrat Ibn Abbas (R.A.A.): "Do you wish that you should be immune from the Hell and enter Paradise,?" Hazrat Ibn Abbas said: "Why not? By Allah I wish to enter Paradise." Hazrat Ibn Umar asked; "Are your parents alive"? Hazrat Ibn Abbas said: "Yes, my mother is living." Hazrat Ibn Umar said: "If you talk with her graciously and look after her comforts, boarding and lodging you shall certainly enter Paradise, provided you avoid major (serious) sins."
>
> *(Al-Adab-Al-Mufrad)*

> Once Hazrat Abu Hurairah (R.A.A.) came across two persons. He asked one of them. "What is the other person to you?" He said, "He is my father." Hazrat Abu Hurairah said; "Be careful, never call him by name, nor walk ahead of him and do not take a seat before he is seated." *(Al-Adab Al-Mu frad)*

Love your parents and this love should be regarded as an honour and means of recompense and redemption in the Hereafter. Hazrat Ibn Abbas narrates the following Hadis of the Holy Prophet (S.A.W.):

> "Dutiful and good natured children who cast one loving and affectionate look at their parents, receive from Allah a blessing equivalent to one approved pilgrimage (Hajj). When the companions asked: "O Prophet of Allah (S.A.W.), what happens if a person looks like that a hundred times a day?" The holy Prophet (S.A.W.) said: "Yes, even if he does so a hundred times: Allah is far greater (benevolent) than your imagination and is not narrow-minded (i.e. He will bestow upon him so much recompense)."
>
> *(Muslim)*

Hazrat Ibn Abbas narrates the following Hadis of the Holy Prophet (S.A.W.) in this connection: "If a man has passed the night having fulfilled the commands of Allah concerning his parents, he will find in the morning two doors of Paradise opened to receive him. If either of his parents is living, one door of Paradise shall receive him. And, if on the contrary he has disobeyed the commands of Allah in this connection, he will find two gates of Hell gaping at him, and, if he has one of his parents living, he will have one gate of the Hell opened for him." The man whom the holy Prophet (S.A.W.) had thus addressed asked: "And if the parents are being unfair to him?" The Holy Prophet (S.A.W.) said, "Yes, even then, even then, even then." *(Mishkat)*

Parents are to be regarded as the owners of your assets, and you should spend your money generously upon them. Holy Qur'an tells us:

> "People ask you as to what they should spend: tell them whatever you spend for good (must go) to parents." (2 : 215)

Once a man presented himself before the Holy Prophet (S.A.W.) and complained that his father takes away everything from his assets whenever he wanted something. The Holy Prophet (S.A.W.) thereupon sent for his father. There appeared an old man, physically weak walking with the help of a stick.

When the Holy Prophet (S.A.W.) asked him, he said: "O Prophet of Allah (S.A.W.), there was a time when this son of mine was weak and helpless, and I was powerful. I had money and he was empty-handed. I never checked him from taking anything from me. Today I am weak and he is strong; I am empty handed and he is rich. Now he hides his money from me. The Mercy of the Prophet (S.A.W.) could not resist his tears on hearing this poignant story and told the son: "You and your wealth belong to your father."

Even if the parents happen to be non-Muslims, they are to be treated well and all courtesy to be shown to them. But obedience in matters of religion should be refused and they are not to be followed if they ask you to do a sin or an act associating somebody with Allah.

> "And if your (non-Muslim) parents press you to associate somebody with Me about whom you have no knowledge, obey them not, and (but) treat them well in the world." (3 : 15)
>
> Hazrat Asma (R.A.A.) says that her mother came to see her during the lifetime of the Holy Prophet (S.A.W.). She was an infidel at the time. Hazrat Asma (R.A.A.) said to the Holy Prophet (S.A.W.): "My mother had come to see me but she abhors Islam. How she should be treated?" The Holy Prophet (S.A.W.) asked her to continue to treat her mother affectionately as a kindred." *(Bukhari)*

Continue to pray for your parents, recalling their kindness; beg for their weal from Allah and His mercies for them.

Allah has said:

> "Always say my Lord! have mercy on both of them, just as they both nourished me when I was a little child." (17 : 27)

That is to say, "O Allah! When I was helpless in my childhood, they nourished me with full attention and devotion, affection and mercy, and for my sake sacrified their comforts. Now in their old age, in helplessness and infirmity, they are more deserving of kindness and mercy, O Allah! I cannot return their kindness. You alone can sustain and patronise them and have mercy upon them."

You should have special regard for the mother who is generally weaker and more sensitive. As such, she needs looking after all the more. Moreover, her kindness and sacrifices (towards the offspring) are greater than the father. Therefore, Islam has laid down greater rights for the mother and has exhorted special treatment for her. The Holy Qur'an says:

> "And We have commanded unto man to treat his parents kindly. His mother carried him (in her womb) with difficulty and delivered him with a pang. The period of carrying him in her womb and sustaining him on her milk is 30 months." (46 : 15)

While the Qur'an has prescribed love and kindness towards the parents, it has described that of the mother in bearing and bringing up a child, very graphically and effectively, and points to the act that in view of her sacrifices and services, the mother is entitled to your service and kindness more than your father. This fact has been elucidated very clearly by the Holy Prophet (S.A.W.).

Hazrat Abu Hurairah (R.A.A.) reports that a man presented himself before the Holy Prophet (S.A.W.) and asked him: "O Prophet of Allah, who is the most deserving of my courteous and kind treatment." The Holy Prophet (S.A.W.) said, "Your mother . "He asked, "Who next ?" The Messenger of Allah (S.A.W.) said: "Your mother," He again asked: "Who next ?" The Holy Prophet (S.A.W.) repeated: "Your mother." The man asked the Holy Prophet

(S.A.W.) for the fourth time, "Then who next ?" The Holy Prophet (S.A.W.) said "Your father." *(Al-Adab -Al-Mufrad)*

The foster-mother also is to be treated and served with love and courtesy. Hazrat Abu Tufail (R.A.A.) narrates the following Hadis:

"I saw the Holy Prophet (S.A.W.) distributing meat at a place called Jaranah. In the meantime a lady came and reached very near the Holy Prophet (S.A.W.). He immediately spread his sheet for her and she sat upon it. I enquired from those present, as to who she was. I was told that she was the foster mother of the Holy Prophet (S.A.W.)." *(Abu Daud)*

Even after their death, the parents should be remembered and repaid their kindness follow this schedule:

(a) Constantly pray for their redemption. The Qur'an has taught us the following prayer for this purpose:

> "Allah! Pardon me and my parents; and (also) forgive all who have accepted the faith, on the Day of Reckoning." (14 : 41)

(b) Hazrat Abu Hurairah (R.A.A.) says that when the position of the dead is exalted after death, he is taken by surprise and asks as to how this could happen. He is told on behalf of Allah that his offsprings (in the world) have been praying for him, and Allah has graced the prayer with acceptance.

Hazrat Abu Hurairah (R.A.A.) has also said:

The Holy Prophet (S.A.W.) said: "When a man dies, the period of his activities in the world ends, but there are three things, which benefit him even after his death; these are firstly a continuing Sadaqah or charity, secondly, the knowledge disseminated by him for the benefit of others; and thirdly, the noble offspring whom he had left behind and who continue to pray for his salvation."

(c) The offspring should fulfil the contracts and Undertakings made by the parents and execute their will. The parents, while alive, would have made promises to individuals, entered into covenant (Nazar) with Allah, promised payment of money to some persons. They might be having some debt, which remains to be repaid, or made some will to be executed. All these are to be fulfilled to the best of one's ability.

Hazrat Abdullah Ibn Abbas (R.A.A.) says that Hazrat Sa'd bin 'Ibadah asked the Holy Prophet (S.A.W.) "O Prophet of Allah (S.A.W.), my mother had made a vow, but she died before fulfilling it; can I do it for her?" The Holy Prophet (S.A.W.) said: "Why not? You should do it for her."

(d) The friends of your father and the female colleagues of your mother should also be well treated. They should be associated and consulted in your matters and their advices be respected. Once the Holy Prophet (S.A.W.) remarked: "The best act of courtesy consists in kindness towards the friends of one's father.

It so happened that once Hazrat Abu Darda (R.A.A.) fell sick and his condition worsened to the extent that there was no hope left for his recovery. Hazrat Yusuf bin 'Abdullah (R.A.A.) undertook a long journey and came to enquire after his health. Hazrat Abu Darda (R.A.A.) felt surprised and asked him as to how he was there. Hazrat Yusuf Ibn Abdullah (R.A.A.) said: "I have come here to see you, as you had very close relations with my father."

Hazrat Abu Dardah (R.A.A.) says that when he went to Madina, Hazrat Abdullah Ibn 'Umar (R.A.A.) visited him and said: "Do you know, O Abu Dardah, why I have come to see you?" Hazrat Abu Dardah expressed his ignorance, whereupon Hazarat Abdullah Ibn Umar said: "I have heard the Holy Prophet (S.A.W.) saying that he who wants his parents to be treated well in the grave, should observe courtesy towards their friends after they are no more." And then he said; "O Brother your father and my father were very good friends and I wish to sustain that friendship and concede their rights." (Ibn Haban)

(e) Kindred relations of the parents should also be treated well and helped by all means. Indifference towards them is indifference towards parents. The Holy Prophet (S.A.W.) has said: "Never be indifferent to your ancestors. Indifference towards parents is like ingratitude to Allah."

Make up for Omission in Treatment of Parents : If by chance you have failed to treat well your parents in their life time, you should not feel disappointed from the mercies of Allah. After their death, pray constantly for them. It is possible Allah will forgive your lapses and accept you as one of the pious persons.

Hazrat Anas has reported the following Hadis of the Holy Prophet (S.A.W.).

> "If a servant of Allah has failed to treat his parents well during their life time, and if either one or both of them has died in this state the son should continuously pray for the salvation of his parents and for their redemption, till Allah writes his name among his good servants."

Rights of the Wife

The exalted and magnificent civilization and way of life which Islam represents, is only possible when we are able to establish a noble and clean society and for this it is necessary that the family life which is the basic unit of the social order is stable, well-knit and organised. The foundation of family rests on the happy relations between the husband and wife. But this is only possible when the husband and wife themselves are aware of their duties and rights as partners for life; these are reciprocal in nature, which they should discharge with all sincerity, trust and affection. We shall first describe the rights and duties of a wife and later on that of the husband.

The Rights of the Wife : A wife has the right to be treated with affection and due consideration. The husband, if necessary, should be ready to make sacrifices for her sake. Allah has decreed:

> "And live with them in a proper manner." (4 : 19)

The Holy Prophet (S.A.W.) on the occasion of the Hajj-atul-wida (the last Hajj) addressing a very large gathering, said:

"Listen to me; O People! Treat your women nicely as they are under your control. You have no authority to maltreat them except when and if they misbehave. If they do so then you ought to separate yourself from them in your bedroom. If you deem it necessary to punish them, then see that they are not severely beaten. And, when they obey you, do not seek excuses thereafter to tease them. Bear in mind! You have certain rights upon your wives and they have certain rights upon you. They owe an obligation that they should not allow people you dislike, to pollute your beds and should not allow persons you do not like to enter your house. And listen it is their right upon you that you should feed and clothe them well." *(Riyaz-us-Salehin)*

That is to say, the wives should be clothed and fed in such a manner as may be appropriate for a unique and intimate conjugal relationship.

As far as possible, you should always entertain a good opinion about your wife. She should be treated with consideration, patience, justice, and high-mindedness; even if the wife suffers from lack of manners, domestic skills, and has bad features, you should put up with her patiently. Her virtues should be considered and her weak points ignored. Allah has said:

> "And harmony is better." (4 : 128)

And the Muslims have been directed:

> "......... For, if you dislike her (for some reasons) it may happen you hate a thing wherein Allah has placed much good (for you.). (4 : 19)

The Holy Prophet (S.A.W.) has explained this point in this *Hadis*:

"A Muslim should not hate his Muslim wife. If he dislikes some habit of his wife, it is just possible that he may like some other traits in her."'

In fact, every woman is likely to have some shortcomings. If the husband starts disliking her on this account, it would be impossible for a household to have any domestic peace or happiness. The right course is that the husband should display broad-mindedness and tolerance and reposing his trust in Allah, adjust himself with the situation and live with her. It is quite possible that the husband may be rewarded by Allah with some blessings, which his short sight had failed to visualize, e.g., the wife may be possessing excellent qualities of faith and nobility, character and manners, which may prove a blessing for the whole household, or she may give birth to a noble child who may benefit mankind, and be a source of beneficence to the father. Or it may be that the wife serves as a means for the reformation of the husband, and bring him closer to Heaven, or that the husband may be blessed through his wife by Allah with increased prosperity and subsistence. In short, one should not go after the outward shortcomings of the wife, and cause disharmony in his domestic life, but should try to make the same as pleasant as possible.

In marital life, adopt an attitude of give and take and forgiveness. The shortcomings, ignorant acts and other faults of the wife should be ignored. The woman is the weaker sex and more emotional, and therefore, she should be dealt with patience, affection, and kindness.

Allah has said : "O who believe! some of your wives and children are your enemies, therefore beware of them. And if you efface and overlook and forgive, then Allah is Forgiving and Merciful" (64 : 14)

The Holy Prophet (S.A.W.) has said:

> "Treat the womankind well. She has been created out of the (man's) rib and the uppermost part of the rib is crooked. If you try to straighten, it will break, while, if you leave it as it is, it would remain crooked. Therefore treat the womankind well." *(Bukhari-Muslim)*

Extend all courtesy and affection to your wife. The Holy Prophet (S.A.W.) has said:

" The most perfect in faith are those Msulims who are the best in their deportment; and the best among you are those who are most conscious of the rights of their wives." *(Tirmizi)*

The field where the noble disposition and good nature of an individual can be tested is his home. It is the members of the family who come into most intimate contact with him and it is here that his temperament and deportment are exposed to the full. And It is a fact that it is that Muslim who is perfect in his faith, who would treat the members of his household with love, affection and kindness.

> Hazrat Ayeshah (R.A.A.) narrates that she used to play with dolls and her female companions also joined her. They all used to hide at the approach of the Holy Prophet (S.A.W.), who used to search and gather them up and send them to her to resume their game.
>
> *(Bukhari-Muslim)*

Once on the occasion of Hajj the camel of Hazrat Safiyah (R.A.A.) sat down, and she was left behind. The Holy Prophet (S.A.W.) saw her crying. He had to stop, and wiped her tears with the corner of his sheet.

Be generous in meeting expenses in connection with the needs and necessities of your life-partners. You should feel happy in having spent your hard-earned money on your family members. Maintenance is the right of the wife and by discharging this responsibility with an open heart, the husband is not only assured of a happy life in this world but he becomes entitled to reward in the Hereafter. The Holy Prophet (S.A.W.) has said, " There is a Dinar which you have spent in the cause of Allah; another is one which you have spent in helping the liberation of a slave; there is another Dinar which you have given as Sadaqah to a beggar; and yet there is a Dinar which you have spent upon your family. The greatest reward is carried by the Dinar which you have spent upon the members of your household." *(Muslim)*

The wife should be taught the principles of Islam and good manners. She should be inducted into the basic principles of Islamic culture so that she may become a good wife, and affectionate mother, and a pious servant of Allah so that she may be able to lead a successful and happy domestic life.

The Qur'an says:

> "O ye who believe! Protect, yourself and your household from the fire of Hell."

The Holy Prophet (S.A.W.) carried on missionary work among his people as well as among his family members. Addressing the wives of the Holy Prophet (S.A.W.), Allah has said:

> "And remember the verse of Allah (Qur'an) and wise talks which are recited in your homes." (33 : 34)

And the Muslims have been commanded through the Holy Prophet (S.A.W.):

> "And instruct your household people to offer prayers and be constant therein."
> (20 : 132)

Holy Prophet (S.A.W.) said :

> "When a man wakes his wife and both husband and wife offer two rakats of prayers together, the name of the husband is recorded in the register of those males who remember Allah and that of the wife in the register of females who remember Allah. *(Abu Daud)*

Hazrat Umar, the second Caliph, prayed at night and in the morning woke his wife asking her to offer prayers, and recited the ayah:

> "And direct your family members to offer prayers and be constant therein." (20 : 132)

If there be more than one wife, all the wives are to be treated equally. The Holy Prophet (S.A.W.) was very particular in treating his wives equally. When he proceeded upon journey, he used to draw lots, and the wife winning the toss would accompany him.

According to Hazrat Abu Hurairah (R.A.A.), the Holy Prophet (S.A.W.) has said:

> "If a man having two wives does not treat them equally and justly, he shall have his half body paralysed on the Day of Judgment. *(Tirmizi)*

By justice and fairplay we mean equal treatment in day-to-day matters and dealings. However, if a man (through natural urge) feels more inclined towards a particular wife, this is beyond the control of human beings and he shall not be made to account for this by Allah.

The Rights of Husband : The wife should obey her husband sincerely. The wife should feel pleasure in obeying her husband as this is the command of Allah. The wife who obeys His command pleases Him.

The Qur'an says:

> "So good women are obedient (to their husbands)."
> (4 : 34)

The Holy Prophet (S.A.W.) has said:

> "No wife should fast without taking permission from her husband." (*Abu Daud*)

Further, highlighting the importance of obedience and devotion to the husband, the Holy Prophet (S.A.W.) has said:

> "There are two kinds of persons whose prayers do not rise above their heads that is, their prayers are not accepted; one is the slave who has fled from his master, till he returns; the other is the wife who has disobeyed her husband's command, till she regresses."
>
> *(Targhib-o-Tarhib)*

The wife should guard her chastity. She should avoid all that might bring a stigma on her chastity. This is the intention of the directives of Allah to the women, and also in order to keep the domestic life happy and successful. If the slightest of suspicion in this connection creeps into the husband's mind, then no amount of service and obedience by the wife would succeed in clearing that doubt. The slightest neglignenece in this regard helps the Devil to create doubts in the hushand's mind. Keeping in view the human weakness in this regard, the wife should be extra cautious, The Holy Prophet (S.A.W.) has said:

The woman who offers prayers five times a day, protects her honour and is obedient to her husband, can enter Paradise from whichever gate she likes." *(Targhib-o-Tarhib)*

The wife should not leave the house without prior permission of the husband. Nor should she visit house where her husband would not tike her to go, nor allow such persons to enter her house whom her husband does not like.

Hazrat M'iaz bin Jabal (R.A.A.) says:

> "The Holy Prophet (S.A.W.) has said: 'It is not lawful for a woman, who believes in Allah, to allow a person whom her husband does not like, to enter the house of

> her husband, nor that she should go out of the house when her husband does not want her to go out, and also a woman should not obey anyone else in her husband's affairs." *(Targhib-o-Tarhib)*

The wife should only obey her husband and should not follow suggestions of others in contravention of the husband's wishes.

The wife should try to please the husband. This is the secret of a successful married life as well as the means of pleasing Allah and attaining Paradise.

> The Holy Prophet (S.A.W.) says: "A woman who died while her husband was pleased and happy with her, shall enter Paradise." *(Bukhari —Muslim)*
>
> There is another Hadis stating that, "If the husband sends for the wife for marital functions and she refuses, causing resentment to the former, the angels send curses upon such a wife whole night."
>
> *(Muslim -Bukhari)*

Love your husband and appreciate his companionship. The love between the couple is the mainstay of life; it is the flower of life, and the beacon-light for a successful living. Be grateful to Allah for a successful living. Be grateful to Allah for this great favour, and appreciate this bounty from the core of your heart. The Holy Prophet (S.A.W.) once said: "There is nothing better than marriage between two persons who love each other."

Hazrat Safiyah (R.A.A.) had great love for the Holy Prophet (S.A.W.). When he fell ill, she spoke with great pathos: "I wish 1 would have been sick in your place." The other wives of the Holy Prophet (S.A.W.) looked with surprise at her, but the holy Prophet (S.A.W.) said: "This is not a showing off; what she speaks is true."

The wife should be grateful to the husband: it is the husband who is her greatest benefactor, who plods the whole day to please the wife and satisfy her wants, and then he feels pleasure in having provided her comfort. Hazrat Asma narrates:

> "Once the Holy Prophet (S.A.W.) passed by me, I was then with my neighbour girl-friends. He greeted us

> and said: Be not ungrateful to your benefactors. You remained unmarried at your parents house till Allah granted you a husband; then He favours you with a baby. And yet, despite all these kindnesses, the wife if she even happens to fly at husband in a fit of temper, says: "I have never seen any kind act from you."
>
> *(Al-Adab-al-Mufrad)*

The Holy Prophet (S.A.W.) cautioning an ungrateful wife has said:

> "On the Day of Judgment, Allah shall not look upon the woman who has been ungrateful to her husband; although a wife cannot do without the husband."
>
> *(Nasai)*

A wife should feel happy by serving her husband, even at the cost of her own comfort. She should try to win his heart and good-will through service. Hazrat Ayeshah (R.A.A.) used to wash the Holy Prophet's clothes, oil and comb his hair, and apply perfume on his persona. This was the routine of the wives of the companions as well.

> The Holy Prophet (S.A.W.) has once said : "A man is not permitted to prostrate himself before another. Were it permitted, the wife would have been commanded to prostrate herself before her husband. The husband has great rights over the wife, so great that even if the whole body of the husband is full of wounds and the wife licks them, the husband's rights will not be repaid.
>
> *(Musnad Ahmad)*

The wife should look after the husband's house and household effects. After your marriage his home should be regarded as yours. Spend your husband's money judiciously and wisely, in order to improve the condition of his house. The improvement and prosperity of the husband should be regarded as your own improvement and prosperity. The Holy Prophet (S.A.W.) praising the womenfolk of the Quraish, said "How nice are the Quraish women! they are very affectionate to the children and guard the household of their husbands so well." *(Bukhari)*

The Holy Prophet (S.A.W.) describing the virtues of a good wife, has said:

> "The most useful and full of blessing bounty for the faithful, after the fear of Allah, is a good wife who would carry out his orders cheerfully, and when the husband looks at her, she pleases him. When the husband swears by the trust he has placed in her, she would fulfil it. When he goes out on a journey, she would guard her chastity and look after his property.
>
> *(Ibn Majah)*

Everything in the house should be arranged properly. Household effects should be arranged decently and should be used in a decent manner. A neat and tidy house well-arranged rooms, good taste in domestic chores; a well-mannered and well-dressed pious wife's smiling looks, is not only rich in love and affection, prosperity and welfare for others, but is also a means to achieve salvation and Allah's pleasure for herself.

Once the wife of Hazrat Usman bin Maz'un (R.A.A.) met Hazrat Ayeshah (R.A.A.), who found the former clothed in very rough clothes and without any decoration or make up. Hazrat Ayeshah felt surprised, and asked: "Has Usman gone out on a journey?" This note of surprise shows how pleasing is the act of personal make up by the wife for the sake of her husband.

> A female companion once presented herself before the Holy Prophet (S.A.W.). She had gold bracelets on her hands. The Holy Prophet (S.A.W.) advised her not to wear them, whereupon she said: "O Prophet of Allah, if the wife does not properly adorn herself, she would lose her importance in the eyes of the husband."
>
> *(Nasai)*

Behaviour with Children

Children ought to be regarded as a blessing from Allah and their birth should be celebrated with zest and exchange of greetings. The arrival of the baby should be welcome with prayers for his or her welfare. Allah may he thanked for having blessed you with an opportunity to bring up one of His creatures and that you will be able to leave behind a successor in this world and the Hereafter.

Pray for Pious Children : If you have no issues, pray for the grant of pious children just as prophet Zachariah (Zakariya) prayed for a noble offspring. The Prophet prayed:

> "Allah give me from your bounty a pious issue; undoubtedly you are the Hearer of the supplication."
> (2 : 38)

Do not feel unhappy on the birth of child on account of straitened circumstances, ill health or other reasons, and do not consider the birth of a child as a sign of misfortune for you.

Abortion should never be practised. The destruction of a child either before or after birth is rank heartlessness, a heinous crime and extreme cowardice. It brings disaster both in this world and in the Hereafter. Allah has said:

> "They are losers who have slain their children foolishly and in ignorance" (6 : 140)

And again we are told that:

> "Slay not your children, fearing a fall to poverty. We shall provide for them and indeed it is We who provide for you. Lo! the slaying of the offspring is a great sin".
> (17 : 131)

During the pre-Islamic (Jahilliya period) the Arabs disliked the birth of a female baby which was considered very humiliating and, therefore, the pagan Arabs used to bury girl babies alive or hurl them from the top of a mountain.

Once a companion asked the Holy Prophet (S.A.W.) "O Prophet of Allah, which sin is the greatest? The Holy Prophet (S.A.W.) said: "Associating a partner with Allah." The Companion asked, "And the next?" The Holy Prophet (S.A.W.) replied: "Insubordination of parents." He asked once again. The Holy Prophet (S.A.W.) replied: "Killing the offspring through the fear that it shall share your food".

Prayers at the Time of Childbirth : The *ayatul-kursi* (verse of the Throne, chapter 2 : 255) and the two ayats from Surah Al-A'araf 17 : 54,55) are to be recited near the woman in labour pain. Surah.

The translation of Ayat ul Kursi is as follows :

> "Allah: There is no Allah save Him, the Alive, the Eternal. Neither slumber nor sleep ovetaketh Him, Unto Him belongeth whatsoever is in the heavens and whatsoever is in the earth. Who is he that intercedeth with Him save by His leave? He knoweth that which is in front of them and that which is behind them, while they encompass nothing of His knowledge save that what He will. His throne includeth the heavens and the earth and He is never weary of preserving them. He is the Sublime, the Tremendous".

And the two translations of two ayats from Surah Al-'araf are as follows:

> "Lo! Your Lord (Sustainer) is Allah Who crated the heavens and the earth in six Days, then mounted His throne of Power. He covers the day with the night, which is in haste to follow it; and has created the sun, and the moon and the stars and made them subservient to His command. Listen: Creation is His job and command is His right. Blessed is the Allah, the Master and Sustainer of the worlds. Beseech your Sustaniner humbly and meakly and secretly. Indeed He does not like aggressors". (7 : 54,55)

The newly-born baby should first of all be given a wash and the Azan should be recited in the right ear and the Iqamat in the left ear. When Hazrat Husain, the maternal grandson of the Holy Prophet (S.A.W.) was born, the Holy Prophet (S.A.W.) recited the Azan and Iqamat in his ears. *(Tabarani)*

The Holy Prophet (S.A.W.) also said that the child in whose ears these two prayers are recited would be safe from the incidence of epilepsy.

Tahnik means chewing the date and rubbing its paste on the skull of the baby. After the Azan and Iqamat, a pious man or woman should be asked to chew a date and the paste of the fruit applied to the skull of the newly born child and that pious person should pray for the welfare of the baby. Hazrat Asma narrates that, when Hazrat Abdullah bin Zubair was born, I placed him in the lap of the Holy Prophet (S.A.W.). He sent for a date, chewed it and applied the saliva to the mouth of Hazrat Abdullah bin Zubair, and its paste on the skull and prayed for the well-being of the baby. According to Hazrat Ayeshah, the Holy Prophet (S.A.W.) performed Tahnik upon the children brought to him and prayed for them.

Name the child with a decent and appropriate name, like that of the Prophets, or Allah's names with the prefix of Abd e.g., Abdur Rahman, Abdullah, Abdur-Rahim, Yusuf, Ibrahim. The Holy Prophet (S.A.W.) has said: "On the Day of reckoning, you will be called by your names; therefore have better names. *(Abu Daud)*

The Holy Prophet (S.A.W.) has further said, "Of your names, Allah likes Abdullah and Abdur Rahman the most, and that the children should be named after the names of the Prophets". The Holy Prophet (S.A.W.) said that the child should be named after him, and not after his patronyms or filionyms.

Name wrongly given should be changed into a good or auspicious one. The Holy Prophet (S.A.W.) used to change bad names. One of the daughters of Hazrat Umar (R.A.A.) was named Asiyah. Her name was changed to Jamilah by the Holy Prophet (S.A.W.) *(Muslim)*

> Hazrat Zainab was the daughter of Hazrat Abu Salmah (R.A.A.). Her name was Barrah which means chaste. When the Holy Prophet (S.A.W.) heard this name, remarked: "You parade your piety yourself". When asked about the other name, he suggested the name, Zainab. *(Abu Daud)*

Aqiqah or the ceremony of shaving off the hair of the infant, should be celebrated preferably on the seventh day after the birth.

Two goats are to be sacrificed for the male and one goat for the female. But even one goat could be sacrified for the boy. Gold or silver equivalent to the weight of the hair should be distributed as alms. The Holy Prophet's *Sunnah* is that the *Aqiqah* should be performed on the seventh day. The name of the child is to be chosen on this very day, and the head shaved.

The prayer to be offered at the time of the Aqiqah is as follows:

> "O Allah: This is the Aqiqah of (Name of the child to be recited). Accept this as Thou hast accepted on behalf of Thine loved one, Muhammad (S.A.W.), and Thine friend, Abraham (A.S.). This offering of blood is the ransom for the blood of the child; flesh is the ransom for the flesh of the child; the hair are the ransom for the hair of the child; and these bones are the ransomfor the bones of the child. O Allah, accept".

Circumcision of the boys may preferably be performed on the seventh day. If on account of some circumstances this may not be possible, it should be done before the boy attains the age of seven years. The circumcision is an Islamic ritual.

Kalima the First Utterance : When the child begins to speak, he should be taught to speak the Kalima Tayyabah, that is:

> *La-Ilaha Il-lal-lahu Muhammad-ur-Rasul-ullah.* (There is no god but Allah. Muhammad is Messenger of Allah).

The Holy Prophet (S.A.W.) has said: When your baby begins to talk, teach it' *La-Ilaha-il-lal-lah*. Then do not worry about its consummation. When the milk teeth of the child have been shed off, command your child to offer prayers. *(Ibn e Sani)*

> The Hadis has it that, when any member of the Holy Prophet's family started talking, he used to teach it the second ayah from Surah Furqan(Chapter 25 : 21, wherein the basic Islamic principle of Oneness of Allah has been succinctly narrated. It is as follows:

"He unto Whom belongs the sovereignty of the heavens and the earth; He has chosen no son nor has He any partner in the sovereignty. He created everying and has meted out for it a role."

Suckling the Child: The child has a right to be fed on mother's milk. It is this bounty of the mother which the Qur'an reminds the child and exhorts him to treat his mother with exceptional love and kindness, in return for this service. It is the duty of the mother to inculcate into the child with each drop of her milk, the concept of oneness of Allah, love for the Holy Prophet (S.A.W.), and devotion for Islam. She should try that this love for Islam should seep into the heart and soul of the child. Responsibility for bringing up the child ought not to be thrown upon the nurse to lighten your burden. The parents should bring up the child themselves and feel spiritual pleasure and happiness in having performed this pleasant religious duty.

Do not frighten the children. Once thrown into a fright it is likely that this fear may persist in them even after their attaining adulthood. Such children are usually rendered incapable of achieving a big success in life.

Note that children should not be chided on trifles. In the first place, too much rebuking loses its effectiveness. In the second, it makes the child feel he is not loved. Therefore, instead of chiding and reproving the child on trivial matters and showing annoyance at their faults, one should try to be affectionate and tactful in handling them. They should be allowed to follow their aptitudes, but on one thing you should be firm that, at no cost, an act, contrary to the Shariat, would be tolerated.

The children should always be treated with sympathy and consideration, and their requirements should be satisfied as far as possible, This will not only make them happy, but would also develop sentiments of obedience and service in them. Once Hazrat Muawiyah asked Hazrat Ahnaf bin Qais as to how the offsprings should be treated. This companion of the Holy Prophet (S.A.W.) replied:

"Leader of the Faithfuls: Our offsprings are the fruits of our desires. They are props for our backs. We ate for them like the earth which is soft and harmless; our existence for them is like the sky which provides them with shade (protection); and through them we are able to perform marvelous tasks. Thus if they ask you for something, give them generously and if they feel sad try to enliven then. As a result of this they would develop love for you and appreciate your paternal affection. Never become an unbearable burden upon them lest they should become disgusted with you and even desire your demise and dislike your association"

Don't be always a dour-faced, stern-looking, hard task master. Be affectionate towards the children, run your hand lovingly on their heads; take them in your lap and fondle with them. An irate and grim attitude does not generate sincere love in the hearts of the children for their parents. and retards their natural growth and development and destroys their self-confidence.

Once Hazrat Aqra bin Habis (R.A.A.) presented himself before the Holy Prophet (S.A.W.) who was kissing Hazrat Hasan. Hazrat Aqra was astonished to see this and said: "O Prophet of Allah: you also cuddle children. I have ten children, yet I have never shown any affection to them". The Holy Prophet (S.A.W.) looked at Hazrat Aqra, and said: "What can I do if Allah has deprived you of love and compassion."

Hazrat 'Amair (R.A.A.) held an important appointment during the caliphate of Hazrat Umar (R.A.A.). He once went to see the Caliph. He saw that Hazrat Umar was lying and some children were riding on his chest and playing with him. Hazrat ' Aamir was somewhat displeased to see this. Hazrat Umar guessed this from the wrinkles on his forehead and asked Hazrat ' Aamir as to how he treated his own children. 'Aamir explaining his views said: "Leader of the Faithfuls: Whenever I enter the house, the inmates get stunned and every body is put to silence". Hazrat Umar spoke with great regret: "Aamir! how unfortunate it is that, even being a Muslim, you do not know that you should treat your kith and kin with affection and kindness."

You should try your level best to impart your children with a decent and befitting education and a dedicated discipline. No sacrifice should be spared in this regard. This is your religious duty and great favour to the children is also good for you.

> *The Holy Qur'an says* : "O ye who believe: Protect yourselves and your family members from Hell's fire."
>
> (66 : 6)

> Safety from the fire of Hell lies only in knowing the basic principles of Islam, and in living according to the commandments of Allah and obedience to the Holy Prophet's Hadis.
>
> And the Holy Prophet (S.A.W.) has said that the best legacy a father can leave for his offspring comprises proper training and good education. *(Mishkat)*

In reality a virtuous and well behaved progeny can only advance your cultural traditions and religious principles after you and it is for this reason, the Muslim aspire and pray for well mannered and virtuous children.

Inducing children to prayers : When the children attain the age of 7 years, they should be induced to prayers and taught how to pray. For this purpose they should be taken to the mosque with a view to creating a liking for prayers. And when they attain the age of ten, they should be forced to pray, and even punished, if they neglect to do so. It should be impressed upon them that this negligence will not be tolerated.

Segregation of children : When the children have attained the age of ten, they should be made to sleep on separate cots. The Holy Prophet (S.A.W.) has commanded:

"Ask your children to offer prayers by the time they are seven years of age. Punish them for (missing) prayers when they are ten and, allot separate beds to them at this age."

Keep the children always neat and clean. Pay special attention towards their personal hygiene, cleanliness, bathing, ablution etc. They should wear neat and clean clothes, but avoid pomposity and ostentation. The dress for girls should be specially plain and unornamented. Expensive and gaudy clothes are likely to spoil the habits of children.

Never express disappointment on reforming and correcting your children on their face. On the contrary, applaud even minor good deeds done by them and be generous in appreciation of any virtue in them. They should he encouraged so as to build up self confidence and courage in them, so that they may achieve a high place in their life.

You must tell your children stories of prophets and pious persons and heroic deeds and sacrifces of the venerable companions of the Holy Prophet (S.A.W.). This is essential for their education and trainintg, character building and inculcating a love for Islam. This has to be done at all costs. Occasionally recite Holy Quran rhythmically before them; and relate incidents, anecdotes teachings and tradition from the life of the Holy Prophet (S.A.W.). This would instil into them an intense love for the Holy Prophet (S.A.W.).

Cultivate the habit of giving and respecting other's rights : On some occasions distribute some food, money, etc., to the poor through the children so that they may cultivate the habit of charity and sympathy for the poor. Similarly, occasions should also be furnished to the children for distributing eatables among themselves, so that they get accustomed to the distribution of things equitably among themselves and do justice to each other by recognising each other's rights and develop mutual cooperation.

Do not concede each and every demand of the children. Tactfully try to dissuade them from this practice. If necessary use force in this behalf and see that they do not become obstinate and self willed by unnecessary cajoling.

How to talk with children : Do not shout at your children, nor talk to them harshly. Likewise, tell them not to talk in this way even among themselves. They should be told to talk in a sweet and mild tone.

Train your children to do their work themselves. They should not look to the servants to do their small chores. Dependence upon servants is likely to make them lazy and even to take up most difficult jobs.

Do not side your children unjustly : If there is fighting amongst children, you should not side your children unfairly. It should be remembered that every father loves his children. You should watch whether your children are to be blamed; if so, then taking into consideration future mishaps, you should try to adopt preventive measures by finding out if it is the misbehaviour of your children which has caused the trouble and take appropriate measures to correct them.

You should treat all your children equally and avoid injustice and unfair attitude in this connection. However, if due to some natural causes you feel more inclined towards a particular child it may be an exception. But in matters of treatment, bestowal of gifts and social matters, strict equality and fair play should be manitained. Never be partial towards a particular child, as which may be noted and felt by other children. This may create inferiority complex, hatred, frustration, and at last, it may develop rebellious attitude in your children. And such sentiments constitute a great hindrance in the growth of the natural capabilities of the children and act as a deadly poison to the evolution of spiritual and ethical progress.

> Once Hazrat Bashir, the father of Hazrat Nauman, presented himself alongwith Hazrat Nauman, before the Holy Prophet (S.A.W.) and said: "O Prophet of Allah: I had a slave whom I have gifted to this son." The Holy Prophet (S.A.W.) asked: "Have you gifted each of your son a slave?" "No, O Messenger of Allah," said Hazrat Bashir. The Holy Prophet (S.A.W.) said, "Then take back the slave. Fear Allah, and treat all your sons equitably." Hazrat Bashir on his return home, took back the slave. According to another version, the Holy Prophet (S.A.W.) said: "Do not make me a witness to a sin: I shall not be witness to an injustice." Still another version has it that the Holy Prophet (S.A.W.) said: "Do you desire that all your children should treat you well?" The Holy Prophet (S.A.W.) then said: "Then do not do such a thing."
>
> (*Bukhari—Muslim*)

Your life is a permanent and silent teacher for your children. They constantly learn and adopt from your life. Never speak a lie before them even as a joke or as a matter of expediency.

Hazrat Abdullah bin 'Aamir narrates that one day the Holy Prophet (S.A.W.) had graced the house of his father in his presence. His mother called Aamir and said: "Come here; I shall give you something." The Holy Prophet (S.A.W.) saw her calling her son, and asked her what she would give to him. His mother said: "I wish to give him dates." The Holy Prophet (S.A.W.) said: "Had you pretended to give him anything, it would have gone as a lie in your account." *(Abu Daud)*

Do not be downcast on the birth of a daughter : The birth of a daughter should be celebrated in the same way as that of a son. Whether it is a son or a daughter, both are gifts from Allah, and He alone knows what is good for you. To frown at the birth of a daughter is not befitting a Muslim. This is sheer ingratitude and disrespect to Allah.

> The *Hadis* has it that "When a daughter is born in a house, Allah sends angels to that house who say: O Ye who reside in the house ! peace be upon you. Having said this, they take the daughter under the protection of their wings, and, moving their hands softly upon her head, say: Here is a frail life, born to another frail being. Allah shall extend His succour to him who will look after her and bring her up. *(Tabarani)*
>
> Girls should be brought up with immense pleasure, spiritual satisfaction and sense of religious devotion pervading our minds and expecting entry into Paradise. The Holy Prophet (S.A.W.) has said; "If a person brings up three daughters or three sisters, educates and teaches good manners to them, and treats them with compassion till they become independent, Allah will certainly admit him to the Paradise." One companion asked: "And if there are only two." The Holy Prophet (S.A.W.) said: "They too will carry the same recompense." Hazrat Ibn Abbas says that the Holy Prophet (S.A.W.) would have given the same Basharat (happy news) for the upbringing of even one girl." *(Mishkat)*
>
> Hazrat Ayeshah (R.A.A.) says that once a woman called upon her with her two daughters and asked for something. Hazrat Ayeshah had only one date with her, which she gave to the woman. She divided the

> date into two pieces and gave one each to her daughters, without eating herself anything. Then she stood up and left. When the Holy Prophet (S.A.W.) came Hazrat Ayeshah narrated the incident to him (S.A.W.). He said: "Anybody who is tested through the birth of daughters and negotiates that test successfully by treating them well, these daughters will serve as a shield against the fire of Hell." *(Mishkat)*
>
> The daughter is not to be regarded as inferior to the son, nor he should be given preference over her in any matter. Both should be loved and treated equally. The Holy Prophet (S.A.W.) has said: "If a man has a daughter born to him, he does not bury her alive, as the pagans did and he has neither treated her with contempt nor preferred his son over her, he would be granted entry into Paradise by Allah." *(Abu Daud)*

Be very careful and pleased to give the fixed share of the girl from your property. This is the share which has been prescribed by Allah, and no one has the right to increase or decrease her share. It is not befitting a devout Muslim to deprive a girl of her share on some excuse, or to give her something less than her due, according to his own calculations, and feel satisfied. This amounts to misappropriation and an insult to the religion of Allah.

Pray for your children : Parents should follow these practical guidelines and pray for their children with the depth of their heart. The most Merciful and Benevolent Allah will certainly grant these heart touching supplication of the parents.

7

Good Company

Deep friendships have great effect and sufficient influence in guiding a man's self and intellect, and their effects are felt on the whole society. The society advances towards economic progress or retards a few steps. Either it gains comfort and peace or pain and distress disturb it.

Islam has given great importance to these connections. Through them, you have connection with some persons and you influence them, and you are influenced by them, and these people remain very near to you for a very long period.

If the basis of these relationships are on sincerity and selflessness, and if they were established with a view to achieving good consequences, Allah will patronise them and bless them with prosperity, otherwise He throws them back at their faces

> Friends on that day will be foes of one another, save those who kept their duty (to Allah). O My slaves! For you there is no fear this day, nor is it you who grieve.
>
> (*Zukhruf : 67, 68*)

Islam is the religion of love and collectivism. The tendency to know the people and to meet each other is the foundation of the Islamic teachings. Its development has not been based on wildness and Bedouinism, nor did it teach its sons to be aloof from the common people. It has not taught them to run away from the difficulties of life, nor has it taught a Muslim to meditate in a monastery, or to be lost in worship only. No, by no means ! Allah has not instituted high ranks for these coward and timid people.

Allah's Prophet (S.A.W.) has said:

> "The Muslim who lives with the people and shows tolerance for the harms received from them is better than the Muslim who does not meet them and does not show tolerance for the harms received from them." (*Tirmizi*)

For whom the congregational prayers have been made compulsory? For whom the Friday prayers have been compulsory? Who will bear the hardships of jihad and who have made the courage to bear the hardships experienced in the way ?

This heavy burden can be borne only by that Ummah, the mutual relations of whose members among themselves are very strong and firm.

Therefore, when Ibn Abbas (R.A.A.) was asked for his opinion about a man who observes fast during the day and offers prayers during the night, but does not attend the daily congregational prayers and the congregational prayers of Fridays. He said:

> "Tell him that he is of the hell." (*Tirmizi*)

It is so because Islam is ardently desirous that its symbols should prove to be the means of mutual sincerity between Muslims, deep love among them and mutual co-operation.

As the collective activities of Muslims will increase Allah's blessings on them will increase in the same proportion. In the hadith it is mentioned:

> "It is better to offer prayers in company with another man than offering it alone, and offering prayers in the company of two men is better than in offering it in the company of one man, and the greater the number, the more would it be liked by Allah." (*Ahmed*)

In another tradition it is stated:

> "The reward of prayers of two men, when one is Imam and another is the follower, is less than the reward of prayers of four men together, and the reward of the congregational prayers of eight men is greater than the reward of the congregational prayers of four men.

> The reward of the congregational prayers of hundred men is greater than the reward of the prayers of eight men, when one is Imam and others are followers." (*Tibrani*)

From these traditions it appears that Islam wants to see a great collective organisation of Muslims, and does not want to see them scattered and separated.

Although sometimes the coming together, the firmness in relationships and the offering of the congregational prayers become rather slack, and their importance in comparison with the other commands and rules becomes less, but this thing is certain that every attempt to live away from the Ummah would amount to run away from the responsibility of the compulsory duty of ordering of the righteous deeds and preventing the commitment of the forbidden things, or it would be a sense of weakness of defending Islam against the enemies. This is such a crime as cannot have any excuse worth considering.

People have different natures. Some people go to well-attended meetings and establish a relationship with others present there, and mix with others with the help of their smiles and friendly conversation. but there are some who avoid the meetings. They build up a wall around themselves, to cross which becomes difficult for others. They look at others with fear and suspicion, and if somebody wants to meet them they try to hide and avoid meeting him.

Islam has guided persons of both these natures in a correct way. To the people of the first group it says "Keep relationship with the people and teach them the points of religion." To the other group it says: "A Muslim should be soft hearted and of good conduct. He should be sympathetic to the people and should be liked by humanity."

It is true that Islam has enjoined upon Muslims to keep away from mischief and corruption. When there is disorder in the country, and the countrymen are busy in assaulting one another for the sake of material gains and cross all the moral limits, at such a time the boycott of this mischief is the best expression of one's disapproval of such a thing, and also the last stage of fighting against the forbidden evil, to which a hadith of the Prophet has made a reference, that is, if you can stop with hands, stop it, otherwise stop it with the use of your tongue, and if even this much you cannot do, then consider it as evil in your heart.

This means that the man who has little power of criticising mischief and corruption with his tongue, to keep silent for such a man is not right. Boycotting is an effective weapon which can be used wisely during the modern times. Weak and backward rations have used this weapon against aggressive and tyrant enemies. But the position of boycott in comparison with the other weapon is the same as that of keeping away from other means and resources, that is its use is right only when other means and resources are not available. Those who have the equipment and wherewithal of extinguishing the fire of mischief and corruption, for them silence and boycott is the worst crime.

After this brief explanation the meaning of the Prophet's hadith can be understood : When he was asked which man was better, he answered

> "That Muslim who strives for the cause of Allah with his life and wealth." He was again asked: "Who else?" He replied : "That man who worships his Lord in a valley secretly." (*Bukhari & Muslim*)

It means that one's liking for seclusion or mixing up cannot be a permanent quality, therefore, a Muslim should divide his timings in such a way that his privacy as well as his company should be beneficial, so that from both benefits may be derived.

Choosing Friends

On this basis we select friends, establish relationships with them or withdraw from any relationship. The foremost condition for the best friendship is that it should be free from all selfish interests and motives, and should have been established for pure truth, and it should develop under the shadow of faith and righteousness. This is the meaning of loving Allah.

When man kindles the lamp of belief and faith in his heart, his bosom is bright with the light of truth of Islam and his tongue is sweet with its sweetness, he looks at all the humans in the world in the same light which he has made his own. He makes friends for the sake of principle and not for the sake of his carnal desires, and he hates for the same principles only, and not on account of deprivation or frustration.

Different groups sometimes gather round the bitter and sweet springs, and sometimes for temporary or permanent worldly interests, and many times these develop into strong relationships, but this love, friendship or acquaintance cannot be considered as the high grade sincere friendship and selfless love which is generated as an outcome of faith.

That is why Islam has given due respect to the feelings of pure friendship, and has induced Muslims to make friends purely for Allah and to keep it going only for His pleasure, and it has fixed the best reward for that. In a hadith Qudsi it is mentioned:

> "Those who love My Majesty will be under the shadow of My Throne, on a Day when there will be no other shadow." (*Ahmed*)

Hazrat Umar bin Khattab (R.A.A.)says that the Prophet (S.A.W.) has said:

> "There will be some slaves of Allah who will neither be from the Prophets nor from the martyrs, but on account of their high position before Allah Prophets and martyrs will envy them." The people asked as to who would they be? The Prophet (S.A.W.)replied: "Those persons who would have loved each other for the pleasure of Allah, even though there was no blood relation among them,nor would they give their wealth to one another. By God, from their faces light will emanate and they will be riding the light. When the people will be shuddering with fear they will have no fear, and when the people will be sad and worried they will have no sorrow." (*Abu Daud*)

> Lo! Verily the friends of Allah are (those) are whom fear comes not, nor do they grieve. (*Yunus ; 633*)

This love for Allah is not a thing of which everybody can be capable, nor is it for making tall claims about. For this it is necessary that man should first acquire some knowledge and understanding about Allah, and this knowledge and recognition should grow so much that in his heart the value of other things should be totally reduced and he should be lost in the thought of Allah. He should prefer to do his work in every condition to say that now he loves for Allah and hates for Allah.

But if he is influenced by the ability and personality of some person or somebody's life and character appeal to him, them this will be a kind of love or friendship of a different kind. This love has no relation with the one which we have mentioned above.

Allah's Messenger (S.A.W.) has said:

> "That man who has three qualities, will taste the sweetness of faith and its deliciousness: For him Allah and His Messenger are more loveable than all the world, he should love for Allah and hate for Allah, for him it should be preferable to jump in the fire lighted in his presence to joining any partner with Allah." (*Muslim*)

Accordingly, love is the last stage of faith, and its result and fruit can be achieved when the warmth of sincerity and selflessness has been completely mixed in the blood, because such a love is the proof of perfection and purity, which deserves reward.

Allah's Messenger has said:

> "When two men love in absence for the sake of Allah, then the man who is more liked by Allah will also be more liked by his companion." (*Tibrani*)

And both the loving friends remain under the security and support of Allah. A *hadith Qudsi* has it:

> "My love is certain for those who love each other for My sake, and My love is fixed for those who meet each other for my sake; and My love is definite for those

> who indulge in dealings (trade) for My sake, and My love is permanent for those who make friends among themselves for My sake." (*Ahmed and Tibrani*)

Effects of Good and Bad Company : One friend exercises a deep influence over the other friend. Therefore it is necessary that a person should be very careful in selecting a friend, and he should examine them properly till he is satisfied about them.

Allah's Prophet (S.A.W.)has said:

> "Man is on his friend's religion. Therefore, man should see with whom he is making friend." (*Abu Daud*)

If the friends are such as help in performance of compulsory religious duties *(faraiz)* and in safeguarding the rights, and keep you away from committing evil and forbidden things, then they are the best friends, their company should be definitely adopted, and you should be desirous of their friendship. But those friends who embellish the paths of evil and misguidance, or are ready to help in indulging in play and amusements, and these is a fear of deception and trickery from them, then you should be careful of them.

A true friend shows the way of success in the world and the Hereafter, a misguided and tricky friend proves wicked and ominous. The number of persons is very large who have suffered heavily the results of evil friendship, and today they are sorry for their past misdeeds

> On the day when the wrong-doer gnaws his hands, together with the messenger of Allah! Alas for me! would that I had never taken such a one for friend! He verily led me astray from the Reminder after it had reached me. Satan was ever man's deserter in the hour of need. (*Furqan: 27-29*)

One nature adopts the habits of other nature. Man very soon tries to follow the path which is liked or is approved of by his dear friend. The law which is operative in connection with the infectious diseases is also operative in connection with the conduct of men. It is observed that compared to virtue, evil spreads much faster. Many times a man who smokes cigarettes influences other persons to fall a prey to this bad habit, and it is very rare that on account of good company, this bad habit is given up by men.

Taking into consideration these bad results, and in order to safeguard good moral conduct and to give protection to good moral practices, the Prophet has commanded that a man of good conduct should be selected as a friend. He has said:

> "The example of a good man is like that of a seller of perfumes; if he does not give you anything, his good smell would at least reach you ; and the example of the bad company is like the oven of the iron-monger, if you are safe from its blackness, then at least its smoke would irritate your noses." (*Abu Daud*)

When this is the position with regard to a friend with whom you come in contact for a very small time during the night or day, then what would be the position with regard to a companion who would share with you your happiness and sadness throughout the life. The friendship of pious and God-fearing men elevates men, while the friendship of foolish and idiotic persons takes to a low level.

> "It is only wrong-doers that are protector, one to another; but Allah is the Protector of the righteous. These are clear evidences to men, and a guidance and mercy to those of assured faith." (*Jathiya : 19, 20*)

It is necessary that the foundation of friendship should be on the strength of beliefs and purity of conduct, and the best of men is he who is attached to his friends and who makes their love a means of success in this world and the next. About such men, the Prophet (S.A.W.) has said:

"He who had dealings with the people and did not ill-treat them talked to them but did not tell a lie, made a promise and kept it, then such a man is of perfect good conduct, is just and righteous, and with him friendship is enjoined."

When the friendship will be for Allah, it will develop only if Allah is obeyed and both the friends keep away from dispute and disunity. If wickedness enters in the character of either or both, their hearts will change and their love will decrease. In the hadith it is writte:

"By the Being in whose hands is my life, when two friends are separated being victims of disruption, its cause is some sin which any one of them has committed."

For this reason the honoured companions of the Prophet considered the advice to be patient and truthful and to be co-operative in righteousness, protector of love and a guarantee for the salvation as Allah:

Abu Qalaba (R.A.A.)narrates: "Two persons met in the market. One of them said to the other: 'Let us pray for Allah's pardon, when others are neglegent.' They did so. Then one of them died, then in the dream he met the other man and informed him: 'You should know that Allah had granted us salvation in the very evening when we had met." *(Ibn Abi Dunya)*

> Anas bin Malik (R.A.A.) says that when Abdullah bin Rawahaused to meet somebody, he used to say: 'Let us revive our faith in our Lord.' (one day he said the same to a man, who got extremely angry, and went to the Prophet (S.A.W.)and complained : 'O Messenger of Allah (S.A.W.) Look at Ibn Rawaha he prefers to have faith in you for a short time to having faith in you all the time.' The Prophet (S.A.W.)said: 'Blessings of Allah on Ibn Rawal a. He likes those gatherings in which the angels take pride.' *(Ahmed and Tibrani)*

Lasting Principles of Friendship : Friends should know each other well so that there is truth and firmness in their friendship. The feelings of love and brotherhood which a friend has for another friend should be conveyed to the other friend. Allah's Messenger (S.A.W.) has said:

> When any one of you may love another person, he should inform him that he loves him. *(Ahmed)*

> Hazrat Anas (R.A.A.) narrates that a man was sitting with the Prophet (S.A.W.) Another man passed from there. This man said to the Prophet (S.A.W.) "O Prophet of Allah ! I love this man." The Prophet asked whether

he had informed him about that. He replied in the negative. The Prophet (S.A.W.)then said: "Inform him that you love him." Therefore he addressed the sitting man and said : "I love you for the sake of Allah." In reply that man said : "I also love you for the salve of that Being for the sake of whom you love me."

(*Abu Daud*)

Allah's Messenger (S.A.W.) has said:

"If a man may love another man, he should try to know the name of that man, his father's name and his lineage, as this thing strengthens love and brotherhood." (*Tirmizi*)

Undoubtedly, similarity of thinking and temperament plays a very important role in strengthening relations and in the foundation of friendships. There is a well known saying that there are many of your brothers whom your mother has not given birth, for in this world you come across may people for meeting whom and talking with whom you are irresistibly attracted, as if you had known them for years, although actually it is not so. Same is the purport of this *hadith*:

"There are thousand types of men, of them, with whomsoever you are introduced, get close to them, and shun away from the ones with whom you do not get introduction. (*Bukhari*)

But in connection with this feeling only belief and the ruling power of that belief can give directions, and these directions become the guidance for a Momin's heart. That is why a Momin loves those persons whom he has not seen on account of distances of time and place between them, for the sake of Allah, though he had not seen their faces, and similarly, he hates those persons whom he never accompanied in travels or in residence. His love and hatred are for the reasons that he loves good persons and hates wicked persons. The guidance of hearts on these lines raises men's ranks and position.

Abuzar narrates ;that he said to the Prophet (S.A.W.) "O Messenger of Allah ! A man loves certain persons,

> but has no ability to work like them." The Prophet (S.A.W.) said : "O Abuzar! You will be with those whom you loved." (*Tirmizi*)

The tradition of Islam in connection with friendship is this that there should be mutual visits. It is necessary that the visits should be free from every interest, and purely for the pleasure of Allah.

> Abu Huraira; (R.A.A.) narrates that Allah's Prophet has said: A man went to visit his brother in a village. Allah sent an angel after him. When the angel went near him, he asked: 'Where are you going?' He replied that he was going to visit his brother in that village. The angel asked: 'Are you going to take compensation for any obligation that you might have done for him?' He replied: 'No. I love him purely for the sake of Allah.' Then the angel told him: 'I am the messenger of Allah and I have come to give you glad tidings that Allah has made you his favourite, because you have loved this man for the sake of Allah'. (*Bukhari*)

The steps that proceed in this path are very auspicious, as are the steps proceeding in the path of jihad for Allah, and attract similar reward.

Allah's Prophet (S.A.W.)has said:

> "When any person goes to see a sick man or visits his brother for the sake of Allah, then a caller gives a call : "to be happy, lucky are your steps ! you have made a house in the Paradise." (*Abu Daud*)

In another tradition it is written:

> "Whenever a person goes to visit his brother for the sake of Allah, then a caller gives a call from the heaven: "Let it be auspicious. Let the Paradise be auspicious for you" and Allah says on Arsh: "My slave visited for my sake and his entertainment is enjoined on Me." Accordingly He is not prepared to give any reward less than the Paradise." (*Muslim*)

"If a Muslim likes that everybody should be benefited, he would like it more that his friends should be benefited more. And if they are benefited, he will be happy, and there is nothing wrong if he remembers his brethren when he is blessed by God

> And forget not kindness among yourselves. Indeed, Allah sees well all that you do. (*Baqarah: 237*)
>
> Allah's Messenger has declared exchange of presents and gifts among friends commendable. He has said: "Give to one another among yourselves gifts, because gift vanishes heart's jealousy." (*Tirmizi*)

"Hazrat Ayesha (R.A.A.) has narrated:

> Allah's Messenger used to accept gifts and in return used to send gifts." (*Bazzar*)

It is true that if in these noble practices the formalities cross the limits, they become undesirable and ignoble, for Islam has come to fight artificiality and to spread convenience and informality, and every method which has narrowness, inconvenience and formality Islam is free from that. Islam wants that for the strength of friendship and for decent behaviour such manifestations and practices be adopted which in their appearance and execution should be beautiful and which also should have their basic excellence, and they should make life easier to live and reduce the hardships of life.

> "For Allah the best individuals are those who are good to their companions, and the best neighbours are those who may prove better for their neighbours."
>
> (*Hakim*)

Islam has permitted joining with the friends in their eating, as we join in eating with our parents, brother and relatives:

"There is no blame upon .... you even if you eat from your houses, or the houses of your fathers, or the houses of your mothers, or the houses of your brothers. or the houses of your sisters,........."

so much so that it permitted to eat—

> (from the houses) whereof you hold the keys, or (from the house) of a friend. (*An-Nur : 61*)

And this is not surprising, because friendship is very important and has far-reaching effects, so much so that if it wire possible to provide one deliverance from the punishment of the hell, the help of a friend could be expected to do that. Allah quotes the words of the polytheists, uttered by them when they are being subjected to punishment

> By Allah, of a truth we were in error manifest when we made you equal with the Lord of the Worlds. It was but the guilty who misled us. Now we have no intercessors nor any loving friend.
>
> (*Ash-Shu'ara:97-101*)

Since great rights are attached to these relationships, Allah's Messenger (S.A.W.) has said:

> "Make only a Momin as your companion, and your food may be caten only by a God-fearing man."
>
> (*Abu Daud*)

Love your friends and in return be loved by them. Such a man is indeed very fortunate. As against this, the man who is shunned by the people and he himself tries to avoid them, is in fact in a pitiable condition. A man without money is not poor, but a man without friends, is the poorest. A friend is an asset and adds zest in our life. He is mainstay in our long march of life and is a bounty of Allah. The Holy Prophet (S.A.W.) has said that:

> "A Muslim is love and affection personified. The man, who neither loves nor is loved in return by others, has no good in him." (*Mishkat, Bab-ush-Shafqat*)

The Holy Quran says:

> "Muslim males and Muslim females are friends and helpers of each other." (9 : 71)

The Holy Prophet (S.A.W.) used to love his companions very much, so much so that each of them considered that he was the most beloved companion of the Holy Prophet (S.A.W.).

Friendship is a Test. You should live with your friends amicably and maintain sincere relations with them. Do not cultivate the 'habit of aloofness or hatred towards them. When a person moves in the circle of his friends, very often he comes across difficult and unpleasant situations; sometimes his sentiments are hurt; at other times his dignity is damaged; at times his rest is disturbed and his routine is affected; or he has to face things which are contrary to his desires and inclinations; and still at other times his patience and forbearance is put on trial or he has to suffer financial loss. In short, he suffers a number of difficulties and torments. But when such a person puts up with these ordeals, his heart is galvanised, noble sentiments are generated and he passes through a process of self purification and spiritual development and attains greater spiritual and moral heights. He , thus gets enriched with sentiments of tolerance, love and sacrifice, sympathy and regard; fidelity and good wishes for others, courage, the faculty to cooperate and do good; chivalry and generosity, and becomes an asset for the society. The people respect him and consider him to be a blessing for them. The Holy Prophet (S.A.W.) has therefore said:

> "The Muslim who lives among his people and puts up with worries and inconveniences created by them, is far better than one who is isolated from others and chafes at the troubles he gets from them." *(Tirmizi)*
>
> Always cultivate friendship with virtuous persons. While selecting people for friendship, see that they are fit for association from moral as well as religious point of view. A well known adage says: "A man is known (judged) by the company he keeps." The Holy Prophet (S.A.W.) has said: "A person is supposed to follow the faith of his friends. Therefore, a person should consider as to what type of man is the person with whom he is going to forge friendship. *(Musnad Ahmad, Mishkat)*

This means when somebody would associate with a person, he is bound to be influenced by the sentiments and ideas of that person, and he will have the same standard of likes and dislikes. Therefore one should be meticulously careful in making friends, and should choose only such persons for this purpose who agree with him temperamentally and have the same ideas in religious matters. The Holy Prophet (S.A.W.) has emphasised to cultivate friendship only with a Muslim and have your social contacts exclusively with him." He (S.A.W.) has said "Move in the company of a Muslim only, and only a virtuous person should join you on your dining table."

Eating on the same dining table brings people closer and develops affection; and as such this relationship should exist between the true believers only; that is to say, people who are good and virtuous. Avoid the company of those who are indifferent towards Allah and are irresponsible, lethargic, and ill-mannered.

The Holy Prophet (S.A.W.) has elucidated this point in a beautiful simile:

"The examples of good and bad friends are like those of a muskseller and blacksmith. From the musk-seller you are bound to gain something. Either you will buy his musk ,or enjoy its good smell. But the foundry of the blacksmith would only burn your house or clothes or its unpleasant fume will harm your brain." (Bukhari; Muslim). In Abu Daud, however, the above hadis is recorded in these words:

"A good friend is like the musk-shop where even if yo do not gain any advantage, you will at least feel the aroma of the musk. And a bad friend is like the fire of a furnace. Even (your clothes) are not burnt they would certainly get smeared with smoke."

Cultivate the friendship for the sake of Allah alone. Allah's chosen servants are only those who unite with each other on the basis of his faith, and strive shoulder to should with unity of heart and soul for the establishment and protection of his religion. The Holy Quran says:

> "Lo! Allah loveth those who battle for His cause in ranks, as if they were solid structure." (61 : 4)
>
> And the Holy Prophet (S.A.W.) has said: "On the Day of Reckoning, Allah shall ask: Where are those persons who loved people only for My sake, I shall give them protection today under My shadow." *(Muslim)*

The Holy Prophet (S.A.W.) describing the covetous and respectable position of such persons on the Day of Judgment has remarked:

"There are a few obedient servants of Allah who although are neither prophets nor martyrs, yet Allah on the Day of Judgment shall elevate them on such ranks, which would be envied even by the prophets and martyers." When the companions asked as to who would be such fortunate ones, the Holy Prophet (S.A.W.) said:

"These are the people who love each other only for the sake of Allah's religion. They were not related to each other, nor did they have any monetary transactions. By Allah! on the Doomsday their faces would be glowing with light; in fact they would be all radiant, while the other people would be trembling with fear, they would be immune from anxiety and worry. When all others would be plunged into grief, they would not be at all sad." Then he recited the following verse from the Holy Quran:

> "Listen! The lovers of Allah shall fear nothing nor grieve (over their past lives)" (10: 64). *(Abu Daud)*

According to Hazrat Abu Darda, the Holy Prophet (S.A.W.) said:

"On the day of Resurrection some persons shall come out of their graves, with their countenance glowing with radiation. They shall be seated upon pearl-studded pulpits, and people would look at them enviously. They shall be neither prophets nor martyrs." A Bedouin asked: "O Prophet of Allah, who are they? Tell us how we could recognise them." The Holy Prophet (S.A.W.) said: "They are those persons who loved each other for the sake of Allah."

Consider the love of the virtuous persons as a means of Allah's pleasure and redemption in the Hereafter. Pray to Allah that He may grant you virtuous friends and their love, and to include you among good people.

Hazrat Abdullah bin Masud narrates:

> "A man once presented himself before the Holy Prophet (S.A.W.) and said "O Prophet of Allah, a man loves a virtuous person on account of his goodness, but he himself does not follow his good acts," The Holy Prophet (S.A.W.) said: "It matters little. A man

> would find himself in the company of the man he loves on the Doomsday." *(Bukhari)*

The Holy Prophet (S.A.W.) one night had a vision of Allah. He commanded the Holy Prophet (S.A.W.) to ask whatever he wished. The Holy Prophet (S.A.W.) submitted the following supplication:

> "O Lord! I request you for the capability for good deeds, and the power to leave the evil acts; love for the poor, and that You may pardon me and show mercy to me. And when You want to engulf a nation in some calamity, take me away from their midst unaffected. I ask for Your love and the love of the person who loves You. I solicit for the favour of capability for such acts which may help me to attain nearness to Your love." *(Musnad Ahmad)*

Hazrat Mu'az bin Jabal says that the Holy Prophet (S.A.W.) said:

> "Allah has said, it is imperative for Me that. I should love those who make friendship with each other for My sake and sit together to remember Me, and do good to each other for pleasure. *(Musnad Ahmad, Tirmizi)*

The Holy Prophet (S.A.W.) draws the happy picture of friendship of two persons in these words.

> "A man started on his way to meet a friend who lived in another village. Allah posted an angel on his way. The angel asked him: "Where are you going?" The man said: "I am going to meet my brother in the other village." The angel asked again: "Does he owe you anything which you are going to receive from him?" The man said: "No I am going thither because I love him for the sake of Allah," The angel thereupon said: "Then listen! Allah has sent me to you to convey you the happy news that He harbours the same amount of love for you." *(Muslim)*

Permanent Friendship: Friendship should be cultivated with persons who are worthy of friendship from the Islamic point of view; and then such a friendship be kept up as long as you live. But it is necessary that for permanent friendship one should have good friends.

The Holy Prophet (S.A.W.) has said:

> "On the Day of Reckoning there will be no shade anywhere except under the throne of Allah. On that day seven kinds of people shall be under the (shadow) of the Throne. One kind shall be of those two persons who made friendship with each other for the sake of Allah; Love for Allah had brought them together, and in this state they would have been separated from each other." That is to say, their friendship was for the sake of Allah and they tried to fulfil the requirements of such friendship. When one of them was about to depart from this world he would have been in the state of friendship.
>
> Have faith in your friends, and be happy among them. Do not be dejected nor make others gloomy. Be frank and free and be jovial among your friends and avoid being reserved and self centred so that your friends do not get wearied of your friendship. Hazrat Abdullah bin Haris says, he never saw a person more smiling than the Holy Prophet (S.A.W.). *(Tirmizi)*
>
> Hazrat Jabir Ibn Samurah says: "I have attended more than a hundred sittings with the Holy Prophet (S.A.W.). In these gatherings, the companions recited poems and also narrated tales of the *Jahilyah* (Pre-Islamic period). The Holy Prophet (S.A.W.) used not only to listen to these attentively, but sometimes even joined in laughing along with his companions. *(Tirmizi)*
>
> Hazrat Suraid says: "Once I was riding an animal sitting behind the holy Prophet (S.A.W.). I recited a hundred verses by Umaiya Ibn Assalt and he asked me to recite more after each verse, and I complied. *(Tirmizi)*

The Holy Prophet (S.A.W.) himself used to narrate stories in gatherings at his house. Hazrat Ayesha reports that he once narrated a story to his family members. A woman remarked that this strange tale was exactly like that of Khurafah. The Holy Prophet (S.A.W.) asked: "Do you know what is the story of Khurafah,?" and then he himself gave an account of the story of Kurafah in detail. Similarly he once related to Hazrat Ayesha an extremely interesting story of eleven women.

> Hazrat Bakr bin Abdullah describes the frank and jovial nature of the Holy Companions, that, on the one hand, in playful manner they threw feelings of water melon upon each other and on the other hand when the time for battle arrived, it was the same companions who used to be in the fore front." *(Al-Adab al-Mufrad)*

> Hazrat Ibn Ziyad says: "I have seen that several families of the noble and virtuous people in old days lived in the same house. Many times it so happened that a guest arrived at one family's quarters, while another family would have a cooking pot ready to serve. The party having the guest, would take away the pot for his guest and the owner of the cooking pot would look for it and ask the people as to who had taken away his cooking pot. The host would then tell him, that he had taken it away for his guest; whereupon the owner of the pot would say; "May Allah bless you and increase the food in the pot." Hazrat Muhammad Ibn Ziyad says, "When people baked their bread, the same thing used to happen."
>
> *(Al-Adab al-Mufrad)*

> Hazrat Ali says: "At times leave the heart free. Think of cheerful titbits; because like your body the heart also gets tired."

Be jovial and full of zest for life. But see that jokes should never exceed the limits, and they should not infringe upon Islamic value of self respect, balance and moderation.

Someone said to Hazrat Sufyan bin Ainiyah that joking is also a curs. He said: "No it is a Sunnah, but for those who know the proper occasions and can make decent jokes."

If one loves a friend, he should tell him so. This will have the psychological effect of bringing him closer, and there will be an increase in affection on both sides as a result of this exchange of mutual liking. Love will then not be a mere sentiment of the heart but will have effects on the practical side of life, and there will be a greater chance of taking personal interest in each other's personal matters and coming closer to each other.

The Holy Prophet (S.A.W.) said: "When a person harbours sentiments of love and affection for his brother, he should express them before him, and tell him that he loves him." *(Abu Dand)*

Once a man passed by the Holy Prophet (S.A.W.) who was then sitting in the midst of his friends; one of those present said: "O Prophet of Allah, I love this man only for the sake of Allah." When the Holy Prophet (S.A.W.) heard this, he asked him whether he had told this to the other person. When he replied in the negative, the Holy Prophet (S.A.W.) said: "Then go and tell him that you love him for the sake of Allah." He immediately got up, and expressed his sentiments to the passerby. The passerby said: "May He for Whose sake you love me, love you."

In order to make friendship more firm and meaningful, and also to become closer to your friends, you should take interest in the personal affairs of friends, as much as permissible, and tell them about your intimacy to them.

> The Holy Prophet (S.A.W.) has said: "When a person joins in friendship with another, he should ascertain his name, his father's name and his antecedents, as this would strengthen the roots of mutual love."
>
> *(Tirmizi)*

Friends should always observe moderation in the expression of love and in mutual dealings. Neither should you behave so coldly that your love and friendship may appear uncertain and doubtful, nor so effusive in the expression of cordiality that it may take the form of a craze, and you may have to repent later. A moderate stance that can be maintained, ought to be adopted.

> According to Hazrat Aslam, Hazrat 'Umar (R.A.A.) once said: "Your love should never take the form of madness and your enmity should not make you adopt cruelty." Hazrat Aslam asked: "How this could be?" Hazrat 'Umar said: "As for example when you love somebody, you tend to become enamoured of him like a child and behave like children; and when you are angry with anyone, you go for his life and property."
>
> *(Al-Adab Al-Mufrad)*

Hazrat Ubayd Kindi says:

> "I heard Hazrat Ali saying, "Be soft and moderate in friendship towards a friend. May be, he turns to be your enemy sometime. Likewise, be on the path of moderation and just towards your enemy: It is quite possible he might become your friend later."
>
> *(Al-Adab Al-Mufrail)*

Friends should be treated with fidelity and sincerity. The best act of sincerity towards a friend is that you should try to improve and better his morals and try to better his prospects in the Hereafter more than in this world.

The Holy Prophet (S.A.W.) has said: "Islam is all and all wishing well for others." By wishing well we mean that we should choose for our friends what we choose for ourselves, as nobody wishes ill for himself.

The Holy Prophet (S.A.W.) has said:

"By Allah Who has my life in His possession, no person can become a true believer unless he chooses for his brother, what he chooses for himself."

Further, describing the six rights which a Muslim has over another Muslim, he said: "And he should do good to his brother, whether, he be present or not." And observed:

"Verily, Allah has made the fire of Hell obligatory upon him and debarred him from Paradise, who, in spite of his having taken an oath, has violated the rights of his fellowMuslim brother!" The Companions then asked: "And what if it is a trivial thing?" The

Holy Prophet (S.A.W.) said: "Even if it be the insignificant salvadova twig."

Join your friends in their bereavements and participate in celebrating festive occasions with them. You should try to lessen the impact of sorrow through kind and sympathetic words and increase their pleasure by participating in their happy celebrations. Every friend expects his friends to be of help to him in need and not to leave him alone and stranded. He also, similarly, expects them to add to his pleasure in celebration of happy events. The following Hadis of the Holy Prophet (S.A.W.) enunciates this point:

> "Muslim, enforcing and supporting one another is like a brick, becoming a help for the other and reinforcing it," "having said this, he put the fingers of one hand into those of the other (and thus demonstrated with the natural relationship and strength of one Muslim with the other). He also said: "Just as when a part of the body becomes sick, the entire body feels the pain, in the same way, a Muslim will feel pain for other Muslims." *(Bukhari-Muslim)*

Receive your friends warmly, welcoming there cheerfully. You should avoid carelessness and indifference towards them; because such a behaviour will cause ill-will between you and your friends. While meeting friends, express your pleasure and happiness. Avoid all expressions of unpleasantness, despondency and abhorrence; your attitude should make your friends thrilled with feelings of joy. They should be made to feel at ease and not as if they constitute a burden. The Holy Prophet (S.A.W.) has said:

> "Do not regard any good as insignificant even though it may be your meeting with your friends cheerfully." *(Muslim)*

> "Your smile when you see a friend, is also a sadaqah (a good deed or charity). *(Tirmizi)*

Soft attitude and polite manners create love and affection for each other, and these virtues help formation and development of good society.

The Holy Prophet (S.A.W.) has said:

> "I tell you the signs of the man upon whom Hell-fire is prohibited. He is the man who is gentle in temper, soft in disposition and soft-natured." *(Tirmizi)*

Several companions have said that, when the Holy Prophet (S.A.W.) addressed himself to someone on the occasion of a visit, he addressed himself fully attentively and when somebody spoke to him he used to listen with full attention.

> Once the Holy Prophet (S.A.W.) was sitting in the mosque. A man came to see him; the Holy Prophet (S.A.W.) moved and collected his body. The man said: "O Prophet of Allah (S.A.W.)! The place is quite spacious. The Holy Prophet (S.A.W.) said: "It is the right of a Muslim that when a brother Muslim sees him, he should move a little. *(Baihaqi)*

The Qur'an has defined a Muslim as follows:

> " They are very merciful among themselves."(48 : 29)

The Holy Prophet (S.A.W.) elucidated this in the following words:

> " The faithful are just and soft-natured like the (tamed) camel who has a string in his nose which, when pulled, draws the animal, and if made to sit upon a stone, sits there. *(Tirmizi)*

In the event of differences between friends, the matter should be patched up immediately. You should have no hesitation in admitting your mistake and seeking pardon.

Hazrat Abu Darda, narrates that once hot words were exchanged between Hazrat Abu Bakr and Hazrat 'Umar. Later on Hazrat Abu Bakr felt sad about it, went to the Holy Prophet (S.A.W.) and said: "O Prophet of Allah! There was some difference between me and 'Umar resulting in exchange of hot words. I felt very much ashamed later, and begged forgiveness from 'Umar, but he is not prepared to forgive me. 1 am much perturbed and in anguish. I have come to you." The Holy Prophet (S.A.W.) said: "Allah shall forgive you." In the meantime Hazrat 'Umar also felt sorry for his mistake and ran to Hazrat Abu Baker's house, where he learnt that Hazrat Abu Baker had left the house to present himself before the Holy Prophet (S.A.W.). He also went to the Holy Prophet's (S.A.W.) and saw signs of displeasure upon the Holy Prophet's (S.A.W.) countenance. When Hazrat Abu Baker saw this, he was much frightened and falling on his knees said in an extremely submissive tone, "O Prophet of Allah: Umar is not at fault. I am to be blamed for having used strong words."

The Holy Prophet (S.A.W.) remarked "When Allah sent me as His Prophet , all of you belied me and only Abu Baker believed in me. He supported me in every way with material support and personal sacrifice. Are you now bent upon causing pain and mental torture to my companion?"

There should be no delay in settling the disputes. The more the delay, the greater is the degree of animosity and ill- will. Prophet Isa (Jesus) (A.S.) has given a very faith inspiring advice in this regard:

"Thus if you are busy offering a sacrifice at the altar, I and there you are reminded hat your brother has some grouse against you, you should leave the offering there, and go to your brother to reconcile with him, and then return to complete your sacrifice."

The Holy Prophet (S.A.W.) has said:

"The muster of the acts of the people are presented on each Monday and Thursday to Allah. Every Muslim is forgiven except the one who bears grudge against his Muslim brother. They are left (out) so that they may reconcile."

Who knows whether the next moment would be that of life or death; will he be able to see next Monday or Thursday. Why then delay in reconciliation? Who would like to present himself before Allah with dark and black heart laden with a malice and animosity?

Also bear in mind that when a friend confesses his fault and begs forgiveness, his explanation should be accepted and he should be forgiven.

The Holy Prophet (S.A.W.) has said: "A Muslim who refuses to accept pardon from his brother, is equal in sin like collector of illegal taxes."

Show Forbearance and Patience. If you hear something from your friend that militates against your good sense, you should control your expression, and should not retaliate; instead try to ward off the topic tactfully and in a friendly way. The Holy Prophet (S.A.W.) has said:

"Prophet Moses (A.S.) asked Allah, 'My Lord! Which of your creature is dearest to You.' Allah replied, "One who has the power to take revenge, but forgives." *(Mishkat)*

The Holy Prophet (S.A.W.) has also said:

"The heaviest roll which shall be placed in the scales of a Muslim on the Day of Judgment shall be his good manners; and one who talks vulgarity and insolence, shall earn Allah's wrath,"

Hazrat Abdullah bin Mubarak has defined courtesy in three ways:

(i) When a man meets another man, he should meet him with a smiling face.

(ii) He should spend upon the poor and the needy people, and

(iii) He should not cause harm to another person.

> Hazrat Ayeshah says: "The Prophet of Allah has said that the worst person before Allah on the Day of Resurrection will be the man whom people avoid meeting because of his foul and annoying language."
> *(Bukhari Muslim)*

One should not neglect, reforming and training his friends on right lines, and should not allow the development if the twin faults of egoism and bride. The friends should be exhorted to realize their weaknesses and to confess them with courage; and to realize that, in not admitting their faults, they would hamper their moral development.

It is in fact very easy to outwardly display humility, humbleness and suavity, but listening to one's faults patiently and to put up with the criticism from friends, is indeed a difficult task. But real friends are only those who keep an alert mind and advise their friends to desist from bride and self-esteem.

The Holy Porphet (S.A.W.) has said:

There are three things which lead to grave consequences:

(i) An intense desire or infatuation that may enslave a person.

(ii) A desire that man may regard as the *sumrnum honum* of life.

(iii) Self-love is the disease that is more dangerous of all the three evils. *(Mishkat—Baihaqi)*

Criticism and assessment are like an operation that expels all harmful and putrid mattter from the body, adds to the ethical vigour, and infuses a new life into it. To feel irritated at the criticism of friends, and to regard oneself immune from all criticism, is very dangerous and to neglect one's duty of pointing out defects of his friends, is also full of evil consequences. All this means that one should welcome criticism from his friends and be prepared to subject himself to a strict accountability. Similarly as a sincere friend he should offer good suggestions to his friends for their improvement and betterment. In fact, the friend who is being offered advice should, instead of being puffed up, offer thanks for the kindness of his friends. The Holy Prophet (S.A.W.) has expressed this through a beautiful simile.

> "Each of you is like a mirror for his borther. If he sees some thing ill in his brother, he should try to dispel it." *(Tirmizi)*

(i) The mirror shows the spots in you only when you stand before it in order to see them, and when you move away, there is nothing to see. Likewise, you should also make apparent to a friend his faults when he offers himself for criticism and provides you with an opportunity for his examination and hears them with patience. If you feel that he is not yet prepared to listen to the criticism, the advice should be postponed for a better occasion. In the meantime, not a word should be said about his weaknesses in his absence because this would amount to back-biting and back-biting instead of joining the hearts separates them.

(ii)The mirror also reflects the spots on the face that are visible not those which are hidden. It shows them as they are; it neither magnifies nor minimises. As such, a friend who is sincere should only point out to the defects he sees without exaggeration. Only defects you come across in the day-to-day life should be pointed out and you should not be curious and inquisitive about his unknown defects. Investigating hidden defects is not a service but an unethical and destructive habit. Once the Holy Prophet (S.A.W.) from the pulpit cautioned the audience in a loud tone:

> "Do not go after the hidden faults of the Muslims. A person who shows inquisitiveness for the hidden faults of his fellow-Muslim brothers, shall have his faults bared by Allah, and, when Allah is determined to expose somebody, such person is sure to be disgraced even if he takes shelter within his own house." *(Tirmizi)*

(iii) The mirror only presents a person's reflection as it is: It does not bear any motive nor it takes any revenge from anybody. You should as such take your friend to account, free from any selfish motive, ill-will or evil intention. The object of your criticism should be to enable your friend to reform himself.

(iv) When you see your own reflection in the mirror, you do not get annoyed and do not feel like breaking it. Instead you start making up yourself, and in your heart of hearts you begin thanking the mirror for pointing out things you knew nothing about them. In the same way, when a true friend points out to you your image as he sees it, you should not feel offended, you should rather thank him and request him to continue advising you in the future as well.

(v) As a last point, bear in mind that every Muslim is a mirror of his brother; a symbol of love for his Muslim brethren. When he sees his brother in trouble, he feels perturbed, and when he sees him happy he also feels happy. His criticism will contain sincerity, sympathy and genuine love. Only such advice helps in uniting hearts and invigorating lives.

Gifts should be exchahged among friends in order to express your loving sentiments and to cement the relationship. The Holy Prophet (S.A.W.) has said: "Exchange gifts with friends this would develop mutual love and remove ill-will."

(Mishkat)

The Holy Prophet (S.A.W.) and his companions used to exchange gifts with each other very frequently.

While presenting a gift, you should keep your financial position in view. A gift need not be expensive; whatever you can afford may he presented. The worth of a present depends upon your sincerity and sentiments of the giver. It is the gift, and not its value that joins the hearts. The receiver should also never regard a gift with contempt but have in mind the love and affection of the giver. The Holy Prophet (S.A.W.) has said:

> "If someone presents me with a leg of the goat as a gift, 1 shall accept it; and if somebody invites me and offers only a piece of cooked leg, I shall accept his invitation." *(Tirmizi)*

You must send a gift when you receive one. The Holy Prophet (S.A.W.) always did this. The gift he most liked was perfume. We should also regard this as a choice gift. In the present circumstances a book is also one of the best presents. With this end in view friends would arrange for common dinners as well. You should invite your friends on dinners given by them; such meetings go to strengthen the existing relationship and mutual affection. But instead of lavish and tasty dishes, more attention should be given to love and affection.

Well Wishing Friends

Look after the welfare of your friends and help them with man and money. Isbahani narrates that a man came to Hazrat Abdullah bin 'Umar and asked him: "Whom does Allah likes most?" Hazrat Abdullah bin 'Umar replied:

"The best man before Allah is one who helps and serves people most, and the deed best liked by Allah is that you should please a Muslim by solving his problems and mitigating his troubles or by satisfying his hunger. I would prefer to go with a brother to fulfil his needs, rather than sit in Itikaf in the mosque of the Holy Prophet (S.A.W.). If a man controls his anger although he had the power to carry it out, he earns Allah's pleasure. If a

Muslim goes forth to fulfil the want of his brother and satisfies it, shall have his steps strengthened on the day when all others would be tottering."

The following Ahadis of the Holy Prophet (S.A.W.) emphasize this point:

> "He who fulfils the wants of his brother, shall have his desires fulfilled by Allah. If he satisfies a want of his friends, Allah shall mitigate one of his troubles on the Day of Judgment." *(Bukhari Muslim)*
>
> Allah keeps on helping a person as long as he is engaged in helping his brother." *(Tirmizi)*
>
> "Hazrat Abdullah Ibn Abbas says that the holy Prophet (S.A.W.) has said, the blessings of satisfying the want of a Muslim are more than the bliss earned by ten years of *Itikaf*." *(Tabarani)*

According to Hazrat Anas (R.A.A.) the Holy Prophet (S.A.W.) has said:

> "Allah shall please the man on the Day of Reckoning, who goes to his Muslim brother with cheerful tidings and makes him glad." *(Tabarni)*

If your friend confides in you, you should prove as the most reliable confidant; should keep the secret in your heart and not divulge it, so that your friend may seek your advice if and when he needs and you may tender sound advice to him.

Winning Others

You should cultivate such a leniency, generosity, forbearance and accommodation in your character and behaviour, that persons of diverse nature and taste, may feel an extra ordinary attraction towards you. You should behave with them judiciously according to the taste and temperament of each of them. You should not try to measure others by your own standard. Diversity of taste and temperament is a gift of nature. Keep every friend in his natural place and take interest in him, and appreciate him accordingly, and thus keep him close to you.

It was the achievement of the universal genius and character of the Holy Prophet (S.A.W.) that persons of all taste and temperament could find relief in his company and were adjusted amicably. When he had love, affection and humility personified in Hazrat Abu Bakr, there was the iron road Hazrat 'Umar as well; there were Hazrat Hassan bin Sabit who hated war, and Hazrat Ali the conqueror of Khaibar, as his companions. There was Hazrat Abuzar Ghifari, the great pessimist who abhorred wealth and also Hazrat Abdul-Rahman bin Auf, the wealthy and handsome person in the company of the Holy Prophet (S.A.W.). But it was the genius of the universal nature of the character of the Holy Prophet (S.A.W.) that all of them had immense and unparalleled love for the Holy Prophet (S.A.W.) and in return was so much loved by the Holy Prophet (S.A.W.) that each of them thought that the Holy Prophet (S.A.W.) loved him most. It was because of this generosity, amiability and statesmanship of the Holy Prophet (S.A.W.) which brought the opposites together. The Holy Prophet (S.A.W.) moulded together a group of companions who in spite of diversity of nature and temperament were the best organisation from all points of view that human knowledge could evolve.

Your acquaintances can be successful and permanent when you develop a sagacious flexibility, exceptional patience and forbearance. In matter of friendship give and take, generosity, sacrifice, mutual cooperation, humility, regard for each other, and selflessness are prerequisite. The following incidents from the life of the Holy Prophet (S.A.W.) show how considerate, large hearted, patient and tolerant he was, while dealing with persons around him.

> The Holy Prophet (S.A.W.) once said: "I come for prayers and feel inclined to lead long prayers. But I hear a child crying, and therefore, I shorten the prayer, because I do not want to put the mother of the child to inconvenience by prolonging the prayer." *(Bukhari)*
>
> Hazrat Malik Ibn Al-Huwairis narrates the following incident. "I, alongwith some other youngmen, presented ourselves before the Holy Prophet (S.A.W.),

and stayed with him for twenty days. The Holy Prophet (S.A.W.) was extremely compassionate and kind towards us. After we had stayed with him for twenty days, he guessed that we had become homesick, he asked us as to whom we had left behind. Each of us told him about the situation of his home. He advised us to go back to our families and teach them what we had learnt from him, and to exhort them to do good deeds, and apprise them of proper timings for prayers; and when time for prayers comes, one of you should call the people for prayers. The most learned and pious among you should lead the prayers." *(Bukhari Muslim)*

Hazrat Muawiyah Ibn Hakam Sullami has described his own experience as follows:

"I was offering prayers under the leadership of the Holy Prophet (S.A.W.). In the course of the prayers one worshipper sneezed, and I forgetting that I was praying said *"Yar Hamak Allah"* in the course of my prayers. Other worshippers began to stare at me as an expression of their annoyance. I said: Peace be upon you: Why you stare at me like this? Then I became quiet. When the Holy Prophet (S.A.W.) finished his prayers, may my parents be sacrificed for him, I have never seen a better teacher either before or afterwards, neither he scolded, nor beat me, nor spoke to me harshly. He only said: "It is improper to talk during prayers as they are meant for reciting His virtues, His Greatness. and reading the Qur'an." *(Muslim)*

Praying for the Friend : Friends in particular should pray for each other. I should pray for them and request them to pray for you. Prayers should be offered in the presence of the friend as well as in their absence by name. Hazrat 'U mar says that he sought permission of the Holy Prophet (S.A.W.). Giving his gracious permission the Holy Prophet (S.A.W.) said: "O My brother, remember me in your prayers." Hazrat 'Umar says that he felt more pleased at this than attainment of the whole world.

The Holy Prophet (S.A.W.) has said:

> "When a Muslim prays for his friend in absentia, Allah grants this prayer. An angel appointed by Allah by his side says, "Amen! You may have for yourself what you desire for your friend." *(Muslim)*

In your ardent prayers, solicit the favour of Allah to clean your hearts of malice and hatred and join them with love and affection, cementing your relationship with mutual cooperation and love. The following prayer from the Qur'an may also be recited:

> "Our Lord! Forgive us and our brethren who were before us in faith; and place not malice and ill-will in our hearts toward those who believe. Our Lord, You are full of pity and Most Merciful." (59 - 10)

Moving in Good Company

While visiting somebody you should be neatly and properly dressed. But you should not be decked in gaudy and costly dress which may give the impression as if you want to overawe the other person.

Meeting with Proper Appointment : It is better to inform the other party of your intending visit in advance and have an appointment. Doing without prior appointment is not a good habit. This interferes with the routine of the person whom you are visiting and may also cause some embarrassment to you as well.

Talk on Useful Matters : When you visit a person, talk topics which may serve some purpose, and do not waste time in random talks. This will make you an unwelcome visitor.

While visiting somebody, permission to enter the house should be sought at the door, and on receiving the permission go into the house and greet the inmates with As-salam-o-'Alaikum. If no reply is received after saying As-salam-o-Alaikum thrice, you should turn back without any displeasure.

Present Gifts : Occasionally, while visiting friends or relatives take some suitable gifts to present. This exchange of gifts enhances mutual love and regard for each other.

If a needy person calls, his request should be carried out as far as possible. If he requests for a recommendation, do recommend him and if you cannot do anything for him, regret your inability politely. One should never be kept on false hopes.

If you visit a person with a request, state it in a civilized manner. In case it is acceded to, thank him; and if the same is refused, greet him and return home without any grumble.

You should not expect other persons always to visit you. You should also call on others occasionally. This develops mutual cooperation and regard for each other. But it should be kept in mind that the believers always meet for a noble purpose.

Removing unwanted things from friends' person : If you find that there is a piece of straw or any other such thing on the person or clothes of the individual you are visiting, do remove it with your hands and if anyone does this for you, thank him and pray for him in this way.

> "May Allah keep you away from things you do not like."

Visiting a Person in the Night : If you have to visit someone at night, have regard for his comfort and convenience, and do not prolong your stay. If you find him asleep, return home without any grouse.

If a group of persons visits somebody, the spokesman, while talking, shoud speak for all and should not ignore the views and interests of others, He should avoid only impressing his personal needs and importance.

When a guest arrives, receive him warmly and express your happiness on his arrival and do not express any sign of indifference or resentment.

The Holy Prophet (S.A.W.) has said:

> "Those who believe in Allah and the Hereafter should be hospitable to their guests." *(Bukhari - Muslim)*

Hospitality includes respect and cordiality, comfort and convenience to the guest; cheer him and make him happy by pleasant conversation; introduce him to your intimate friends and serve him personally. All this is known as the Ikram-e-Zaif (honour for the guest).

The Sunnah of the Holy Prophet (S.A.W.) tells us that the Prophet himself used to entertain his guest and insisted on his eating till he was full.

Attending the Visitors

When the guest arrives, he should first be greeted and enquiries made about his welfare.

The Qur'an says :

> "Hath the story of Abraham's honoured guests reached thee (O Muhammad) when they came unto him and said; Peace! he answered peace!" (51 : 25)

Hospitality Should be Generous : The guest should be entertained generously and lavishly with the best possible fare that may he available. When guests came to Prophet Abraham, he immediately set himself to arrange for their food; he picked up a well-fed and fat calf and slaughtered it to prepare roasted meat for them.

The Holy Quran says;

"Then he hastened to his house and (slaughtered) a well fed and fat calf and prepared a roast for his guests."

It is also implied that Prophet Abraham went to his house to arrange for the food quietly, so that the guests might not know about it, otherwise considering the host's inconvenience, they might formally refuse to eat., and it would not be possible for the host to have the honour of entertaining his guests.

The Holy Prophet (S.A.W.) has emphasised the importance of hospitality and this has been graphically described by Hazrat Abu Shuraih:

> "These two eyes and these two ears of mine have seen and heard the Holy Prophet (S.A.W.) saying, "Those who believe in Allah and the Hereafter should entertain their guest well. The reward of entertaining

> the guest is the prized first day and the first night (of his stay)." *(Bukhari—Muslim)*

"The First day and the first night" requires an explanation. Just as one who gives away a reward or a prize, does so with great pleasure and spiritual satisfaction, the host also feels the same way when he entertains his guest on the first day and the first night. The receiver of the award feels happy and appreciates the gesture of the giver, the same sentiments should be expressed by the guest.

Convenience of the Guest : When the guest arrives, his physical needs require looking after. Arrangements for bathroom and toilet conveniences should be made forthwith. After the guest has taken his bath and made himself easy, ask him for meal although it may not be time for a meal, and this should be done in such a way that the guest may not refuse formally. Thereafter, the room where he is to stay should be shown to him.

Allow the Guest, Time for Rest and Privacy : Keeping in view the convenience of the guest, he should be given some time to be alone and you should not be with him all the time lest he should be feeling bored or inconvenienced or may be in need of rest particularly at night when he likes to go to bed early. When guests came to the house of Prophet Abraham he left them alone for a while, looking after their comforts and needs.

Feel happy on the arrival of guest and express your joy on his taking his meals with you, and you should not feel annoyed on his arrival. A guest is not a source of trouble, but a blessing sent by Allah. When He sends a guest to you, He also provides his food; and the guest eats at your dining table only his share of food which has been already predestined for him.

The honour and prestige of the guest should be guarded as your own and an attack upon his honour should be regarded as an attack on your honour.

The guest is to be entertained lavishly and with an open heart for three days. This is the right of the guest. A Muslim should be very generous in the discharge of this duty. The first day is the special day for entertaining the guest, who should be treated very well. It does not matter if the same arrangements could not be made on the next two days.

The Holy Prophet (S.A.W.) has said:

> "And hospitality is for three days, after which whatever the host does is Sadaqah (favour)".
>
> *(Bukhari—Muslim)*

Service of the Guest : The guest should be looked after by the host personally instead of being left to the care of the children or servants. The Holy Prophet (S.A.W.) used to entertain the guests himself.

When Iman Shafi stayed as Imam Malik' guest, the latter provided him with all comforts and made him sleep in a separate room. At dawn the guest heard someone knocking at his door and said in a very affectionate voice -May Allah bless you! It, is the prayer-time." Imam Shafi got up and saw Imam Malik himself holding a water jug for ablution. Imam Shafi felt embarrassed which Imam Malik guessed, but the host said in a tone full of love: 'Do not mind this, brother. The guest has to be served."

After making guest comfortable in his room show him the toilet and the water pot. He should be furnished with a prayer mat and the place marked for prayer, and shown the direction of the Qiblah. Imam Malik's servant after having settled Imam Shafi in his room, did like this.

How to Handle the Guest at the Dining Table : At the meal time, the host should go to the dining place with his hands already washed thoroughly. He should then help the guest or guests to wash hands. When Iman Malik followed this practice, Iman Shafi asked him the significance for this, who said: "The host should wash his hands first and then prepare to welcome the guests in the dining room. After the dinner is over, the host should wash the hands of the guests first but wash his own last, lest some guests may drop in.

Make arrangements of fare, crockery, etc., a little more than the guests, so that you may not be put to embarrassment if another guest arrives. If the extra. arrangement exists, the new host would naturally feel pleased and honoured.

The guest should be provided with all comfort, even at the cost of your own comfort, and convenience.

Once a man presented himself before the Holy Prophet (S.A.W.) and said: "O Prophet of Allah, ! I am very much hungry." The Holy Prophet sent sword to one of his holy wives to send whatever eatable may be available with her. Her reply was: "By Allah who sent you as His Prophet, there is nothing but water with me." He then sent word to another wife and the same reply came from her. He sent word to other wives one by one, and they sent the same negative reply. Then he addressed his companions: "Who volunteers to accept this guest for this night." One Ansar companion said: "O Prophet of Allah"! 1 accept him."

The companion took the Holy Prophet's (S.A.W.) guest to his house and said to his wife: "I have with me the Holy Prophet's (S.A.W.) guest, entertain him."His wife said: "I have food sufficient for the children only." The companion said: "Then put the children to sleep by some excuse. But when you place the food before the guest, put out the lamp on some pretext, and sit near him, so that he may think that we have also joined him in eating."

> The guest thus ate to his fill, while the hosts passed the night without food. When the same companion presented himself before the Holy Prophet (S.A.W.) next morning, he said: "What you both did for the guest last night, has been greatly appreciated by Allah.
> *(Bukhari—Muslim)*

Hospitality to be Shown under All Circumstances : Even if your guest might have been discourteous to you in the past, you should treat him well.

Hazrat Abul-Ahwas Jashmi says that his father once asked the Holy Prophet (S.A.W.), "If a person fails to extend his hospitality to me, and later on comes to me as a guest, should I extend hospitality to him or teach him a lesson for his indifference and misbehaviour?" The Holy Prophet (S.A.W.) said: "No, you must fulfil your duty and be hospitable to him." *(Mishkat)*

The guest should be requested to pray for the host, especially if the former be a scholar or a 'virtuous and religious person.

Hazrat Abdullah Ibn Busar narrates the following story in this context:

"The Holy Prophet (S.A.W.) once graced the house of my father by his stay. We offered him Harisah. He ate a little and then we offered him dates. He ate the dates and threw the stones holding them with two fingers. This was followed by a beverage, of which he drank a little, and passed it on to the person sitting on his right. When he was about to leave, my father caught hold of his bridle and requested him to pray for him. The Holy Prophet (S.A.W.) prayed for him in these words."

> O Allah! Bless the food Thou hast given them. Forgive them and have mercy upon them."

If you go as a guest, you should take with you, according to your financial position, gifts for the host or his children suiting to their taste and liking. Exchange of gifts and presents help increase mutual love and regard and it creates a place in the heart of the person receiving the gift for the one who presents it.

Except under special circumstances or under vehement pressure from the host, one should not stay with the host for more than three days. The Holy Prophet (S.A.W.) has said: "It is not proper for a guest to stay as long as to embarrass the host."

(Al-Adab Al-Mu frad)

> Another hadith says: "The Holy Prophet (S.A.W.) has said that "It is not proper for a Muslim to so much prolong his stay with his brother as to render him a sinner." The companions asked, "How, O Prophet of Allah, will the guest make the host a sinner?" The Holy Prophet (S.A.W.) said: "If he stays with him so long that he has nothing to offer." *(Muslim)*

Invite Others Also to be Your Guests : **You should not always be a guest** of others; invite others also to be your guest and entertain them lavishily.

While travelling by land or sea, the guest should make it a point to invariably take with him necessary clothes and bedding according to the season. During winter in particular, one should not go to another's house without warm bedding. This will obviate considerable inconvenience and embarrassment to the host.

The engagements and avocation of the host should be kept in mind and the guest should see to it that he does not disturb him.

Avoid making demand of different kinds from the host. He should be thanked for what he does for your entertainment and comfort.

Do Not Violate Purdah : If the guest is not related in blood with the family of the host, he should not converse with the female mambers in the absence of the host unnecessarily nor he should try to hear their talk. He should stay there without causing any inconvenience to them and violating their privacy.

Pray for the Host : If the guest for some reason or the other does not want to eat with the host or is on fast he should tactfully apologize and pray for the host's welfare.

The guest, when invited, should pray for the abundance of means welfare, Allah's blessings and mercy for the host after the meal.

Hazrat Abu Al-Haysam bin Tayhan once invited the Holy Prophet (S.A.W.) and the companions. When the meal was over the Holy Prophet (S.A.W.) said: "Repay your brother! The companions asked: "What repayment should we make?" The Holy Prophet (S.A.W.) said: "When a man goes to the house of his brother and eats, he should pray for his welfare and prosperity. This is his repayment." (*Abu Daud*)

The Holy Prophet (S.A.W.) once graced the house of Hazrat S'ad bin Ubadah. Hazrat S'ad offered him bread and olive, which he ate, and then said the following prayer:

> "May those who fast, break their fasts at your place, may pious people eat here, and may angels pray for mercy upon you and forgiveness for you."

Serving the Patients

Visiting the sick is important not only from social point of view and developing mutual affection and cooperation, but it is also the religious right of a Muslim over another Muslim and an essential expression of love for Allah and a lover of Allah cannot remain isolated or indifferent with the affairs of the servants. Negligence in visiting the sick is equivalent to His neglect of Allah. The Holy Prophet (S.A.W.) has said:

"On the Day of Judgment Allah shall say 'O son of Adam! You did not visit me when I was sick". The servant shall say, 'O Almighty Allah! You are the Creator of the Universe, how could I visit you?" Allah shall then say; "When such and such creature of Mine fell ill, you visited him not. Had you visited him, you would have found Me there (i.e.you would have earned My pleasure and blessings)."

That is, if a sick person is visited, it pleases Allah immensely. The Holy Prophet (S.A.W.) has further said:

"There are six rights which one Muslim has over the other." Some one asked to enumerate them; "O Prophet of Allah, what-sights are these." The Holy Prophet (S.A.W.) replied:

(i) When you meet a fellow-Muslim, offer salutations to him.

(ii) If invited by him to meal, accept the invitation.

(iii) When he requests you for an advice, be good to him, and give him a sound advice to his advantage.

(iv) When he sneezes and says Al Hamdo Lillah, say Yar Hamuk Allah.

(v) When he is sick, visit him and enquire about his health.

(vi) When he dies, participate in his funeral.

And the Holy Prophet (S.A.W.) has also said:

"He who visits his sick Muslim brother, shall have his abode in the upper chamber of Paradise."

(Al-Adab Al-Mufrad).

Hazrat Abu Hurairah narrates the HolyProphet (S.A.W.) said: "When a man visits his brother Muslim, or goes to meet him, it is announced from the Paradise 'You have done a good deed; your visit has been fruitful and you have made an abode for yourself in the Heaven." *(Tirmizi)*

When a sick person is visited, the visitor should move his hand gently over his head or body and say words of consolation and encouragement, so that his attention is drawn to the blessings and rewards of Hereafter and he may not utter any words of impatience or complaint.

Hazrat Ayesha bint Sa'd reports that once her father fell seriously ill in Makka. The Holy Prophet (S.A.W.) graced him with visit. Her father said: "O Prophet of Allah, I am leaving considerable property, and have only one daughter. May I will two thirds and leave one third for my daughter?" The Holy Prophet (S.A.W.) said, "No" He then asked: "can I will one-half and leave the other half to the daughter?" The Holy Prophet (S.A.W.) said, "No". He then asked. "O Prophet of Allah! Can I will one-third?" The Holy Prophet (S.A.W.) said, "Yes, will one-third, this is quite sufficient."

Thereafter the Holy Prophet (S.A.W.) placed his hand upon his forehead and, moved it over his face and stomach, and prayed for him, "O Allah! Grant health to Sa'd and enable him to complete his migration. Hazrat Sa'd said that thereafter, whenever I am reminded of that incident I feel the coolness of the Holy Prophet's hand upon my heart." *(Al-Adab Al-Mufrad)*

Hazrat Ibn Abbas says:

"Whenever the Holy Prophet (S.A.W.) visited any sick person, he used to sit near his head and recite the following prayer seven times:

> "I beg Almighty Allah, the Lord of the Throne (Grand Heavens) to grant you health," And he said: "The recitation of this prayer for seven times would cure the sick, unless he is destined to die." *(Mishkat)*

How to Talk to the Patient : While visiting a sick person make enquiries about his health and pray for his recovery. Whenever the holy Prophet (S.A.W.) visited an ailing person, he used to ask him "How do you do" and then he (S.A.W.) would condole him and say, "Don't worry, Insha Allah you would be cured, and this ailment would prove a means for the condonation of your sins." And moving his right hand over the place of the pain he would recite the following prayers:

"Allah! Take away this ailment. O, the Sustainer of the human beings, help him recover his health. You are the Giver of health. Only You can cure him, and a cure which may completely cure him."

You should not sit near the patient too long nor create noise near him. However. if the patient happens to be very intimate and close friend or relative and is desirous of having your company for sometime more, then only you may stay with him a little longer. According to Hazrat Abdullah Ibn Abbas, 'Not to sit too long with a sick person and not to create noise', is a practice of the Holy Prophet (S.A.W.)

Meet the Relative of the Patient Also ; The condition of the patient should be enquired from his relatives also and express your sympathies, and do whatever you can do to alleviate their difficulties, e.g., to afford medical help by bringing a doctor, securing medicines, etc., and, if necessary, financial help.

Also visit non-Muslim sick persons, and wisely request them to study and embrace Islam. When sick, a peson is more inclined towards Allah and he is likely to accept Islam.

Hazrat Anas has it that a Jewish boy used to serve the Holy Prophet (S.A.W.). It so happened that once he fell ill and the Holy Prophet (S.A.W.) graced him with his (S.A.W.) visit. Sitting by his side, the Holy Prophet (S.A.W.) invited him to embrace Islam. The boy looked towards his father who was present, as if asking for his opinion. The father said: "Son follow what Abdul-Qasim says." The son thereupon embraced Islam. The Holy Prophet (S.A.W.) came out saying: "We are thankful to Allah, who has made safe this boy from hell." *(Bukhari)*

While visiting a patient, you should not throw your random looks all over; and see that you sit in such a way that your eyes do not fall upon the women folk.

Don't visit persons known for their atheism Persons who are known for openly insulting Islam and shamelessly violating the commands of Allah, do not deserve a visit. Hazrat Abdullah bin 'Umar says: "Do not visit drunkards when they fall ill."

> While visiting a sick person, request him to pray for you, the prayer of the sick is like the prayer of the angels." This means that the angels only pray when it is so willed by Allah and as such their prayers are graced with acceptance. *(Ibn Majah)*

Sufferings and griefs should be borne with equanimity. One should not lose heart, and expression of grief and sorrow should never be allowed to exceed the limits of moderation. There is no person in this world who is immune from some sort of failure, frustratiom calamity, sorrow and deprivation. The difference between the Muslim and the infidel is that the latter, succumbing to the tide or grief, gives himself up totally to grief; at times even committing suicide. A Muslim bears even greater calamities with composure and gives a good account of himself in forbearance and resignation. He considers that whatever has happened is according to the Will of God: none of Whose commands is without significance and wisdom, and that whatever He does is for the betterment of His creatures, having some positive aspect. A Muslim begins to feel a kind of spiritual tranquility and peace and its soothing effect in the midst of grief, and this aspect of destiny makes things easier. The Holy Qur'an says:

"All the sufferings that befall on earth, and all the tribulations which you face, are predetermined and recorded in a book. Undoubtedly it is easier for Allah, so that you may not bewail which has escaped you." (57 : 22)

The Holy Prophet (S.A.W.) has said:

"Unique is the attitude of the Muslim. He sees good in every situation. If he is faced with bereavement, ailment, or hardship, he bears it up with resignation, and such a trial proves a blessing in disguise for him. If on the other hand, he gets happiness and prosperity, he offers thanks to Allah and this prosperity becomes a cause of good for him."

Facing Odds

When one bears a news communicating a bereavement, death, loss or some other such bad event, one should immediately recite.

Inna Lillahe Wa Inna Ilaihe Raje'oon.

Verily we belong to Allah and to Him we shall return.

(2 : 156)

In other words all that we have belongs to Allah. He has given all that we have and He can take them away, We all belong to Him and will return to Him. We are under all circumstances resigned to His Will, all His commands are based upon some purpose, wisdom, and justice, and He does everything for some greater goal. The obedient servant is one who never grumbles at any time.

The Holy Prophet (S.A.W.) has said :

"When a person recites *'Inna illahe'* in the face of some suffering, Allah mitigates his suffering, grants him with a good end, and awards him in return the thing he likes."

One night a lamp in the room of the Holy Prophet (S.A.W.) got extinguished. The Holy Prophet (S.A.W.) immediately said, Inna Lilahe wa inna ilaihe Rajeoon. When someone asked: "O Prophet of God, is the putting out of the lamp a calamity?" The Holy Prophet (S.A.W.) said: "Yes, whatever torments or causes inconvenience to a Muslim is a calamity."

The Holy Prophet (S.A.W.) has also said:

"If a Muslim bears patiently any trouble of the body of heart, ailment, sorrow or bereavement, may it be so minor as pricking of a thorn, Allah forgives his sins. *(Bukari — Muslim)*

Allah has said:

"And We shall certainly test you with fear and hunger, loss of life and property, and (O Prophet,) give glad tidings to those who show patience in the face of such ordeals and say, 'We are from Allah and to Him we have to return.' They shall be rewarded generously by their Sustainer and their Lord's favour and blessings on them. Verily, such people are on the true path."(2 : 156)

According to Hazrat Anas, the Holy Prophet (S.A.W.) has said:

"The severer the suffering, the greater would be the recompense. When Allah loves some people, in order to purify them, He puts them under trial. As such those who acquit themselves well in this trial, with them Allah is pleased, and those who grumble and express displeasure with Allah, with them Allah becomes displeased. *(Tirmizi)*

Hazrat Abu Musa Ash'ari quotes the Holy Prophet (S.A.W.) as having said:

"When a person loses his child, Allah enquires from the angels, "Did you take away the life of the child of My servant ?" The angels say, "Yes, O Lord :" Allah asks again: "Did you extract the life of his dearest child ?" The angels reply in the affirmative. He then asks: "What did My servant say'?" The angels submit "In his hour of trial, he praised Thee O Lord, and recited *'Inns Lillahe wa Inna ilaihe raje'oon'*.

(Verily we belong to Allah and shall return to Him).

Allah then commands: "Build a house for this servant of Mine, and name it the 'House of Thanks' *(Tirmizi)*

Be Discreet in the Expression of Sorrow : It is but natural to express sentiments of sorrow on some trouble, mishap or bereavement; but it should be borne in mind that the expression should not be unbridled and out of proportion, patience and composure should reign supreme throughout.

And example of forbearance and indomitable courage in the face of heart-rending bereavement is provided by the Holy Prophet (S.A.W.) himself. Hazrat Ibrahim, the son of the Holy Prophet (S.A.W.) was breathing his last in the lap of his august father. In this poignant situation the Holy Prophet's (S.A.W.) eyes started shedding tears, but he only said: O Ibrahim, we are rent by grief at thy departure, but our tongue shall express only those words, Which will be according to the Will of Allah. *(Muslim)*

Thus one should never complain about the disease or speak ill of it. Fortitude should be shown and hope pinned in the reward of the Hereafter. Bearing ailments and sufferings with fortitude, washes off the faithful's (Muslim) sins, cleanses him, and rewards him on the Day of Judgment. The Holy Prophet (S.A.W.) has said:

> "Allah sheds off the sins committed by a faithful (Muslim) when he suffers through a physical affliction or a disease, just as the tree sheds off its leaves."
> *(Bukhari — Muslim)*

Sickness Purifies a Person : The Holy Prophet (S.A.W.) one day saw a lady shivering. The Holy Prophet (S.A.W.) asked: "O Umm Sa'ib (or Musayyab), why you are trembling. The lady said: "I am suffering from fever. May it be cursed." The Holy Prophet (S.A.W.) said "Do not speak ill of fever, because fever purges the offspring of Adam of sins as the fire purifies the iron by removing its dirt." *(Muslim)*

Hazrat Ata Ibn Ribah describes an episode thus:

"Once I met Hazrat Abbas near the Ka'ba who asked me whether I would like to see a lady marked for Heaven. I expressed my eagerness to see her. Hazrat Abbas, pointing to a woman said: "This blackish woman once presented herself before the Holy Prophet (S.A.W.) and said: O Prophet of Allah, I am suffering from such severe fits of epilepsy which makes me totally unconscious, so much so that I become stark naked. She requested the Prophet of Allah (S.A.W.) to pray for her. The Holy Prophet (S.A.W.) said: "If you keep on bearing this ordeal with fortitude, Allah shall recompense you with the Paradise. If you wish I shall pray for your recovery and Allah shall make you well. She said 'O Prophet of Allah (S.A.W.). I shall bear this disease with fortitude, but do pray for me that I may not shed off my clothes in the course of a fit." The Holy Prophet (S.A.W.) prayed for her," Hazrat Ata says that he saw this lady, Umme Rafz on the stairs of the Ka'ba.

Do not Exceed the Limits of Moderation in Sorrow : When overcome by grief, do not commit an act which may imply ingratitude or complaint, it may be contrary to the Shariah. Among these acts are loud lamentations, rending off clothes, slapping of cheeks and breast. The Holy Prophet (S.A.W.) has explicitly said:

> "He who slaps his cheeks, tears off his clothes, and laments like the people of the period of ignorance, does not belong to my Ummah. " *(Tirmizi)*

When Hazrat Jafar Tayyar was martyred, and this news reached his home, the women-folk of his house began wailing loudly. The Holy Prophet (S.A.W.) sent words that they should not bewail loudly. But they continued their screaming. He (S.A.W.) again ordered them to stop, but they persisted. The Holy Prophet (S.A.W.) then ordered to stuff their mouths with dust."

(Bukhari)

Once the Holy Prophet (S.A.W.) was attending a funeral. A woman was accompanying the funeral procession with burning fire in a brazier. He (S.A.W.) reprimanded her so severely that she had to run away. He further commanded that nobody should follow a funeral procession with burning fire or any kind of music. *(Sirat Un-Nabi, Vol.6)*

There was a custom in the pre-Islamic Arabia that when people walked behind the coffin, they used to throw away the cloak and only kept the shirt. The Holy Prophet (S.A.W.) once saw them in this state and said:

"You are following the practice of the infidels. I feel like cursing you so that your faces become deformed."

The people immediately put on their clothes and never did like this again.

(Ibn Majah)

Never extend the period of mourning beyond three days. It is natural to feel sorrow at the death of a relative, but the period of mourning ought not to go beyond three days. The Holy Prophet (S.A.W.) has said:

"It is not permissible for a Muslim to mourn the demise of anybody for more than three days; however, the period of lamentation for a widow is four months and ten days. During this period she should not put on coloured clothes, nor apply scent to her clothes and body nor decorate herself."

(Tirmizi)

When the brother of Hazrat Zainab bint Jahsh, a cousin of the Holy Prophet (S.A.W.) died, some women visited Hazrat Zainab on the fourth day to offer their condolences. She dabbed herself with some scent in their presence and said, "It was not at all necessary for me to do so, yet I have rubbed "it just because the Holy Prophet (S.A.W.) has said that it is not permissible for any woman to mourn for any relation except, her husband, for more than three days."

Condolence : We should try to condole each other on the occasion of a bereavement. When the Holy Prophet (S.A.W.) returned from the battle of Uhad, women presented themselves before Him (S.A.W.) to inquire the welfare of their relations. When Hazrat Hamana bint Jahash appeared, the Holy Prophet (S.A.W.) counselled patience and told her to bear the loss of her brother, Hazrat Abdullah, with fortitude, whereupon she recited *Inna Lillahe wa inna ilaihe Raje'oon,* and prayed for her brother's salvation. Then the Holy Prophet (S.A.W.) asked her to put up with the loss of Hazrat Hamza her maternal uncle as well, and she prayed for him too.

> Hazrat Abu Talha had a son who was sick; he had to go to work, leaving him sick. Shortly after his departure the son died. His wife asked Hazrat, Talha's friends that the news of the death of the son should not reach the father. When Hazrat Talha returned home in the evening, he asked about the son. The wife told him that he was more comfortable than before, and served food to her husband. He took his meal in peace and went to sleep. In the morning the noble lady conveyed the sad news to her husband in a sagacious way by telling that if some body wanted his thing back from the borrower, can the latter refuse it ? Thereupon Hazrat Talha said: "How can the borrower claim that right?" The forbearing lady said. "Then be resigned to (the bereavement of) your son." *(Muslim)*

All ordeals that are faced for the sake of the truth and supremacy of faith are to be welcomed, and borne with fortitude and smilingly. Instead of being overwhelmed by feelings of sorrow and disappointment, we should thank Almighty Allah, for his favour for the acceptance of our sacrifices.

The mother of Hazrat Abdullah Ibn Zubair, Hazrat Asma, (the daughter of Hazrat Abu Bakr) once fell ill. Her son Hazrat Abdullah, came to see her. His august mother, on this occasion said: "O son, it is my prayer to Allah that I be alive till I have witnessed two things: either I should hear the news of your death in a battlefield as a martyr and I should, on hearing this news, secure the blessings of fortitude or that you should be the victor in a battle and I should feel the coolness in my eyes on seeing you as the victor". As it happened, Hazrat Abdullah bin Zubair died fighting in a battlefield during the life time of Hazrat Asma, and Hajjaj bin Yousuf had his corpse hung from a gibbet. Hazrat Asma had become old by that time, but despite her frailty, she went to see the dead body of her son, and instead of lamenting on the unfortunate death of her son, she addressed Hajjaj and said: "Has the time not yet come for this rider to dismount?"

Participation in the Bereavements of Friends : A Muslim should make it a point to condole and sympathise with each other in sorrow and bereavement. Join your friends and relatives in their tragedies and catastrophies to mitigate their pain and sorrow. The Holy Prophet (S.A.W.) has said:

> "The entire Muslim nation is like a single human body. If the eye suffers pain, the whole body is affected; and when the head aches, the whole body feels the pain."
>
> *(Muslim)*
>
> When the Holy Prophet (S.A.W.) learnt about the martyrdom of Hazrat Jafar Tayyar, he said, "Send food to the house of Jafar, because his people, overcome by sorrow, will not be able to cook any food today."
>
> *(Abu Daud)*

According to Hazrat Abu Hurairah, the Holy Prophet (S.A.W.) once said:

> "A person who offers condolences to a woman who has just lost her child, shall be admitted to Paradise and covered with a sheet from Heaven." *(Tirmizi)*

He (S.A.W.) further said:

> "He who comforts a bereaved person, shall have as much recompense as the sufferer himself." *(Tirmizi)*

The Holy Prophet (S.A.W.) has commanded participation in funerals. Hazrat Abu Hurairah reports that the Holy Prophet (S.A.W.) has said:

> "He who has joined a funeral procession and participated in the funeral prayers shall have one qayrat worth of recompense, and he who has stayed till the burial of the coffin, shall have two qayrats worth of reward." On being asked how much two qayrats would be, the: Holy Prophet (S.A.W.) said: "They would be equal to two mountains." *(Bukhari Muslim)*

One must seek solace and succour from Allah, in the face of multitude of grief and sorrow. One should supplicate Allah after prayers with all humility. The Quran hay said:

> "O believers (in the face of ordeals and tests) seek relief through patience and prayers" (2 : 153)

Prayers When Faced with Grief : Hazrat Abu Hurairah has narrated the following:

Whenever the Holy Prophet (S.A.W.) was beset with worries and anxieties, he lifted his head towards the sky and said:

Subhan-All-hil Azim.

"Allah is Glorified and Magnificent."

When, however, sorrow was on the increase and the devotion in prayers also gained the upper hand, he used to say.

"Ya Hayyu Ya Qayyum. "

O thou Everlasting and Eternal. *(Tirmizi)*

Prayers in Difficult Situations : Whenever one is beset with intense grief and extreme difficult situation, he should recite these supplications. Hazrat Sa'd bin Waqas reports that the Holy Prophet Yunus (Jonah) when swallowed by a huge fish, recited the following payer for his deliverance.

"There is no god but Thee. Thou art Glorified and Spotless and indeed I myself have done wrong to me."
(21 : 87)

As such, a Muslim who when faced with tribulations, prays to Allah in this way, is surely to be blessed with the acceptance of his prayers.

Hazrat Abdullah Ibn Abbas has said that the prayer offered by the Holy Prophet (S.A.W.) on such occasions was:

"There is no god but Allah, the Lord of the great Throne; There is no god save Allah, the Lord of skies and the Lord of earth, the Lord of the Magnificent Throne."

Hazrat Abdullah Ibn Masud says:

"The Holy Prophet (S.A.W.) said that if a person afflicted with some trouble or difficulty, offers the following prayer, Allah will transform his sorrows into cheerfulness:

O Allah, I am Thy slave and son of Thy slave and the son of Thy slave girl. 'My forelock is in Thy hand, Thy command operates in my matters. All Thou commands in relation to me are just. I beg of Thee in every name which is Thine and with which Thou has taught to any of Thy creatures, or which Thou has preferred to keep among Thy secret knowledge, to make the Holy Qur'an the spring of my heart, the light of my eyes, and a means of dispelling my grief and a remover for my anxiety."

Bereavement

When you have to see somebody on death bed, continuously recite loudly the Islamic article of faith:
(Kalimah)

"La-ilaha illal-ahu Muham-madur Rasulullh.

"There is no god except Allah and Muhammad (S.A.W.) is His Messenger."

> The Holy Prophet (S.A.W.) has directed that "When you go to a man who is on death's door keep reciting the *Kalimah*." *(Muslim)*

When somebody is in the agony of death, recite Surah Yasin from the Holy Qur'an. The Holy Prophet (S.A.W.) has instructed that: "Recite Surah Yasin by the side of those persons, who are having their last breath."

And when the person has expired and till his dead body is bathed, the Holy Qur'an should not be recited near the dead body; and those persons not clean and need washing, and the females in menses or passing after birth discharge, should refrain from going near the dead body.

On hearing the news of death you should say:

"Verily we belong to Allah and shall return to Him."

The Holy Prophet (S. A.W.) has said that one who recites this verse will have three rewards from Allah:

(i) Firstly he gets Allah's blessings and peace from Him.

(ii) Secondly he becomes entitled to recompense for the search of truth, and

(iii) Thirdly he is indemnified for the loss he has suffered and gets a better replacement of the loss.

As soon as one has breathed his/her last straighten his/ her, body, arms and feet, close the eyes, and passing a bandage below his/her chin, knot at the head. The toes of the feet fastened together with a strip of cloth, and cover the body with a sheet. All those present should recite.

"Bismillahe wa ala millate Rasul-ullah."

(In the name of Allah and on the millat of the Holy Prophet of Allah (S.A.W.)

All concerned should be informed of the event. While lowering the body in the grave also recite this supplication.

Only good deeds of the dead person should be recounted and not bad ones. The Holy Prophet (S.A.W.) has directed:

"Narrate only virtues of your dead persons and do not mention their evils." *(Abu Daud)*

He has also said: "When somebody dies and his four neighbours testify that he was a virtuous man then Allah says "I have accepted your testimony, and have forgiven him for those things which were not known to you." *(Ibn Hibban)*

Once the companions of the Holy Prophet (S.A.W) recounted the good deeds of a person in his presence. The Holy Prophet (S.A.W.) stated:."Gentlemen, since you are the witnesses of Allah on earth (on your testimony) this person has been allotted the Paradise (by Allah). When you call a dead person as good, Allah admits him into the Paradise, and whom you call bad, Allah sends him to the Hell."

(Bukhari Muslim)

The Holy Prophet (S.A.W.) has further said: "Whenever you pay a visit to a sickman or accompany a funeral procession, always have good words on your tongue, for the angels ditto you and say amen (it may be so).

Wash entire dead body without loss of time. For bathing prepare mild warm water with some strawberry leaves in it, if possible. Put the dead body on a neat wooden plank, remove his clothes and cover the lower part of his body with a sheet of cloth. Cover your hands with hand gloves or a piece of cloth. Then clean his private parts first, and see that the sheet continues to cover the same. Thereafter, perform the ablution of the dead body. In this you need not put water into the mouth and the ears. While giving a bath, plug the ears and nose so that water may not enter into the body through these holes. Then wash the head with soap or any other thing. Then tilt the body a little towards the left, and rush water on the right side from head to feet and repeat this process on the other side. Now remove the water-soaked sheet and replace it with a dry one. Lift the body from the plank and place it on a cot wrapped with coffin.

The Holy Prophet (S.A.W.) has said "Allah forgives forty grave sins of a person who has given bath to a dead person and kept secret of his or her shortcomings or defects; and one who has lowered the dead body into the pit is like a person who has provided a house to the dead person till the Resurrection. *(Tabarani)*

Last Journey

A medium quality cloth of white colour should be used for the shroud of a dead person. it should neither be too costly nor of a very low quality. For males there should be three pieces of the shrouds one sheet (*or outer garment*), one piece (or tahband) to cover his lower part, and a pieced to be used as shirt or "*Kafni*" The sheet should be longer in length and a bit wider so as to fully cover the dead body and its ends may be tied covering the head and the feet.

For females, in addition to these three pieces, arrange a piece of cloth (Sarband) a little more than a meter in length and a little less than a meter in breadth, to cover the head and the hair; and another piece called seena band (chest cover) of sufficient length to provide additional covering from the arms-pit to the knee.

The Holy Prophet (S.A.W.) has said: "Anybody who clothes a dead body with coffin, will get a dress of *Sundus* and *Istabraq* (a fine variety of silken cloth interwoven with silver and gold thread) in the Heaven." *(Hakim)*

Take the funeral procession to the cemetery with a bit fast steps. The Holy Prophet (S.A.W.) has said: "Be quick in taking the funeral procession (to the graveyard)." Hazrat Ibn Mas'ud enquired from the Holy Prophet (S.A.W.) "O Prophet of Allah (S.A.W.), at what speed we should march with the dead to the graveyard?" The Holy Prophet (S.A.W.) replied. "A little less than running. If the dead person was a virtuous man, he should be carried to his good end hastily. If he was not a good person, hasten to remove him from your surrounding." *(Abu Daud)*

Walk on foot when accompanying a bier : Once the holy Prophet (S.A.W.) was accompanying a funeral procession. He noticed some persons riding. He reprimanded them and said: "You ought to feel ashamed, whereas angels are walking on foot you are riding on the back of animals." You may, however, use some means of transport while returning from the graveyard. The Holy Prophet. (S.A.W.) accompanied the funeral procession of Abu Wahidi on foot and returned riding a horse.

Stand up on Seeing Bier : When you see a funeral procession coming, stand up, and if you do not have time to accompany it, wait for some time till the procession has gone ahead. The Holy Prophet (S.A.W.) has said: "When you see a bier, stand up, and those who are accompanying it should not sit till it is placed (on the ground)."

Participation in Funerals : You should make it a point to offer funeral prayers, and Accompany the funeral procession to the graveyard and lend your shoulders to carry the bier to the graveyard . . . . .

The grave should be dug according to the direction of Qibla, and the dead body should be lowered into the pit from the side of Qibla. If the body is not heavy, two persons would be enough to lower it, otherwise, three or four persons may have to be employed for the purpose. While lowering the body, turn its face towards the Qibla. After having laid the body untie the knots of the shroud.

Don't be Desperate : If you get involved in some serious worries and calamities which may make your life quite miserable; even then you should not lose hear nor ever try to commit suicide, for this is not only sheer cowardice but misappropriation of Allah's trust and munificence and this is a sin as well. Under such circumstances have recourse to Allah and regularly recite this prayer;

> "O Allah, with Your knowledge of the Unseen and Your power over Your creatures, keep me alive, as long as You know it is good for me to live, and grant me death when You know, it is better for me to die."
>
> *(Musnad Ahmad)*

Whenever you see somebody in distress, recite the following invocation, Hazrat Abu Hurairah quotes the holy Prophet (S.A.W.) as having said that whosoever recites this supplication on seeing somebody in trouble, he by the Will of Allan, himself remains immune from trouble.

> "Thanks be to Allah Who has kept me safe from this ordeal in which you are involved, and has granted me supermacy over many of His creatures."

Observe Purdah to Bury a Female : When lowering the body of a female in the grave, arrangements should be made for Purdah (Seclusion or keeping away women from the sight of strangers).

While covering the pit with earth, start from the side of the head. Gather soft clay with both the hands and throw it on the grave three times. For the first time while throwing soil say:

> *Minha khalq-na-kum* (We created you from this very earth;.

While throwing the earth second time say:

> Wa fiha n'ueedu hum (And We are retruning you to the same),

And when throwing the same for the third time say:

> *Wa minha nukh-riju-kum taratan ukhra.*
>
> (And We shall raise you again from this earth).
>
> (20 : 551)

Do not build the grave too high nor make it like a quadrangle. Only so much earth should be thrown over the grave, which has been excavated from the pit. When the grave has been filled with the earth some water may be sprinkled over it.

After having finished the burial, stay for some time near the grave praying for the salvation of the deceased and recite verses from the Holy Qur'an for the repose of the departed soul. Other people should also be asked to join in the prayers for the deceased.

> The Holy Prophet (S.A.W.) used to pray for the dead person after his burial and also asked others. "This is the time for the reckoning of accounts. Pray to Allah

> for the stead-fastness of your brother, and beg for Allah's mercy for him." *(Abu Daud)*

Send Cooked Food to the Bereaved Family : In case of a death taking place among your relatives or neighbours, arrange to send cooked food for one or two times, to that house, as the bereaved family would be too much grieved and upest to think of preparing food. This is a token of sympathy and love with the grieved family.

Give something according to your means in charity for the peace of the departed soul. But refrain from indulging in irreligious and unauthorised practices and rituals.

Participation in Funeral Prayers : You should make it a point to invariably attend funeral prayers. Participation in funeral prayers is like beseeching Allah for the peace of the soul of the dead person, and this is an important right of the deceased. In case there is a danger that the prayer is likely to be missed if you have to perform ablution, then you should perform Tayammum and join the prayer.

> The Holy Prophet's (S.A.W.) injunction in this regard is: "Offer funeral prayers, such a prayer may move you and soften your heart. A tender-hearted person remains under the shadow of Allah and he welcomes every good act." *(Mustadrak Hakim)*

> And the Holy Prophet (S.A.W.) has also said " A dead body for which three rows of Muslims offer prayers will certainly go to heaven. *(Abu Daud)*

The Holy Prophet (S. A.W.)) has further remarked "When a person participates in the funeral of another person, and offers funeral prayers for him, the former will get a recompense equivalent to one qayrat and one who takes part in the burial as well, will get recompense equal to two qayrat. Some one asked about the volume of two qayrat the Holy Prophet (S.A.W.) replied "they will be equal to two mountains." *(Bukhari - Muslim)*

The bier should be set in such a way that the head of the dead person should face North and the feet South; and the face mould be in the direction of *Qibla*.

If you are leading a funeral prayer, stand in such a way that you may be facing the chest of the deceased.

The number of rows of participants in a funeral service should be odd. If there are a few persons, only one row should be formed, otherwise set up more rows, but their number must be odd.

Niyyat (Intention) : When you begin funeral prayers, affirm in your heart (Niyyat) that you are praying for the salvation of the dead person from Allah. The Most Compassionate of the compssionates. Both the *Imam* and the followers should make this affirmation.

In a funeral prayer the Imam and the congregation should recite the same supplication. The followers should not remain quite. The Imam may call the Takbir loudly and the followers should repeat them slowly.

Modus Operandi of Funeral Prayers : In a funeral prayer four *Takbirs* (Allah-u-Akbar) are recited loudly. With the first Takbir raise your hands upto your ears and thereafter fold them, and recite the following sana (eulogy).

> "Allah! Thou art Pure and sublime alongwith their praise and laudation. Thy Name brings good and blessings; and Thy Greatness and Magnitude are highest, Great is Thy Praise, and there is no god but Thee."

Now recite the second Takbir but do not raise your hands nor make any sign with your head. After the second Takbir the following Salat may be recited:

> "Allah! vouchsafe Thy compassion upon Muhammad and his descendents; just as Thou hadst mercy and Thou sent peace and blessed and hadst compassion on the descendents of Abraham. Verily Thou art praise-worthy, the Great."

The third Takbir is to he said without raising of hinds and the prescribed prayers is to be recited for the dead.

Prayers Prescribed for the Occasion : If the body is of an adult man or woman, the following prayers is to be offered after the third Takbir:

> "Allah! forgive our living and dead; those present and those who are not present; our minors and elders; our males and females. Allah! those whom Thou keepest alive, may they be kept alive in the fold of Islam; and those whom Thou deems fit to send death, may they die in faith."

The following prayer is to be recited in case the body is that of a boy:

> "Allah make this male child a means for our salvation; and make him a means for our reward a store (for our reward) in Hereafter, and make him the intercessor whose intercession may be accepted.

If the body is that of a minor girl, the prayer to be offered is given below:

> "Allah make this female child a means for our salvation, and make her a means for our reward store (for our reward) in Hereafter, and make the intercessor whose intercession may be accepted.

Finally the fourth Takbir is to be said and the Salams s are to be said in both directions, (right and left.).

Reflection upon Death : While accompanying a funeral, we should always reflect upon our destiny and consider that just as you are going to bury some one today, so some day you too will be buried by others and a funeral procession will march for you. We should, for that while at least have time to reflect upon (our end) and the hereafter and purge ourselves of the base emotions of the world.

Accompany a bier to the graveyard, and participate in the burial of the deceased. Apart from this, you should visit graveyards quite often, as it revives the remembrance of the Hereafter, as well as helps us prepare ourselves for the journey of life after death.

> The Holy Prophet (S.A.W.) once accompanied a funeral procession to the graveyard, where he wept by the side of a grave so much that the ground became wet. Addressing the Companions, he said: "Brethren! prepare yourself for this day (of death)." *(Ibn Majah)*

On another occasion, sitting by the side of a grave, he said: "The grave daily declares in a very frightening tone: Children of Adam, have you forgotten me? I am the house of solitude; the place of isolation and nightmare; the abode of insects and worms; and shortness and ordeals, (for you) except for those blessed ones for whom Allah make me broad and wide. For all men I am a source of torture".

> And he (S.A.W.) further said: "Either grave is a pit among the pits or the Gardens or the Paradise."
>
> *(Tabarani)*

Grave as a Source of Lesson : A visit to the graveyard should infuse into you the imagery of life after death.

While entering a graveyard, the following prayer may be recited"

> "Peace be upon you, O Obedient faithfuls, the dwellers of this place, God willing, soon we shall join you. We Pray to Allah for you and ourselves, that He may keep us safe."

A graveyard is not a place where you may indulge in irresponsible and loose talks; cut jokes, laugh and chit chat on worldly matters. The grave is the gateway to the Hereafter on seeing which you should feel overwhelmed with the feelings remorse and repentance, which may bring tears in your eyes.

> The Holy Prophet (S.A.W.) has said: "I had asked you not to visit the graveyard to save you from shirk. If you now like, can go (to see the graves) since graves revive the memories of the Hereafter. *(Muslim)*

Graves not to be Built as Permanent Structures : The Holy Prophet (S.A.W.) has specifically prohibited from making graves as permanent structures or decorating them. When the Holy Prophet (S.A.W.) was near the end of his (S.A.W.) worldly life, and felt much pain and uneasiness so much so that at times he covered his face with his sheet and then uncovered his face alternately. In this state of pain and restlessness Hazrat Ayesha heard him saying "Allah's curse be upon the Jews and Christian who had converted the graves of their Prophets into places of worship."

Praying for Dead : You should go to the graveyard and pray to Allah far salvation of the dead. According to Hazrat Safyan, "Just as the living persons are in need of food and water, so the dead are in great need of prayers."

> According to a tradition, when Allah elevates the status of a virtuous servant in the Paradise by one degree he asks Allah, "O Lord, how did I get this elevation'?" And Allah answers: "Because of your son, who has been praying for thy salvation." *(Tabarani)*

8

Art of Discussion

The tongue and the language are great gifts of Allah. These gifts that Allah has given him makes him superior to all other creatures

> "The Most Gracious Allah has taught the Quran; He has created man; He has taught him speech."
>
> (*Ar-Rahman : I-4*)

The greater the gift, the higher would be its repayment. Being grateful for it is as necessary as being ungrateful is reprehensible.

Islam has explained how people can derive benefit from this unparalled blessing, and how the speech that flows from their tongues throughout the day be used for goodness and truth. People who are never tired of talking are not few in number.

If you examine their talks you will find that most of these consist of senseless, absurd and trash things, whereas Allah has not given men their tongues for this purpose, nor these capabilities were given for such a purpose:

> "In most of their secret talks there is no good; but if one exhorts to a deed of charity or justice or conciliation between men, (secrecy is permissible): to him who does this, seeking the good pleasure of Allah, We shall soon give a reward of the highest (value)."
>
> (*An-Nissa : 114*)

Islam has given special attention to speech, its style, its etiquette and rules, because the talk that comes out from a man's mouth discloses his intellectual level and moral nature, because the etiquette of speech in a group reveals its general standard, and shows the standard of decency in their environment.

Take an Account of Yourself : Before addressing others take a glance at yourself, and ask yourself whether this is an occasion which demands speaking. If the answer is in the affirmative, then speak, otherwise silence is much better. To avoid talking unnecessarily on appropriate occasions is a worship of great rewards.

Abdullah bin Masood says:

> "By the Being other than whom there is no God, on this earth there is none more deserving of long imprisonment than the tongue." (*Tibrani*)

Abdullah Ibn Abbas says : "Five things are more valuable than the horses with the black-striped legs

1. Do not indulge in senseless talk, because it is. useless and absurd, and I am uncomfortable from the fear of your committing a sin.
2. Talk purposefully when there is an occasion for it, for there. are many people who talk without an occasion. This is a drawback.
3. Do not indulge in hot discussion with an intelligent man or with a fool. If he is intelligent, he will be angry with you and will hate you, and if he is a fool and uneducated, he will try to harm you.
4. In the absence of your brother speak of him in the same words in which you would like him to speak of you in your absence, and consider him innocent of 'the thing which you would like him to consider you innocent of.
5. Act like a man who thinks that he will be rewarded for a good deed and will be punished on committing a crime."

(*Ibn Abi-al-duniya*)

A Muslim can develop these attributes in himself only when he keeps his tongue in control, and is able to keep silent wherever necessary. He should be able to hold the reins of his tongue in his hand ; wherever necessary he should speak, and wherever it is not necessary he should keep quiet.

Those who are ruled by their tongue, they are pushed back, and in the fields of life they receive insults and disrepute.

Golden Rule of Silence

One loses sense in talking absurdities and aimlessly. Those who want to impress others in meetings by their talk, they speak so glibly and endlessly that the words come out from their mouth like rainwater. Although they try to convince others that they are very wise, intelligent and far-sighted, but sometimes the impression created by their long-winding speeches is quite the contrary, and from their talks people feel that there is no relation between what they want the people to believe about them and what actually they are.

When a man wants to contemplate over his position and wants to organize his religious thoughts, he runs away from the atmosphere of noise and uproar and takes shelter in a quiet place. And therefore if Islam recommends silence and considers it a means of civilized training, then it is not at all surprising.

The Prophet had, among other things, advised Hazrat Abuzar in this way

> "Adopt silence. This is a way of causing Satan to run away, it is a support to you in the matter of your religion." (*Ahmed*)

Undoubtedly the tongue is a rope in the hands of Satan. He turns it anywhere he likes. When a man is unable to control his affairs, his mouth becomes a passage for all the negative talk which contaminates the heart and covers it with the sheet of negligence.

> The prophet has said: "The faith of a man cannot be straight unless his heart is straight, and his heart cannot be straight unless his tongue becomes straight." (*Ahmed*)

The first stage of this straightness and correctness is that man should wash his hands off all the irrelevant matters and he should not interfere in those things about which he is not answerable.

> "It is the excellence of a man's faith that he gives up meaningless work." (*Tirmizi*)

Avoidance of Nonsense : To avoid irrelevant and nonsensical things is a condition for success and is a proof of perfection. Quran has mentioned it in between two essential duties (Faraiz) of Muslims, which give an idea of its importance:

> "Successful indeed are the believers who are humble in their prayers, and who shun vain conver sation, and who are payers of zakat." (*Al-Muminoon : 1-4*)

If all the men of the world count their efforts which they make in indulging in vain conversation and acts, they will come to realize that a very large part of the long-winding tales and stories, widely circulated news, narratives, speeches and broadcasts comprises of vain, meaningless and useless things, which are eagerly watched, and heard, but no benefit is derived from them.

Islam has expressed its disapproval of the meaningless talks and things, because the superficial and useless things have no value in its eyes. It dislikes that man should not busy himself in matters for which he has not been created and instead he should waste his life in involving himself in other irrelevant matters.

The more distant a Muslim will be from an absurd and irrelevant thing, the more high will be his rank before Allah.

Anas bin Malik says that when a man died another man passed a remark about him in the presence of the Prophet that he would go to Paradise. The Prophet stopped him and said:

> "Do not you know? It is likely that he might have indulged in meaningless conversation or might have been miserly in spending his wealth, although this does not effect any reduction." (*Tirmizi*)

A vain talker, on account of the weak co-ordination between his thought and his tongue, blurts out whatever comes on his tongue. Sometimes he says something which places him in danger, and he ruins his future. It is said that the more one talks, the more one commits mistakes. An Arabic poet has said:

> "The youth dies by the fault of his tongue whereas from the faltering of the feet death does not occur."
>
> In the tradition it is stated: "A man says something so that those present may laugh, although on account of it he is thrown to the most distant region between the earth and the sky. The faltering of the feet cause much less harm than the faltering of the tongue." (*Baihaqui*)

Heart-warming Speech : When a man has to speak, he should say something good and worthwhile. He should accustom his tongue to indulge in good, decent and respectable conversation, because the best manifestation of the thoughts and feelings demeanours and mind is the classical literature, with which Allah has blessed the followers of all the religions.

Quran has clearly mentioned that the covenant which Hazrat Moosa had taken from Bani Israil also included the condition that they should indulge in good and worth-while conversation

> "And (recall) when We took a covenant from the Children of Israil, (saying): "Worship none save Allah, be good to parents and kindred and orphans and those in need; and speak aright and kindly to people, and establish salat and pay Zakat." (*Baqarah: 82*)

Clean and decent conversation impresses both friends and foes, and its sweet fruits can be readily enjoyed. It guards love between friends. It strengthens their friendship and makes it durable and defeats all the tricks of the devil for weakening their relations and for sowing the seeds of discord between them

> "Say (O Prophet !) to my slaves to speak which is kindlier. Verily, the devil sows discord among them. Verily, the devil is for man an open enemy."
>
> (*Bani Israil: 53*)

The devil is hiding in ambush against man. He tries to sow the seeds of discord, enmity and jealousy among them. He wants that the ordinary disputes be converted into big bloody battles, and that no spanner should be thrown in his works by means of good, decent and kindly talk.

It you would talk gracefully with your enemies, their enmity would disappear, and their tempers will be cooled, or at least a distinct difference can be witnessed in their hostile attitude.

> "The good deed and the evil deed are not alike. Repel the evil deed with one which is better, then surely, he, between whom and you there was enmity (will become) as though he was a bosom friend."
>
> (*Ha-Meem-Sajda : 34*)

To make Muslims in all conditions well-behaved and of good manners, the Prophet has said : "You will not be able to rule over the people through your wealth, but through good appearance and good manners you can win their hearts."—(Al-Bazzar). In the eyes of Islam not to give a gift to somebody while behaving in a decent way and with good manners is better than giving it in an indecent manner, and by giving him pain.

> "A kind word with forgiveness is better than charity followed by injury. Allah is Free of All Wants and Most Forbearing." (*Baqarah: 263*)

Decent conversation is such a habit that it is counted among the virtues and good attributes, and one who, adopts this habit becomes worthy of pleasing Allah and for him is written eternal bliss.

Anas narrates that one man asked the Prophet to teach him such an act as would enable him to enter the Paradise.

> The Prophet replied : "Feed the poor, practise salutation (salaam) in the night when people are enjoying sleep, offer prayers, you will enter Paradise with peace." (*Al-Bazzar*)

Allah has commanded us to adopt decent and serious manners of speaking when we may discuss matters with the followers of other religions. It should not have intensity nor heat and anger. However those who are aggressive against us, it is necessary to put a stop to their aggression

> "And argue not with the People of the Book unless it be in (a way) that is better, save with such of them as do wrong." (*Ankabut : 46*)

Great men always take care in all conditions that no extra and useless word comes out of their mouth, and they do not adopt an attitude of pride and foolishness with every specie of creatures.

Malik has reported that Yahya bin Saeed has told him that Hazrat Issa (Christ) one day passed by a pig, and he addressed it: "Pass on peacefully." He was asked : "You talk to a pig in this manner !" He replied: "I am afraid my tongue may not be habituated to rude talk."

Answer to the Uneducated : Some people remain ill-mannered, hot-tempered and lewd talkers for the whole of their lives. Their faith and belief are not at all disturbed by these evils, nor does their morality admonish them on their attitude. They have no hesitation in telling others things which are disagreeable to them. Whenever they find a suitable field tro let on their steam, their tongues run away with vulgar and obscene talks like reinless steeds. No cries stop them nor does any voice inhibit them.

The attitude of a gentleman with such people should be that he should not engage himself in any discussion with them, because any provocation would lead to great disturbance, and it is necessary to seal this source of trouble. For this reason Islam has commanded to ignore the foolish and unwise people.

Once one of these illiterate persons stood at the door of the Prophet's house with a view to entering it. The kind Prophet treated him very decently and managed to persuade him to go away. There was no other go besides this, for tolerance and forbearance is the cloth by which the uneducated and the fool can be gagged. Had the Prophet allowed him to do whatever he intended to do, then he would have had to hear all the trivial and the rubbish talk from which his ears thus remained safe.

Hazrat Ayesha says that one man sought the Prophet's permission to enter the house, and the Prophet remarked: "What a bad man is he of his family!" When he came in, the Prophet talked to him pleasantly and softly. After he went away, she asked him 'O Messenger of Allah! You heard this man talking in this way, yet there was no sign of perturbation on your face, on the contrary you talked to him pleasantly ?' The Prophet replied

> "O Ayesha! when did you hear me talking vulgarly ? On the Day of Judgment before Allah the worst man would be the one for avoiding whose vulgar talk people stopped meeting him." (*Bukhari*)

This policy is such that its truth is borne out by our daily experiences, for how can a man like that could tarnish his good manners by hobnobbing with a badmannered person ? If he starts teaching manners to every uneducated and foolish person, then his life will become a bundle of troubles.

Man swallows his anger once, twice, but later on he bursts.

But a well-behaved Muslim is expected by Islam to tolerate more troubles and adversities, so that consequently the evil should not be able to stand firmly on its ground.

> Sa'eed bin Musayyeb says : "When the Prophet was sitting with his companions one person used insulting words against Hazrat Abu Bakr, causing him pain, but Abu Bakr was silent. For the second time also he used the bitter words against him, and still Abu Bakr was silent. When for the third time he hurt him with his tongue, Abu Bakr tried to answer him. The Messenger of Allah got up. Abu Bakr asked him : 'Are you displeased with me, O Messenger of Allah! The Prophet replied : 'No, but from the heaven an angel had come down and he was denying that man's talk, and when you started to answer that man, the angel went away and the devil sat down. And I cannot sit where the devil is sitting'." (*Abu Daud*)

To pay respect to the foolish and unintelligent people does not mean that their low and superficial acts should also be accepted. In these two conditions there is a very great difference.

The first thing means that man should have control over his self in the presence of folly and unintelligence, and he should not give them a chance to show their true nature which is the bearer of anger and wrath, and be provoked to take revenge.

While the second aspect has quite the contrary sense. In that condition it amounts to allow the self to submit to folly, meanness and disrepute, and to accept those low things which no wise and decent man would be ready to accept.

The holy Quran has treated the subject of respect to the unintelligent people and the hatred of their low and mean acts in this maner

> "Allah does not like that evil should be noised abroad in public speech, except where injustice has been done; for Allah is He Who hears and knows all things. Whether you express a good deed or conceal it or cover evil with pardon, verily Allah does blot out (sins) and has power (in the judgment of values)"
>
> (*An-Nissa : 148-149*)

Silver Rule of Speech

The commands that Islam issued to keep the tongue safe from baseless and absurd things is to declare polemical discussion and controversial debating and to shut its doors upon Muslims, irrespective of whether the polemical debating is correct or otherwise.

It is so because here such conditions arise that a man tries to score a point and to overcome his opponent. As he wants to defeat his adversary by his talk, he takes the support of even dubious and unreliable things which can strengthen his argument, and he quotes such statements unhesitatingly which help him in his task. In such a gathering people give more importance to winning than on expressing truth. This is likely to result in rancour and disturbances, in which clarification and satisfaction have no place.

Islam hates all these conditions and considers them a danger for the religion and morality.

> The Prophet has said: "He who has given up controversial discussion in senseless and false matters, for him there will be built a house in the lower section of the Paradise ; and he who has corrected his morals, for him there will be built a house in the upper section of the Paradise." (*Abu Daud*)

There are some people whom Allah has gifted the power of tongue and has made them expert in that line. This prompts them to exercise their expertise over all people, educated or uneducated. It becomes a burning desire in their hearts, and they do not rest content with out satisfying this desire.

When this group makes others a victim of their power of speech and shows their expertise, they hurt their feelings, and when this quality is required to be employed in expressing the religious realities then all the beauty and grandeur of their speech vanishes.

Islam is extremely displeased with nonsensical talkers who shout at the top of their voices, and admonish them very severely.

> The Prophet has said : "Before Allah the most hated are the quarrelsome debaters." (*Bukhari*)

> In another tradition it is stated : "After receiving guidance no community went astray and did not deviate from the path it was following, except when debaters turned them away from it." (*Tirmizi*)

On account of the speed of its tongue, this group does not stay within the limits. 1t goes on talking, feels conceited and struts along. For this group the position of words is of first importance, their meaning takes the second place. As regards the great and clean purpose, many times it is demoted to the last place, and sometimes in this hullabaloo it does not get any place at all.

> It is narrated that once a deceitful man, wearing beautiful clothes, went in the presence of the Prophet and during conversation raised his voice higher than the voice of the Prophet. When he went away, the Prophet said : "Allah does not like people of this type. They work their tongue in the way a cow does when it chews the cud. In the same way Allah will twist their faces and mouths on the Doomsday in the fire of hell." (*Tibrani*)

When in the fields of religion, politics and other branches of learning the so-called orators and expert writers come forward for indulging in polemics and debates, then the spirit of religion receives a setback. The face of politics, learning and sciences is disfigured. And possibly this helped in hastening the decline of our civilization and culture, in the formation of groupism of the schools of Fiqh, division of the Ummah on the sectarian basis and other diseases of disruption. In other matters of religion and worldly affairs also this controversial debating spread its poison.

Controversial debating is words away from pure, clean discussion, and sober and pleasant argumentation.

A number of companions of the Prophet have reported that once they were discussing and debating some religious point, when the Prophet arrived; he was terribly angry. He was never seen so angry before. He admonished them and said:

> "Stay put, O Ummah of Muhammed! Nations before you were destroyed by this only. Give up this debating. The portion of good is very little in it. Give up this discussion and argumentation, for this is not a quality of a Momin. Avoid this polemic and disputation, for the loss sustained by one who indulges in it becomes complete. For your being a sinner it is sufficient that you are a debater. Give up this debating, because on the Day of Resurrection there will be none to intercede for the debater. Wash off your hands of this wicked habit, for in Paradise I will lead only to three kinds of houses, its lower floor, middle floor and the upper floor, which will be for that man who has given up debating truthfully and with good intention. Keep away from this bad habit because after idolatry, the first thing that my Lord has forbidden is this very debating."
>
> (*Tibrani*)

Such gatherings of men are arranged where novel and attractive talks drive men towards them. Islam dislikes such gatherings, where people sit and waste their time, and where people always lap up news and defects of others. They have wealth in excess under whose shadow they try to have good time. They have no other work besides this that they seek pleasure in the affairs of other people.

> "Woe to every (kind of) scandal-monger and backbiter, who piles up wealth and lays it by, thinking that his wealth would make him last forever! By no means ! He will be sure to be thrown into that which breaks to pieces." (*Humaza : 1-4*)

In modern times such gathering in mehfils and clubs are the order of the day.

This is a calamity that has caused the society to be infected with a number of diseases. This calamity is found in abundance in big towns and small cities, even though there is no religious necessity for this thing.

It is mentioned in the hadith : "Avoid sitting on the roads." The people said: "O Messenger of Allah! What would happen to our those gatherings without which there would be no life for us." He said : "If you insist on having gathering, then do due justice to them." People asked : "What is their due, O Messenger of Allah ?"

> He answered : "To keep your eyes down, to remove harmful things, to give answer to salutation, to command performance of good things and to prevent commitment of evil things." (*Muslim*)

Always speak the truth, and never hesitate to do so, whatever the consequences.

Open your mouth when it is necessary, and, whenever you talk, speak something useful. Incessant and unnecessary talk is against the norms of seriousness and decency. We have to answer for every word we utter and the angel appointed by Allah notes our conversation.

> "No sooner a word is uttered by the tongue the angel remains ready to note it." (60 :18)

Whenever you talk, talk softly and with a smile : Speak in a voice neither too low that the listener may not be able to hear, nor so loud that the listener may feel you are trying to overawe him. The Quran has:

> "Lo! the harshest of all voices is the voice of the ass." (41 : 19)

Do not pollute your tongue with vulgar words : don't abuse, backbite or complain against any person; don't imitate or ape others, or ridicule anybody or indulge in self praise or tall talks; do not make false promises. Avoid arguing unnecessarily and playing to the gallery. Do not pass sarcastic remarks nor call anybody with a bad name. Nor you should swear frequently.

Always speak what is just, even though you or your friends, or kinsfolk may have to suffer. The Holy Quran says:

"And when you say a thing with your tongue, say what is just, even though the person might be your relation."

If women have to talk with men, they should not talk coquettishly but in a straight-forward and rough manner, lest the man should indulge into harbouring lustful thoughts.

Don't Enter into Argument with Illiterate Persons : When illiterate persons try to entangle you in unnecessary talk, take your leave from such people and quit the place. Such people are among the worst lot of the people.

If you are explaining something to a man, bear in mind his mental capacity and intelligence, and then explain the matter to him accordingly. If he does not follow, explain to him again without getting irritated.

Always talk to the point and with brevity. It is not wise to prolong conversation.

Explain religious points in simple and appealing style. If you have to explain some theological point to some religious edict, do so in a manner that is both simple and appealing.

Seeking a name through oratory, or to impress people with the flow of the words and to deliver speeches just for fun and enjoyment or as an expression of pride, is a despicable habit that blackens the heart.

Never flatter or talk in a way smacking of sycophancy. Always keep your self-respect upper most in your mind and do not degrade yourself.

Never interrupt conversation between two persons. If you have to speak out at all, do so with their permission.

Talk deliberately and with dignity in an appropriate manner. Do not talk rapidly nor indulge in loose talk or cut jokes too often. This will belittle you.

Reply to aquestion after due consideration. If you are asked a question, listen to it attentively and then reply after due consideration. It is extremely undesirable that a random and unthoughtful reply should be given. And if someone else is being asked a question, do not take upon yourself to reply.

Never anticipate what other is saying. If you are being told a thing, do not show by expression or words that you already know what he is saying. It is quite possible that he may come out with something new or may he be able to move you by some particular fact or style of narration. The earnestness and grace of the conversationalist also has its effect on the listener.

While talking, do not point towards third person lest he becomes suspicious. Similarly never try to overhear or eavesdrop other people's conversation.

Try to listen to other persons more, and talk as little as possible. Do not reveal anything that is secret. Confiding your secret in others and expecting that it would be kept secret is a foolish expectation.

Expressing through Letters

Bismillah-ir Rahman-nir Rahim i.e., in the name of Allah, the Most Beneficent, the Most Merciful. The Holy Prophet (S. A.W.) has said that a work which does not commence with Bismillah remains incomplete and without blessing. Some people write 786 in place of Bismillah. This should be avoided, as only wards appoved by Allah are blessed.

Invariably write your address in each letter : Don't neglect it thinking that the addressee already knows your address. It is not necessary that, if the addressee has been communicated your address earlier, he would still remember it or have it in his record.

Either below your address or on the top of the right side write the date of the letter.

Write appropriate appellation. Having put down the date, address the addressee in a simple and direct manner with proper appellation. He should be addressed in a manner that reflects sincerity and affection, avoiding appellation indicating artificiality and adulation. In the next line greetings should be offered in the form of "As-Salam-o-Alaikum."

End your letter with proper subscription. After having written the heading and the address, write down the object of writing the letter. Once the text of the letter is over, it should he ended with a proper subscription, e.g. "Yours Sincerely," "Yours Truly," "Faithfully," "Affectionately," etc.

The letter should he legible, simple in style and neatly written which may he appreciated by the addressee.

Some hints for writing letters : The following guidelines will help you in writing a good letter.

(a) It should be precise and to the point it may not be lengthy but must contain necessary details.

(b) The status of the addressee should he kept in mind throughout.

(c) The tone of the letter should be suave and dignified throughout. Non-serious topics should be avoided.

(d) Never write a letter when you are heated or extremely angry. Ensure that no improper words are written. Write when you are cool and in proper mood.

(e) A general letter should not contain any secret matter.

Reading another person's letter without his permission is ethical misappropriation.

Be regular and prompt in writing letters of your welfar to your relatives and friends.

Write letter of sympathy when necessary. If somebody falls sick or meets with an accident or gets involved in some difficulty, do write a letter expressing your concern and sympathy.

Similarly when there be a happy event; you must congratulate the person concerned.

Post letter before mail leaves. If a letter has been given to you for posting, be particular in posting it well in time.

Send stamps for reply. While writing to unfamiliar person within the country and from whom a reply is solicited, it is desirable to enclose stamps or a stamped reply envelope or post-card.

Do not confine your letter to the matters of interest to you alone; but keep in view the sentiments and interests of the addressee as well; while you write about your family members' welfare, do ask him about the health and well being of his relatives also. And mind that you do not pester the addressee with numerous demands. Too many demands degrade a person.

9

Propagation of Beliefs

> And who is better in speech than him who calleth towards Allah, And Doeth Right and sayeth.
>
> Lo! I am of those who surrender (unto Him). (41: 33)

Journey of Thoughts

1. Develop full appreciation of the position conferred upon you. You are the successor to the mission of the Holy Prophet [S.A.W.] and you have to discharge the same duty of communicating the message of Allah, testifying the truth through your practical life and propagating the teachings of Islam which the Holy Prophet [S.A.W.] performed all through his holy life. Try to develop the same degree of zeal and fervour for the propagation of Islam which was the unique and distinctive characteristic of the Holy Prophet [S.A.W.].

   The Holy Qur'an affirms:

   > "He hath chosen you and hath not put you in any hardship in the matter of faith; follow the faith of your father Abraham. He hath given you the nomenclature of Muslim long ago and in this (Scripture) too, that the Prophet of Allah [S.A.W.] may testify the truth before you and that you may stand witness to the whole of Mankind."

   In other words, the Muslims are the successors to the mission of the Holy Prophet of Allah [S.A.W.] and required, therefore, to discharge the same duty which the Apostle of Allah performed during his auspicious life. In the same manner as the final Prophet of Allah [S.A.W.] struggled day and night by his words and action and made the way of total submission to Allah clear to the people, the adherents to Islam have also to preach Islam, the religion of Allah, to all the people of the world and what is more, they have to practise it in their every day life and testify.

Call to Religion and prove it the religion of truth with the same high sense of duty and missionary zeal.

2. Always keep in view your real position in this world and constantly endeavour to order your life accordingly. You are not like the other people of the world. Allah has conferred on you a distinction and a privilege. You have been vested with the honour of leading the affairs of the world. You don't believe in extremes and are expected to keep yourself firm on the straight path of Allah with moderation.

   The Holy Qur'an affirms:

   > "Thus we have appointed you a middle nation that ye may be witnesses against mankind and that the Messenger may be a witness against you." (2: *143*)

3. Seek knowledge of the real purpose and aim of your life and try to achieve it with confidence and conviction. The real mission and task before the Muslims is to establish and enforce the religion as a whole which the Holy Prophet Muhammad [S.A.W.] communicated to the mankind-a religion which contains divine guidance and injunctions in each and every aspect of life such as beliefs and worship, morality, and social, economic and political spheres etc. The Holy Prophet [S.A.W.] during his auspicious days enforced Islam with all its details. The Holy Prophet [S.A.W.] taught beliefs, principles of morality and the modes of worship; he [S.A.W.] established and organised a society on the principles of Islam and brought about countless favours and blessings to the people.

   Allah has affirmed:

   > "He hath ordained for you that religion which He commended unto Noah,and that which We inspire in

> Thee (Muhammad), and that which We commended unto Abraham and Moses and Jesus saying: Establish the religion and be not divided therein." *(42: 13)*

4. Always remain determined to eliminate evil and establish good. This is an obligation you owe to your faith to justify your existence as upholders of the truth. Live to achieve this aim and idea serving this mission. Allah has named you as the best people on earth only because you live to uphold the truth and sacrifice even your life for this noble cause.

> "Ye are the best Community that hath been raised up for mankind. Ye enjoin right conduct and forbid indecency and ye believe in Allah." *(3: 110)*

The Holy Prophet [S.A.W.] has affirmed:

> "I swear by Him Who has power over my life you must enforce virtue and curb evil, otherwise Allah shall send very soon such calamity over you that you will cry and seek mercy from Allah but you will get no response." *(Tirmidhi)*

5. Develop, missionary zeal and exemplary fervour and enthusiasm for the propagation of the message of Allah and to save the people of Allah from the fearful torment of Hell. The Holy Qur'an has acknowledged the unique fervour and abounding zeal of the Holy Prophet [S.A.W.] in the following words:

> "Yet it may be, if they believer not in this statement, that thou wilt torment thy soul with grief for them." *(18: 6)*

The Holy Prophet [S.A.W.] has himself described his feeling in these words:

> "I am like a person who lit a fire and when the surrounding area became bright with light, the moths and insects began to drop in fire. The person is now trying with all the force at his command to stop these moths and insects from dropping in the fire, but the moths and insects are rushing towards the fire

> rendering all his efforts ineffective. Likewise, I am trying my level best to draw you back and keep you away from the fire, yet you are bent upon falling in it." *(Mishkat)*

One day Hazrat 'A'isha [R.A.A.] submitted to the Holy Prophet [S.A.W.]: "O Prophet of Allah [S.A.W.]! Have you passed a harder day than the day of Uhud in your life?" The Holy Prophet [S.A.W.] observed: "Yes, 'Aisha! The day of *'Aqabah* was the hardest in my life." This was the day when, dismayed with the people of Mecca, the Holy Prophet [S.A.W.] had visited Ta'if to convey the message of Allah to the people there. Their chief 'Abd Yalil set ruffians after the Prophet [S.A.W.] who hurled stones at him in response to his message of blessing and salvation. The Prophet of Allah [S.A.W.] sustained serious injuries. His whole body was stained with blood and he fainted. Deeply grieved and frustrated, the Holy Prophet. [S.A.W.] returned to Mecca. When the Prophet [S.A.W.] arrived at Qarn Aththaalib, he had overcome his grief. Allah sent the angel of calamity to the Prophet [S.A.W.]. The angel of torture submitted: "O Prophet of Allah [S.A.W.]! If you wish I shall collide Abu Qubais with Jabal Ahmar and crush all the wicked between the two mountains. The benefactor of the world [S.A.W.] observed:

> "No, no, let me warn my people of the torments of Allah. May Allah open their hearts to accept the truth and concede to the Divine Guidance or else their succeeding generation may submit to the truth." *(Bukhari, Muslim)*

The Meccans were constantly busy conspiring against the Holy Prophet [S.A.W.]. Some said that the Prophet [S.A.W.] should be exiled from the city while others counselled that he should be assassinated. In the mean time a famine struck Mecca. It was such a terrible calamity that the Quraish were constrained to eat leaves and bark of the trees. The children suffered from the terrible agony of hunger and the elder felt restless but helpless over the affliction of their children.

The benefactor of the mankind [S.A.W.] was deeply moved by the heart rending distress of the people. His devoted companions [R.A.A.] could not bear the grief and uneasiness of the Holy Prophet [S.A.W.]. The Holy Prophet [S.A.W.] conveyed his heartfelt sympathy to his deadly foes who had always been after him to harm and tease him and its unhappy memories were still fresh in his mind. The Holy Prophet [S.A.W.] sent a sum of five hundred dinars to Abu Sufyan and an equal amount to Safwan with the instruction that the money should be distributed among the famine-stricken people.

Truly speaking, to be sorry for the misguided, to feel disturbed over their wickedness and distress, to be anxious to save them from the wrath of Allah, to be distressed at their affliction and to have an extraordinary craving for their right guidance- such are the attributes of a missionary of truth which create irresistible attraction in his life and an impression uncommon in history.

6. Serve your people with selfless devotion and do not ask for any recompense for your devotion from anybody. Do whatever good you can only to win the favour of Allah and expect reward and blessings from Him only. The desire to earn the favour of Allah and to demand reward and blessings from Him alone lends weight to a man's word and makes him dynamic. Allah has always been-and will remain for ever. He neither sleeps, nor dozes off. No move or activity of man is hidden from Him. He never lets the reward of any of His devotees go waste. He pays more than ones labour and never deprives any one of His blessings. The Prophets (peace be upon them) repeatedly observed to their people:

"I demand not any reward or recompense from you.
My reward lies with the Lord of the worlds."

Do acquire a deep understanding of Islam and be sure that Islam is the only true religion in the eyes of Allah. No mode of worship, except the one enjoined by this true religion has any worth before Allah. Allah holds only that religion as true and valid which He has revealed in the Holy Qur'an and which the Holy Prophet [S.A.W.] translated into practice during his auspicious life. The Holy Qur'an enjoins upon the Prophet of Allah [S.A.W.] to make it clear to the people that he had adopted his path with careful deliberation and full awareness.

> "Say, this is my way. I call on Allah with sure knowledge, I and whosoever followeth me-Glory be to Allah! and I am not of the idolators." *(12: 108)*

Allah makes clear affirmation:

> "And whosoever seeketh as religion other than the surrender (to Allan) it will not be accepted from him and he will be a loser in the Hereafter." *(3: 85)*

> "The only religion unto Allah is the surrender (unto Him)." *(3:19)*

And beware it is for the performance of this grand task that Allah had sent Prophets (peace be upon them) one after another—and be convinced in your own heart that this wealth of religion which the Almighty has vouchsafed to you is the key to attain excellence and honour in the world and Hereafter. The worldly pomp and show which is transitory and short-lived can not be compared with the eternal and inestimable wealth of religion! The holy Qur'an affirms:

"And We have bestowed upon you seven oft-repented verses and a great book, the Qur'an. Hence care not for this mundane wealth Allah, have conferred on others." Addressing the believers of other Revealed Books before Qur'an, the Holy Qur'an says:

> "Say: O People of the scripture! I guidance till ye observe the Torah and the Gospel and that which was revealed unto you from your Allah." *(5: 68)*

9. Make constant efforts to grasp the real spirit of religion and the wisdom it contains. The Holy Prophet [S.A.W.] has observed.

> "Allah endows, whomsoever He wishes to bless with good the real understanding and deep insight into religion." *(Bukhari, Muslim)*

As a matter of fact, it is tire real knowledge of religion and insight into the spirit of religion which is the fountain-head of all goodness and the man who is deprived of this goodness is deprived of the blessings of this world as well as of the world Hereafter. Such a man can never achieve balance and consistency in life, nor can he truly represent religion in any walk of life.

10. Whatever you wish to proclaim to the world, address it to your self first. Tell yourself first what you wish to tell others and perform in your won life what you preach to others. The distinction of a missionary of true religion is that he tries to project in himself the true model of his preachings. His deeds and character stand testimony to his words. He himself yearns for the truths he propagates to other as a source of goodness. Whenever the Prophets (peace be upon them) rose to call the people to surrender themselves before Allah they proclaimed Ana awwalul muslimin (I am. the first to surrender before Allah).

    Testify by spoken as well as written word that truth is what you represent. Make it evident through your individual life, family relations, social dealings and through your national and political activities that piety can only be developed by adopting the way of life as enunciated by Islam. This system guarantees stability of homes, emergence of a morally oriented society and a culture and civilisation based on justice and equity. Those who ignore the duty of reforming and training their own character and ruminate over the reformation and training of others are completely devoid of common-sense. Their own house is on fire, yet they are carrying about buckets of water looking for a blaze anywhere else to extinguish. Such people are losers not only in this world but in the Hereafter also. Their inaction in this world will render all their preachings ineffective and weightless and in the next world they shall undergo the most deterrent punishment. It is most hateful in the sight of Allah that they do not practise what they preach and tell others to do what they themselves do not do.[1] The Holy Prophet [S.A.W.] has warned such missionaries of Islam who do not do what they preach, of the most fearful punishment. The Holy Prophet [S.A.W.] observed:

> "A man shall be brought on the Day of Judgement and will be thrown into the Fire. His intestines will spill out due to the Fire. He will then carry around his intestines as a donkey goes round the mill. On seeing him the denizens of hell will gather around him and enquire: "O man, what has become of you! Are you not the one who preached to us in the world to perform virtuous deeds? Are you not the one who dissuaded us from the performance of evil acts? How did you come into this place despite having performed such pious deeds?" The man will answer: " I did teach you piety, but never cared for it myself. I forbade you to do evil, but performed evil deeds myself."
>
> *(Muslim, Bukhari)*

The portentous account of the night of Ascension which the Holy Prophet [S.A.W.] related to the people contains a warning for the misguided to reform themselves. The Holy Prophet [S.A.W.] observed:

> "I beheld some people in the night of Ascension whose lips were being clipped with scissors of fire. I enquired from Jibrail [A.S.]: "Who are these people?" Jibrail [A.S.] replied: "They are the orators of your Ummah. They preached piety and fear of Allah to people, but forgot to follow these teachings in their personal lives."
>
> *(Mishkat)*

The illustrious companions [R.A.A.] also used to issue stern warnings to such misguided and hypocritical people who did not follow what they preached. On one occasion, a person said to Hazrat 'Abdullah b. 'Abbas [R.A.A.]: "Hazrat I desire to instruct people in piety and forbid them to commit evil deeds. I wish to propagate religion among the people." Hazrat

'Abdullah enquired: "Have you acquired the proper qualifications for becoming a preacher?" The person submitted: "Yes, I believe I am capable of performing the task of a missionary." Hazrat ibn 'Abbas [R.A.A.] observed: "If you do not apprehend any condemnation in the light of three verses of the Holy Qur'an, do preach Islam." The person enquired: "Which three verses do you mean?" Hazrat ibn 'Abbas [R.A.A.] answered:

The first verse is:

> 'Enjoin ye righteousness upon mankind while ye yourselves forget to practise it.?" *(2: 44)*

Ibn 'Abbas [R.A.A.] then enquired: Do you follow this verse in your practical life fully?" The man replied: "No." Ibn Abbas [R.A.A.] then recited the second verse:

> "O ye who believe! Why say ye that which ye do not do? *(61:2)*

Hazrat ibn 'Abbas [R.A.A.] then asked: "Are you sure you are following this verse" The man replied: "No." Hazrat ibn 'Abbas [R.A.A.] observed: The third verse is:

> "I desire not to do behind your backs that which I ask you not to do." *(11 . 88)*
>
> "Tell me now, have you fully carried out the instruction contained in this verse. The man submitted: "No." Whereupon Hazrat Abdullah observed: "Go then and instruct yourself in piety first and forbid your own self from evil."

11. Perform your prayers with full devotion keeping in view its rules, regulations and conditions. In addition to them also offer supererogatory prayers.

    No one can propagate religion without establishing a close communion with Allah. Prayer is the sure means-a means prescribed by Allah Himself-of establishing a deep connexion with Allah. Allah affirmed through a revelation to the Holy Prophet [S.A.W.].

"O thou wrapped up in the raiment! Keep vigil the night long, save a little-a half thereof, or abate a little thereof, or add (a little) thereto and chant the Qur'an in measure, for We shall charge thee with a word of weight."

(74: 1-5)

'Charge thee with a word of weight' implies 'Propagation of the Religion of Truth' and truly this responsibility is the most burdensome and heavy of all duties in the world. In order to be able to discharge this duty, it is important for you to derive strength from prayer and establish a firm connexion with Allah.

12. Develop a fondness for and interest in the study of the Holy Qur'an and recite the Book regularly. Recite the Qur'an slowly and with deep concentration during the prayers as well as during the period other than prayers. When the Qur'an is recited with a interest and concentration, it becomes easy to understand and reflect upon the meanings of the Holy Qur'an. As soon as one starts appreciating the charms of the word of Allah, his interest and inquisitiveness increases and he goes deeper and deeper in the Book of Allah. The Holy Qur'an is the only source of guidance and warning. It has been revealed to make the people ponder over its contents and derive benefit from its guidance and warnings, so ponder over the meanings of the Holy Qur'an and learn wisdom from it. Recite the Qur'an with a firm determination to mould your own self as well as your society as a whole according to the injunctions of the Holy Qur'an. Only those can establish the rule of Allah who mould their own thought and action according to the teachings of Qur'an. He, who forsakes Qur'an, can no longer maintain his allegiance to the faith, nor can he contribute any way in the struggle to establish Islamic system of life. Readers of the Qur'an have been advised:

"(This is) a Scripture that We have revealed unto thee, full of blessing-that they may ponder its revelations and that men of understanding may reflect."

(38: 30)

Moreover, the readers have been instructed: "Read the Qur'an slowly with pauses." (73: 4)

The Holy Prophet [S.A.W.] affirmed:

"These hearts get rusted as the iron rusts when water is poured over it." The people submitted: "O Holy Prophet [S.A.W.]! Tell us then what cleanses the rust of the hearts?" The Holy Prophet [S.A.W.] observed: "The rust of the hearts is cleansed when one remembers death frequently and secondly studies the Qur'an often." (Mishkat)

13. Be grateful to Allah under all circumstances. Look towards those who are below you in terms of material prosperity and social status. It will help you develop a sense of gratitude to Allah.

The Holy Prophet [S.A.W.] observed:

"Look at those who are below you in terms of material prosperity and social status. (You will then feel grateful to Allah). Do not look at those who surpass you in material riches, lest you depreciate the bounties and blessings that Allah has conferred upon you (as it may foster ingratitude to Allah)."

14. Abstain from pleasure-seeking and luxurious living. Be a watchdog of truth who is always on guard and never drops vigil.

The Holy Prophet [S.A.W.] observed:

"How can I live at ease or seek pleasure in life when I know that Israfil stands ready with the trumpet close to his mouth, to sound the call for Doomsday to descend as soon as he receives the Command of Allah." Addressing the Believers, Allah affirms in the Holy Quran:

"Make ready for them all thou canst of (armed) force and of horses tethered that thereby ye may dismay the enemy of Allah and your enemy, and others beside them whom ye know not. Allah knoweth them whatsoever ye spend in the way of Allah. It will be repaid to you in full and ye will not be wronged."

(8: 60)

15. Be prepared to sacrifice everything for the sake of religion and if needed, be prepared even to migrate from your homeland. Check up yourself off and on as to what extent you have developed this devotion. Giving an account of the emigration of Hazrat Ibrahim [A.S.], the Holy Qur'an has urged believers to be prepared to emigrate and offer sacrifices in the following verses:

"And make mention (O Muhammad) in the scripture of Abraham, Lo! he was a saint, a Prophet. When he said unto his father: O my father! Why worshippest thou that which heareth not nor seeth, nor can in aught avail thee? O my father! Lo! there hath come unto me the knowledge that which came not unto thee. So follow me, and I will lead thee on a right path. O my father! Serve not the devil. Lo, the devil is a rebel unto the Beneficent. O my father! Lo! I fear lest a punishment from the Beneficent overtake thee so that thou become a comrade of the devil. He said: Rejectest thou my gods, O Abraham! if thou cease not I shall surely stone thee. Depart from me a long while! He said: Peace be unto thee! I shall ask forgiveness of my Allah for thee. Lo! He was ever gracious unto me, I shall withdraw from you and that unto which ye pray beside Allah and I shall pray unto my Allah. It may be that, in prayer unto my Lord, I shall not be unblest."

(19: 41-48)

16. Develop a burning zeal striving in the way of Allah, a spirit of fighting with all your means and soul and a pious desire to attain martyrdom in the cause of Allah. Truly speaking, 'Jihad' is the test of faith and the heart which is devoid of the spirit of Jihad is devoid of faith and right guidance and may be compared to a desolate ruin in the wilderness. It is really a great privilege to be able to reach the field of Jihad and to

gain an opportunity of sacrificing one's life and property in the way of Allah. In case, the circumstances prevent you from availing of the opportunity to participate in the Jihad; if you lack means or wherewithal to prove your conviction in the field of Jihad, even then you may be counted among those soldiers in the eyes of Allah, who either attained martyrdom while fighting for His cause or returned from the field as the winners provided your heart is filled with the zeal of setting out in the way of Allah, you always take into account the feelings and sentiments which stir a man to perform heroic deeds in the way of Allah. On his return from the battle of Tabuk, the Holy Prophet [S.A.W.] addressed his illustrious companions [R.A.A.] on the way and observed:

> "There are some people left behind in Madinah who did set out with you and traversed the valley and remained with you throughout the battle." The companions [R.A.A.] were astonished end submitted: "Did they do all this while staying behind in Madinah all the time!" The Holy Prophet [S.A.W.] observed: "Yes, they did all this even while staying behind in Madinah all the time, for circumstances forced them to stay back, otherwise they would not have held themselves back of their own accord."

In the Holy Qur'an, Allah has also praised those people who could not take part in Jihad, despite their burning zeal and were ever afterwards smitten with sorrow over this deprivation.

> "Nor unto those whom, when they came to thee (asking that thou shouldest mount them thou didst tell) I cannot find whereupon to mount you. They turned back with eyes flowing with tears, for sorrow that they could not find means to spend." *(9: 92)*

> The Holy Prophet [S.A.W.] observed: "The man who died without waging a struggle in the way of Allah or had no yearning in his heart to wage such a struggle, has died in a state of hypocrisy." *(Muslim)*

In fact anybody whose heart is devoid of the spirit of fighting in the way of Allah and of sacrificing his life and resources for the cause of the Almighty is not a true believer.

Propagation

1. Observe prefect decorum and propriety while preaching and propagating Islam. Adopt such an appropriate, dignified, and calculated technique to communicate your message as to generate fervour and zeal in the listener.

   The Holy Qur'an affirms:

   > "Call to the way of thy Lord with wisdom and fair exhortation and reason with them in the better way."
   >
   > *(16: 125)*

   This comprehensive verse of the Holy Qur'an contains instructions regarding three principles:

   (i) The call must be made in the most appropriate manner.

   (ii) The instruction and guidance must be provided in the best possible way.

   (iii) Discussion and reasoning should be fair and courteous.

   Calling in a wise manner means to communicate your message according to the situation and circumstances aptitude of the people, their intellect and understanding and their social environments and status. Do not waste this precious treasure of knowledge and wisdom in a haphazard way. Address each class, group or individual according to their ability, capacity, and their mental level. Always start your discussion from such universal truths as are mutually conceded to and pave the way for mutual understanding and agreement.

   Arouse one's best sentiments with sincerity and devotion. Create and develop in him an urge and desire to know the truth. Thus he will not only achieve peace of mind but adopt and accept the faith as his own inner urge. It will serve as a source of nourishment for his soul and a tranquiliser for his passions and sentiments.

To be courteous in criticism, and discussion means that you should offer constructive criticism. Your criticism should reflect your earnestness and sincerity. Your style should be so convincing and simple that the intransigence, hate, obstinacy, prejudice or pride may get no inlet. Your approach should be so rational and impressive and your discussion so charming and thought provoking as to make the listener think over your arguments and to feel an irresistible attraction towards the truth. Whenever you feel intransigence in attitude and reasoning, stop discussion and take leave.

Propagate religion as a whole and do not add to or expunge anything from its teachings or principles of your own accord. The preacher of Islam has no discretion to project what he thinks fit and to withhold what he does not think fit to project.

Allah affirms:

> "And when Our clear revelations are recited unto them they who look not for the meeting with us say: Bring a lecture other than this, or change it. Say (O Muhammad): It is not for me to change it of my own accord. I only follow that which is inspired in me: Lo' if I disobey my Lord I fair the retribution of an awful day. Say: If Allah had so willed I should not have recited it to you nor would He have made it known to you. I dwelt among you a whole lifetime before it (came to me). Have ye then no sense? Who doeth greater wrong than he who inventeth a lie concerning Allah and denieth His revelations? Lo! the guilty never are successful. *(10: 15-17)*

However unfavourable the circumstances may be, the preacher must propagate religion in its true and whole form. It is a hideous crime to introduce innovations into or to make alterations in the principles and teachings ordained by Allah to suit the prevailing trends. The people who are guilty of such alterations are the losers in this world as well as in the world Hereafter. Islam is a religion ordained by Allah who is All Knowing and Omnipotent. His knowledge is eternal and there is nothing beyond His knowledge of whole of this universe right from beginning to the end. Whatever be the human conquests in the field of science and technology, discoveries and explanations, all are subject to the supreme Will of Allah. Nobody has got any right to make any addition or alteration in the Code of life ordained by Him. So much so that the Holy Prophet [S.A.W.], through whom this code of life has been conveyed to us, has been introduced to us as the most ideal servant of Allah who follows what is ordained to him in letter and spirit and dares not overrule His mandate.

3. Convey the message of Islam in a natural way, so that it may not be taken as an unnatural burden. The people may take it as a remedy for all their ills and sufferings instead of feeling scared and developing hatred against it. You should be so polite and rational in conveying the message of Islam to the people that they may feel an irresistible attraction towards Islam. Hazrat Mu'awiya ibn Hakam [R.A.A.] states: "Once I was saying prayers behind the Holy Prophet [S.A.W.] when a man sneezed. I responded to the sneeze by saying in the course of the prayer. The people began to star at me. I said: "May Allah bless you! Why are you staring at me? The People indicated to me by gestures to keep quiet. I kept quiet. When the prayer was over, the Holy Prophet (peace and blessings of Allah be upon him) and may my father and mother be sacrificed for him, never did I see a better guide and teacher before or after him) neither reproached me, nor beat me, nor blamed me. He only said to me "Look. This is prayer and it is not admissible to talk during the prayer. Prayer is meant to acknowledge the purity, supremacy and exaltedness of Allah to recite the Holy Qur'an."

4. Be moderate in your writing, speech and conversation while conveying the message and call of Islam so that the listeners may feel hopeful as well as seized with awe. Neither overstress the terrifying aspects of the punishment for sins, lest the people should lose all hopes of mercy from Allah and consider salvation not only difficult but impossible; nor should you present such a rosy and one-sided picture of the kindness

and forgiveness of Allah that people become fearless and irresponsible in their actions and feel free to transgress the divine commands trusting upon the Munificence and Forgiving Nature of Allah.

Hazrat 'Ali [R.A.A.] observed:

> "The best scholar is he who invites the people to obey and submit before Allah in such a manner that people do not lose hope in Allah; he neither gives them allowances to commit transgressions against the Law of Allah nor makes them fearless of Divine punishment."

5. Observe perseverance and constancy in missionary activities. Continue implementing your programme with fortitude and a high sense of responsibility. Avoid the habit of abandoning your programmes half way and chalking out new schemes. Do little, but do it steadily.

   The Holy Prophet [S.A.W.] has observed:

   > "The best deed is the one which, however little it may be, is done constantly and regularly."

6. Meet all hardships and trials that confront you while preaching and propagating Islam cheerfully and with patience and fortitude:

   The Holy Qur'an affirms:

   > "And enjoin kindness and forbid iniquity and persevere whatever may befall thee." *(31:17)*

   Hardships and difficulties do come in the way of truth and submission to Allah. These trials and hardships strengthen faith in Allah and season one's character and morals. This is why Allah puts those to trial who claim to be His servants and the trial gets harder and harder for those who are better seasoned in faith and devotion.

   Allah affirms:

   > "And most certainly shall We try you by means of same fear, and hunger and loss of worldly goods, lives

> and fruits, and glad tidings to the patient who, when adversity overtakes them, say: Surely Allah's we are, and unto Him we are to return. It is they, upon whom there are blessings of their Lord and (His) mercy and it is they alone who are guided aright" *(2: 155-57)*

'Hazrat Sa'd [R.A.A.] submitted to the Holy Prophet [S.A.W.]: "O Prophet of Allah [S.A.W.]! Which person is put to the severest trial?" The Holy Prophet [S.A.W.] observed:

> "The persons who are put to the severest trials are firstly the Prophets of Allah [A.S.], then those who are nearest to the prophets in conviction and devotion, and then those who are next to them in their faith and submission. In fact one is tried according to his conviction and devotion. Whoever is firm in his conviction and devotion is put to a hard test and whoever is weak in faith and submission is confronted with a mild trial and these trials continue till a man is purged of all traces of sin." *(Mishkat)*

Recounting his own experience, the Holy Prophet [S.A.W.] observed:

> "Never was a man more persecuted in the way of Allah than I was and never was a man more threatened in the way of Allah as I was. We spent thirty days and thirty nights in such state that Bilal [R.A.A.] and I had nothing that a living being could eat, save some little provisions in the small pack which Bilal [R.A.A.] kept under his arm." *(Tirmidhi)*

The Holy Prophet [S.A.W.] also affirmed:

> "And person who will make an effort to be patient shall be granted patience by Allah. And there is no blessing which encompasses more good than patience." *(Bukhari, Muslim)*

In fact, trials are essential for strengthening and carrying forward the movement. No movement can achieve success without passing through periods of trial, especially a movement which calls for a universal revolution in human society and plans to raise the social structure of human life on entirely new foundations.

Reminiscing about the days when the stone-hearted Meccans were perpetrating endless tortures on the Holy Prophet [S.A.W.] and his illustrious Companions [R.A.A.], Hazrat Khabbab ibn al-Arat [R.A.A.] related:

> "The Holy Prophet [S.A.W.] was resting with a sheet placed under his sacred head in the shade of Bait-Allah (House of Allah) when we reached his presence with the complaint: "O Prophet of Allah [S.A.W.]! Don't you seek aid for us from Allah! Don't you pray for an end to this oppression! (How long will this period of trial continue and when will it come to an end!) The Holy Prophet [S.A.W.] heard our complaint and observed: There had been people before you who faced unprecedented trials and oppressions. Often one of them was made to stand in a pit, half buried in the ground, and his body was sliced into two parts with a saw like a log of wood, yet the man refused to renounce his faith. Their flesh was pierced through with steel combs till the iron nails reached the bones and the fibres, yet the devotees of Allah did not resign from truth. By Allah, Islam shall prevail and you will see (such a state of peace and security) that a man riding from San'aa (the Capital of Yemen) to Hadramut will have nothing to fear on the way except Allah. The shepherds will only fear the wolves lest they should carry off their goats. But, alas, you show impatience."
>
> *(Bukhari)*

> Hazrat Mu'awiya [R.A.A.] relates: "I have heard the Holy Prophet [S.A.W.] observing, "There shall always remain a group among my Ummah who will defend Islam and their faith. Those who do not support them or oppose them shall never be able to destroy or eliminate them till the final word from Allah. These defenders of Faith shall remain firm in their conviction.
>
> *(Bukhari, Muslim)*

7. Do not show undue toleration, or shower undeserved praise on any one, nor sacrifice principles under any circumstances. In affirmation of a virtue of the believers, the Holy Qur'an says:

   "They deal strictly with the non-believers."

   In other words, the believers are extremely strict about matters of religion and principle and under no circumstances do they compromise their principles or tolerate wrong-doing. They can bear anything, but cannot sacrifice their religion or principles. Allah has transmitted through the Holy Prophet [S.A.W.] the following to the Muslims:

   "Unto this then summon (O Muhammad). And be thou upright as thou art commanded, and follow not their lusts."

   Accommodation for wrong-doing, undue toleration and compromise with falsehood are the weaknesses that destroy one's faith and religion.

   The Holy Prophet [S.A.W.] has observed:

   "When the tribe of Israel began to transgress the commands of Allah, their learned men checked them, but they did not refrain from their wicked deeds. Their learned men instead of boycotting their society, continued to attend their company and ate and drank with them. Consequently Allah equated these pious Ulemas with the transgressors and cursed them through His Prophets, Hazrat Dawud and Hazrat 'Isa [A.S.]. Allah cursed the Israelites because they followed the path of disobedience to Allah and went too far on this way." The reporter of this Tradition 'Abdullah b. Mas'ud [R.A.A.] relates: "The Holy Prophet [S.A.W.] changed his reclining posture and sat erect and observed: No, I swear by Him Who hath power over my life, you will certainly continue to enforce virtue and curb evil and you will hold the hand of the oppressor and bend the tyrant before truth. If you do not act as you must, you too shall assimilate with them and Allah shall withhold all His blessings and guidance from you and forsake you completely, just as He deprived the Israelites of His clemency.

8. To train and reform your children and to prepare them for the duty of establishing religion is not only your foremost obligation, but a logical sphere of your activity. On the other hand, it is unwise and unnatural to ignore your children and get yourself busy in missionary activities outside. It is a gross negligence and an escape from duty. It is as if you leave your own family writhing in agony of hunger and thirst during famine and go out in search of the needy to distribute grain among them to display your munificence. It shows that you are quite incapable of perceiving the suffering of hunger and thirst and are devoid of the sense of kinship and love; nor can you appreciate the wisdom that lies behind the act of distributing grain. The Holy Qur'an enjoins upon the believers:

 "O Believers! Save yourselves and your families from the fire of Hell."

 The Holy Prophet [S.A.W.] has elucidated the same verse as follows:

 "Each one of you is a guardian and is charged with a respon- sibility, and each one of you shall be held accountable for those who have been placed under your care. The ruler is a guardian and he shall be held to account for the affairs of his subjects. The husband is the guardian of his family; the woman is the guardian of her husband's home and children. So each one of you is a guardian and charged with a responsibility and each one of you shall be called to account for the affairs of those who have been placed under your care." *(Bukhari, Muslim)*

9. Expend some care upon reforming and cultivating your neighbours and the people living around you and consider this task as a part of your duty.

The Holy Prophet [S.A.W.] delivered a sermon one day and in the course of his sermon praised some Muslims and then observed: "Why is it so that some people do not impart religious knowledge to their neighbours and do not season them in religion, neither do they warn them of the fearful consequences of their ignorance of religion, nor restrain them from committing evil deeds? And why is it so that some of you do not care to learn religion from their neighbours and do not acquire an understanding of its purpose and spirit, nor do they try to ascertain the fearful consequences of remaining ignorant of religion. By Allah! The people must teach religion to their neighbours and inculcate an understanding of religion in them. The people should guide their neighbours, give them good counsel and restrain them from wrong and evil. Besides, it is the duty of people to learn religion and accept their counsels or else I shall punch them soon." The Holy Prophet [S.A.W.] then descended from the pulpit concluding his sermon.

Those who were present there enquired from each other: Against whom the Holy Prophet [S.A.W.] delivered this warning?" The others said, "The Holy Prophet [S.A.W.] was alluding in his speech to the people of the tribe of Ash'ar. These people are well-versed in religion, but their neighbours, who live in the Oasis, are ignorant yokels." When the people of the tribe of Ash'ar came to know of the sermon delivered by the Holy Prophet [S.A.W.] they presented themselves before the Holy Prophet [S.A.W.] and submitted: "O Prophet of Allah [S.A.W.]! You were pleased to shower praise on some people and expressed your displeasure towards us. Kindly let us know what is wrong with us?" The Holy Prophet [S.A.W.] observed: "It is the duty of the people to teach religion to their neighbours; they ought to preach to them, educate them and restrain them from wrong and evil. Likewise it is the duty of the people to learn religion from their neighbours and to accept their counsels. They should also cultivate an understanding of religion, otherwise I shall punish them soon in this world." The people of the tribe of Ash'ar again submitted: "O Prophet of Allah [S.A.W.]! Should we inculcate the spirit of religion among others?" The Holy Prophet [S.A.W.] observed: "Yes, indeed, it is your duty." Thereupon the people submitted: "O Holy Prophet [S.A.W.]! Allow us a grace period of one year." The Holy Prophet [S.A.W.] granted them a grace period of one year within which they were to teach religion to their neighbours and inculcate an understanding of religion in them. The Holy Prophet [S.A.W.] then recited the following verses:

> "Those of the children of Israel who went astray were cursed by the tongue of David, and of Jesus son of Mary. That was because they rebelled and used to transgress. They restrained not one another from the wickedness they did. Verily evil was they used to do."
>
> *(5: 78,79)*

10. Respect and give due regard to the religious beliefs and sentiments of the people among whom you are performing your pleasant duty of preaching and propagating religion. Do not desecrate the names of their forbears or leaders; neither attack their beliefs, nor denounce their religious doctrines. You should preach your religion in a positive manner with sense and wisdom. Your criticism, instead of provoking the listeners, shall be earnestly aimed at driving home your preachings to them. Impassioned criticism and disparaging speech never succeeds in bringing about the desired change in the addressee. On the other land, there is an ever present danger in this case that feelings of pride in ignorance and prejudice may be ignited in the listener and under their influence he may pass impudent remarks upon Allah and religion and instead of drawing near to religion may go farther astray.

    The Holy Qur'an affirms:

    > "(O Believers!) Do not revile those whom they call besides Allah lest they should unknowingly take to reviling Allah out of enmity."

11. When you become a missionary for spreading the message of Allah, you should confine your activities to calling people

towards Allah and nothing else. Do not call the people of Allah towards anything other than Allah; do not issue your call in the name of a country, people, race, or language; nor call them on behalf of a party. The objective of the believer is to obey the Will of Allah. Call people towards total submission to Allah and cultivate an assurance among them that the slave's duty is to worship his Creator and Master, be it in the sphere of his individual or family life or in social and political affairs. The slave should obey in all spheres of his life the order of his Lord and Creator and submit to His Law with sincerity and devotion. A Muslim can have no objective before him other than this. He should, therefore call others also to achieve this objective. Whenever a believer should dare turn his back upon the Commands of Allah and set up anything else than obedience to the Will of Allah as his objective, he shall be condemned and rejected in both the worlds.

> "Who is better in speech than he who calls people towards Allah, acts righteously and says 'I am surely of those who submit."

Structural Setup

1. Form a strong organisation for propagating religion and make a concentrated and collective struggle to establish Islamic order.

   > And there must exist at least a group among you which should call people towards goodness enjoining good and prohibit the evils.

   "*Al-Khair*" denotes all that is naturally good and which has always been regarded as good by human nature and which has been attested as good by the revealed Books. A comprehensive and systematic form of all that is good and virtuous is the religion of Allah which the Apostles (peace be upon them) have been transmitting to the world in every successive epoch and whose final, complete, authentic and fully preserved form is the Qur'an and Sunnah which the Holy Prophet Muhammad [S.A.W.] bequeathed to the Ummah.

To call people towards this good and to enrich the world with virtue it is imperative that Muslims should form a party and perform this duty in an organised manner. They should forge strong and well-kint front and launch a well-organised and concentrated struggle to eliminate the wrong and evil from every sphere of life. Allah describes this unity and strength of the Muslims with appreciation and praise and lauds their collective and concentrated struggle.

> "Verily Allah loves those who fight in His cause arrayed in ranks as though they were a structure cemented with molten lead."

Stressing the importance of collective struggle and advising Muslims to live as an organised body, the Holy Prophet [S.A.W.] observed:

> "Three men who live in a jungle are forbidden to live together save they choose one from among themselves as their Amir (Chief)." *(Muntaqa)*

Further the Holy Prophet [S.A.W.] observed:

"The person who wishes to secure a dwelling place in the centre of Paradise ought to remain firmly attached to the "Aljama'at" for the devil haunts a single person, but if two persons join together, the devil runs away as far as possible."

"Al-Jama'at" implies a well-organised society of Muslims which is governed by the rule of Ṣhariah under a Muslim Caliph and the Muslims as a whole agree and concede to his authority and leadership. In such a situation there is no justification, whatsoever, for any Muslim to keep himself away and aloof from such a society. In case such a society and such an organisation does not exist make an all-out concentrated and collective effort to bring about such a society which is called Al-Jama'at in Islamic terminology.

2. Make Islam the foundation of your unity and organisation as the distinguishing feature of an Islamic organisation is nothing but total submission to Allah. Any organisation, unity or alliance based on any thing other than total submission to

Allah shall not be termed as Islamic, as it is not based on the foundation of Islam. The real base of brotherhood and bond of unity is Islam and Islam only. Anything other than Islam cannot cement relations of brotherhood and unison. It will rather disperse and disintegrate the people and instead of forming a powerful and well-knit unit and organisation with singularity of purpose and procedure, they will be divided into several sects and factions.

Call to Religion if you form a party, the only objective before you should be to establish the rule of Allah and all your struggle and efforts should be devoted to achieve this goal only.

The Holy Qur'an affirms:

> "And hold fast all of you together to this rope of Allah and do not separate. And remember Allah's favour unto you how ye were enemies and He made friendship between your hearts so that ye became as brothers by His grace." *(3: 103)*

"The rope of Allah' means Islam, the 'Religion of Allah'. According to the Holy Qur'an, it is Islam which forms the basis of the unity and organisation for Muslims. Anything else will only divide them into a number of factions instead of uniting and unifying them.

3. Love those working for the cause of Islam from the core of your heart and consider this connexion as the most important and the most inestimable of all connexions.

   Describing the characteristics of the believers, the Holy Qur'an affirms:

   > "They will not find folk who believe in Allah and the Last Day loving those who oppose Allah and His Messenger even though they be their fathers or their sons or their brothers or their clan." *(58: 22)*

4. Extend support and counsel to your colleagues in the party and keep alive the spirit of mutual guidance and advice in your party life, for this is the real key to success.

> "By the time, surely man is ever in a state of loss except those who believe and do righteous deeds and exhort one another to preach Truth and exhort one another to be steadfast."

5. Observe party discipline with full care, and do not consider it only a means of strengthening your party, but deem it as a religious duty.

   Allah affirms:

   > "They only are true believers who believe in Allah and His Messenger and when they are with him on some common errand go not away until they have asked leave of him. Lo! those who ask leave of thee, those are they who believe in Allah and His Messenger."
   >
   > *(24: 62)*

   Party discipline and loyalty and devotion to the leader is not only a legal point, but an important issue. The Holy Qur'an has affirmed the true faith of those who are loyal to party discipline and in no case abandon their party duty without leave of their leader.

6. Extend sincere co-operation in all the good works that are being carried out by the party and exert yourself to the maximum in this effort. Do not stain the purity of your moral character by entertaining any evil sentiments such as selfishness, or personal motives and self-glorification.

   The Holy Qur'an enjoins upon the believers:

   > "And co-operate with each other in good works of piety and Allah-fearing."

7. Maintain cordial relations with your colleagues. If at times a difference of opinion arises, resolve the dispute at once and keep your heart clear of any feelings of grudge.

   > "So fear Allah and maintain cordial relations among yourselves."

8. Obey the Amir of the Islamic Party with all sincerity and in good spirit and remain loyal and devoted to him.

The Holy Prophet (S.A.W.) has observed:

> "It is the duty of the Muslims to listen to and obey the order of their leader, regardless of the consideration whether such an order is agreeable or disagreeable to them, provided such an order does not constitute a transgression of Allah's law. In case no such order is issued as is repugnant to Allah's law, it should not be listened to, nor obeyed. *(Bukhari, Muslim)*

Hazrat Tamim Dari reports that the Holy Prophet [S.A.W.] observed:

> "Religion means devotion and loyalty." The Holy Prophet [S.A.W.] repeated this observation three times. Thereupon we submitted: "Devotion and loyalty to whom?" The Holy Prophet [S.A.W.] observed: "Devotion and loyalty to Allah, His Messenger, His Book, the leaders of Muslims and the mass of Muslims." *(Muslim)*

9. Avoid party chauvinism, bigotry and factionalism. Cooperate with everyone with an open heart and in good cheer. Esteem those who are working for the cause of religion. Deal with them in good faith and sincerity and consider them as your colleagues and comrades. All those who work for the cause of religion are in reality supporters and helpers of one another. The goal of everyone of them is the glory of religion and all of them wish to serve religion according to their lights. It is auspicious and fruitful to point out each other's faults in a spirit of friendship and understanding and to focus attention on correct mode of thought and action. On the other hand, it is below the dignity and office of the preachers of religion to indulge in such despicable conduct as hatred, friction, envy, grudge, confrontation and hostile propaganda against each other. The character of the preachers must be clear of all these blemishes who sincerely and truly wish to expend their energies and talents in the way of Allah and to render some service to the cause of Islam during their lifetime.

Choice of Leader

1. To lead and guide the Islamic party choose a person who excels others in piety and fear of Allah. Heritage nor wealth is the basis of leadership or eminence in Islam. The best person in Islam is he who fears Allah most.

   The Holy Qur'an affirms:

   > "O mankind! Lo! We have created you male and female, and have made you nations and tribes so that ye may know one another. Lo! the noblest of you in the sight of Allah, is the best in conduct." (49: 13)

2. Regard the election of a leader as a sacred duty and use your vote as a trust from Allah only in favour of person who in your view is best qualified to discharge the onerous responsibility of leadership.

   Allah affirms:

   > "Lo! Allah Commandeth you that you restore deposits to their owners." (4: 58)

   This is a precise principle which encompasses all kinds of trusts. In the context of this Chapter 'trusts denote the responsibilities of an Islamic Party i.e. the duty of leadership should be vested by open choice in such a person who is the best qualified among you to discharge the onerous responsibility of leadership. To cast your vote in this case in a partisan spirit or to show undue favour or to act under the influence of other extraneous factors is a breach of trust. The character of a believer must be free from the taint of breach of trust.

3. If you are to lead an Islamic Party, you should be fully conscious of your responsibilities and should discharge your duty with complete honesty, diligence, sense of responsibility and energy.

The Holy Prophet [S.A.W.] observed:

> "Allah shall ban the entry of that person into Paradise who is entrusted the duty of administering the affairs of Muslim society and he betrays their trust."
>
> *(Bukhari, Muslim)*

The Holy Prophet [S.A.W.] also observed:

> "The person who accepts the charge of administering the affairs of Muslims and then does not serve their interests and does not tire himself out in their service to the same extent that he tires himself out to fulfil his own personal needs, Allah shall throw such a man headlong into the fire of Hell." *(Tabrani)*

4. Treat your subordinates with tenderness, affection, fairness and largeheartedness so that they may cooperate with you willingly and Allah may grant your Party the favour of rendering some service to Islam. Describing the virtues of the Holy Prophet [S.A.W.] the Holy Qur'an says:

> "It was by the mercy of Allah that thou west lenient with them (O, Muhammad). for if thou hadst been stern and fierce of heart they would have dispersed from round about thee." (3: 159)

Moreover, Allah has urged the Holy Prophet [S.A.W.]:

> "And lower thy wing (in tenderness) unto these believers who follow thee." (26: 215)

In the course of a speech, Hazrat 'Umar b. Khattab [R.A.A.] remarked:

> "O people! You owe us a duty to support us sincerely in our absence and assist us in performing deeds of piety."

Furthermore he observed:

> "Officers of the government! No tenderness is greater before Allah and more profitable than the tenderness and leniency shown by the head of the executive. Similarly, no lack of wisdom and ineptness is more damaging, dangerous and despicable than the indiscretion, whimsical nature and haphazard actions of the executive head."

5. Realise the importance of your collegues. Respect their sentiments and pay due regard to their needs. Treat them in

such a fraternal way that they should look upon you as their greatest well-wisher.

Hazrat Malik ibn Huwarith relates: "Once some of us young men who were of the same age group went to stay with the Holy Prophet [S.A.W.] and lived in his auspicious company for twenty days. The Holy Apostle of Allah was no doubt extremely kind and tender-hearted. When the Holy Prophet [S.A.W.] felt that we were homesick, he [S.A.W.] enquired from us: "What relations have you left behind at home?" We submitted details, whereupon the Holy Prophet [S.A.W.] advised us: "You should now return home and live with them and teach them what you have learnt and propagate good deeds among them. Tell them the exact hours of prayers and when the time of prayer approaches, one of you should announce the call and he who excels all others in learning and character among you should lead the prayers."

6. Appreciate the worth and importance of your colleagues and considering them your real assets, take pains to train them in right earnest. Do not underrate them as poor and destitute nor covet those upon whom Allah has bestowed worldly pomp, grandeur and wealth.

   "Restrain thyself along with those who cry unto their Lord at morning and evening, seeking His countenances and let nor thine eyes overlook them desiring the pomp of the life of the world." *(18:29)*

   In fact the people who have devoted their lives and resources to the propagation and preaching of religion are the veritable assets of a religious party. The duty of the party leader is to realise the value of these people and concentrate all his attention on their education and training.

7. Settle and execute all party matters in consultation with your colleagues. Try to develop their interest in the party and consolidate their support for the activities of the party. Allah, in praise of the believers, also affirms that they settle their affairs by mutual consultation.

   "And their affairs are (settled) by mutual consultation."

Allah has urged the Holy Prophet [S.A.W.] to consult his companions in matters of special importance.

"And consult them in (important) matters."

8. Display generosity and selflessness in party matters. Do not seek to advance your own or your family's interests in any party matter. On the other hand, show a liberal and unselfish conduct so that your colleagues may always be prepared to make all sacrifices with a willing heart and may not feel disillusioned with the party or severe their connection with it or may not be moved to act with selfish and interested motives. Hazrat Abu Bakr [R.A.A.] once observed to Hazrat 'Umar [R.A.A.]:

   "O son of Khattab! I have chosen you and appointed you over Muslims so that you may deal with them with kindness. You have been a companion of the Holy Prophet [S.A.W.]. You know how the Holy Prophet [S.A.W.] used to prefer our interests to his own interest and that of our family to his family, so much so that we often returned as a gift to the Prophet's family whatever we received from him in excess of our needs and requirements." *(Kitab al-Khardj)*

9. Always avoid partiality and nepotism and never show undue regard and toleration. Hazrat Yazid b. Sufyan [R.A.A.] relates: "When Hazrat Abu Bakr [R.A.A.] appointed me chief of the army and sent me towards Syria, he gave me the following instructions:

   'O Yazid! You have some kinsmen and relations. It is possible that you may feel tempted to prefer them to others for appointment to offices of trust. This is what I fear most about you."

   The Holy Prophet [S.A.W.] observed: "Allah will accept no compensation or consideration from a person who is responsible for the affairs of the Muslims and appoints a man to an office of authority over Muslims merely on the basis of kinship or friendship, so much so that Allah shall consign the guilty person to Hell."

(Kitab al-Khardj)

10. Maintain strict party discipline as far as is possible and do not show weakness or leniency in matters of discipline.

    Allah affirms:

    > "So, if they ask thy leave for some affair of theirs, give leave to whom thou wilt of them, and ask for them forgiveness of Allah." *(24: 62)*

    In other words, when the members of the party assemble to attend to some party business and later some members begin to seek permission to leave on account of their personal needs or disabilities, it behoves the leader of the party to accept the requests of those people only whose personal needs are really more pressing than the matters confronting them in the meeting or of those whose disabilities justify their leave by canonical law and, therefore, must be considered and conceded.

10

Conclusion

Like other divine religions, Islam also keeps the reform of man's self as the first item in its programme of refoms. It makes the human self as the first target of its efforts and sows the seeds of the Islamic teachings in its depths, so that self and training become inseparable.

The teachings of the Prophets lasted till the Doomsday and around them gathered the group of faithful people. Its secret was this that the self of man was the objective of all its work and it was the axis of all its activities. Their teachings were not like something externally pasted that they could be separated from men in the movements of their daily life. These were not like the paint or varnish that could be worn out by the passage of time. They had imbibed their principles and teachings into the depths of man's hearts, which had turned into a very strong power that could keep it safe from the wickedness of men's nature and could rule over their decisions.

Many times some divine religions raised objections against the society and its culture and governments and its nature, and also presented remedies for the ills which had appeared in these quarters.

In spite of this, the nature of all the divine religions has been this that they kept righteous self as the basis of all their programmes of reform, and considered firm and strong moral character as a permanent guarantee for the establishment and upkeep of every civilization.

But this does not mean that the importance of those who are striving for the construction of a better government and society is being reduced, or that their efforts are considered to be less important. No. Not at all. Here an attempt is being made to make the people realize the value of the reform of man's self for the safety of life and for the security of healthy and virtuous living.

The self that has become wicked can only spread disruption and disorder in the system of government, and can make use of the enforcement of the laws of that system for meeting its mean and wicked objectives. But a purified and noble self will perform the responsible task of stitching the tears in the garment of the environment and repairing it. It will try to enhance society's greatness and decency. It will consider it its responsibility to bring in regularity in the use of power, and to remove all kinds of defects from the government.

It is like a judge. If he is well trained and decent, he can reform the defects of the law by his selfless decisions and just orders. But a cruel and unkind judge can show indifference to the correct commands and authorities. Same is the condition of the self, when it is confronted with my ideas and views about world, and personal likes and interests.

That is why the reform of the self is the first foundation pillar of the supremacy of virtue in this life.

If no attention is paid to the reform of the individuals (selves), this world becomes the dominion of the dark forces, men's present and future will be ruled by corruption. That is why Allah says:

> "Verily, Allah will never change the condition of a people until they change it themselves. But when Allah wills a people's punishment, there can be no turning it back, nor will they find, beside Him any to protect."
>
> (*Ra'ad : 11*)

Stating the cause of the corrupt communities, Allah says:

> "Like (the deeds of) the people of Pharaoh and of those before them ; they rejected the signs of Allah and Allah punished them for their crimes ; for Allah is Strong and Strict in punishment; because Allah will never

> change the Grace which He has bestowed on a people until they change what is in their (own) souls."
>
> (*Anfal: 52-53*)

From the viewpoint of reform and training, Islam considers this matter in its two aspects:

The first aspect is this : Every self has a decent and pure nature in itself which rushes towards righteousness and good, and feels happy on getting it. It hates wickedness and evil. It becomes sad and sorry on committing it. It sees the extension and development of its existence and the health of its life in truth and justice.

With this there is its second aspect also. Every self is in its exciting emotions and Satanic inclinations, which turn away from the right path. The present harm is in a glamorous way and throw it into the pit of meanness and lowliness. We are not interested in talking a survey of the principles and elementaries of these harmu inclination from a historical point of view so that it may be ascertained whether these emotions or desires enter the human nature from outside or whether they are ingrained in the nature itself. We are concerned with the fact that both these conditions are found in men, which are locked in mutual struggle for attaining leadership for guiding man's life. And whatever kind of leadership man accepts decides his final destination.

Allah says:

> 'By the soul, and the proportion and the order given to it; and its enlightenment as to its wrong and its right; truly he succeeds who purges it, and he fails who corrupts it." —(*Shams: 7-10*)

The achievement of Islam is this that it helps man fully, so that he may be able to make his nature strong and firm, he may make its rays more bright and more illuminating, and in its guidance and leadership may successfully complete his long journey of life.

Similarly it also prepares man to be free from the ways of wickedness and the inciting of the devil, because these try to mislead him and turn him away from the right path, and finally cause him to fall from his high rank.

Nature of Faith

Islam has called itself a 'Natural Religion' which is free from all these impurities

> "So (O Prophet !) set your face steadily and truly to the faith. (Establish) Allah's nature on which He has framed mankind. There is no change in what Allah has created; that is the standard religion; but most among mankind do not understand." (*Rum : 30*)

The function of the eye is to see until there is some disturbance in it. The ear hears the sound till it becomes deaf. The function of the nature is to follow the right path, and to rush towards it with such alacrity as the water rushes down from a height, unless it is overcome by corruption and wickedness, which may take its reins in hands and turn it away from the path of righteousness and blessings.

The disturbing things which corrupt nature are sometimes the result of the past centuries or sometimes they are the creation of the lowly environment and habits and customs, or both these things together are responsible for the disturbances. These things are a great danger for the nature of man. They cause a variety of diseases in it. The real jihad of a reformer is to fight these inhibitions and customs and to weaken their strength. He tries to relieve Nature of these dangers in order that its original purity may be regained and it may be able to fulfil its real responsibility. Islam has given a full clarification of this method.

After explaining the natural religion in the abovequoted verses, the holy Quran says immediately thereafter:

> "Turn back in repentance to Him, and fear Him ; Establish regular prayers, and be not you among those who join gods with Allah, those who split up and become sects, each party rejoicing in that which is with itself." (*Rum : 31-32*)

To encourage faith in place of disbelief, righteousness in place of wickedness, to adopt the policy of fearing God, in place of disturbed thoughts in respect of Allah the righteous people's unity of thought and action-these are the manifestations that show that man has remained on the righteous nature.

This has been clarified in the following verse of the Quran:

> "We indeed created man in the best of moulds, then we have abased him to be the lowest of the low, except such as believe and do righteous deeds."
>
> *(At-Teen : 4-6)*

What is the best mould or form of man? The understanding of Truth and adopting it, fulfilment of its requirements and meeting of its demands. This is called the attachment to virtuousness and decency, and consideration of these two good qualities in man's individual and collective life is the real achievement. And attempts to make them operative in all the departments of life is the real mould and form.

But there is a very large number of people who do not reach this high level. They remain attached to the earth only. They follow their own desires, and express disobedience of God's commands. In this way they fall to the lowest level. Quran has called this "Asfala safileen (lowest of the low), to which Allah has thrown such people.

To throw the men of such nature to the lowest level is according to the divine law regarding guidance and transgression. And these laws are true and based on justice. The holy Quran mentions them as under :

> "And Allah will not mislead a people after He has guided them, to order that He may make clear to them what to fear (and avoid) for Allah has knowledge. of all things." *(Tauba : 115)*

In Surah A'raf this law of guidance and transgression has been mentioned thus

> "Those who behave arrogantly on the earth in detance of right-them I will turn away from My signs; even if

> they see all the signs, they will not believe in them; And If they see the way of right conduct, they will not adopt it as the way of error is the way they will adopt; for they rejected Our signs, and 'failed to take warning from them."
>
> (*A'raf:146*)

Who is it then that remains on the 'best mould' and keeps himself away from the indignities of the world ? In the verses of the Surah At-Teen occurring immediately after those quoted above the answer is given

> "Except such as believe and do the righteous deeds."
>
> *(Al-Teen)*

In the foregoing pages we have seen that the outcome of Faith and the Righteous Deeds is the excellence of moral character.

Eradication of All Evils

Islam's stand vis-a-vis man's pure nature and its strength and firmness has been discussed. As regards its dealings with the devil-like natures, that has also been made clear. Islam warns mischievous-natured people. It entrusts its reins in the hands of the healthy intellect ; it encourages it to bow down to the pure nature and to surrender itself to Allah.

The prophet has hinted at some of these kinds of natures:

> "The son of Adam reaches the old age and two of his habits do not leave him. One is greed and the second is the unending succession of hopes." (*Muslim*)
>
> "The worst evil found in man is the frightening cowardice and the undignifying miserliness."
>
> (*Abu Daud*)
>
> "If the son of Adam is given a valley of gold, he will desire to have another one. And if the other is also given, he will be greedy to have the third one. The hunger of Adam's son will not be satisfied except when his remains are mixed with the dust. And the one who turns to Allah, Allah accepts his repentance."
>
> (*Bukhari*)

The holy Quran has mentioned some of the habits in the Surah Ale Imran:

> "Fair in the eyes of men is the love of things they covet, women and sons ; heaped up hoards of gold and silver ; horses branded (for blood and excellence) ; and (wealth of) cattle and well-tilled land. Such are the possessions of this world's life ; but in the nearness to Allah is the best of the goals (to return to)."
>
> *(Al-e-Imran : 14)*

The first thing Islam wants man to pay attention to is this that to run after the carnal desires of the self and to follow its unending demands will never satisfy self and make it contented. Truth and right path will not be acceptable to it.

The condition of the self is that when its one desire is satisfied, it immediately demands to have some other desire satisfied. It is always busy in eating, drinking, and having a good time, and greedy with desire to have more and more of everything. It has no hesitation in committing sin and acts of aggression and cruelty. Therefore, Quran has forbidden men to follow the desires that have been considered haram

> "Nor follow you the lusts (of your heart), for they will mislead you from the path of Allah; for those who wander astray from the path of Allah, is a penalty grievous, for that they forget the Day of Account."
>
> *(Saad: 26)*

The policy of the infidels and the necessity of opposing it and its importance have been mentioned in these words:

> "If the Truth had been in accord with their desires, truly the heavens and the earth and all beings therein would have been in confusion and corruption! Nay, We have sent them their admonition, but they turn away from their admonition." *(Muminun: 71)*

It is necessary that a distinction be made between the forbidden desires of myself and the lawful desires, because some so-called religious people have mixed up these two very dangerously.

If man wants to enjoy the goods of the world, then there is nothing wrong in it, but it is a very serious error that this kind of lawful demands and desires have also been included in the list of forbidden, wicked acts.

Its consequence is this that man satisfies his lawful and respectable desires, but his conscience becomes like the conscience of those people who accept crimes as lawful and adopt them willingly. In this way their conscience becomes a victim of a great error.

When he realises that he has committed a mistake, and that sin is an inevitable part of his life, then he commits more serious sins and indulges in the strictly forbidden acts. In other words this time he becomes a criminal and a sinner in the real sense of the word.

The holy Quran has paid special attention to this aspect and has very clearly declared the pure desires of the self and the lawful wishes as proper and lawful, and provided it with a chance to use halal and clean things. It declared any interference of narrowness and inhibition in this respectable and lawful sphere by way of any checks on the self as bad and obscene, because it opens. the gate for obscene acts and sinning.

> "O you people I Eat on earth what is lawful (halal) and clean (tayyib) and do not follow the footsteps of Satan. Indeed, he is an open enemy for yours. He will command you (to do) what is evil and indecent and induce you to say about Allah that which you do not know."
>
> —(*Al-Baqarh : 168-169*)

It is a fact that to put restrictions on the consumptions of what is lawful (halal) and clean (tayyib) is nothing but levelling false charges against Allah, and this thing amounts to evil and indecency which Satan commands men to do.

Islam does not like to repress such natures and inclinations with force and punishment, nor does it want to placate or flatter them, but Islam follows a balanced method which is free of any kind of excess.

Morality holds the reins : As the rules and regulations of the healthy nature are secure in faith and reform and they have no connection with heresy and agnosticism, similar is the case of the rebellious natures and habits.

In both the cases only a strong and firm moral character can control it. Where the holy Quran has mentioned man's weakness, his anxiety, his richness and indifference, there it has also made it clear that the remedy of these indignities lies in following the path of religion.

> "Truly man was created very impatient ; fretful when evil touches him ; and niggardly when good reaches him ; not so those devoted to prayer, those who remain steadfast to their prayer ; and those in whose wealth is recognised right for (the needy) who asks him and who is prevented(for some reason from asking) ; and those who hold to the Truth of the Day of Judgment ; and those who fear the displeasure of their Lord, for the Lord's displeasure is the opposite of peace and tranquillity ; and those who guard their chastity."
>
> —*(Al-Ma'arij : 19-19)*

It is common knowledge that good moral character does not develop suddenly. Nor does it become strong and firm in the beginning. It requires consistency and gradualness. And in strengthening it there come many stages.

That is the reason why in its nourishment and growth it is required to perform such acts that have to be repeated. The quality that is developed should have consistency, e.g. prayer, fasting, Hajj, Zakat, and the performance of other forms of worship, confirmation of the Day of the Judgment, and to be fearful of its punishment, etc.

When the rebellious natures insist on their acts and are steadfast on their wrong stance, and continue to attempt to traverse the wrong path from time to time, then to check and prevent it no fixed and temporary remedy can be found.

Their transgression and intensity can be brought to the normal level only by such an activist who is more strong and powerful than they and who may be able to bring them to a balanced level.

The long and short of the discussion is that Islam respects the human nature and considers its teachings as the voice of that nature. It warns the rebellious natures and reforms their point of view. Those forms of worship which have been made compulsory in Islam are such as strengthen the human nature and turn the wind of desires to the right direction. And these forms of worship do not perform their duties satisfactorily and the desired objective cannot be obtained from them unless they generate the excellent moral character and the tendency to exemplary treatment of others.

Moral Conduct Codified

To generate goodness in someone by coercion and to call him a man of good moral character is not possible. Similarly no faith can be developed in any person by means of force or terrorism. Only personal and intellectual freedom is the sole basis of responsibility and accountability.

Islam understands this reality and respects it. It builds up its edifice on the foundation of the excellent moral character.

Where is the need for Islam to use force and coercion to bring man to the right path and to make him run towards righteousness, when it has full confidence in the human nature and is certain that if the obstructions before man are removed then the best generation can be developed ?

Goodness is ingrained in the human nature. It does not mean that it cannot do anything except good, but it means that only good can co-ordinate with his original nature and offer resistance. The nature wants to attach itself to good only and wants to function in its light, like the bird that after getting free from the cage flies round and round in the sky in ecstasy in accordance with its foremost wish.

According to Islam the right method is to break nature's checks and chains. After this when man falls down to the ground, and has no strength to rise and walk, then he should be considered as sick and efforts should be made to treat him.

Islam does not order such kind of sick persons to be thrown out of society, provided his existence is not harmful and damaging to others.

Within the limits of this sphere, Islam fights against moral crimes. At first it imagines that every man wants to lead a decent life and wants to live by the sweat of his brow and enjoy luxuries on what he earns from his own labours, that is he does not depend on thefts and looting.

Then what thing compels him to take to thieving? In order to provide him for the necessities of life, therefore, Islam says that the necessities and the means should be in such abundant quantities that they may make him indifferent and above taking wrong steps.

This is the responsibility of the society. If it is deficient and compels the individual to steal, then the responsibility for this crime falls on the deficient society, and not on the head of the wrong-committing individual.

But if the society provides his requirements, and after this the individual advances in the wrong direction, then the actual condition of the individual should be ascertained before inflicting any penalty (Hudd) on him. Probably there may be such extenuating circumstances that may save him from the punishment. As it is, Islam desires delay in inflicting punishment. The Messenger of Allah his reported to have said : "It is better if the Imam pardons somebody by error than he penalises him by error."

Fixation of penalties : When after examining the conditions and problems it is ascertained that the individual's nature is bent on rebellion, and that the society which has brought him up and had provided for him is being subjected to his depredations and he wants to repay its kindness with disturbance of peace, then if that society inflicts some penalty on this kind of an individual and wants to cut away that harmful limb, it cannot be criticised or blamed.

The holy Quran has termed a theft deserving the penalty of cutting the hand as the theft of tyranny and corruption, and about such a thief it has stated as under

> "But if the thief repent after his crime, and amend his conduct, Allah turns to him in forgiveness ; for Allah is Oft-Forgiving, Most Merciful." *(Maids : 42)*

The penalty which Islam inflicts is in reality for saving the reformist, welfare, and just society from the damage that a harmful member may cause it. A criminal who repays justice with cruelty and reform with corruption — who would like to consider him deserving of mercy ?

Appeals to the hearts : I have mentioned this example merely to show that the penalties for moral crimes have not been fixed with a view to generating forcefully goodness in society, nor does it amount to coerce people to follow the right path.

For Islam the better way is to appeal to the hearts of men, to awaken their sleeping nature, to stir their repressed inclination and desire towards progress and perfection, to return them to the presence of God, and to adopt such a method that would have convincing arguments and the sweetness of love and brotherhood. The moral values should be explained and clarified in such a way that the heart may be convinced that it is necessary to adopt them for attaining the good and the righteous qualities.

In such an environment the rule of that law is necessary which helps in nourishing the human capabilities and in developing excellent habits and good moral character.

There is nothing wrong if this useless and profitless limb is cut and thrown away, because in the society we are undertaking farming of various kinds of produce. The purpose is growth and nourishment, whether it may involve the clearance of the wild plants or the thornbearing shrubs.

The security of the interests of common man and their safety is not a thing of less importance, Therefore, there is no reason for being critical of these penalties. which are inflicted by Islam. This thing has been mentioned in the Torah, and all the divine religions have placed emphasis on this.

Responsibility of the society : According to Islam the society itself plays a very important role in the spread of good or evil that spreads in that society. It (Islam) wants to attain power because it wants, with other things, to form a society in such a way that it may be helpful in encouraging chastity, righteousness, aversion from wickedness, proliferation of good acts, indifference to love for world, steadfastness for the right path and consistency.

The Prophet has told the story of a murderer who wanted to repent for his crimes. He inquired of the address of the greatest learned man of the land. His name was given to him, whom he saw and said

> "I have committed hundred murders. Is there any chance of repentance for me?" He was told: "What thing can come between you and repentance. Go to a particular place, where some good slaves of Allah reside and are always found worshipping Him. You also join them in worshipping, and do not return to your village, because it is a bad place." —(*Bukhari*)

In another version, it is narrated that he went to a monk and related his whole story and placed his difficulty before him. The monk told him

> "You have committed a big mistake. How am I concerned with this ? However, there are two villages. One of them is named 'Nasrah' that is supporter of Allah and the other one is named 'Kufrah' that is rejector of God. The people of Nasrah perform the deeds of the people of the paradise. Any person who follows other methods cannot stay there. The citizens of Kufrah perform the deeds of the people of the hell. If you stayed there and worked like those people, then there would be no doubt about the acceptance of your repentance." (*Tibrani*)

For this reason Islam says that for the safety of the healthy nature and for the training and reform of the rebellious tendencies the care and vigilance of the environment is necessary, and in the formation of the good moral character it plays a very important role.

We are sure that if all these aspects are taken care of, then a clean and tidy society can be brought into existence, in which pure qualities and chaste character may be nourished.

Behaviour with Non-believers

Every religion has its characteristic symbols, which make it distinct from every other religion.

Undoubtedly there are certain fixed forms of worship in Islam which have been made compulsory for its followers. Besides there are certain values prevalent among the followers which have no relation with the Non-Muslims.

But the moral teachings do not come under this category or within the sphere of this principle. Every Muslim has been made responsible to employ good manners in dealing with all the citizens of the land unhesitatingly. For every Muslim it is necessary that he should be truthful in dealing with the NonMuslims. Similarly good qualities like charity, keeping one's promise, tolerance, decency, generosity, co-operation, etc. are to be brought into play while dealing with Muslims and NonMuslims alike.

The holy Quran has commanded us not to indulge in such debates with the Jews and the Christians that may encourage mutual enmity, clashes and quarrels. It says:

> "And do not indulge in disputation with the people of the Book except in a refined way, unless it be with those of them who inflict wrong, and say: 'We believe in the Revelation which came down to us and in that which came down to you: Our Allah and your Allah is one; and it is to Him we bow'. *(Ankabut : 46)*
>
> And the followers of Moosa and Isa (Moses and Jesus) were asked, expressing wonder, whether they were indulging in this kind of argumentation and polemics? "Say: `Do you argue with us about Allah when He is our Lord as well as your Lord ? We are accountable for our deeds and you for yours ; so we are sincerely (dedicated) to Him'." *(Baqarah : 139)*

It is a famous incident of the biography of the Prophet that he owed something to a Jew. The Jew demanded repayment and in a very harsh tone said : "O Son of Abdul Muttalib ! You people unnecessarily delay the repayment of your loans." At that place Hazrat Umar bin Al-Khattab was also present. He decided to teach the Jew, who insulted the Prophet, good manners, and drew his sword from the scabbard. But the Messenger of Allah silenced Umar saying : "I and he deserve better treatment. Teach him to demand his money in a better way and advise me to repay it in a refined manner."

Islam has commanded to deal justly and fairly even if the opponent may be a wrong-doer or an infidel. ,Allah's Messenger has said:

> "The prayer of the oppressed is answered. If he is wicked and wrong-doer, his ill effects will go against him." (*Ahmed*)

In another Hadith it is stated : "Even if the oppressed person is an infidel, there is no obstruction between his prayer and its answer. Give up doubtful things and adopt those matters in which there may be no doubt."

In the light of these authorities and the commands, Islam has advised its followers not to maltreat their ideological and religious opponents.

In connection with the insistence on treating the followers of the other religion kindly, there is one more *hadith*:

> Hazrat Ibn Umar says that a goat was slaughtered in his house. When he came home he inquired whether the gift was sent to the neighbouring Jew or not? He further says : "I have heard the Messenger of Allah as saying 'Jibril' had been regulary insisting on me to treat kindly my neighbours, so much so that I surmised that the neighbour would be made a recipient of the inheritance." (*Bukhari*)

Similarly Islam has ordered that its followers should be kind to their relatives, even though they may have rejected this religion which they have made their own. Therefore, following the Truth does not mean that the rights of the relatives may be usurped

> "And bear them company in this life with justice (and consideration), and follow the way of those who turn to Me (in love); in the end the return of I meaning) of all that you did." (*Luqman : 15*)

Need of morality for the nation and the country : This discussion was on the importance of morality at the level of individuals. As regards the importance and need of morality at the public and collective level, Islam says that the progress and the survival of the nations, the nourishment and the development of their civilization and culture, and the consolidation of their power and strength depend on morality. If the people have good and excellent moral character, then all these good qualities will be found in them, but if their moral character is a lower level, then kingdom and rule will soon end.

"Nations live till their morality lives.When their moral character declines, they also decline." This reality is fully explained in a hadith in which the Prophet says to the people of his nation that although they have control over the whole of Arabia, and are in a position to decide the fate of the people of the country, as they hold an important position, their power can be maintained on the pillar of morality only.

Anas bin Malik says: "We were sitting in a house where some members of the Ansar and Muhajir were present. The Messenger of Allah came into the room and everybody tried to make room for him near his own seat. Then he proceeded towards the door and stood taking support of the door and said:

> "The leaders will be from the Quraish, and I have great right on you and they have also a right on you as they would do. When they would be requested to show mercy, they would show mercy. When they would give a judgment, it would be based on justice. And when they would make a covenant, they would honour it. He who does not do like this, there would be on him the curse of Allah, of the angels and of all the people." (*Tibrani*)

This *hadith* unambiguously shows that any person, community, nation or government would be deserving of as much honour and respect as they would be the representatives of the best qualities in this world and would be striving to achieve high objectives.

If a government flaunts the label of Islam and Quran but the people are not satisfied with it, if it does not decide their matters justly, if it is not kind to the needy and does not honour its covenants, then it should be understood that in this government Islam and Quran are merely names, and this government is bereft of Islam's basic values and it deserves to be cursed from every corner of the earth and the skies.

Hazrat Husain narrates that the Messenger of Allah has said

> "When Allah wants to deal kindly with a nation, He entrusts its reins in the hands of the wise men, gives wealth to its generous people ; and when He wants to deal with a nation harshly, he entrusts its wealth to its miserly men." —(*Abu Daud*)

It is a famous saying of Imam Ibn Taimiyah : "Allah guards the justice-loving government, even if it is the government of the infidels, and destroys the tyrant government, even if it is the government of Muslims."

In the light of the holy Book and the Sunnah, morality is the perfect religion and also the perfect world. If any nation loses its honour in the eyes of Allah or commands no respect among the people, it so happens because of its losing good moral character and becoming deprived of decent and honourable traits.

Bibliography

Aiyer, Sir Sivaswamy *Evolution of Hindu Moral Ideals,* Calcutta University Press, 1935.

Amery L.S. "Thoughts on Constitution", Oxford, 1956.

A.K. Brohi, *Islam in the Modern World,* Karachi, 1968.

Ahmad, Aziz, *Studies in Islamic Culture in the Indian Environment,* Oxford, 1964.

Anawati, G.C. and Gardet, Louis, *Mystique Musulmane,* Paris, 1961.

Arnold, Sir Thomas, *The Preaching of Islam,* Lahore, 1956.

Arnold, Sir Thomas, *The Calilhate,* London, *1965.*

Asborn Eide, *"Human Rights in World Society"*, Oslo. 1977.

Browne, E.G., *A Literary History of Persia,* Cambridge, 1957.

Burckhardit, Titus, *Introduction to Sufi Doctrines,* Lahore, 1959.

Corbin, H, *Avicenna and the Visionary Recital,* W. Trash, New York and London, 1960.

Dorothy Pickles, "Democracy", Mathuen and Company, London, 1970.

F. Schuon, *Islam: the Perennial Philosophy,* London, 1976.

Faris, Nabith A., *The Book of Knowledge,* Lahore, 1962.

Faruqi, Bherhan Ahmad, *The Mujaddid's Conception of Tauhid, Lahore,* 1940.

Fennessy R.R., *"Burke, Paine and the Rights of Man"*, Martiness Nijhaoff Hague, 1965.

Field, Cland H., *Al-Ghazali : the Alchemy of Happiness,* London, 1910.

Foster, W., *The English Factories in India,* Oxford, 1927.

Friedmann, Johanan, *Shaykh Ahmad Sirhindi,* Montreal, 1971.

Frykenberg, R.E. (ed.,) *Land Control and Social Structure in Indian History,* Wisconsin, 1969.

Gairdner, W.H. Temple *Al-Ghazzali's Mishkatu'l-anwar, The Niche for Lights,* London, 1915.

Gilsenan, Mechael, *Saint and Sufi in Modern Egypt,* Oxford, 1973.

Halepota, A.J, *Philosophy of Shah Waliu'llah,* Lahore.

Hanson, D.W. *"From Kingdom to Commonwealth,"* Princeton, London, 1970.

Haqq, En'amul, *Muslim Bengali Literature,* Karachi, 1957.

Hasrat, B.J., Dara Shikoh : *Life and Works,* New Delhi, 1982.

Henderson J.J. Craik, *"Parliament—a Survey"*, George Allen and Unwin London, 1965.

Hodgson, *G.S. The Order of Assassin,* The Hague, 1955.

Husaini, S.A. Q. *The Pantheistic Monism of Ibn al-'Arabi,* Lahore, 1970.

Ikram, S.M., *Muslim Civilization in India,* New York.

Iqbal, Ali Shah, *Islamic Sufism,* London, 1933.

Iqbal, Sir Muhammad, *The Development of Metaphysics in Persia,* Lahore, 1964.

Irfan Habib, *The Agrarian System of Mughal India,* Bombay, 1963.

Jois, M.R., *Human Rights and Indian Value*, National Council of Teacher Education, New Delhi, 1998.

Ja'far Sharif, *Islam in India, or the Qamun-i-Islam,* tr., by G.A. Herklots, New Delhi, 1972.

Jalbani, G.N., *Teachings of Shah Waliyullah of Delhi,* Lahore, 1973.

Jennings, Sir Ivor, *"Approach to Self-government"*, Oxford, London.

Kernig C.D., *"Marxism Communism and Western Society"*, New York 1972.

Landau, R., *The Philosophy of the Ibn'Arabi,* London, 1959.

Lord Northbourne, *Religion in the Modern World,* London, 1963.

Lewis, Bernard, *Islam,* New York, 1974.

Luckner, R.C., *The Bhagvad Gita,* Oxford, 1969.

Lings, Martin, *A Sufi Saint of the Twentieth Century,* London, 1971.

M. Lings, *Ancient Beliefs and Modern Superstitions,* London, 1965.

McCarthy, R.I., *The Theology of al-Ash'ari,* Beirut, 1953.

MacDonald, D.B., *The Religious Attitude and Life in Islam,* Beirut, 1965.

Maryam Jameelah, *Islam versus the West,* Lahore, 1968.

Mayne, P. *Saints of Sind,* London, 1965.

Mcllwain, Charles Howard, "*Constitutionalism*", Great Seal Books, New York, 1947.

Mir Valiuddin, *Love of God,* Hyderabad, Deccan,1968.

Mohaghegh, Mahdi and Landolt, *Collected Papers on Islamic Philosophy and Mysticism,* Tehran, 1971.

Mole Marigan, Les *Mystiques Musulmans,* Paris, 1965.

Moreland, W.H., *India at the Death of Akbar,* London, 1920.

Mujeeb, M., *The Indian Muslims,* London, 1969.

Muni, S.D. and Kalim Bahadur (eds.) *Domestic Conflicts in South Asia,* South Asia Publishers, New Delhi, 1986.

Murthy, T.S. *Assam: The Difficult Years,* Himalayan Books, New Delhi, 1983.

Nageeb al-Attas, Syed, *The Mysticism of Hazmali Fansuri,* Kuala Lumpur, 1970.

Nasr, Seyyed H., *Three Muslim Sages,* Cambridge, Mass., 1964.

Nicholson, R.A., *The Mysteries of Islam,* London, 1914.

Phadmis, Urmila *Ethnicity and Nation-Building in South Asia,* Sage, New Delhi, 1990.

Padwick, C.E., *Muslim Devotions,* London, 1960.

Petersen, E.L., *'Ali and Mu'awiya in Early Arabic Traditions,* Copenhagen, 1964.

Philips, E.C. ed., *Politics and Society in India,* London, 1963.

Phillips, O. Hood, "*Reform of the Constitution,*" London, 1970.

Qureshi, I.H., The *Administration of the Sultanate of Delhi,* Karachi, New Delhi, 1971.

Ray, Samirendra *Judicial Review and Fundamantal Rights,* Eastern Law House, Calcutta, 1974.

Rafiqi, A.Q., *Sufism in Kashmir,* Delhi, 1977.

Raverty, H.G., *Selections from the Poetry of the Afghans,* London, 1862.

Religious and Intellectual History of the Muslims in Akbar's Reign, Delhi, 1975.

Riazu'l Islam, *Indo-Persian Relations,* Tehran, 1970.

Rizvi, S.A.A., *Muslim Revivalist Movements in Northern India in the Sixteenth and Seventeenth Centuries,* Agra, 1965.

Russel, Ralph and Khurshidu'l Islam, *Three Mughal Poets,* Cambridge, Mass, 1968.

Saxena, K.P., (ed.) *Human Rights: Perspective and Challenges in 1990s and Beyond,* Lancers Books, New Delhi, 1994.

Seervai H., *Constitutional Law of India,* N.M. Tripathi & Co., Bombay, 1967.

Singh, Nagendar *Human Rights and International Cooperation,* S. Chand & Co., New Delhi, 1969.

S.H. Nasr, *The Encounter of Man and Nature, The Spiritual Crisis of Modern Man,* London, 1968.

Saran, P., *Provincial Government of the Mughals,* Allahabad, 1941.

Schacht, J., *The Origin of Muhammadan Jurisprudence,* Oxford, 1950.

Sharif, M.M., *A History of Muslim Philosophy,* Wiesebaden.

Sharma, R.S. and Jha, V. (ed.), *Indian Society : Historical Probings,* Delhi, 1974.

Shehadi, F., *Ghazali's Unique Unknowable God,* Leiden, 1964.

Shemesh, A.B., *Taxation in Islam,* Leiden, 1958, 1965.

Siddiqi, M.Z., *Hadith Literature,* Calcutta, 1961.

Smith, M., *Rabi'a The Mystic and her Fellow Saints in Islam,* Cambridge, 1929.

Spear, P., *Twilight of the Mughals,* Cambridge, 1969, New Delhi, 1970.

Storey, C.A., *Persian Literature: A Bibliographical Survey,* London, 1927-58.

Subhan, J.A., *Sufism : Its Saints and Shrines,* Lucknow, 1960.

T. Izutsu, *The Concept and Reality of Existence,* Tokyo, 1971.

Tarachand, *Influence of Islam on Indian Culture,* Allahabad, 1963.

Temple, R.C., *Legends of the Punjab,* London, 1893-1901.

Thomas, W.F., *Mutual Influence of Muhammedans and Hindus in India,* Cambridge, 1892.

Tripathi, R.P., *Some Aspects of Muslim Administration,* Allahabad, 1959.

Tritton, A.S., *The Caliphs and their Non-Muslim Subjects,* Oxford, 1930.

Underhill, E., Mysticism : *A Study in the Nature and Development of Man's Spiritual Consciousness,* New York, 1956.

Wahed Husain, *Administration of Justice during the Muslim Rule in India,* Delhi, 1977.

Waheed Mirza, *The Life and Works of Amir Khusrau,* Calcutta, 1935.

Watanmal, L., *The Life of Shah' Abdul Latif,* Hyderabad, Sind, 1889.

Willoughby W., *"Principles of the Constitutional Law of the United States",* Baker Voorthis and company, New York, 1938.

Yusuf Iblish and Peter Lambron Wilson, *Traditional Modes of Contemplation and Action,* Tehran, 1977.

Zaehner, R.C., *Hindu and Muslim Mysticism,* London, 1960.

Index

□□□